COLLECTED WORKS OF ERASMUS

VOLUME 63

Lucubrationes title-page
Strasbourg: Matthias Schürer, September 1515.
Universitätsbibliothek, Basel

COLLECTED WORKS OF
ERASMUS

EXPOSITIONS OF THE PSALMS

edited by Dominic Baker-Smith

ENARRATIO IN PRIMUM PSALMUM, 'BEATUS VIR'
COMMENTARIUS IN PSALMUM 2, 'QUARE
FREMUERUNT GENTES'
PARAPHRASIS IN TERTIUM PSALMUM, 'DOMINE
QUID MULTIPLICATI'
IN PSALMUM QUARTUM CONCIO

translated and annotated by

Michael J. Heath

University of Toronto Press

Toronto / Buffalo / London

The research and publication costs of the
Collected Works of Erasmus are supported by
University of Toronto Press.

© University of Toronto Press 1997
Toronto / Buffalo / London
Printed in Canada

ISBN 0-8020-4308-9

Printed on acid-free paper

Canadian Cataloguing in Publication Data

Erasmus, Desiderius, d. 1536
[Works]
Collected works of Erasmus

Partial contents: v. 63. Expositions of the Psalms.
Includes bibliographical references and index.

ISBN 0-8020-4308-9 (v. 63)

1. Erasmus, Desiderius, d. 1536. I. Title

PA8500 1974   876'.04   C74-006326-x rev

University of Toronto Press acknowledges the financial assistance to its
publishing program of the Canada Council and the Ontario Arts Council.

Collected Works of Erasmus

The aim of the Collected Works of Erasmus
is to make available an accurate, readable English text
of Erasmus' correspondence and his
other principal writings. The edition is planned
and directed by an Editorial Board, an Executive Committee,
and an Advisory Committee.

Contents

Preface

Erasmus' expositions of the Psalms make up a substantial part of his writings on spiritual counsel. Although he wrote on only eleven of the psalms, and spread these works out over a period of twenty years, they nevertheless fill some 385 columns in volume 5 of the great Leclerc edition of his works, by any standards a formidable body of print. As his only excursions into the field of Old Testament exegesis these writings in any case merit close study, but an additional interest derives from the period of twenty years when they were composed, that is 1515 to 1535, the last two decades of Erasmus' long life, which also witnessed the beginnings of the Reformation and the gradual

* * * * *

Works cited frequently are referred to in the notes in abbreviated form; a list of abbreviations and full bibliographical information is given at 278 below. References to Erasmus' correspondence are to the English translation of the letters in CWE, where these have already been published, or to the Latin edition of Allen.

The following shortened titles are adopted for individual expositions of the Psalms:

Enarratio allegorica in primum psalmum: In psalmum 1
Commentarius in psalmum 2: In psalmum 2
Paraphrasis in tertium psalmum: In psalmum 3
In psalmum quartum concio: In psalmum 4
Concionalis interpretatio in psalmum 85: In psalmum 85
In psalmum 22 enarratio triplex: In psalmum 22
Consultatio de bello Turcis inferendo, et obiter enarratus psalmus 28: De bello Turcico
Enarratio psalmi 33: In psalmum 33
Enarratio in psalmum 38: In psalmum 38
De sarcienda ecclesiae concordia [in psalmum 83]: De concordia
Enarratio in psalmum 14 qui est de puritate tabernaculi: De puritate tabernaculi

Those expositions which have yet to be published in CWE volumes 64 and 65 are referred to by means of the appropriate column numbers in LB V; these can easily be followed in ASD V-2 and V-3.

break-up of Christian solidarity and doctrinal consensus. In his meditations
on the Psalms Erasmus had a powerful opportunity to express his hopes
and anxieties about the future and to convey his proposals for restoring
charity among Christians. As the history of their publication reveals, the
Expositions of the Psalms had only a limited impact, and Erasmus' conciliatory
tone was drowned in a more aggressive clamour; yet it may be suggested that
they have acquired a new force and relevance in our time, read within the
context of ecumenical respect and understanding. Erasmus was in no sense a
relativist, but he invariably regretted the precipitate imposition of judgment.

    Out of the eleven commentaries on individual psalms only the final
two have previously been translated into English. The first of these was *An
exposicyon of the xv psalme*, an anonymous (and tendentious) translation of *De
puritate tabernaculi* (1535) which was printed in London by John Wayland in
1537. This, together with a lost translation of *De sarcienda ecclesiae concordia*
by Richard Taverner dating from 1545, was part of the propaganda issued by
the government of Henry VIII to defend aspects of its ecclesiastical policy.[1]
But apart from these Tudor versions, to which must be added two modern
translations of *De concordia*,[2] these important and highly characteristic biblical
commentaries by Erasmus have not previously been available in English.
It is the hope of those associated with the three volumes of the Collected
Works which will contain the *Expositions of the Psalms* that wider access to
these neglected writings will enrich appreciation of Erasmus and clarify the
nature of his mature religious thought.

    In arranging the *Expositions* for publication in three volumes the de-
cision has been taken to depart from the precedent set by Leclerc (LB) and
followed by the Amsterdam editors (ASD), so that instead of printing the expositions according to the sequence of the psalms they will be printed in the
order of their original publication. This, it is hoped, will enable the reader
to form a clearer picture of the development of Erasmus' expository habits
and of his dominant concerns. So far as volume 63 is concerned this creates
few surprises, and it contains the *Expositions* of Psalms 1–4, which were the
first to engage Erasmus' attention; but volume 64 will accordingly contain
those on Psalms 85, 22, 28 (*De bello Turcico*), and 33, and volume 65 those
on Psalms 38, 83 (*De sarcienda ecclesiae concordia*), and 14 (*De puritate tabernaculi*). It should be noted that, in accordance with Erasmus' own practice, the

* * * * *

1 E.J. Devereux *Renaissance English Translations of Erasmus: A Bibliography to 1700*
   (Toronto 1983)
2 In J.P. Dolan *The Essential Erasmus* (New York 1964) and R. Himelick *Erasmus
   and the Seamless Coat of Jesus* (Lafayette, Ind 1971)

Vulgate numbering of the Psalms has been followed throughout; while for the most part he follows the familiar Vulgate text there are occasional departures from it, and the reader will find a recreation of the psalm text before each exposition.

Any undertaking of this kind inevitably accumulates a comprehensive indebtedness to the learning, skill, and benevolence of others. Since I have been engaged on it for so long a time I would like to offer my gratitude to those (many, I fear) whose acts of assistance do not receive formal acknowledgment here. How long a time has been felt with particular sharpness by Michael Heath, whose translations, prepared in the flush of youth, now see the light as he settles into a professorial chair; to him it can only be said that he has been as Patience, 'Gazing on kings' graves and smiling / Extremity out of act.' It is also appropriate to recall here the interest taken in the *Expositions* by the late Beatrice Corrigan, the initial coordinating editor for cwe, as well as the generous guidance on textual matters provided by the late Sir Roger Mynors. Hans Trapman, Secretary of the Erasmus Commissie of the Koninklijke Nederlandse Akademie van Wetenschappen, made the asd texts available to us at the earliest opportunity and has been a constant source of help and encouragement. A debt is also due to the readers of the University of Toronto Press, whose comments and suggestions have proved so helpful. An invaluable opportunity to advance the preparation of volume 63 was provided by a period as Visiting Scholar at the Centre for Reformation and Renaissance Studies, Victoria University in the University of Toronto, with its fine collection of Erasmiana, and I am grateful to the then curator, David Galbraith, for his enthusiastic support. J.K. McConica csb and R.M. Schoeffel have provided unwavering support and practical guidance on behalf of the Collected Works, while Mary Baldwin, as copyeditor, has demonstrated the creative potential of vigilance; David Smith also made a number of helpful suggestions which have found their way into the final text. Marion Lea, of King's College, London, took on the important task of preparing the index, and Ity Siesling of the University of Amsterdam provided much-needed computer support. I should close with a word of thanks to my department at Amsterdam, who have come to accept over the years that a professor of English should spend so much time studying a Dutchman.

Introduction

In light of the central place in the career of Desiderius Erasmus accorded to his Greek-based Latin New Testament text of 1516, the *Novum instrumentum*, it is hardly surprising that relatively little notice has been taken of his *Enarratio in primum psalmum*, which preceded it by half a year. Yet this work, dedicated to Beatus Rhenanus and printed by his fellow Alsatian Matthias Schürer in a volume of *Lucubrationes* – literally, 'works by lamplight' – is in fact Erasmus' first published commentary on a biblical text. As such it marks a new phase in his intellectual preoccupations. 1515 was, in any case, a year of ambitious and creative activity which included the important political additions to the extended *Adagia* printed by Johann Froben at Basel during the spring, as well as intensive work preparing the New Testament and the edition of Jerome. This first commentary, that on Psalm 1, initiates a series of eleven writings on individual psalms over a period of twenty years, so that the last one, on Psalm 14, was completed only shortly before his death in July 1536. In fact, given the gap of seven years between that first venture into discussion of the Psalms and the subsequent commentary on Psalm 2, Erasmus' expositions can be described as works of his mature years, the last six of them appearing in the 1530s. Only the commentary on Psalm 1, in other words, predates the controversies provoked by Luther's attack on the established practices of Catholic Christianity. The greater part of Erasmus' discussion of the Psalms must, therefore, be set in that period when he was distrusted and increasingly criticized both by the reformers, who regretted what they saw as a failure to respond to the challenge of the times, and by the more aggressively orthodox among the traditionalists, who had always detected a subversive tendency in his ideas. This may in part account for the relative neglect of the psalm commentaries after his death, at any rate in formal accounts of the religious thought of Erasmus. Yet if there is one note that becomes increasingly audible in them, it is one of irenical concern for those things which the warring factions might share in common. Outside a limited following this was not a popular line, yet the psalms, the traditional expression of corporate prayer in the church, were also a basic element in the lay piety encouraged by the reformers. These texts, at least, were a common possession, a shared source of self-understanding which might resonate across the frontiers of credal allegiance.

Nevertheless, in spite of a certain initial popularity, it is clear that interest fades at much the same period as hopes for reconciliation between the warring churches. The failure in 1541 of the Diet of Regensburg, where Julius Pflug, the dedicatee of the commentary on Psalm 83, played a prominent role among the conciliatory Catholic theologians, can be seen as a watershed. This commentary, *De sarcienda ecclesiae concordia*, was the most successful of all Erasmus' attempts in this genre, at least so far as publication was concerned. In the year of publication, 1533, no fewer than seven Latin editions were printed, together with German and Dutch translations. Four more Latin editions appeared prior to the *Opera omnia* published by Hieronymus Froben and Nicolaus Episcopius in 1538–40, and in addition to a second German version there were translations into Danish, French, and English. The two German versions, interestingly enough, are attributed to Wolfgang Capito (Strasbourg 1533) and to Georg Witzel (Erfurt 1534), both of them admiring correspondents of Erasmus who, along with Julius Pflug, would be drawn into the preliminary discussions which led to Regensburg. The English version by Richard Taverner, a late arrival on the scene in 1545, can be associated with the complex ecclesiastical manoeuvring which preceded the death of Henry VIII.[1] The last exposition of the Psalms, that on Psalm 14 with its highly topical title *De puritate tabernaculi sive ecclesiae christianae*, was dedicated to Christoph Eschenfelder in February 1536, five months before the death of Erasmus. Yet four editions appeared in that year, and in 1537 it was printed by Froben and Episcopius at Basel together with *De concordia*. Here again, the number of translations is impressive, Dutch, English, and German versions appearing within a year and a Czech one in 1542. In all no fewer than six Dutch printings are recorded, four from the sixteenth century (Antwerp 1537, 1554, 1556, and Utrecht c 1595) and two from the seventeenth (Delft 1611, Rotterdam 1616), which suggests a link to specific debates over toleration both in the Spanish Netherlands and later in the nascent Dutch Republic. But such interest was not confined to the later commentaries: in the period up to the 1540 *Opera omnia*, Psalm 1 achieved fourteen editions,

* * * * *

1 On the Regensburg discussions see P. Matheson *Cardinal Contarini at Regensburg* (Oxford 1972) chapter 1. Taverner has been called 'the most prolific popularizer of Erasmus whom England produced'; see J.K. McConica *English Humanists and Reformation Politics* (Oxford 1965) 117.

including one in Venice (G. de Gregoriis 1523); Psalm 2 achieved nine; the paraphrase on Psalm 3 – despite Erasmus' misgivings – managed twelve; Psalm 4, the longest thus far, only attained five. Of the remainder, the commentaries on Psalms 22, 33, 38, and 85 each appeared in only a single edition prior to the *Opera omnia*, the odd one out here being the *Consultatio de bello Turcico* of 1530, ostensibly a commentary on Psalm 28, which had six Latin editions and a German translation within a year of its publication by Froben. This reinforces the impression that it made good commercial sense for the publisher to embellish a scriptural commentary with some topical title. Indeed, it is very noticeable that of the psalm commentaries which Erasmus produced after 1525 – after, that is, the numerical sequence was abandoned – only those with some such title went beyond a single edition in his lifetime. Even *De puritate tabernaculi*, published in 1536 as Erasmus was close to death, ran through five editions in the same year. To read a clear pattern into the afterlife of these texts would be to strain the evidence, but some suggestive features can be discerned. Consider the translations: while Dutch and German versions remain a constant feature of the publication history, Spanish interest includes Psalms 1, 2, 4, and *De bello Turcico* but then ceases after 1530. From that date on the various editions and versions appear in settings marked by a degree of religious instability. Moreover, after the Froben-Episcopius *Opera omnia*, in effect a memorial volume which contains the only complete printing of the expositions of the Psalms prior to Leclerc's Leiden edition, the list of later printings becomes startlingly thin. The failure of the Regensburg discussions is symptomatic: the 1540s witness a hardening of attitudes among the disputing orthodoxies which allows little space for Erasmian spirituality. Six of his expositions (on Psalms 83, 85, 28, 1, 22, and 33) were reprinted in Leiden between 1644 and 1652 by J. Maire, and these individual items were followed by Leclerc's great *Opera omnia* of 1703–6, but one must conclude that Erasmus' appeal now was almost exclusively to small groups of like-minded readers who might find in his pages some support for their own reservations about institutional rigidity.[2]

'Who indeed has not written on the Psalms?' asks Erasmus, almost wearily, in a letter to Sadoleto in 1530. His primary concern on this occasion was to explain those considerations which, in spite of urgent and influential pleas, have kept him from attempting an exposition of the entire Psalter: for one thing he is deficient in Hebrew, and for another there is a real danger

* * * * *

2 Further details of the printed editions can be found in the 'Introduction générale' to ASD v-2. For the background to the later publishing history see Bruce Mansfield *Phoenix of his Age* (Toronto 1979).

that the accumulation of commentaries will sink the text.[3] Yet there are signs that initially Erasmus had contemplated a complete treatment of all one hundred and fifty psalms, and such still seems to be his idea in the letter dedicating his *In psalmum quartum concio* to Bishop John Longland in 1525; here he refers to Longland's repeated urgings that he produce a commentary on the Psalms, and offers the work in question as a sample. If the bishop approves he will press on. However, when the next exposition appeared in 1528, duly dedicated to Longland, it was a commentary on Psalm 85. The idea of a series had been abandoned. Nor is this surprising when the length of the expositions is taken into account; economy is not one of their more obvious features.

If the departure from a sequential series of expositions suggests a degree of uncertainty in Erasmus' mind about the exact nature of his undertaking, this impression is reinforced by the variations in the titles which he allocates to them. While Psalm 1 is provided with a conventional enough 'exposition' (*enarratio*), Psalm 2 is given a 'commentary' (*commentarius*), Psalm 3 is presented in the form of a paraphrase (*paraphrasis*), and the two subsequent expositions, of Psalms 4 and 85, are described as 'sermons' (*concio, concionalis interpretatio*). But the six expositions which follow return to the original title of *enarratio*. This indicates some searching on the part of Erasmus for a fully satisfactory format in which to present the extended discussion of a psalm text. The term *commentarius* means in effect a discontinuous narrative, elucidating philological and theological interests, and it has an academic ring about it.[4] The *Paraphrasis in tertium psalmum* (1524) was undertaken at the request of Melchior Matthaei of Vianden, who presumably saw this as a natural extension of the New Testament paraphrases, which had been concluded in that same year with the publication of Mark and Acts. No doubt one practical consideration for Erasmus and his publisher was to take advantage of the extensive readership which these earlier works had won. This attempt at a follow-up does, incidentally, bring out the special status accorded to the Psalms, uniquely among the books of the Old Testament, as a resource in the spiritual life of Christians, but it overlooks the very real difficulties inherent in achieving a convincing paraphrase of an implicitly dramatic text in which different voices have to be distinguished by the reader. Even the playful tones of Erasmus' dedicatory letter admit 'that this subject simply does

* * * * *

3 Allen Ep 2315:171–80
4 Kenneth Hagen 'What Did the Term *Commentarius* Mean to Sixteenth-century Theologians?' in *Théorie et pratique de l'exégèse* ed Irena Backus and Francis Higman (Geneva 1990) 13-38

not lend itself to paraphrase,' and he goes beyond the conventional gestures of self-deprecation to insist on the problems of handling the Psalms – the provision of technical and contextual information, the identification of the speaker(s) or personae, and the discernment of the spiritual sense. Erasmus instinctively sees the expositor in a mediating role, keeping the material under his personal control, and this is not so easily achieved in paraphrase.[5] Instead, in the succeeding expositions on Psalms 4 and 85, he adopts the sermon mode, no doubt conscious of Longland's reputation as a preaching bishop but also anxious to preserve the flexibility of his own performance, unravelling obscurities where necessary while maintaining the essential note of spiritual exhortation.

The return in the later expositions to the title *enarratio*, that used typically by St Augustine in his writings on the Psalms, probably reflects his conviction that the rhetorical overtones of *concio* failed to mesh with the more intimate style of textual elucidation which he follows. *Concio*, according to the definition given by Lorenzo Valla, refers to a popular gathering of the people (ἐκκλησία) drawn together to hear matters pertaining to the public good; of its nature it demands the use of deliberative oratory, persuading to the adoption of a specific policy or course of action. While a sermon might well develop along such lines, relying on persuasion and sound sense, it is not a particularly satisfactory term to apply to the unravelling of a text, even when the outcome is intended to be the adoption of a way of life. Both the paraphrast and the preacher, though they may point back to an authoritative text, distract us by their performance. By using *enarratio* Erasmus is signalling the adoption of a homiletic style, one designed to convey the significance and force of a scriptural passage to a small, clearly defined congregation.[6] This is certainly more apt for the character of a printed exposition, and in any case it glances back at important patristic antecedents, above all at the exegesis of Origen. Mediation of the text is the key feature: in his *Ecclesiastes* Erasmus suggestively refers to Christ, the Word, as *enarrator* of the mind of

* * * * *

5 See 152 below. Erasmus had already acknowledged the difficulties of the form in his dedication of the *Paraphrase on Matthew* to Charles v in 1522 (Ep 1255); for a discussion of the issues see Terence Cave *The Cornucopian Text* (Oxford 1979) 38–9, 88–90.

6 On Erasmus' adoption of *concio* from deliberative oratory, as well as his use of *enarratio* as the virtual equivalent of *homilia*, see John W. O'Malley sj 'Erasmus and the History of Sacred Rhetoric: The *Ecclesiastes* of 1535' *Erasmus of Rotterdam Society Yearbook* 5 (1985) 14–22; that he was not unduly concerned about the issue is clear from Ep 2261, where he refers to *In psalmum 22 enarratio* as a *concio*, no doubt reflecting the fact that it is devised as an oral presentation.

God,[7] so that the accommodation of the divine and the human in the second Person of the Trinity is a model for the work of exegesis. The exegete must move freely between historical or philological questions and that spiritual understanding which for Erasmus is the real purpose of all engagement with the Old Testament; the material conditions of the psalm text are a legitimate concern only so long as they help to open out the prophetic meaning, which is Christ. For Christ is already present as David's intended meaning, and through him the drama of the psalms touches the lives of all those who, united in his mystical body, work for his kingdom in the ages to come. This insistently practical, and in a special sense sacramental, view of scriptural interpretation is the most striking feature of Erasmus' exegesis, and it offers some comment on the fact that three of the later expositions carry additional titles. These are the expositions of Psalm 28, *A Discussion Concerning Proposals for War Against the Turks* (1530), of Psalm 83, *On Restoring the Unity of the Church* (1533), and of Psalm 14, *On the Purity of the Christian Church* (1536). While these certainly qualify as psalm commentaries, they give particular attention to contemporary dilemmas, the Turkish threat and the effects of the Reformation, using these as the pretext for an examination of Christian society. So again it is a question of the prophetic linked to the contemporary, and Erasmus finds the freedom of the *enarratio* – its informal transition from sermon to essay – the most appropriate medium in which to draw out the full significance of his text and apply it to the circumstances of his readers.

What did the Psalms mean for Erasmus on the personal level? David Knowles has suggested that an important factor in Erasmus' career was his departure from the observance of a canon regular, since this left him anxious to prove that, far from representing backsliding or an evasion of spiritual challenge, his disengagement from the community at Steyn had actually freed him to pursue a more effective apostolate.[8] Public recitation of the Psalms in the divine office was the central feature of all monastic life, canons regular included, so that life outside the cloister meant a new way of using the psalms specified in the official worship of the church. The private breviary had been introduced in the course of the thirteenth century as a consequence of the new style of religious life represented by the mixed apostolate of the mendicant orders; while preserving a framework of monastic observance this allowed for greater freedom to meet the pastoral commitments taken on by the friars. In effect, the obligation of the office devolved from the religious community to the individual; the Franciscans, in particular, worked to popularize use

* * * * *

7 LB V 772D
8 *The Religious Orders in England* 3 vols (Cambridge 1948–59) III 148

of the private breviary among the secular clergy, while abbreviated versions were devised for lay use. One example of this *Psalterium abbreviatum* was translated into Italian by no less a figure than Marsilio Ficino for the use of Lorenzo de' Medici's wife Clarice.[9] While Erasmus presumably continued to attend public singing of the office in chapels or collegiate churches, his way of life suggests that for most of the time he had to replace liturgical performance with private recitation. In a sense, this shift in his own practice anticipates the new style of religious institute which emerges in the 1520s, that of clerks regular such as the Theatines in 1524 or the Society of Jesus in 1534, since one of their novel characteristics was exemption from the obligation to public recital of the office. Private reading of the office was less obviously 'ecclesiastical' and it could be developed to meet the aspirations of a wider lay audience and to cohere with those traditions of subjective devotion which, in the spirit of Augustine's *Confessions*, saw the psalms as a dramatization of inner conflict.

The Book of Psalms, deriving from the chants and songs used in the Temple, was central to the startling hermeneutical shift whereby the canon of Judaic scripture was taken over and appropriated for Christian use. Such a recontextualization was inevitable once Christ was seen as the fulfilment of the messianic yearning voiced in the prophetic books of the Old Testament. Rather than remain open-ended as in Jewish expectation of a Messiah yet to come, Christian exegesis sees the events and roles of the Old Testament as types realized in Christ, historically fulfilled in him but still reapplicable as signs in the life of the church. Thus in 1 Peter 2:6 Christ, 'our living stone,' is recognized as the 'corner-stone of great worth' of Isaiah 28:16, and in turn the Christian reader is instructed, 'Come, let yourselves be built, as living stones, into a spiritual temple.' This spiritual temple, the 'city of righteousness' of Isaiah 1:26, is identified as the New Jerusalem to be established by Christ at the end of time. Such a random example illustrates two important tendencies in early Christian exegesis: one is the habit of treating the Old Testament as a repertory of types – events or roles – which find their true, spiritual meaning in the antitype, Christ, so that in a sense the Old Testament can fairly be described as 'an intellectual dress rehearsal for the New.'[10] The second tendency is, by a process of interiorization, to read the history of Israel in terms of the spiritual struggle of the individual believer, so that those events and utterances which look to the future and are realized in Christ are also

* * * * *

9 Eugene F. Rice Jr *Saint Jerome in the Renaissance* (Baltimore and London 1985) 193
10 R.P.C. Hanson *Allegory and Event* (London 1959) 204

re-enacted in the lives of those who are members of his mystical body. As we shall see, such a view was especially compelling for biblical humanism. The first books of the Old Testament to be taken over in this way were, inevitably, the prophetic books, since these set the context within which the claims of Christ can be demonstrated, and the Psalms were included among them on account of their messianic content. The most striking instance of such a use, though maybe not the earliest in textual terms, is the adoption by Christ of the opening verse of Psalm 21, 'My God, my God, why hast thou forsaken me?' in the passion narratives of Matthew and Mark.

The text of the Old Testament used for the most part in the early centuries of the church was based on the Septuagint, a Greek version of the Hebrew canon prepared for the Hellenistic Jewish community of Alexandria in the early second century BC and named after its legendary seventy translators. This was the version adopted by Paul and the New Testament authors generally, yet it increasingly fell from favour among Jewish exegetes. In fact by the time of Origen (c 185–c 254) the Septuagint was an established Christian text, regarded by many as inspired and yet cut off from its Hebrew source, a status not unlike that of the Vulgate in the early sixteenth century. Although Origen's knowledge of Hebrew was limited, he was able to rely on the assistance of Jewish scholars in his efforts to probe the relation between the Septuagint and its Hebrew sources, as well as other Greek translations; the result was his massive *Hexapla*, a presentation of the Old Testament in six versions, set out in parallel columns. These were the Hebrew text, then a transliteration of it into Greek, followed by four existing Jewish Greek versions, that of Aquila, that of Symmachus, then the revised Septuagint, and finally that of Theodotion. In the case of the Psalms Origen was able to unearth yet further versions so that, according to Eusebius, as many as seven were given side by side.[11] Although the *Hexapla* at an estimated 6500 pages was not exactly an enchiridion, it did establish an important point about the critical study of sacred texts which was to have implications for Erasmus.

Meanwhile, those parts of the Roman empire in which Greek was not familiarly used developed their own Latin versions. It seems likely that the first Latin translations were prepared in Africa, but they were also circulated at an early date in Gaul and Italy. In his *De doctrina christiana* Augustine recommends the *Itala*, a version that has not been conclusively identified,[12]

* * * * *

11 M.F. Wiles 'Origen as Biblical Scholar' in *The Cambridge History of the Bible* I: *From the Beginnings to Jerome* ed P.R. Ackroyd and C.F. Evans (Cambridge 1970) 458

12 *De doctrina christiana* 2.15.22 PL 34 46

and in his psalm commentaries he uses a text which is almost identical to
the Verona Old Latin Psalter. In either case, the source was the Septuagint.
Inevitably in such a situation variants multiplied, leading the exasperated
Jerome to complain that there were as many versions as codices, and the
need for standardization became urgent. Thus, during Jerome's second stay
in Rome (382–5), Pope Damasus commissioned him to revise the Old Latin
Bible in the light of the Greek 'original,' a project which resulted in, among
other things, the so-called Roman Psalter. But Jerome's brilliance as a linguist
led inexorably towards examination of the sources, and his next review of the
Psalms was undertaken in the light of Origen's *Hexapla*, making full use of
its resources to emend the Greek out of the Hebrew text .The outcome on this
occasion became known as the Gallican Psalter, and it was this version which
was to be incorporated into the Vulgate and so become the standard Latin
form of the Book of Psalms for a thousand years. It says much for the sense of
familiarity generated by popular use that the Gallican version was retained
in spite of the availability of Jerome's third rendering of the Psalms, this time
directly from the actual Hebrew text, his *Psalterium iuxta Hebraeos* or Hebrew
Psalter.[13] In any case, Jerome's evolving commitment to the Hebrew Old
Testament (referred to as *Hebraica veritas* 'the Hebrew verity') was the object
of considerable suspicion and led to charges of Judaizing; Augustine, for one,
was worried by the implications for the inspired status of the Septuagint.
Jerome's insistence on delving back to the original source was thus directly
comparable to the strategy of Origen, and the controversy that it stirred
would have been recognized by Erasmus as he faced the opposition to his
own revised Latin text in the *Novum instrumentum*. If Erasmus identified
with Jerome and consciously endeavoured to create a hieronymian image for
himself, this was not so much an act of vanity as a statement of policy.[14]

    The assimilation of the Gallican Psalter into the Vulgate did not, how-
ever, mean that the Hebrew dimension was lost, even when the language was
largely unknown outside the Jewish community. In liturgical use the Gallican and Roman Psalters predominated, the latter surviving in Italy until the
post-Tridentine reforms of Pius v (and in St Peter's until modern times), but
Jerome's three versions remained in circulation, frequently in the form of

* * * * *

13 Erasmus distinguishes between the 'ancient version' still used in the liturgy
   and the revisions available for private study in Ep 456:98–102.
14 On the Jerome image see Lisa Jardine *Erasmus, Man of Letters* (Princeton 1993)
   55–82 and passim. In fact Erasmus' relationship to Jerome is defined by the issue
   of scriptural revision; see Mark Vessey 'Erasmus' Jerome' *Erasmus of Rotterdam
   Society Yearbook* 14 (1994) 62–99.

triple psalters, and were a constant provocation to textual comparison and, indirectly, to a sacred philology. When in the course of the fifteenth century interest in Christian antiquity developed it would owe much to the humanist cult of St Jerome.[15] As an example we can take the Florentine Giannozzo Manetti (1396–1459), who studied the classical tongues and Hebrew and saw Jerome as his model; his attempt at a revised psalter comprised three texts, Jerome's Gallican and Hebrew versions, together with his own rendering of the *Hebraica veritas*. Needless to say, this intrusion of his own efforts into the privileged space of Jerome was widely criticized.[16]

But if Manetti's effort had only limited impact, due in part to problems of manuscript circulation, the advent of printing offered new standards of accuracy and control to support the philological effort of humanists like Lorenzo Valla, whose *In Latinam Novi Testamenti interpretationem adnotationes* Erasmus discovered in manuscript and prepared for the press in 1505. An interesting example of this combination is the 'polyglot' psalter edited by the Carmelite Johannes Crastonus, the first such biblical text to benefit from the new technology, which was printed at Milan in 1481 with the Greek wording alongside the Latin translation. Crastonus' insistence in his preface that the Latin Bible should be corrected in the light of the Hebrew and Greek verities may, indeed, reflect the influence of Valla. Another example, of greater virtuosity, is the *Psalterium octaplum* of the Dominican Agostino Giustiniani, published at Genoa in 1516, the year of Erasmus' *Novum instrumentum*, and like it dedicated to Leo x. This elegantly produced book complements the Vulgate with versions in Greek, Hebrew, Arabic, and Aramaic, together with word-for-word Latin renderings of the Hebrew and Aramaic, and a commentary derived from rabbinic sources.[17] Less ambitious but more representative were the efforts of the Jewish convert Felice da Prato, whose *Psalterium ex Hebraico Latine redditum* appeared with papal approval in 1515 and was certainly known to Erasmus.[18] It remained, however, for the Dominican protégé of Savonarola, Fra Santi Pagnini, to complete a translation of the entire Hebrew Bible, complete with numbered verses, in 1528. What does emerge, even from a perfunctory survey, is that of all the books of the Old Testament

* * * * *

15 Eugene F. Rice Jr *Saint Jerome in the Renaissance* (n9 above) 85

16 C. Trinkaus *In Our Image and Likeness* 2 vols (London 1970) II 581–95

17 For Crastonus and Giustiniani see W. Schwarz *Principles and Problems of Biblical Translation: Some Reformation Controversies and their Background* (Cambridge 1955) 77n and 106; Giustiniani's contacts with Erasmus are summarized in Ep 906:529n and in CEBR II 102–3.

18 Ep 456:103

the Psalms were a special focus for scriptural scholarship during the revival of philology and were so on a scale comparable to the Gospels and the
Pauline Epistles. Moreover, it should be emphasized that this philological interest is inseparable from a general movement towards pastoral renewal and
ecclesiastical reform.[19] Few clearer statements of this link can be found than
Erasmus' own formulation in the dedication of his New Testament to Leo,
a pope whose childhood studies with Poliziano gave him genuine humanist
credentials:

> Our chiefest hope for the restoration and rebuilding of the Christian religion,
> our sheet-anchor as they call it, is that all those who profess the Christian
> philosophy the whole world over should above all absorb the principles laid
> down by their Founder from the writings of the evangelists and apostles, in
> which that heavenly Word which once came down to us from the heart of the
> Father still lives and breathes for us and acts and speaks with more immediate
> efficacy, in my opinion, than in any other way. Besides which I perceived that
> that teaching which is our salvation was to be had in a much purer and more
> lively form if sought at the fountain-head and drawn from the actual sources
> than from pools and runnels.[20]

The quest for authentic texts is here clearly associated with a regeneration
of Christian life, the hope that all Christians may 'absorb' their Founder's
teaching; the verb used, *imbibant*, literally that 'they may drink in,' fits with
Erasmus' habitual use of verbs of nutrition to describe the reception of the
Scriptures.

Very much the same attitude is implicit in the *Quincuplex psalterium* of
the French humanist Jacques Lefèvre d'Etaples, first printed by Henri Esti-
enne at Paris in 1509. This book was widely disseminated: Beatus Rhenanus
reported enthusiastically on its combination of liberal learning and theology,
Luther made use of it in his own work on the Psalms, and we can with a
fair degree of confidence suppose Erasmus to have studied it.[21] Its dominant

* * * * *

19 On this aspect of prereform see L. Polizzotto *The Elect Nation: The Savonarolan
   Movement in Florence 1494–1543* (Oxford 1994) 141–67; a useful survey remains
   G.V. Jourdan *The Movement Towards Catholic Reform in the Early XVIth Century*
   (London 1914).
20 Ep 384:44–55
21 *Briefwechsel des Beatus Rhenanus* ed A. Horawitz and K. Hartfelder (Leipzig
   1886) 22–3; for Erasmus' familiarity with the New Testament commentaries of
   'that learned and industrious man Jacques Lefèvre' see his references in Epp
   334:172–8 and 456:105–6.

features are entirely representative of biblical humanism: a concern for textual authenticity on the one hand and a spiritual or prophetic mode of interpretation on the other. Lefèvre, who went to some trouble to consult ancient codices, prints the three versions of Jerome, plus an Old Latin text derived from Augustine's *Enarrationes in psalmos*, and a *Conciliatum* which is basically the Vulgate corrected in the light of Jerome's Hebrew version. It is scarcely a radical approach, but it does at least imply that the Vulgate is open to improvement. More interesting, however, is Lefèvre's manner of exegesis, and this he outlines in the preface addressed to Cardinal Guillaume Briçonnet.[22] His approach may fairly be described as pastoral: genuine theology for Lefèvre is marked by the sweetness and fervour which it generates, and these responses in their turn provide the dynamic of the spiritual life. It follows that when divine studies decline, devotion cools. This characteristic link between scriptural study and growth in the spiritual life is backed by a direct appeal to experience; recalling monks whom he had questioned about their devotional reading, Lefèvre notes that those who had approached the Bible, and the Psalms in particular, through the literal sense had found only aridity and depression. He is scathing about what he terms this pseudo-literal or carnal sense which reads the psalm as a record of events in Jewish history, since it blocks the true-literal or prophetic sense which looks forward to Christ. If, as he believes, the Scriptures are the true food of the spiritual life, that is only when they are read within an appropriate exegetical frame: Christ is the key to the Psalms. The actual process of appropriating the Psalms sets up a tension between their Jewish historical context and the Christocentric signification by which they are received by the believing community; thus Lefèvre, in order to contrast his two kinds of 'literal' sense, takes the example of Psalm 2, 'Why did the nations rage?': in the carnal or pseudo-literal sense it refers to the rebellion against David, but in its proper literal sense, following the reading of Acts 4:25–6, it refers to the alliance of Herod and Pilate, of the Jews and the Gentiles, against Jesus.

As we have seen, such a distinction between the historical sense of Scripture and the spiritual sense is wholly traditional; Augustine had written in *De doctrina christiana* of 'a miserable servitude of the spirit' by which the

* * * * *

22 The cardinal, a widower, should be distinguished from his son Guillaume, bishop of Meaux, who appointed Lefèvre to assist in the reform of his diocese. The preface is printed as Epistle 66 in *The Prefatory Epistles of Jacques Lefèvre d'Étaples* ed Eugene F. Rice Jr (New York and London 1972) 192–200; an English translation of the preface is printed in H.A. Oberman *Forerunners of the Reformation* (London 1967) 297–301.

signs of spiritual things are read as if they were the things themselves.[23] Though Lefèvre may seem to be muddying the waters by referring to a 'twofold literal sense' (*duplex sensus litteralis*), his aim is to establish the prophetic sense – that which sees the Psalms fulfilled in Christ – as an integral part of the intended meaning of the text, thus liberating it from the restrictions of its original cultural matrix as well as restoring an affective dimension to exegesis. Read properly, that is with due awareness of its signification, the psalm opens the way to a direct encounter with the divine, to that spiritual insight which must be the goal of all true theology. In polemical terms, Lefèvre is dismissing both what he terms the rabbinic sense and the distracting subtleties of conventional fourfold interpretation, since these lead away from a devotional response. By the rabbinic sense Lefèvre is not thinking necessarily of Jewish commentators but in all probability of Nicholas of Lyra, the outstanding Christian Hebraist of the scholastic era – significantly he did not know Greek – whose influential *Postilla super Bibliam* was the first biblical commentary to be printed (Rome 1471–2). Nicholas' design was to counter the more indulgent flights of allegorical reading by arriving at an exact understanding of the literal sense, and to this end he drew on Jewish scholarship, especially the work of Rashi (Rabbi Solomon ben Isaac), which represented within the Jewish tradition a similar reaction against allegorical exegesis. While the biblical humanists do make surreptitious use of Nicholas, they usually cover their tracks with care, and their public attitude to him is hostile; in their eyes his work was of a piece with the frigid objectivity of scholastic exegesis and thus weakened the affective and volitional force of the Scriptures, as was the case with Lefèvre's despondent monks. While Nicholas aimed to establish a more exact understanding of the literal-historical sense in order to check the vagaries of allegory, both Lefèvre and Erasmus tend to treat it as a distraction from the prophetic reading which is focused on Christ.

The multiple signification of the Old Testament text had been implicit in the very first appropriation of the Psalms by St Peter as he addressed the crowd in Jerusalem at Pentecost (Acts 2:25–36); here Peter interprets verses 8–11 of Psalm 15 (16) as a prophecy of the risen Christ, distinguishing between the literal application of the psalm to David himself and its prophetic fulfilment: 'What [David] foresaw and spoke about was the resurrection of the Christ: he is the one who was *not abandoned to Hades*, and whose body did not *experience corruption*.' An identical interpretive practice is deployed

* * * * *

23 *De doctrina christiana* 3.5.9 PL 34 69

by Lefèvre: 'I have tried to write a short exposition of the Psalms with the assistance of Christ, who is the key to the understanding of David and about whom David spoke, commissioned by the Holy Spirit, in the Book of Psalms.' This idea of David as 'commissioned by the Holy Spirit,' abbreviating as it does the entire Christian accommodation of the Old Testament, reveals the Pauline inspiration of biblical humanism. The attempt to return to the fountain-head, to recapture the authenticity of early Christian practice, included asserting the Christocentric reading of the prophetic books, and on this basis the Psalms were deemed to hold a special relationship to the New Testament canon. A succinct statement of this position can be found in *De laudibus et materia psalmorum* by Agazio Guidacerio, published at Paris in 1530, the same year that he was appointed Hebrew lector in the newly instituted Collège Royal. As early as 1513 Guidacerio had been teaching at the Sapienza in Rome, together with Fra Santi Pagnini, and in 1521 there was an attempt to lure him to a post at the Collegium Trilingue at Louvain, a proposal which Erasmus supported with unusual warmth (Ep 1221). Although this came to nothing, he was driven northwards by the sack of Rome in 1527, staying first with Sadoleto at Avignon before moving on to Paris. *De laudibus* celebrates his appointment and gives some display of its scope; indeed, given the hostility of the theological faculty towards the philological bias of the Collège, there is something distinctly provocative about Guidacerio's defence of Hebrew studies: 'For what could be more fitting for the Christian than to speak in the native tongue of Christ our Lord and God?'[24] But the central concern of his book is to assert the relevance of the Psalms to Christian life, leading to the question whether they should be classed properly among the *hagiographa* – that is, those books not collected under either the Law or the prophets, where Jewish tradition would normally place them – or with the prophetic writings. The answer, as we might expect, settles for the latter. The Jewish commentators, and indeed some Christian ones, rely on an external sign of prophetic inspiration, 'The Lord said to Moses' or some comparable formula indicative of reported speech; David, by contrast, through the internal inspiration of the Spirit foresees and prophesies the incarnation of Christ the Messiah, his passion, death, descent into hell, resurrection from the dead, and ascension into heaven. More than any other of the prophets David points to the mysteries of Christ and his church, and the Psalms thus form in a special sense a bond between the two Testaments,

* * * * *

24 *De laudibus et materia psalmorum* (Paris: G. de Gourmont [1530?]) fol Aii verso. On the clash with the theologians see J.K. Farge *Orthodoxy and Reform in Early Reformation France* (Leiden 1985) 205–6.

a source of healing for all human ills. In the light of Guidacerio's fierce assertion of David's prophetic role one can see why Lefèvre is so insistent on what
he calls the true-literal sense, that which captures the intended prophetic
meaning and reveals the operation of the Spirit. For Erasmus, too, the spiritual rendering of the sense requires that David – and with him the literal
sense – be constantly subsumed in the figure of Christ: 'So I shall not waste
any time in considering how individual parts of the psalm may be applied to
history; let us investigate instead the extent to which it applies to our David,
that is Jesus Christ, about whom it was unquestionably written'; Christ is
'our king David,' 'our own David,' 'our true David.'[25] The historical, Davidic
sense can even be compared to the outward form of the Silenus image, that
paradoxical focus for physical revulsion and spiritual wonder which is so important to Erasmus, which we open up through Christ in order to grasp the
mystery.[26]

The displacement of David is, therefore, the first step in opening the
psalm text to a spiritual interpretation. Commenting on Psalm 2, verse 6,
Erasmus writes:

> On the literal level, this verse is appropriate enough to David, who defeated the
> Jebusites and built his palace on Zion (that is, the citadel of Jerusalem), but let
> us dismiss such an insipid, watered-down interpretation, a product of 'the letter
> which kills'; we prefer to drink from the new wine of our king. What interest
> have we in David, who rules a precarious kingdom, soon to be destroyed, in
> Palestine, a mere dot on the map?[27]

Yet the opening of a 'spiritual' or 'mystical' reading, emancipating
the text from its original conditions of production, also has its inherent
dangers; what had been weighed down by historical reference is now liable
to drift off into fantasy. It was to meet this particular danger that the
various strategies of Christian hermeneutics were devised, culminating in the

* * * * *

25 *In psalmum 2* 80 below; *In psalmum 4* 176 below; *In psalmum 22* LB V 313A; *In
psalmum 38* LB V 418D; *In psalmum 14* LB V 295A. On the hermeneutic significance
of David see Edward A. Gosselin *The King's Progress to Jerusalem: Some Interpretations of David during the Reformation Period and Their Patristic and Medieval
Background* (Malibu 1976).
26 'If we open the Silenus, we shall see that in the human David there is hidden
another, more sublime David ...' (*In psalmum 33* LB V 371B; see also 381B,
where the suffering victim of Psalm 21 is identified as the 'Silenus of history').
Erasmus' most extensive use of the Silenus motif is in *Adagia* III iii 1.
27 119 below

elaboration of a fourfold sense of Scripture. So the prophetic interpretation of the Old Testament evident in the early church was soon broadened to embrace allegory, following the Jewish precedent of Philo of Alexandria, who used it to transmute the historical sense into moral or philosophical concepts. Such an enterprise was not without its opponents, but by the time of Origen allegory was established as a necessary resource in scriptural study, one which could be justified by the Pauline contrast between the letter which kills and the Spirit which gives life.[28] This basic dichotomy can be said to underlie all the variant schemes that emerge, since threefold or fourfold modes of explication involve no more than increasingly subtle divisions of the 'spiritual' or 'mystical' sense. Thus while Origen may on occasion fall back on a simple dichotomy between the literal and the allegorical, very much in the spirit of St Paul's injunction to fix our eyes 'not on the things that are seen, but on the things that are unseen' (2 Cor 4:18), in formal terms he adopts a threefold scheme which matches the trichotomous human nature of the Platonists but is nevertheless rooted in the Pauline adoption of an identical division into body, soul, and spirit (1 Thess 5:23). Applied to the business of interpretation, this results in the threefold division into literal, moral, and spiritual readings. As the body achieves its meaning through the soul, so the materially conditioned text is opened to spiritual understanding. The proper reading of the Scriptures, then, in its ascent from the body of the text to the hidden meaning which animates it, may be said to comprehend the full scope of the human person. This view of biblical reading as intimately bound up in the spiritual growth of the believer has important resonances in the exegesis of Erasmus; to transcend the letter is to enter on a spiritual journey: 'If someone loves the Holy Scriptures, he is enraptured, changed, transfigured into God.'[29]

The actual business of enumerating the senses of Scripture can be an arbitrary business, as de Lubac makes clear: a threefold scheme may be suggested by the Trinity, a fourfold one by the rivers of paradise, and so on; provided the spiritual principle is recognized the multiplication of

* * * * *

28 2 Cor 3:6, alluded to in the passage just cited from *In psalmum 2*; writing to Luther in May 1519, Erasmus observes, 'that was how Paul did away with the Jewish law, by reducing everything to allegory' (Ep 980:46–7). Yet it is clear from his editorial efforts that Origen did not disdain the literal.

29 *In psalmum 1* 25 below; the mention of rapture should not distract us from the initial encounter with a text. For Augustine's sense of reading as 'both an awakening from sensory illusion and a rite of initiation' see Brian Stock *Augustine the Reader* (Cambridge, Mass and London 1996) 1–19.

senses is not important.[30] In *De utilitate credendi* Augustine proposes one fourfold scheme based on history, aetiology, analogy, and allegory,[31] but while he was often given credit for defining the four senses, something far more like the traditional form can be discerned in his contemporary John Cassian (c 360–435), an important figure in monastic history and a mediator of Origen's influence. In his *Collationes* use is made of what would become the classic division into four senses, one literal and three spiritual: thus the tropological sense derives moral instruction from the text, the allegorical sense traces God's workings in history, and the anagogical sense looks to the final end of all things in God. In Cassian's example Jerusalem is *literally* a Jewish city, *tropologically* the soul, *allegorically* the church, and *anagogically* the heavenly Jerusalem, the city of God.[32] In fact this systematic approach was intended both to stimulate reflection on the broader spiritual or mystical sense and to introduce some necessary order into the ramblings of figurative interpretation. As a monk Cassian saw the fourfold approach operating within the context of *lectio divina*, that meditative-ruminative reading of the biblical text which was itself a form of spiritual exercise. In a passage which confirms the major tradition, St Gregory the Great compares the Scriptures to square-hewn stones which can stand on four sides: 'For in every past event that they narrate, in every future event that they foretell, in every moral saying that they speak, and in every spiritual sense they stand, as it were, on a different side, because they have no roughness.'[33] But once exposed to the intellectual thrust of scientific theology in the medieval universities, the four senses hardened into a rigid scheme which stifled subjective response and obscured narrative continuity. The reaction of humanist exegesis, consequently, was to collapse the four senses into a comprehensive spiritual or mystical sense, referring where appropriate to tropological or allegorical perspectives, as indeed Erasmus does, without compromising the integrity of the text as the

* * * * *

30 Henri de Lubac *Exégèse médiévale* 4 vols (Paris 1959–64) IV (part 2/2) 36; in his *Life of Jerome* Erasmus dryly observes that 'It was an attractive idea to have four Doctors of the church and likewise four senses of Holy Scripture, to correspond of course with the four evangelists. To Gregory they assign tropology, to Ambrose allegory, to Augustine anagogy, and to Jerome, to assign him something, they leave the grammatical and literal sense' (CWE 61 53).

31 *De utilitate credendi* 3.5 PL 42 68–9; Augustine's four senses are described in Brian Stock *Augustine the Reader* (n29 above) 165–9.

32 *Collationes* 14.8 PL 49 964A, on which see Beryl Smalley *The Study of the Bible in the Middle Ages* (Oxford 1952) 28.

33 *Homiliae in Ezechielem* 2.9.8 PL 76 1047A–B

word of God.[34] That there should be similarities between monastic *lectio divina* and the exegesis of prereform can be explained by their common reliance on patristic commentary and, most importantly, by the fact that both see the biblical text as a means to personal transformation rather than to intellectual demonstration.

It is, then, this combination of textual scholarship with an affective mode of exegesis which is typical of the movement sometimes awkwardly termed prereform, but perhaps more aptly described as biblical humanism. Lefèvre's mention of the religious who found psalms dispiriting when read according to the letter matches Erasmus' own comments about such inadequate approaches; as early as the *Enchiridion* he deplores the impoverishment of monastic devotion: 'I think the principal reason why we see that monastic piety is everywhere so cold, languid, and almost extinct is that [religious] are growing old in the letter and never take pains to learn the spiritual sense of the Scriptures.'[35] A decade later in the *Enarratio in primum psalmum* he complains about the religious who 'beat the thin air,' mumbling their way through psalms they do not understand, as well as those scholastic commentators who 'wring the neck' of the Scriptures, fragmenting them into arguments for *quaestiones*: both remain outside the text.[36] At this juncture Erasmus is discussing the second verse of the psalm, 'and he will meditate on his law day and night'; the significant term is 'meditate,' *meditabitur*, since this indicates a process of assimilation. So it is not by chance that Erasmus draws an analogy with eating; to meditate is to penetrate the shell and take in the transforming nourishment of the kernel: 'Eat and you will be transfigured into the image of Christ.' Failure to grasp the true sense may be the outcome of inattention or of a lack of education; either way it is a failure to meditate. Returning fifteen years later to this theme of meditation in his *In psalmum 22 enarratio triplex*, Erasmus refers back to the same verse of Psalm 1: 'What I have here described as digestion, the First Psalm calls meditation.' The basis for the comparison is the law of God, seen as the food of the soul which must be assimilated into our innermost being. In the later commentary the occasion is a hostile glance at enclosed religious, 'those who recite a great string of psalms every day but with the tongue only, not with the spirit.' This is described as one of the most widespread and serious faults among

* * * * *

34 An interesting variant can be found in *In psalmum 22* LB V 313D where Erasmus proposes a four-fold *spiritual* reading based on the distinction between Christ as head of the church and its members as his mystical body.

35 CWE 66 35

36 *In psalmum 1* 29–30 below; cf 46.

religious, inducing weariness of spirit and a loss of integrity: 'Almost all our nuns are such that whatever constancy they have is due to iron bars.' This characteristically Hieronymian judgment is qualified when Erasmus goes on to lay the blame squarely on those responsible for the spiritual guidance of the nuns, but the complaint recurs in the *Life of Jerome* when he contrasts the circumstances of holy women like Paula with the iron grillwork behind which enclosed nuns now must lurk like savage beasts: 'I grieve ... that the purity of virgins must be secured through the constraint provided by iron bars and prison walls.'[37] The polemical point is clear: monastic life devoid of spiritual meaning – lived in the letter as it were – is no better than incarceration. This literal existence is the fate of those who fail to meditate on the psalms, 'those who remain stuck at the outer layers of Scripture in the manner of the Jews, without ruminating on the mystical wisdom hidden within.' Within the pastoral context of Psalm 22 Erasmus works out an intricate analogy between the cud-chewing by which sheep gain their nourishment and the proper reading of the Scriptures:

> But Christ's sheep have for palate their understanding, which they use in simplicity to take in health-giving doctrine; they mash it for a while with serious consideration, turning it over in their minds; then they commit it to their upper stomach, that is, their memory. Then refreshed by drinking from the spirit, they withdraw from the tumult of worldly cares, and lying down in the pastures of the Lord they recall to the understanding those things which they have stored in their memory and chew them over again with more careful consideration. Then finally they send it down to the stomach, so that from there it may be absorbed into the whole body and become the substance of the mind.[38]

So far does Erasmus take this pastoral theme as a model for the working of the Scriptures in spiritual growth that he can even compare Christ to the salt lick which sharpens the appetite of the sheep for sustaining food.

The underlying ground for Erasmus' criticism of the church in his time – 'this most turbulent century' as he would call it in 1528[39] – is its pastoral failure, that is, its failure to support the spiritual growth of those placed in its care. A particular duty of the bishop's office, as he constantly reiterates, is to minister the word of God, and in his numerous assaults on the slackness of the clergy he never loses sight of the metaphorical source of pastoral care in

* * * * *

37 CWE 61 31
38 *In psalmum 22* LB V 338D–340A
39 *In psalmum 85* LB V 544B

the figure of the good shepherd.[40] As the curious allegory of ovine rumination makes clear, the shepherd must ensure that the sheep have the means to eat properly, but the actual process of assimilation is a deeply personal one: it is not enough to see or hear the Scriptures in a passive way any more than it is enough to stare at the consecrated host at mass. In both cases it is the personal reception of the spiritual reality which is actually transforming. Christ's sheep, once they have ruminated the cud of God's word, consign it to the stomach:

> Our stomach is our inner disposition [*affectus*]; if we love what we have learned and believe it, we have sent food to our stomachs. And if we have begun to practise through acts of charity what we have received, then by vigour and activity we show that the food has become the substance of the spirit.[41]

What is striking here is the identification of the spiritual 'stomach,' the organ that distributes vital energy, with the inner disposition or *affectus*, the term commonly used in the Latin rhetorical tradition to describe the potential self, that shadowy meeting point of aspiration, instinct, and subjectivity which together with its related term *affectio* is the target for the persuasive arts of rhetoric.[42] This faculty rather than the rational judgment is the real force behind our actions, so that the point of the allegory is that the word of God must penetrate to this level to be effective; it must not stay lodged in the intellect, heard only by the outer ear. The image of feeding, standing as it does for the meditative assimilation of God's word, is central to Erasmus' account of the place of the Scriptures in the Christian life, and the quasi-sacramental nature of the act of reading can be sensed in the commentary on Psalm 1 as he advises the Christian teacher to immerse himself in the Scriptures day and night: 'Let him drink deeply of them, let him learn them by heart; nor merely learn them, but meditate on them, that is, apply them to his mental attitudes, his feelings, his morals, and his life' – *hoc est in habitum animi, in affectus, in mores ac vitam traiiciat*.[43] The Latin verb *traiicio*,

* * * * *

40 On the obligation of bishops to meditate on and teach the Scriptures see 33, 43 below; cf *In psalmum 33* LB V 337E–338C and *In psalmum 38* LB V 421F.

41 *In psalmum 22* LB V 339C. That charitable acts demonstrate the assimilation of Christ's teaching matches the concept of double justification; see lxiii–lxv below.

42 In the *Tusculan Disputations* (5.16.47) Cicero attributes to Socrates the view that 'as was the disposition of each individual soul [*qualis cuiusque animi adfectus est*] so was the man.'

43 44 below; on meditation as preparation for action see 28.

which is used here to convey the sense of 'to transpose' or 'to apply,' is used elsewhere by Erasmus for the ingestion of 'heavenly bread,'[44] and this process of absorption into the inner self of 'attitudes' and 'feelings' demonstrates the rhetorical basis for this kind of meditative reading. It could well have been while he was at work on this commentary that Erasmus drafted that passage in the *Paraclesis* which puts the matter most succinctly, as he describes how in the philosophy of Christ, 'located as it is more truly in the disposition of the mind [*in affectibus situm*] than in syllogisms, life means more than debate, inspiration is preferable to erudition, transformation is a more important matter than intellectual comprehension.'[45] If the whole enterprise of deliberative rhetoric is designed to make words issue in action, then the ruminative reading of the Scriptures is a species of internalized rhetoric directed towards action. In the *Exposition of Psalm 38* Erasmus underlines the point: 'The word *meditatio* here does not mean "deliberation" but is synonymous with the Greek word μελέτη, in other words, a passionate desire to do something.'[46]

One intriguing detail in Erasmus' elucidation of the pastoral topoi in Psalm 22 is the contrast he draws between Christ's sheep, which, since they ruminate, are gentle creatures, 'incapable of biting, because they have teeth only in their lower jaw,' and the doglike Pharisees: 'Whatever food they were given by the Lord they tore at with their teeth, using it to slander him.'[47] The point clearly is that the Pharisees do not meditate, their reading is confined to the literal sense, they are not transformed by it. To ruminate, to open one's being to the spiritual scope of the Scriptures, is to encounter Christ – the faithful shepherd – and to imitate him. The inevitable association in this psalm of food with doctrine offers a valuable indication of how Erasmus sees the working of the Bible in the economy of the Christian life; just as the figure of Christ the shepherd is central to the pastoral responsibilities of the church, so the idea of feeding is an appropriate image of its functioning, one associated in the first place with the effective presentation of divine teaching. In fact, in order to elucidate this most pastoral of the psalms, Erasmus draws on an associative cluster which he had earlier used in his *Paraphrases on the Gospels* when narrating Christ's miraculous feeding of

* * * * *

44 In the *Paraphrasis in Joannem* LB VII 547C, 549D
45 *Paraclesis* in *Desiderius Erasmus Roterodamus: Ausgewählte Werke* ed Hajo Holborn and Annemarie Holborn (Munich 1933; repr 1964) 144–5, trans J. Olin *Christian Humanism and the Reformation* 3rd ed (New York 1987) 104
46 *In psalmum 38* LB V 444F; for the Platonic source of μελέτη see Screech 81.
47 *In psalmum 22* LB V 339B

the crowds.[48] In the *Paraphrase on Mark* it is suggested that the crowds, simple folk, were drawn in their search for Christ by hunger for saving doctrine; they are like lost sheep, disregarded by the priests, Scribes, and Pharisees, so Christ out of pity becomes their shepherd and gives them spiritual food before he satisfies their physical hunger. In all the accounts the multiplication of the loaves is treated as a sign of the spread of the gospel: Christ is the *convivator*, the master of the feast, and the apostles are his assistants, setting the model for bishops as they distribute his bounty unadulterated by human teachings. As might be expected, the most complex and suggestive account of the miraculous feeding is that to be found in the *Paraphrase on John*, the Gospel which makes the richest use of pastoral metaphor. Chapter 6 of John describes how Christ, shortly before the feast of Passover, multiplies barley loaves to feed the crowd of five thousand before crossing the Lake of Galilee to Capernaum, where, in the synagogue, he delivers his discourse on the heavenly bread which gives everlasting life. The discourse becomes a commentary on the multiplication of the loaves, and, in contrast to the Synoptics, John's account presents a tension between the secular concerns of the Jewish crowd and the enigmatic teaching of Christ, a contrast which Erasmus exploits. Christ's words in the synagogue set the spiritual nature of his teaching against the material and political ambitions of some among his followers; they are 'still dreaming about the belly's business,' whereas he offers them 'heavenly bread, which is the divine word.' As so often in John, Jesus' hearers are stuck on the literal sense, failing to distinguish the sign of the loaves from the reality they signify. Foreshadowed by the manna in the desert, this bread, which stills all hunger and is eaten 'not with an open mouth but with a believing soul,' is Christ himself, the word of the Father:

> If anyone lets this bread pass into the bowels of his soul he will be quickened and will grow strong into eternal life. But if you, being unspiritual, do not yet understand spiritual matters, I will say something simpler and related to the flesh. This flesh that you see is also living bread, which I shall pay and hand over to death to ransom the life of the whole world. Believe, take, and live.

In his paraphrase Erasmus is distinguishing the two possible lines of interpretation that tradition had found in the Johannine text: on the one hand there is the bread which is the word of God, 'eaten with a believing soul,' while on the other there is an apparent reference to Christ's human body,

* * * * *

48 On these episodes see Jane E. Phillips 'Food and Drink in Erasmus' Gospel Paraphrases' *Erasmus of Rotterdam Society Yearbook* 14 (1994) 24–45.

which would suffer on the cross 'to ransom the life of the whole world' and which is, by implication, consumed in the Eucharist.[49] While Erasmus allows the second possibility, it is the first reading with its emphasis on the saving word of God that he regards as the more satisfying. One can suspect that this particular interpretation of Christ's enigmatic words on the bread of life is of some importance for his own sense of the church: two years after the *Paraphrase on John* it reappears in *A Sermon on the Fourth Psalm* on the authority of 'the earliest commentators'; it is then added as a note to the 1527 *Annotationes* and, as we have seen, the issue surfaces again in the *Exposition of Psalm 22*, where the food given to the sheep is identified with Christ's teaching.[50] It is not so much that Erasmus disregards the second interpretation and its Eucharistic associations but that he sees it subsumed within the more comprehensive idea of the church as driven and sustained by the spiritual reception of the gospel. Thus what emerges from his treatment of the 'puzzling statements' of John 6 is a strong assertion of the Scriptures – the 'heavenly bread, which is the divine word' – as a means of spiritual access to Christ which operates in a manner analogous to the sacraments. Hence the importance given to metaphors of eating in his account of reading the Scriptures: they reiterate that spiritual mode of reception which Christ had demanded of the disciples at Capernaum:

> By my flesh and blood I mean my teaching; if you take it eagerly through belief and pass it through the bowels of your mind, it will quicken your souls and make you one body with me so that by my spirit you live forever, just as the members of a single body live by their shared breath as long as they are joined together. And I shall leave my flesh and blood as a mystical symbol of this union, though it will do you no good to have received that unless you receive it in spirit.[51]

When we find Erasmus here referring to the Eucharist as 'a mystical symbol' of Christ's union with his members it is clear that he sees this symbol as something more substantial than a mere aid to recollection. In 1532, while writing his commentary on Psalm 83, *De sarcienda ecclesiae concordia*,

* * * * *

49 The quotations are taken from the paraphrase on John 6:26–59 CWE 46 81–7.
50 His appeal to 'the earliest commentators' is probably based on Origen, Chrysostom, and Tertullian; see 209 and n208 below. For the annotation see *Erasmus' Annotations on the New Testament: The Gospels* ed A. Reeve (London 1986) 242; for Psalm 22 see LB V 322d. See also CWE 46 86 n69 (page 277)
51 CWE 46 88

Erasmus faced the contemporary dispute over the nature of the sacrament with characteristic restraint, using conciliatory language but only in order to endorse authentic tradition; the mass is a true participation by 'mystic rites' in the unique sacrifice of Calvary, and Christ is indeed present under the forms of bread and wine, but he is so 'in order that he may be consumed with absolute purity of mind, not that he may be exhibited, or carried around at celebrations or public processions, or borne round fields on horseback.' If the abuses of a carnal religion are exposed here, Erasmus is equally severe on those like the Sacramentarians who reduce the Eucharist to a purely subjective event, 'since what is performed only by mental processes and with no external sign is not worthy of the name of sacrament.'[52] Spiritual food, the cud chewed in meditation, must be grounded in a material sign, whether this be bread and wine or the letter of God's word; what is necessary is that it be received 'in absolute purity of spirit' so that the process of digestion may begin. Thus the conversion of food into energy provides a key paradigm for the transformation of material signs into spiritual truth, not only in the sacraments but also in that interpretative process which reveals the mystical meaning hidden in the literal sense. Since the main purpose of his religious teaching is precisely to reanimate the signs of the Christian life, it is only logical that Erasmus should endeavour to preserve the objective content while giving prominence to the need for subjective response; to take a sentence from the *Ecclesiastes* which echoes the theme of John 6, 'It is not absurd to believe that the Holy Spirit also desired Scripture to suit the disposition of each reader, just as manna tasted as each one wished it to.'[53] This is so because the proper understanding of the word of God – which so many of Christ's hearers at Capernaum failed to achieve – entails a dynamic interaction between the individual believer and the received body of divine teaching, a process so intimate that it can best be conveyed by the metaphor of eating.

The opening section of the *Exposition of Psalm 33* achieves a particularly rich development of the theme of spiritual, that is Christocentric, perception: the reader is urged to pray for 'the eyes of a pure heart to see the things of the spirit, and pure ears with which to perceive the secrets of heavenly

* * * * *

52 LB V 503F–504B. Both extremes might be said to take the Eucharist out of context; Erasmus' stance does not appear to be reductive, as Chomarat argues (*Grammaire et rhétorique chez Erasme* 2 vols [Paris 1981] I 697), but conciliatory.

53 LB V 1047; relevant here is J.B. Payne's observation that Erasmus follows the Franciscan notion of a sacrament as a free (*ex pacto*) grant of grace marked by a sign, rather than the Thomistic idea of intrinsic efficacy (*Erasmus: His Theology of the Sacraments* [Richmond, Va 1970] 98).

wisdom.'[54] In effect this means the capacity to open the Silenus figure and reach beyond the literal sense of historical narrative to its Christocentric application: the section centres on Christ both as the antitype who fulfils the Old Testament signs, the true manna which gives eternal life to body and soul, and as the companion who 'opened the Scriptures' for the two disciples on their journey to Emmaus. To the question 'What is the meaning of "opened"?' Erasmus answers, 'It means that he showed them the allegory hidden in the history.' The emphasis falls on the act of opening; the verb *aperit* (not found in the scriptural source, which simply states that Christ 'interpreted' Moses and the prophets) can best be understood – in the light of the recurrent use of references to opening throughout the section – as an allusion back to the Silenus figure, which must be opened to reveal its divinity.[55] Indeed the act of opening is a fitting analogy for the reading of the Scriptures, since it implies the imminence of an encounter; the reader is placed in a comparable situation to the disciples at the breaking of bread in Emmaus: 'Then their eyes were opened and they recognized him.' To enter, to engage the text and penetrate beyond the letter is to recognize the divine presence within it.[56] Sacred Scripture is at the heart of Erasmus' spirituality because in it he discovers the workings of divine grace, the guiding hand of providence which brings meaning to the scattered events of history and even to the fumbled efforts of the individual life.

It is certainly no accident that Erasmus' commitment to biblical studies appears to develop at much the same time as his interest in Platonism. This is not to say that he ever becomes a technical Platonist in the sense that he adopts it as a formal system; rather it furnishes him with a highly effective rhetorical resource for conveying the eternal and unchanging in its relation to the transient, precisely what so absorbs him in his 'mystical' interpretation of the Bible. The two most persistent figures of thought which he derives directly from Plato are allegories of transcendence, the paradoxical Silenus used in the *Symposium* to characterize Socrates and the parable of the cave from the *Republic*. Evidently both impressed him deeply: they

* * * * *

54 LB V 369B
55 LB V 371A–B: '. . . as we open (*expandimus*) the Silenus . . .'; 'If we open the Silenus . . .'; at 371C the expository process is treated as the opening of doors. I am grateful to Dr Emily Kearns for alerting me to this sequence.
56 Terence Cave *The Cornucopian Text* (n5 above) 86: 'Instead of himself penetrating the text in an attempt to extract meaning, or imposing alien senses on it, the reader is penetrated by it, transformed into it . . . he is himself a place of plenitude, the place where the virtual productivity of Scripture becomes actual.'

have a prominent function in the *Enchiridion*, his earliest attempt to reanimate Christian observance, and they are still central to the commentaries on Psalms 33 and 38 three decades later. Reanimation is an apt term to describe the aim of his efforts at reform; just as his attacks on secular abuses are directed at practices which have become hardened in custom and divorced from their originating purpose, so in the Christian life his goal is to recover the spiritual vision – the animating principle – which alone gives the ceremonial and juridical aspects of the church validity. This accounts for the informal alliance between the Scriptures and Neoplatonic epistemology which is a recurrent feature of his spiritual writings.[57] Presumably he first encountered Plato in the Latin translation of Ficino, which would certainly have been available to him during his residence at Paris between 1495 and 1500, the period when he began work on the *Antibarbari*.[58] Apart from a lifelong admiration for Socrates as a midwife of the soul – a pioneer of the exegete's role – the most lasting thing to emerge from this encounter was the pneumatic emphasis which Erasmus instinctively expresses in dichotomies: outer and inner, darkness and light, body and soul, letter and spirit. The terms he uses are Pauline, but they are handled in a manner which can be called Platonic: 'Just as there are two laws, of the flesh and of the spirit, so there are two worlds. The world in which we live teems with vanities; another will follow, in which the phantoms will be scattered, and all will be revealed.'[59] In this passage the warring principles of flesh and spirit look back to St John and the Pauline Epistles, but the distinction of worlds echoes Plato's theory of ideas: just such a spatial transition from a world of shadows to the glaring light of authentic vision is that enacted in the allegory of the cave.

Plato's fable in the *Republic* (7.514A–517B) describes the human condition in terms of prisoners shackled in a cave with their backs to the light, unable to perceive any reality except the shadows thrown on the face of the rock by the figures which move behind them. As Erasmus adapts the allegory in the *Enchiridion*, they are the crowd, *vulgus*, 'who, chained by their own passions, marvel at the empty images of things as if they were the true reality.'[60]

* * * * *

57 Cf J.B. Payne 'Towards the Hermeneutics of Erasmus' in *Scrinium Erasmianum* ed J. Coppens, 2 vols (Leiden 1969) II 17–20; it needs to be stressed that the alliance is informal.

58 See M. Cytowska 'Erasme de Rotterdame et Marsile Ficin son maître' *EOS* 63 (1975) 165–79; also P.O. Kristeller 'Erasmus from an Italian Perspective' *Renaissance Quarterly* 23 (1970) 1–14.

59 *In psalmum* 4 244 below; cf John 6:63, Romans 8:1–2, 1 Cor 3:6, *Moria* CWE 27 152.

60 CWE 66 86

The cave myth had a compelling force for Erasmus, and he returned to it frequently both as a telling image of the dangers of conventional evaluation and as an incitement to break loose from it, for Plato's account goes on to describe those exceptional individuals who escape from their bonds and discover the upward ascent into the full light of reality. It is this aspect of the myth which is developed in the *Moria*, where the folly of the crowd is contrasted with the apparent insanity of those who no longer accept the conventions of the shadow world; as Erasmus later explained it to Joris van Halewijn, 'The passage which troubles you in the *Moria* ... will be clear if you remember the Platonic myth about the cave and the men born in it, who wondered at the shadows of things as though they were the reality. What we apprehend with our senses does not really exist, for it is not perpetual, nor does it always take the same form. Those things alone really exist which are apprehended by the contemplation of the mind.'[61] If on the one hand Erasmus had found in Lucian an effective model for exposing the pseudo-values of a fallen world, on the other he found in the Platonic tradition an effective rhetoric for pointing beyond them. That is not to say that he was uncritical – Origen's errors are squarely blamed on his Platonic leanings – but Erasmus' loosely Platonic orientation provided the basis for the distinction he repeatedly draws between carnal or institutional forms of religious life and the spiritual reality which should validate them. In the *Moria* Folly evokes the cave myth by her description of the crowds which focus on the mass as a physical performance and neglect the spiritual invitation which it proffers, in contrast to the devout man 'who throughout his life withdraws from the things of the body and is drawn towards what is eternal, invisible, and spiritual.'[62] A constant motive in the religious writings of Erasmus is the recovery of the spiritual purpose behind the public forms of contemporary Christianity, forms which under the pressure of custom had so often become ends in themselves. The key term *pius* – possessing the quality of *pietas* – is not easily translated into English, having little to do with such conventional phrases as 'objects of piety'; rather it conveys the idea of being receptive to the Spirit. Touching on a topic that will require our scrutiny later, Erasmus condemns worship of Christ through visible things for the sake of visible things as 'a kind of Judaism,' that is of blindness to the Spirit.[63] Against the background of the contemporary preoccupation with ritual and public

* * * * *

61 Ep 1115:5–11, referring to *Moria* CWE 27 150; cf *Institutio principis christiani* CWE 27 212, *In psalmum 38* LB V 453A–B, *Ecclesiastes* LB V 939E.
62 CWE 27 152
63 CWE 66 74 see xlix–lv below.

ceremony, he repeatedly draws attention to the dangers of detaching signs from their original signification and making them self-referential. This may be a matter of ritual action, of fasting, or of religious dress: whatever the case, the sign must be transcended if its proper function is to be realized.

The Platonic model also had relevance in matters of textual interpretation. As early as the *Enchiridion*, composed as he first began to engage seriously with scriptural studies, Erasmus recognizes that 'the same rule applies for all literary works, which are made up of a literal sense and a mysterious sense, body and soul as it were, in which you are to ignore the letter and look rather to the mystery. The writings of all the poets and the Platonist philosophers belong to this category, but especially the sacred Scriptures, which like those images of Silenus mentioned by Alcibiades enclose unadulterated divinity under a lowly and almost ludicrous external appearance.'[64] Thus the ascent from the cave also provides an analogue of the process of interpretation whereby a psalm which in its literal sense relates to Jewish history can be read as a prophecy of Christ; one incidental interest of the passage cited is that it seems to render any dramatic conversion of the young Erasmus from literary studies to divinity superfluous since it suggests a natural progression from one to the other. Whatever the case, the later months of 1501 do appear to mark an important juncture in his sense of personal commitment to the Scriptures: at Saint-Omer he made the acquaintance of Jean Vitrier, warden of the house of Franciscan Observants there, and in the course of the winter which he passed at Courtebourne he gave himself to the study of Greek and a course of theological reading. Central to this was the figure of Origen, and Erasmus' enthusiasm for his writings – 'I learn more of Christian philosophy from a single page of Origen than from ten of Augustine,' he would write ten years later – seems to owe much to Vitrier, whose unconventional admiration for the Greek Father had clearly impressed him.[65] From the library of the Observants at Saint-Omer he was able to borrow a number of books, including a copy of Origen's homilies which was perhaps, as Godin suggests, a manuscript of a Latin version by Jerome or Rufinus. This may not have been his first encounter with Origen, but its impact was strongly evident in the *Enchiridion*, which he began work on at this time, and it seems to have prompted his earliest exegetical attempt, a lost commentary on Romans.

* * * * *

64 CWE 66 67–8
65 Ep 844:272–4; as with other such sweeping statements, a mystical reading seems wiser than a literal one. For Vitrier see Ep 1211:29–33. For a full account of Erasmus' relationship with Vitrier, and the discovery of Origen, see A. Godin *Erasme lecteur d'Origène* (Geneva 1982) 13–28.

As the *Enchiridion* makes clear, Erasmus' response to Origen was assisted by the Platonizing disposition which they shared. But in terms of his theological understanding Erasmus' most important debt was to Origen's teaching on incarnation. The dualism of flesh and spirit is persistently used by Erasmus, usually when an ethical point is being made; that is how it operates in the *Enchiridion*, and there most notably in 'the fifth rule' with its depreciation of visible things. But even in this work he introduces the trichotomous anthropology by which Origen reconciles Platonic duality through the Pauline scheme of 1 Thessalonians: spirit, soul, and flesh.[66] As options, spirit and flesh are totally opposed, but in the paradox of human nature they may be reconciled through the mediating function of *anima* 'soul,' so that the body is no longer a disruptive force but may become a temple of the Spirit. In exegesis, similarly, the carnal or literal sense may be charged with spiritual significance through the figurative and and symbolizing powers of language. At the root of these mediations is, for Erasmus, the extraordinary reality of the Incarnation, by which Christ relates the material events of history to their spiritual purpose. It was from Origen that he derived not only this recognition of the centrality of the Incarnation but also the idea that it was in a sense extended through the Scriptures, that the word of God truly grasped is a means by which Christ's presence reaches through history.[67] As the divinity of Christ was hidden in human form, so the sacred meaning of Scripture is lodged within the fragile vessel of human language. The office of the genuine theologian, therefore, is to reveal the presence of the Word in words, a function which is allied not so much to philosophy as to prophecy, intending not so much to inform as to transform.

In all three synoptic gospels the parable of the sower draws attention to the challenge of interpretation within the New Testament text itself; in response to the disciples' question 'Why do you speak to them in parables?' Christ makes a distinction between those who can both see and hear and those who 'look without seeing and listen without hearing,' an obtuseness which is emphasized by his adoption of Isaiah's ringing denunciation: 'You will listen and listen again, but not understand, see and see again, but not perceive' (Matt 13:3–14; Isa 6:9). Clearly, proper understanding of Christ's teaching depends

* * * * *

66 For example CWE 66 41 and 51; cf *De taedio Iesu* LB V 1288A.
67 For the theme in Origen see R.P.C. Hanson *Allegory and Event* (London 1959) 194, 325; on the Erasmian perspective see Manfred Hoffmann *Rhetoric and Theology: The Hermeneutic of Erasmus* (Toronto 1994) 82. Erasmus' assimilation of Origen has been comprehensively analysed by G.J. Fokke *Christus Verae Pacis Auctor et Unicus Scopus: Erasmus and Origen* (Leuven 1977).

on the auditor's disposition. In his *Paraphrase on Matthew* Erasmus conveys the full force of this passage, giving it a characteristic twist: for those who receive his words with an apt disposition Christ speaks openly, but for those who have no wish to grasp his teaching he shrouds his words in obscurity, 'that so I may actually stir in them a desire to learn and look further.'[68] The provocation of the text can induce a new willingness to respond in which the intricacies of exegesis are matched by a growing subjective involvement. It is instructive to place this Erasmian idea of biblical reading alongside the hermeneutic scheme of a twentieth-century exponent like Hans-Georg Gadamer, to whom the text – whether secular or religious – will always transcend its context, forever opening itself to new significations and thus to new relationships. In consequence Gadamer shows himself just as hostile as Erasmus to the idea of a fixed historical reading and insists, rather, on the two-sided exchange generated by inscription, one which converts what is dead and alien into simultaneity and familiarity. If the act of interpretation revivifies what is received, it equally modifies the attitude of the recipient: 'To reach an understanding with one's partner in a dialogue is not merely a matter of total self-expression and the successful assertion of one's own point of view, but a transformation into a communion in which we do not remain what we were.'[69] *Applicatio*, the act of accommodating the world of the text to that of the reader, is conveyed with brisk economy by John Donne a century after Erasmus: 'This is *scrutari scripturas*, to search the Scriptures, not as though thou wouldest make a concordance, but an application; as thou wouldest search a wardrobe, not to make an *Inventory* of it, but to finde in it something fit for thy wearing.'[70] Not, therefore, that frigid exegesis which views the text as a historical narrative or as a quarry of *loci* for disputation, but a rhetorical exegesis which unravels the text as a personal communication. In accordance with patristic teaching, Erasmus recognizes, in the *coitus* of the divine and the human which begets Christ, the *sermo* or Word of God, an empowering of language to extend the Incarnation, an idea which is active in Origen's theology and equally colours Augustine's understanding.[71] To study Scripture is, in effect, to engage with

* * * * *

68 LB VII 77F
69 *Truth and Method* (London 1975; English translation based on the 1965 ed) 341
70 *The Sermons of John Donne* ed G.R. Potter and E.M. Simpson (Berkeley and Los Angeles 1953–62) III 367
71 For *coitus* see *Paraphrasis in Lucam* LB VII 290B and W.M. Gordon *Humanist Play and Belief* (Toronto 1990) 242. On speech and incarnation in Origen see n67 above; in Augustine see M. Colish *The Mirror of Language: A Study in the Medieval Theory of Knowledge* (New Haven and London 1968) 35.

redeemed speech and by its means to enter into a dialogue with Christ, the Word. What provides the driving force behind Erasmus' biblical enterprise is this sense that God's saving power is primarily transmitted to humankind through the gift of language; thus the divine utterance must be published in terms which can cohere with the individual life. In the case of the Old Testament, in particular, this means detaching the text from the contingency of its origins and applying the Christological frame so strongly asserted by biblical humanism in order to generate new accommodations. This was the truth which Lefèvre's despondent monks failed to grasp; they had halted at the historical predicament of David instead of passing on to the controlling symbol: 'We have done well to leave David,' Erasmus declares, 'and come to Christ. We have left the letter that kills, and found the spirit that gives life.'[72]

To find the spirit means, among other things, to move beyond the literal sense and reach out towards that *sensus mysticus* which is the goal of all Erasmian exegesis. Yet Erasmus is always careful to insist on a coherent approach to interpretation, one that will hold all the possible senses in harmony. Thus, given his concern with spiritual apprehension of the text, it is important to recognize the controlling function which he allots to the literal sense; while it is necessary to go beyond the letter, it is by no means wise to lose sight of it. The immediate sense, whether it be called literal, historical, or grammatical, is to be taken as the starting point for spiritual elaboration: 'The historical sense is as it were the base and foundation which does not exclude but rather supports the mystical sense.'[73] The wording here is precise and it expresses Erasmus' cautious approach to figurative interpretation: to stay preoccupied with the literal sense and disregard allegories and tropes verges on Judaism, but to wing off on allegorical flights, as Origen is prone to do, is to substitute human ingenuity for true understanding.[74] The coherence of Scripture is a fundamental tenet, and it flows from the conception of the written word of God as an extension of Christ's incarnation. It follows therefore that the most appropriate basis for unravelling the text is internal cross-reference within the biblical corpus; at the conclusion of his exposition of Psalm 38 Erasmus concedes the charm and utility of allegory but warns of its dangers: 'I consider it to be the mark of a good teacher at no point consciously to depart from the true sense of Scripture, and if this is not absolutely clear it is better to refrain from making dogmatic assertions and

* * * * *

72 *In psalmum 33* LB V 381B
73 *In psalmum 85* LB V 511A; cf *In psalmum 2* 78 and 144 below, also *Ecclesiastes* LB V 1229C–D.
74 *In psalmum 38* LB V 427B; cf *Ecclesiastes* LB V 1038E.

not to mention everything that can be said when the opportunity arises but only those things which seem closest to the truth when compared with other scriptural passages and accommodated to the continuity of sense in the argument as a whole.'[75] The crux here is the 'true sense,' the *sensus germanus*, a term which reflects confidence both in the unity of revelation and in the unity of interpretive tradition. At the same time he can compare the Scriptures to a wonderful painting which yields more delight to the viewer the longer it is contemplated, a simile which affirms the personal and subjective nature of the quest.[76]

To progress beyond the literal sense is to recognize the intricacies of the painting and thus to become absorbed in the workings of God's redemptive scheme. After God himself, Erasmus writes in the *Ecclesiastes*, the church's most treasured resource is God's word.[77] While he acknowledges the traditional four senses of Scripture he tends to associate these with the *neoterici*, and his preference is for the looser twofold scheme of the *prisci doctores* which simply distinguishes historical from spiritual, the latter a flexible category encompassing those readings which might otherwise be characterized as tropological, allegorical, or anagogical.[78] In the pastoral concern which dominates his exegesis he is more concerned to alert the reader to the Christological dimension than to introduce intellectual distinctions. None the less, the formal terms do occur. In the exposition of Psalm 1, composed in 1515 while Erasmus was heavily engaged in writing on ethical themes, it is not surprising to find that he gives prominence to the tropological level, because it fits 'that reform of morality which is my principal aim.'[79] Moreover, this remains the dominant preoccupation throughout Erasmus' treatment of the Psalms: there is scarcely any part of the Scriptures which cannot be given a tropological application, he claims in 1522 in the commentary on Psalm 2, and in his final commentary, that on Psalm 14 published in 1536, he moves on from allegory and anagogy to the moral sense, 'which may perhaps seem less exalted but is in my opinion more useful.'[80] It is both *humilior* and *utilior*. Precisely because he is relaxed about the modality of the spiritual sense, Erasmus is able to give the tropological a broad connotation, so that it becomes in effect that reading

* * * * *

75 *In psalmum 38* LB V 468E; on the harmony of the Old and New Testaments see ibidem 427C–D.
76 *In psalmum 33* LB V 394A
77 LB V 801F
78 *Ecclesiastes* LB V 1034D
79 See 11 below.
80 *In psalmum 2* 78 below; *De puritate tabernaculi* LB V 301B

which relates to personal growth in holiness and spiritual perception. The exposition of Psalm 4 is consequently arranged in two stages: the first treats the psalm as an allegory of the general scheme of redemption, applying it to Christ as head and to the church as his body; the second more extensive section then turns to the moral sense: 'What I am about to say should be studied especially closely because it relates to each one of us individually, and deals with the conduct of our everyday lives.'[81] The tropological reading, in other words, covers a good deal more than the strictly ethical; it includes the cooperation of the individual with the promptings of grace, and Erasmus' evident preference for it reflects the priority allotted to pastoral goals in the wider context of biblical humanism. The individual *persona*, however, is never isolated from the wider relationship of Christ with the church. While this is implicit throughout the psalm commentaries it is given special prominence in the *Enarratio triplex* on Psalm 22, triple because it comprehends Christ as head, the church as Christ's body, and the individual Christian as *alter Christus*. The initial reading impersonates Christ as redeemer, offering a prayer of gratitude to the Father; this is followed by the application to the church, the Lord's own banquet; finally comes the transition to the moral sense with its personal application: 'Let each of you consider that this psalm is relevant only to himself; let each of you ask himself whether he is really a sheep belonging to Christ, whether he can sing this psalm not only with the voice of his tongue but with that of his heart.'[82]

Grammatical discussion throughout the expositions of the Psalms is confined to an ancillary role, nor is this surprising in view of Erasmus' insistence on the character of the biblical text as utterance, the word of God directed to the receptive reader. For this very reason he is always alert to the issue of context and impatient of that kind of theological practice which pilfers Scripture for isolated phrases or relies on digests to bolster an argument.[83] Any scriptural passage must be considered in terms not only of what is said but also by whom it is said, to whom, the words used, the temporal setting, the occasion, and what precedes and follows it.[84] God's word is thus seen as something vocal, a totality addressed to the inward ear of every Christian and incarnate in Christ. Attention is given to matters of textual obscurity or

* * * * *

81 See 212 below.

82 *In psalmum* 22 LB V 333C; for the application to Christ see 314B–315D and to the church 315E–333B.

83 See 29 below.

84 *Ratio* ed Holborn (n45 above) 197 and 285; *Ecclesiastes* LB V 782E; *In psalmum* 85 LB V 511A

disputed interpretation, but this is kept to a minimum in order to avoid any rupture in the elucidation of the spiritual sense. A typical sequence occurs in the exposition of Psalm 2 where, prior to venturing further across 'this ocean of exposition,' Erasmus touches on certain points designed to assist the reader in plotting a consistent course, so that to start with the issue of the speaker or speakers is tackled, and then the problem of anthropomorphic attributions to God is given some light, in this case his scornful laughter.[85] In fact Erasmus shows little interest in the philological perspective while dealing with the Psalms, and his comments on the Hebrew are minimal. The essential spirit of his exegesis can be be effectively illustrated by two representative passages. The first is found in the treatment of Psalm 4:2, where a number of variants occur; all of them are briefly listed, but Erasmus shows little inclination to resolve the issue: while the original inspiration of the Spirit was unambiguous, God has allowed these variants to develop through the multiplication of manuscripts and translations in order to challenge us and wake us from torpor. Such vicissitudes in the career of the text are no threat to salvation; the essential requirements are that our reading should promote virtue and that it should be in harmony with other passages of Scripture.[86]

In the same way, commenting on Psalm 33, Erasmus is unruffled by discrepancy over the name of the priest who gave the consecrated loaves to David; such inconsistencies are common enough in secular histories, a consequence of human fallibility. But the Scriptures cannot stumble or deceive, so that once textual scholarship has failed to resolve a difficulty we must conclude that the apparent inconsistency is the sign of a mystery and must pray for the grace of understanding.[87] The constant impression is given of an exegesis geared to personal devotion, to attainment of that condition of awareness or constant prayer which is held up as the ideal in the explication of Psalm 33. A Christian whose mind is 'imbued with true piety' does all things, waking or sleeping, to the praise of God; in such a condition, 'one who sets aside his prayers to render his wife her due, praises the Lord in the very action of not praying.'[88] For Erasmus the Psalms have a vital role in the process of

* * * * *

85 See 100–4 below; on anthropomorphism as synecdoche see 111.
86 See 239 below.
87 *In psalmum 33* LB V 378B–C
88 *In psalmum 33* LB V 388B. On the theme of constant prayer see J. Trapman 'Erasmus's *Precationes*' in *Acta Conventus Neo-Latini Torontonensis* ed A. Dalzell, C. Fantazzi, and R.J. Schoeck (Binghamton, NY 1991) 769–79; for contemporary ideas on the marriage debt see Thomas N. Tentler *Sin and Confession on the Eve of the Reformation* (Princeton 1977) 170–4.

growth through which Christians are enabled to realize spiritual maturity in whatever sphere may be their calling; when dedicating the *Explanatio in omnes psalmos* of the Carolingian monk Haimo of Halberstadt to the Carthusian Jan of Heemstede in 1533, Erasmus describes a monk as one who represents all the Christian virtues in their highest form, yet on this very basis he concludes that whoever has attained inner tranquillity may be a monk, whether in the courts of princes, civic assemblies, or the bustle of affairs. In a sense, anticipating the dedication of *De puritate tabernaculi* to Christoph Eschenfelder two years later, he is reclaiming the Psalms for a lay readership.

That Erasmus' guiding motive in exegesis is spiritual rather than philological is clearly demonstrated in his treatment of the Old Testament. His feelings about it were ambivalent. At the height of the Reuchlin affair in 1517 he could even wish that it were done away with altogether if that might restore harmony among Christians; a year later, writing to Wolfgang Capito, he regrets that the latter's talents were taken up with Hebrew rather than Greek: 'If only the church of Christians did not attach so much importance to the Old Testament! It is a thing of shadows, given us for a time; and now it is almost preferred to the literature of Christianity.'[89] The obvious hyperbole should warn us against taking this too seriously, yet it does hint at the difficulties that Erasmus experienced in his encounters with Hebrew and the culture of Judaism. There may even be a note of personal frustration in his remarks to Capito, since his own efforts to tackle Hebrew do not appear to have been especially successful. He was, clearly enough, committed to the ideal of competence in the three tongues, Hebrew, Greek, and Latin, which had special relevance to theology – the three swords and triple shield of Geryon as he calls them[90] – and he missed no opportunity to promote their cause. Still, while his own study of Greek flourished, competence in Hebrew evaded him: writing to Colet in 1504 he reports his progress in Greek but adds that his effort to take up Hebrew has faltered through lack of time and the strangeness of the language. He would later claim in the *Apologia adversus Petrum Sutorem* that prior to writing on the Psalms he consulted Hebrew scholars, and this is borne out by a letter of 1516 from Colet which refers to his continued study of the language; yet all the evidence points to the accuracy of his own frank assessment, that his knowledge of the language was 'only a brief taste ... with the tip of my tongue as the saying goes.'[91] But if one considers the psalm commentaries as a whole, there are very few

* * * * *

89 Epp 701, 798:347–8
90 Ep 541:142–3
91 Ep 181:41–5; LB IX 770F; Ep 423:65–6; *Adagia* III i 1 CWE 34 182

occasions when an appeal is made to the Hebrew text, and then it is usually based on standard authorities, 'those who know Hebrew,' 'students of Hebrew,' or some such phrase.[92] There is the distinct possibility that he worked from a polyglot text, since this would help to explain those odd lapses when he appears to treat the Septuagint Greek as if it were the original.[93] The fact is that he did not feel at ease with Hebrew, a handicap in commenting on the Psalms as he freely admitted to Sadoleto in 1530.[94]

But this did not deter Erasmus from making a substantial contribution to the contemporary literature on the Psalms, nor was this inconsistent: as he treats them in his expositions the Psalms are effectively Christian texts, largely disengaged from their setting in Jewish history and culture. His mature and considered assessment of Hebrew can be found in the *Ecclesiastes*, written at the very end of his career, where he considers it to be the first language in dignity but of limited relevance to the Christian scholar.[95] There may be an element of sour grapes in this judgment, but it merely expresses in modified terms the much stronger comment of the exposition of Psalm 2 where, after alluding by way of Nicholas of Lyra to the Jewish tradition reported by Rashi or 'Rabbi Solomon,' he adds that although he does not wholly disapprove of studying the Hebrew commentators he does not expect much profit to ensue, 'since I observe that their commentaries are pretty well stuffed with vapourings and old wives' tales, not to mention their desire to discredit our interpretations, and their hatred of Christ.'[96] There are indeed two distinct strands in Erasmus' treatment of Hebrew. On the one hand the philologist is alert to the complexities and idiomatic challenge of an unfamiliar tongue and is anxious to illuminate it where possible, as when he tries to explicate the problematic term *Selah* by reference to Greek comic conventions; but the obverse side of this is an often undisguised impatience: 'No language is more confusing, or more open to misinterpretation and disagreement among its translators.'[97] On the other hand, we can detect a deeper concern by which Erasmus as an ardent follower of St Paul, 'that doughty defender of evangelical liberty,' is fearful of any drift back towards a Jewish

* * * * *

92 For examples see 40, 214, 249 below; on the issue see Chomarat (n52 above) 1 321–44.
93 Eg *In psalmum 85* LB V 547B–C where verse 16 is glossed from the Greek, and *Adagia* II ii 74 where Psalm 90:6 is quoted in Greek
94 Allen Ep 2315:171–80
95 LB V 855B
96 See 80 below.
97 See 246 and 225 below; cf the pun on *bar-barbari* at 142.

mentality, anything that might compromise the Christocentric appropriation of the Hebrew Scriptures. This is why his interest in the Old Testament is primarily directed towards those books which are open to prophetic reading and so cohere with the New.[98]

Nowhere is this coherence more powerfully expressed than in *De concordia*, where Erasmus takes Luke's account of the Transfiguration as a figure for this particular aspect of concord: in the sight of Peter, John, and James, Christ appears in glory flanked by Moses and Elijah, who speak to him of his coming passion. Here the Law and the prophets find their direct fulfilment in Christ as the minister of the new, spiritual covenant. Such concord is not to be found in the synagogues, 'where the law is twisted to refer not to Christ but to some other Messiah, for whom the unfortunate people have been waiting in vain all these years'; equally, it is not to be found in the 'tabernacles' of such as the Manichees, who reject the Old Testament and thus forfeit the dynamic unfolding of God's word.[99] This conformity of the two Testaments is established by an authentic, spiritual understanding of the Scriptures and consequently it provides a criterion for all true orthodoxy; those who fail to recognize it are guilty of false reading. Thus the most radical charge that Erasmus brings against Judaism is its failure to interpret the spiritual meaning within its own sacred books; they are 'fighting the law in their zeal for the law.'[100] Those other features which particularly draw his criticism, such as preoccupation with ritual observances or legalistic minutiae, the symptoms of a 'carnal' religious practice, all reflect this initial exegetical failure. It is revealing that in the biographical sketch of Jean Vitrier, a man whose fiercely Pauline spirituality had left its mark on his own development, Erasmus could remark, 'A spark of his teaching still glows in the heart of many, compared with whom you could say that other people are not Christians but Jews.'[101] The profound spontaneity of Vitrier's pastoral style is set against the rigid observance of conventional forms, and seen from this perspective Christians are just as likely to be 'Jewish' as the Jews – the term comprehends an attitude, even a culture, rather than an ethnic designation.

Erasmus' attitude toward Judaism has received considerable scrutiny in recent years, and here a quick review of the issue as it arises within the

* * * * *

98 See for example *Ratio* ed Holborn (n45 above) 211:14–17, 293:31–29.
99 *De concordia* LB V 478B
100 *In psalmum 85* LB V 543B–C
101 Ep 1211:265–7; this famous letter with its double portrait of Vitrier and Colet is in a sense a Pauline manifesto.

writings on the Psalms must suffice to clarify his stance on this sensitive issue. Guido Kisch was one of the first to open up the question, detecting in the writings tendencies of an anti-Semitic character.[102] Undoubtedly one negative factor in the debate has been the image of Erasmus as an apostle of toleration, a concept which emerges in the aftermath of Reformation excesses and is canonized by the Enlightenment. As an image it is misleading: Erasmus opposed the use of force as the means to resolve religious conflicts, but that is not to say that he did not seek their resolution. Coexistence was for him a necessary evil at best, a temporary condition which would be rendered obsolete by the passage of time and the eventual recognition of truth. It is this, more than anything else, which distinguishes his position from modern attitudes; multiculturalism was, quite simply, not a sixteenth-century option. To Erasmus the ideal social community was Christian, the mystical body of Christ in its temporal manifestation. Any individual or corporate force which resisted assimilation into this unity, be it corrupt bishops, heretics, Jews, or Turks, had to be opposed. It is true that by opposition Erasmus did not primarily understand force, though he recognized that it might come to that in extreme circumstances; rather, he envisaged charitable persuasion and the power of example. This is the central point of his essay on Psalm 28, *De bello Turcico*, that 'the more the church's original piety was alive in her, the more she shrank from wars and executions.'[103] One feature of this clemency, which Erasmus cites from the seventh-century Council of Toledo, was a refusal to invoke the death penalty for relapsed Jewish converts. The Jewish reader may well have mixed feelings about clemency of this sort, especially since Erasmus appears to endorse the council's decree that stubborn relapsed Jews might be subjected to ecclesiastical penalties and their children removed. If we are to grasp his position and that of his fellow biblical humanists it will be helpful to draw a line, albeit a fine one, between anti-Semitism and anti-Judaism. The former attitude, with its often horrific overtones, is rooted in centuries of ethnic distrust and misrepresentation; it views the Jewish people

* * * * *

102 *Erasmus' Stellung zu Juden and Judentum* (Tübingen 1969). See further C. Augustijn 'Erasmus und die Juden' *Nederlands Archief voor Kerkgeschiedenis* ns 60 (1980) 22–38, repr in *Erasmus: Der Humanist als Theologe und Kirchenreformer* (Leiden 1996) 94–111; S. Markish *Erasmus and the Jews* trans A. Olcott (Chicago and London 1986); H.O. Oberman *The Roots of Anti-Semitism* trans J.I. Porter (Philadelphia 1981); Chomarat *Grammaire et rhétorique chez Erasme* (n52 above) I 331–44; A. Godin 'L'Antijudaisme d'Erasme' *Bibliothèque d'Humanisme et Renaissance* 47 (1985) 537–53; H.M. Pabel 'Erasmus of Rotterdam and Judaism' *Archiv für Reformationsgeschichte* 87 (1996) 9–37.

103 LB V 356A–C

as an economic and political danger, and it is prepared to use violent action to attain its ends. Anti-Judaism, on the other hand, derives from the apostolic appropriation of the Jewish Scriptures which sees them fulfilled in Christ; it is a legacy of the birth struggle of early Christianity by which it broke loose from the obligations of Mosaic observance, a struggle recorded in the New Testament canon and perpetuated in the liturgy. The distinction, it has to be said, is a narrow one since it is evident that, historically, anti-Judaic statements have been adopted to lend a sort of respectability to raw anti-Semitic prejudice. Nevertheless, the Pauline fervour characteristic of biblical humanism, hostile as it undoubtedly was to Jewish beliefs and customs, did not intend to damage the civil status of Jews or to threaten their physical integrity.

Erasmus believed in the accessibility of divine truth to all races, even to the most primitive natives of the New World, though historical factors might affect their freedom to respond. In the case of the Jews the initial failure to recognize the Son of God had been hardened over the centuries into stubborn resistance. Erasmus saw in this rejection of Christ the most striking historical manifestation of a tendency which is perennial in human affairs, the closing of the heart to grace. This is why he so often detects examples of 'Judaism' within Christian institutions; the blindness of the chosen people serves as a metaphor for all human obduracy. A simple instance of this occurs in his exposition of Psalm 4, where God's rebuke of the Jews is clearly intended to be read as applicable to the Christian reader. In this case one may accept Markish's claim that for Erasmus Judaism is 'first and foremost a moral category, not a historical or religious one.'[104]

But Erasmus' reaction to Jewry is more complex than this may suggest. Apart from those characteristics of literal-mindedness and preoccupation with external observance which he invariably associates with the self-righteousness of the Pharisees and the doctors of the Law, the Synagogue represents for him a corporate threat to the realization of the *philosophia Christi*. Judaism is not only a danger within the heart of the Christian, it is also a potential contamination from without. Erasmus' most offensive remarks about the Jews tend to be found in his letters rather than in the published works, and most densely clustered within the period of the crisis over Johann Pfefferkorn and his attack on Reuchlin, an episode which does not show Erasmus in a good light. One of the letters from this period which has drawn hostile attention voices a complaint about those who are trying to stir

* * * * *

104 *In psalmum* 4 below 187–8; Markish (n102 above) 26

up war against France, which to Erasmus seems the least contaminated part of Christendom: 'France alone remains not infected with heretics, with Bohemian schismatics, with Jews, with half-Jewish marraños, and untouched by the contagion of Turkish neighbours . . .'[105] Despite first appearances this passage is not about racial purity, rather it is concerned with the ideal of a Christian polity: in France at least, Erasmus implies, the realization of a truly Christian community will be hindered solely by the laxity and wickedness of the church's own members and not by the negative presence of hostile forces. On this occasion, certainly, Judaism is more than a metaphor for moral blindness: it is an agency for those powers which work to overthrow Christ's kingdom.

What is, perhaps, the most widely cited of all Erasmus' remarks about the Jews can be found in the lengthy polemical letter which he sent in 1519, while the Reuchlin affair was still simmering, to the Dominican Jacob of Hoogstraten: 'If it is Christian to detest the Jews, on this count we are all good Christians, and to spare.' The sharp irony here finds its echo a decade later in *De bello Turcico* where, after surveying the lamentable state of Christendom, Erasmus concludes, 'And yet, all the while, like true Christians, we hate the Turks!'[106] It is precisely because he is capable of such ironical perception that Erasmus can go on to specify a yet more loathsome race of Turks – those hidden passions which invade the hearts of Christians and which must be driven out before Christendom can respond to the political threat of Islam. In both these examples the irony has the effect of dissolving any clear line of moral distinction between Christians and Jews or Turks; indeed, Heiko Oberman has justly regretted that the reproof of the church implicit in the letter to the inquisitor Hoogstraten did not become the criterion for a new outlook on the Jews.[107] All the same, we should not underestimate the degree of self-irony involved, the literary enactment of a self-criticism. Erasmus' attitude towards the Jewish world was complex, and it may well be that he struggled with an instinctive antipathy towards Jews; at the same time, despite his formal conception of Judaism as a threat to the church of Christ, his most considered statements favour a policy of toleration. It is intriguing to see, as M.A. Screech has pointed out, that the longest note to be excised

* * * * *

105 CWE Ep 549:12–16; for examples of abusive language see Epp 694, 697, 700, 701, 709.
106 CWE Ep 1006:149–50; *De bello Turcico* LB V 357C
107 Oberman (n2 above) 40; the underlying paradox is spelled out in Ep 1202:158–9: 'The cross of Christ brought salvation to the world; and yet we abominate the men who crucified him.'

from the 1527 printing of the *Annotationes in Novum Testamentum* was a gratuitously nasty speculation about the fiscal obligations of the Jews to the Holy Roman Emperor.[108] This certainly suggests a degree of self-criticism at work. To say that Erasmus tolerated the Jews of his time, then, is not to say that he approved of them, or felt any degree of warmth towards them, but simply that he wished them no actual harm; in the forefront of his mind is the Pauline hope of their ultimate conversion, and in the meantime Christians will do well to emulate the forbearance of God.[109]

The emotive charge of deicide, central to so much anti-Jewish polemic, is not one that Erasmus pursues with any vigour. In the exposition of Psalm 2 the issue is directly addressed, primarily because that psalm is read as a prophecy of Christ's passion: there can be no doubt, he asserts, that the Jews bear ultimate responsibility for the shedding of Christ's innocent blood and for the painful and humiliating nature of his death. But it is characteristic that the passage is more concerned with the paradox of Christ's triumph over his persecutors than with dwelling on the question of guilt; in fact the reader is encouraged to feel love for Christ rather than hatred for those who killed him.[110] The references to the Jews are essentially rhetorical, in the sense that they are designed to provoke pity for the sacred victim and to dramatize the overthrow of merely human expectations; moreover, though the Jews will be shamed in the next world, so will all rulers and all philosophers who have similarly resisted the sign of Jonah.[111] Clearly, it is the defect in perception that is held against them rather than ethnic identity, and if they are blamed for Christ's death the real guilt lies with the Pharisees, who, driven by ambition and spite, have led them astray. Even so, Erasmus is not reluctant to universalize the issue, observing that no period in history has been without its own Caiaphas or Herod, its own Pilate or its Pharisees.[112] If the Jews are to blame, even so they should not despair, 'your crime was, in part, an error.'[113]

Their error lay in a misreading of the messianic prophecies – they looked literally for a mighty king and deterred by Christ's humble origins

* * * * *

108 *Erasmus' Annotations on the New Testament: The Gospels* ed A. Reeve (London 1986) x and Appendix A (on John 19:15)
109 On God's tolerance see *In psalmum 85* LB V 546B–C, *De bello Turcico* ibidem 355F–356A, also the gentle example set by St Peter Ep 1202:73–100.
110 See 109–10 below.
111 *In psalmum 85* LB V 551B–C; cf *In psalmum 3* 165 below.
112 *In psalmum 2* 99 below; cf *In psalmum 85* LB V 544B.
113 *In psalmum 4* 188 below

failed to recognize his divine mission: 'We killed a man; we did not know that he was God.'[114] As we have already seen, to read the Scriptures properly is for Erasmus an ethical challenge: interpretation may be vitiated by greed, vanity, or any form of self-regard. So the failure of the Jews to grasp the new covenant held out to them is a warning, the most vivid embodiment of humanity's failure to respond to grace. That is why he is not really interested in pillorying the Jews or insisting on their guilt, except in so far as they present Christians with an insight into their own weakness. He expresses this with particular force in the last of the commentaries, *De puritate tabernaculi*, where the Jews are attacked for making righteousness virtually dependent on outward forms; but, he goes on, it applies equally to Christians, 'for although we do not sacrifice animals, we do still have forms of worship and rites which give a marvellous impression of piety, and some people perhaps rely on these things and do not trouble themselves about purity of mind.'[115]

Much of the fierce denunciation which Erasmus directs at Jewish practices is in reality aimed at those which threaten to pervert Christian practice. The mentality encouraged by outward observance of the law can easily be detected in such acts as pilgrimages, the endowment of monasteries, or the donation of spectacular artifacts to churches. It is even more the case with the monastic or mendicant orders, where literal-minded adherence to institutional forms is too often confused with sanctity. In all such cases the spirit of pharisaism has infiltrated the church. So there is a sense, then, in which Erasmus sees Judaism as a constant threat to the church of Christ, and Paul's struggle against the imposition of the Law on gentile Christians is still a relevant issue. In the *Enarratio psalmi 33*, which betrays an unusual intensity of preoccupation with Judaism, the unhappy Jews are described prowling around the fold of the church, envious of the gifts which God has lavished on it; but their fate will also be that of those Judaizing Christians 'who are inwardly devoid of faith and love, and boast of their diet, their observances, and like formalities, saying, "We are rich and lack nothing; we have such a huge supply of good works that we can enrich others with them."'[116] The cruelty of the Pharisees' actions against Christ is repeated by all those who exploit their position in the church for cynical ends, and this kind of charge is not directed simply at the conservative forces within the established church –

* * * * *

114 *In psalmum 85* LB V 543F
115 *De puritate tabernaculi* LB V 309B–C
116 *In psalmum 33* LB V 401D; the Judaizer is 'the man who trusts in his own strength' (ibidem 410F).

the superstitious reverence of the Sabbatarians in Bohemia is also condemned as a new kind of Judaism.[117]

Enough has perhaps been said to indicate the context within which we have to read the often acerbic references to the Jews which occur in Erasmus' treatment of the Psalms. If he betrays prejudice, this is directed in the first place at those cultural or cultic tendencies – the *animus Judaicus* – which in his view had deprived Israel of its destined fulfilment. The racial factor is overshadowed by the religious one, and it is instructive to compare his warm admiration for such scholarly converts as Paulus Ricius or Matthaeus Adrianus with his seething hostility towards a very different kind of convert, Johann Pfefferkorn. Ricius, on account of his work to reconcile the two Testaments, is accorded the accolade of a true Israelite, one who demonstrates the full significance of the name.[118] Pfefferkorn, by contrast, who was exploited by the Cologne Dominicans, turned against his Hebrew heritage and denounced biblical humanism and is accordingly condemned as a fifth columnist. It would be misleading to take the Pfefferkorn episode as an index of Erasmus' deepest convictions; these are concerned rather with Christian reception of the Jewish inheritance, its impact for good or ill on the practice of the *philosophia Christi*. On a polemical level this may result in his instinctive association of rabbinical obscurantism with the ways of his scholastic opponents, those 'reverend rabbis' who presume to decide who is truly a Christian.[119] But at a deeper level it reveals his fear of a negative distemper which might spread from the maimed body of Judaism to infect the teaching of the gospel. In the *Scholia* on *De esu carnium* he puts this quite explicitly: 'What I call Judaism is not the impiety of the Jews but the anxious obedience of Christians with respect to their own observances'; the true Christian will turn to God in a spirit of trust rather than accumulate ritual merit in a spirit of fear.[120] There is an interesting distinction made in the *Annotations on Romans* between two groups among the Jews: there are those who have nothing in common with Abraham except circumcision, and there are those who have that but also share his faith; following Paul's lead Erasmus sees only the second as true sons of Abraham.[121] Whatever the superficial variations in his expressed views on the Jews, there can be

* * * * *

117 Ibidem 408D; on Sabbatarians see *De concordia* LB V 505F–506A.
118 Ep 549:12–17
119 On scholastic 'rabbis' see Epp 1126:374, 1153:160, 1234:17 and n2.
120 ASD IX-1 74:245–6; in the *Enchiridion* it is implied that monastic observance teaches how to tremble, not how to love (CWE 66 127).
121 CWE 56 114 (on Romans 4:12)

no doubt that he sees the *philosophia Christi* as the fulfilment of Abraham's trust.

It has already been remarked that only the exposition of Psalm 1 predates the radical challenge to Roman authority posed by Luther in 1517. The issue of peace among Christians was a growing preoccupation with Erasmus, reaching its most urgent expression in the last two psalm commentaries, *De sarcienda ecclesiae concordia* on Psalm 83 in 1533 and *De puritate tabernaculi sive ecclesiae christianae* on Psalm 14 which appeared in January 1536, just six months before his death. What stands out in these writings – and gives them a particular interest in modern times – is their irenical stance; Erasmus is persistently concerned to stimulate a controlled discussion of the controversial issues in which differences can be charitably examined. No doubt an important figure for him in these years was Irenaeus of Lyons, whose *Adversus omnes haereses* he edited in 1526 and whose very name suggested to him the peacemakers whom Christ calls the sons of God.[122] If Erasmus found in Irenaeus – *Irenaeum meum* as he calls him – a model to follow in times of religious upheaval, then it was one far removed from the hesitant and even vacillating tolerance which has sometimes been attributed to him. Irenaeus laid particular emphasis on the continuity of tradition within the ecclesial community, and Erasmus likewise repeatedly upholds the church as the community or consensus of believers. Moreover, given the priority of spiritual encounter with Christ through the Scriptures, it is the church as an interpretive community – one that conserves the basic doctrinal framework within which the material signs of Christ's availability can be activated and work spiritual transformation – which dominated his thinking. This means that he is primarily concerned with authority in the church as a guarantee for the authenticity of received tradition, a position which admits the primacy of the Roman church but is light years away from the *deus in terra* of the more extreme canonists.[123] In his dedication of the *Adversus haereses* to Bernhard von Cles, Erasmus notes that Irenaeus had not hesitated to rebuke Pope Victor I for his high-handed treatment of the Quartodecimans,

* * * * *

122 Allen 1738:1–5; Erasmus expresses his confidence that 'God in his unsearchable wisdom will turn the present turmoil in the church into a good outcome, and raise up for us a number of Irenaeuses who by healing our divisions will restore peace to the world' (lines 259–630). For Irenaeus' possible influence on Erasmus' Christology see Boyle 25.

123 For the 'more powerful origin' (*propter potentiorem principalitatem*) of Rome as a focus for unity see Irenaeus *Adversus haereses* 3.3.1–2; some of the more extreme claims of papal canonists are given in G. Tavard *Holy Writ or Holy Church? The Crisis of Protestant Reformation* (London 1959) 47–51.

'so dedicated was he to concord among the churches';[124] a precedent which in 1526 had an obviously topical reference. And yet, quite apart from the examples of Christian antiquity, Erasmus' active pursuit of concord among the warring parties is exactly what one might expect from his handling of the linguistic foundations of Christian teaching: his lifelong distrust of scholastic methodology sprang from its assumption that human language could provide an adequate medium for the exploration of divine truths. In the words of his 1523 letter to Jean de Carondolet, 'The sum and substance of our religion is peace and concord. This can hardly remain the case unless we define as few matters as possible and leave each individual's judgment free on many questions.'[125] This theme of human fallibility finds its most extensive – and most radical – treatment in the *Exposition of Psalm 38*, where Erasmus surveys the ranks of the theologians, from Origen to Jean Gerson, and concludes that in some respect all have wandered from orthodoxy. Even the decrees of popes and councils show inconsistency; only the canon of Scripture can be relied upon as the teaching of the Spirit.[126]

Given his sense of the church as, in effect, a community of readers, Erasmus has little patience with the pyramidal version of the canonists; in a much-cited passage from the adage *Sileni Alcibiadis* he insists that the church is made up of the entire Christian people and not just the clergy, who are in reality only its servants.[127] And in the same year, in the commentary on Psalm 1, this is taken even further: to become blessed like the upright man of the psalm it is necessary to 'meditate on the law of the Lord'; this is not a requirement just for theologians but for all, ploughmen as well as scholars. The passage has a rhetorical optimism about it, but the underlying argument is objective enough: that our engagement with language shapes our humanity, and thus engagement with godly language will draw us towards God. On this premise, regardless of those who stress only the dangers, he argues for the general availability of the Scriptures in the vernacular; proper understanding of the biblical text calls for a particular inner disposition rather than some

* * * * *

124 Ep 1738:56–62
125 Allen Ep 1334:217–19 / CWE Ep 1334:232–4; 'concord' is *unanimitas*. The qualification 'as possible' was added in 1535.
126 LB V 432B–435E; cf *In psalmum 22* LB V 323D, *In psalmum 33* LB V 413B–C.
127 *Adagia* III iii 1 CWE 34 272; in the exposition of Psalm 22 the priest consecrates the bread and wine, while 'the offering is made in common by all the faithful' (LB V 331C). It is interesting to see that Erasmus was alert to issues of inclusive language, so that 'Blessed the man' (*Beatus vir*) includes 'woman'; see 14–15 below and *De concordia* LB V 489B.

arcane intellectual skill: 'Essentially you need piety rather than ingenuity to understand the Scriptures; the Spirit explains them, not Aristotle; grace, not reason; the breath of God, not syllogisms.' Again, such an argument may seem open to the charge of naivety, but it is necessary to weigh against that the kind of 'meditation' Erasmus is advocating, that is, reflective discussion within the consensus of the believing community, informed by received tradition, and illuminated by the Spirit: 'If an understanding of their mystical meaning depends on the help of the Holy Spirit (what Paul calls the gift of prophecy), why do we cut off the great mass of Christians from a share in this gift?'[128] Given his understanding of Christ's words in John 6 about the 'living bread' of his teaching, how could Erasmus really argue otherwise? Clearly what he has in mind here is not some licence to private interpretation, since the individual process of 'rumination' assumes the ecclesial community: the happy man of Psalm 1, *beatus vir*, has 'always taken his stand on Christ, always clung to the evidence of Holy Writ, always accepted the decrees of the church, and never "walked in the council of the impious." '[129] This is why the general availability of the Bible in the vernacular is part of a wider conception which includes a reformed and revitalized episcopate to distribute the living bread of Christ's teaching, in the manner of the apostles at Capernaum.

The role of the bishop can scarcely be overemphasized in Erasmus' idea of the church; nothing in his view has done more to damage the Christian community than neglectful, worldly bishops who pass on their spiritual duties to hirelings; nothing is more requisite to its revival than pastoral bishops who have assimilated Christ's teaching in the Scriptures and can transmit it to the faithful. The first duty of the bishop is meditative study of the Bible, so that he will be equipped to guide the faithful; and this precedes even the administration of the sacraments.[130] In the *Exposition of Psalm 38* the figure of Idythun (Jeduthun), whom David chose to make music to the Lord, is taken both as the Platonic sage who has leaped out of the shadows of the cave to perceive with eyes of faith the forms of all that is truly good, and also as the model for the successors of the apostles: 'For such men ought always to produce prophetic sounds concerning the law of the Lord, not only with their cithara when they instruct the people, but also with their harp

* * * * *

128 *In psalmum 1* 31–2 below
129 Ibidem 17 below
130 Episcopal duties thus incorporate those of the true theologian; see *Ratio* LB V 84A and *Paraclesis* LB V 140E (trans Olin [n45 above] 102). In *De bello Turcico* the failure of 'the shepherds of the church' is the chief ground for God's abandoning Christendom (LB V 357B).

when they rebuke those who have gone astray, or with the tambourine when they try to drum some sense into those who are stubbornly resisting the truth.' The bishop must, like Idythun, have risen above human desires, and be able to sing prophetically 'expounding faithfully the mystical sense of Scripture.'[131] It is necessary to keep in mind this elevated conception of the episcopal office when faced by those passages in which Erasmus appears to be undermining the formal structures of authority by asserting the spiritual dignity of the simple believer: one familiar section of the *Paraclesis* expresses his desire that the New Testament might be a familiar part of common life, so that the farmer might sing words from it at the plough, the weaver hum them, the traveller lighten his journey with them;[132] but of equal force is his picture in the dedication of his edition of Arnobius' *Commentarii in psalmos* to Adrian VI in 1522 of how 'in the olden time nothing was nearer to the hearts of the people than the Psalms of David: they gave the ploughman something to sing at the plough-tail, the helmsman at his tiller, the sailor at the oar, the digger at his trench, the weaver at his loom, and his wife at her distaff; even children in arms longed to sing some scrap of the Psalms to their nurses before they knew how to talk – so great was the love for this divine music in the old days, in every heart – and now the majority even of priests are tired of it.' The contrast of past and present, *olim* and *nunc*, is a rhetorical flourish: in fact it sets up an ideal of popular, spontaneous devotion against the frigidity of clerical learning. And yet, Erasmus continues, 'it is generally agreed that among all the books of Holy Scripture, none is so full of such recondite mysteries as the book of Psalms, and no other book is wrapped in such obscurity of words and meaning.' How can children long to sing such songs, which priests find tedious? The answer lies in the *sensus mysticus*, the spiritual reading of the Psalms, 'by which we might be changed into a frame of mind worthy of Christ, provided only that there is someone at hand who can wake the strings of this psaltery with proper skill.' This would be Idythun, the Davidic type of the bishop, and while Erasmus concedes that believers who are practiced in 'the detection of mystic meanings' may explore the psalms without outside help,[133] the process does presuppose instruction and guidance, in the first place from the bishops, 'truly devout teachers,'[134] or when that is impossible by meditative reading and discussion. In fact this shared interpretive activity can be seen as the bond which holds together the

* * * * *

131 For Idythun as Platonic sage see LB V 453A, C, and D; as bishop 421F and 423C.
132 *Paraclesis* LB V 140B–C (trans Olin [n45 above] 101)
133 Ep 1304:105–2, 262–4, 428–30, 501–3
134 See 33 below.

varying elements within the church, and it is in such a hermeneutic context that we should understand the polemical assertion in the *Paraclesis* that 'all can be theologians.'[135]

No part of the church, in other words, has a passive role; all contribute. But at the same time the unity and inclusiveness of the ecclesial community is persistently emphasized in terms of the mystical body of Christ:

> The head forms one person, so to speak, with the whole church of the saints who have existed since the beginning of the world and will do so until its end. This person never ceases to cry out, 'Preserve my life, for I am holy.' The head cries out on behalf of its members, the members cry out in the person of their head, the members cry out on behalf of other members.[136]

In an elaborate allegorical reading Erasmus can even link the words of Psalm 22, 'You have anointed my head with oil,' with the ointment which in Psalm 132 is poured on the head of Aaron and flows over the collar of his vestments; this ointment, 'the fragrance of Christ,' conveys the spread of grace as it runs through time and reaches to the ends of the earth.[137] It is what is needed to prepare us for the banquet of Christ's body and blood, and the fragrance, as it spreads through the house, flowing from its divine source to the young girls attracted by its sweetness, enacts the opening idea of Psalm 132, 'How good it is and pleasant for brothers to live as one.' This spiritual community, fired by the spirit of the Gospels and confirmed by charity, may seem remote from the institutional face of the church at which Erasmus directed severe criticism and, on occasion, mordant satire. Nevertheless, the real motive of all his religious writing is to reanimate the forms of the church, to restore the prophetic vision which should drive them. The negative picture he offers of the institutional church is in effect of a body without its soul; there is no suggestion that the soul can operate independently of the body, only that the accretions of secular interest must be stripped away and primitive simplicity restored. Hence the charges, already discussed, that the church is in danger of lapsing into a form of neo-Judaism, where ceremonial and outward form replace the promptings of spiritual understanding. Perhaps the most lasting insight that Erasmus had derived from his early encounter

* * * * *

135 *Paraclesis* LB V 141F (trans Olin [n45 above] 104)
136 *In psalmum 85* LB V 517B; cf ibidem 544A–B, also *In psalmum 3* 164 below, *In psalmum 4* 269–70 below, *In psalmum 22* LB V 315E–316A. The devil too has his perverted mystical body; see *In psalmum 22* LB V 320D.
137 *In psalmum 22* LB V 330C–331A

with the satire of Lucian was the recognition that human institutions have an irresistible tendency to substitute public forms and ritual acts for their originating functions. Thus his persistent excoriations of a secular-minded and ceremonial church are best understood as attempts to strip away the deposit of human custom which always threatens to clog the operations of grace. As with the letter of the Scriptures, so with the church: material signs must recover their spiritual signification.

Proper reading of the word of God will foster spiritual renewal in the church. At the same time such reading must be in harmony with the collective experience of the ecclesial community and its historical inheritance. Writing in 1530, in the commentary on Psalm 22, Erasmus faces the question 'How can I know if I am within the unity of the church?' To belong to the church means to be in charity with God and with your neighbour; only you can effectively remove yourself from the church. Such an answer may on the surface seem evasive, but it is entirely consistent with Erasmus' vision of the church as an interpretive community; the first obligation in conscience is to God, and after that to one's fellow believers, a bond formalized in 'the outward fellowship of the Catholic church.' This 'outward fellowship' may require the toleration of unworthy ministers, but behind them is Christ: 'Even though he who administers the sacraments may be a hireling, "a thief and a robber," the sheep are not without their shepherd, who lavishes grace upon them even when he uses evil men to dispense his mysteries.'[138] What is interesting in this passage is the terms Erasmus uses to express the association of Christians: it is *consortio* 'a partnership or fellowship,' or *contubernium* 'a dwelling together,' terms which convey a sense of shared concern. Typically he sees the church as a community rather than a hierarchy; this arises not from egalitarian sentiment but rather from his reserve about the capacity of human institutions (language included) to give adequate and final expression to spiritual truths; unravelling the meaning of the sacred text in time is necessarily a provisional activity.[139] Erasmus' church is thus a pilgrim church, and for its members safety comes by travelling in company.

Holiness, for Erasmus, is the outcome of a process rather than imputed; inevitably therefore there is a discrepancy between membership of the visible institution of the church and those who will be recognized in

* * * * *

138 *In psalmum* 22 LB V 337A–D
139 'The responsibility to gauge the text obliges interpreters to take measure of themselves and observe moderation not only in view of the text but also in relation to other persons' (Manfred Hoffmann 'Language and Reconciliation' *Erasmus of Rotterdam Society Yearbook* 15 [1995] 79–80).

eschatological terms as members of Christ's mystical body. No doubt he would share Thomas More's view that Luther's concept of the church militant was 'somehow imperceptible and mathematical – like Platonic Ideas.'[140] For Erasmus the church militant is a provisional community, embracing both authentic and apparent Christians, and yet despite the personal inadequacies of its ministers it remains the vessel of divine grace and instruction. In other words, it always has the potential to be the mystical body of Christ. That is why Erasmus demands adherence to the visible institution, defective though it may be, and if in 1515 the *beatus* of Psalm 1 is described as faithful to the decrees of the church, this is unsurprisingly a theme that gains in urgency in the later commentaries. In 1525 *In psalmum quartum concio* does refer to the need for reconciliation, though in discreetly general terms,[141] and there are signs that Erasmus is wrestling for a formulation of the doctrine of justification which could satisfy at least moderate opinion on both sides of the Reformation divide. When it is asserted that salvation comes from faith, not works, this is set in the context of an attack on Jewish ceremonial observance; when reference is made to those who confuse 'the sacrifice of righteousness' with going on pilgrimage or entering the monastic life, it is carefully emphasized that there is nothing wrong about such acts, but they may lead to an erroneous reliance on ritual and external performance.[142] In a passage that would later be censured, Erasmus proclaims that true righteousness consists in confessing our unrighteousness and in glorifying God's righteousness in fulfilling his promises, while at a later stage in the text he returns to it as 'trusting in God's promises.'[143] The issue is really one of *theologia rhetorica*, a theology alert to the persuasive resources of language: while the preacher may be attempting to lead his listeners through a psychological process which begins with rejection of the self (the 'sacrifice of righteousness' of Ps 4:5) and leads to complete trust in a loving God, the theological censor is on the watch for formulations that may be misconstrued or promote error. In the case of the former, using language to achieve subjective effect, it will be the cumulative attitude generated rather than the single statement that will provide the test of orthodoxy. What does seem clear is that Erasmus is not seeking compromise so much as entering on a dialogue in the hope of salvaging from Luther some insight which

* * * * *

140 Thomas More *Responsio ad Lutherum* ed J.M. Headley *The Complete Works of St. Thomas More* v part 1 (New Haven and London 1969) 167
141 See 271–2 below; for what may be the earliest glance at growing tensions see *In psalmum* 2 133–4 below.
142 *In psalmum* 4 187, 219, 259 below
143 192 and 220 below

may help to restore authentic tradition. So it is in his treatment of Psalm 4 that he first proffers the scheme of double justification which was to assume major importance for irenical initiatives in the 1530s and 1540s. Resting on the basic Pauline tenet that justification is by faith, not works, Erasmus presents this as just the first step: 'It is not enough to be free of guilt unless this be followed by the fruits of the good works which faith works through love'; in other words, there must be a social issue of faith in the form of charity towards our neighbour. As in a tree where sweet fruit comes from a healthy root, so works must come from genuine faith.[144] Such good fruits, therefore, are the products of grace, which gave the root in the first place; divine initiative is preserved, together with the cooperative acquiescence of the believer.

     This acquiescence is a critical refinement in the search for a balance between *sola fides* and the merit-broking of much popular piety. In the *Explanation of Psalm 85* (also dedicated to Bishop Longland), which followed in 1528, attention is turned on those who consider their obligations fulfilled because they have faith: 'I can live free from anxieties and there is no reason for me to torture myself with good works.'[145] God will indeed protect us, but only if we do all in our power to maintain vigilance. On the other hand there is the danger of Pelagian self-reliance, which attributes to free will what ought to be acknowledged as the work of grace.[146] What dominates Erasmus' concern here is not so much the wish to soothe controversy as his pastoral ambition to induce an appropriate attitude in the reader, one which is before all else a complete trust in God. Therefore it is important for him to stress the utter gratuitousness of divine mercy, since this will encourage the appropriate subjective response; at the same time, this is balanced by a restrained reminder of human obligation: 'The Lord desires to rescue you, but to rescue you as you cry out.'[147] In the place of a competitive asceticism the Christian is asked only to contribute a mental state of responsiveness to grace; the human cooperative role may be a restricted one, but it remains essential. It is characteristic of Erasmus that in the *Exposition of Psalm 33* he tries to reconcile the alternative schemes by using the organic model of bones, sinews, and flesh, a theme suggested by verse 21 of the psalm, 'The Lord guards all their bones: not one of them shall be broken'; the bones which support the body are faith, the sinews which bind the parts are love, and the enveloping flesh is good works, 'which are inseparable from faith

* * * * *

144 258–9 below
145 *In psalmum 85* LB V 518F
146 Ibidem LB V 536C
147 *In psalmum 33* LB V 394B–C

and love.'[148] The significance of the bodily metaphor is that it merges the
constituent parts into a common function, the epitome of concord. Although
those whose bones of faith have been broken, Jews and heretics, remain
outside the church, what of those Fathers, figures like Irenaeus, Jerome, and
Augustine, whose teachings in some respects depart from what has later been
seen as orthodoxy? As opposed to broken bones, therefore, some may be
said to have dislocated or wounded bones, susceptible of treatment. Erasmus
may seem to strain the reading of this verse, but his drift is clear enough;
intellectual differences, those which have not hardened into hostile attitudes,
may yet be brought back into harmony with the church; but to insist on
absolute conformity in the intellectual formulation of doctrine frustrates the
church's healing function.

This appeal for a more flexible handling of the Reformation crisis is the
keynote of the two great commentaries which mark his final years, *De sarcienda ecclesiae concordia* on Psalm 83, which was published in the summer of
1533, and *De puritate tabernaculi sive ecclesiae christianae* on Psalm 14, which
appeared early in 1536, six months before his death. The dedications of these
two commentaries are of interest: *De concordia* to Julius Pflug, who as adviser
to Duke George of Saxony was a tireless Catholic advocate of reconciliation,
and *De puritate tabernaculi* to the layman Christoph Eschenfelder, a customs
official at Boppard near Koblenz. Thus these two exercises in pastoral exegesis commemorate an irenical theologian and a devout family man who, as
Erasmus points out in the dedication to *De puritate tabernaculi*, exemplifies in
his secular calling those virtues that many would confine to monasteries.[149]
What emerges from them is a clear picture of the ideals of Catholic reform,
that is, retention of the unity and historical continuity of the ecclesial community while submitting its institutional practices to critical inspection. It is,
one might say, a matter of restoring the text of the church rather than rewrit-
ing it. Erasmus is insistent on the received essentials of Catholic faith while
warning against the kind of overhasty reaction which judges orthodoxy by
outward forms, in other words, by conformity to the letter rather than the
spirit. In a situation where 'one side allows nothing to be changed, the other
leaves nothing alone,' guilt is attributed by association – as in the tale of the
theologian who, on seeing a man deep in conversation fail to raise his hat to
a crucifix, wagers that he is a Lutheran.[150]

* * * * *

148 Ibidem LB V 412F–413A
149 For biographical details see CEBR; also J.V. Pollet *Julius Pflug (1494–1564) et la
    crise religieuse dans l'Allemagne du xvie siècle* (Leiden 1990).
150 *De concordia* LB V 501F; cf those who cry 'Heresy, heresy! To the fire, to the fire!'
    (499C).

Erasmus' stance at the conclusion of *De concordia* can be described as a radical conservatism: radical both in its curtailment of non-essential elements in religious practice and in its actual demands on the faithful – from pope to layman, 'let each one of us be what he ought to be' – yet also conservative, in that while he calls for concessions in the interest of concord, these must never be at the expense of those things 'handed down to us by the authority of our forebears and established by the usage and agreement of many centuries.'[151] We find him once again turning to the central issue of the freedom of the will and its part in justification, seeking for a formulation that can foster common understanding. While it is evident that his preference would be for such contentious issues to be left well alone, nevertheless, 'if it is necessary to investigate any aspect of it, it should be discussed soberly in theological debates.' Meanwhile – and this is a term of particular importance in the context – certain things can be agreed. Those which Erasmus enumerates are an attempt to reconcile the positive elements that he recognizes in both camps, allowing for the reformers' assertion of God's absolute power while preserving some role for the received tradition of human cooperation in the workings of grace. He looks back, in fact, to that *duplex iustitia* which he had carefully defined in the *Exposition of Psalm 22*, distinguishing between the preliminary restoration of innocence through faith and baptism, and its active expression through deeds of charity.[152] From a Catholic perspective he preserves the idea of sanctification as a transforming process, while reaching out to Luther's apprehension of the irrelevance of human works in the face of God's mercy. It is an attempt to build a bridge between the conflicting churches by giving priority to the affective impact of doctrine. As such it provides a classic formulation of that moderate Catholic position which Pflug and Contarini would occupy at the Diet of Regensburg but which was finally disowned at Trent in 1547.[153]

It is entirely in keeping with his irenical concerns that the last two expositions that Erasmus wrote should deal with psalms that celebrate God's presence among human kind: 'O Lord, who may lodge in thy tabernacle? Who may dwell on thy holy mountain?' (Ps 14), 'How dear is thy dwelling place, thou Lord of Hosts! I pine, I faint with longing for the courts of the Lord's temple' (Ps 83). The Greek term that he employs to express the healing

* * * * *

151 Ibidem LB V 500B
152 Ibidem LB V 500C–D; *In psalmum* 22 LB V 325B
153 On the moderate position see Peter Matheson *Cardinal Contarini at Regensburg* (Oxford 1972), especially 108, 171–81; through their focus on a subjective understanding of justification by faith the moderates tended to overestimate the common ground.

spirit of accommodation which should direct dealings between the churches, συγκατάβασις, literally 'a going down to meet,' had been used to express the idea of Christ's incarnation, a divine condescension to the human.[154] What stands out in the final section of *De concordia* is Erasmus' effort to separate the essentials of Christian life from those elements which are indifferent, the so-called *adiaphora*. Here, as in the business of exegesis, one is made aware of the interpenetration of cultural forms and spiritual meaning: only through alertness to the spirit can the forms be adequately interpreted. Yet the human ascent to spiritual truth depends on a material medium: provided spiritual awareness is present, considerable flexibility is permissible in the use of liturgical resources, ritual acts, music, or religious images. This holds also for devotional practices such as prayer to the saints or for the dead; abuses are possible, but properly handled such practices can be a means of grace. Where indifferent matters are concerned there should be the latitude to follow those customs which prove helpful – idolatry is always wrong, but a truly spiritual use of images can be tolerated. The divine accommodation of the incarnate Christ confirms the spiritual value of material things appropriately used. In essential matters Erasmus is less concerned with precise definitions of doctrine than with a common appropriation of received tradition, which is exactly what might be expected of his sense of the church as an interpretive community. Those who depart from tradition, like the Sacramentarians or the Sabbatarians, are condemned (though not with severity), but for those who can share a common inheritance, 'there should be no dispute over the words while we agree on the reality.'[155] One can sense that for Erasmus the central doctrines of orthodox Christian faith should stimulate an attitude, a mode of relating to God, while the verbal formulations are always prone to restrict and even distort the reality they are attempting to convey. Such statements as 'Whatever man's deeds, he can do nothing but sin' may be, as Erasmus admits, in a *certain sense* true ('in aliquo sensu vera sint') but they are likely to be gravely misunderstood by the unsophisticated. It is, in fact, an assertion that takes us right to the heart of Luther's protest against a religion based on the calculation of merits and rewards, displacing human works with the transcendent power of divine love. For Erasmus there is no doubt that the statement may have a subjective truth which is an important step in the believer's discovery of an all-powerful yet merciful God, but to those who read it literally it may seem to promote despondency or moral apathy.

* * * * *

154 *De concordia* LB V 500B, 505B; G.W.H. Lampe *A Patristic Greek Lexicon* (Oxford 1961) sv
155 *De concordia* LB V 500D, 504B (Sacramentarians), 506A (Sabbatarians)

It is true, in other words, only when read by someone able to place it within the wider frame of Christian self-understanding as that has developed in the consensus of the faithful over the centuries, a concept that Erasmus, adapting the words of Ps 83:5, expresses as 'the nest of the church.'[156]

The essential criterion in all the religious practices which Erasmus reviews at the conclusion of *De concordia* is spiritual awareness on the part of the individual Christian. He can recognize the righteous anger of the iconoclasts, and yet like Plato he appreciates the psychological power of images, which may be harnessed to profitable ends. Confession is a particularly interesting example of the way in which he handles controversial issues: those who doubt that it was instituted by Christ should nevertheless preserve it out of respect for its antiquity and its evident value when properly used.[157] 'But its safety and acceptability are largely up to us': in other words the penitent must avoid either scrupulosity or the ritual evasion of guilt, and contrition must be directed in the first place to God, though a wise confessor can also be a source of guidance in the moral complexities of daily life. Ancient custom is preserved, but purged of superstitious accretions. It is clear here that Erasmus is trying to break out of the adversarial attitudes which locked the opposing sides in their intransigence; until the issues can be settled by a council – and provided that the basic tenets of the Creed are acknowledged – Christians should be prepared to tolerate a variety of observances according to tradition and personal inclination. This repeated reference to the council to come, a hallmark of the centrist position, does prompt a question: Just how confidently did Erasmus look to such a universally accepted resolution of the profound issues opened up by the reformers? How far is his repeated appeal to a council a positive proposal, how far is it a rhetorical device to lower the tension, as it were, and permit Christians to make an objective appraisal of what should be understood as the church and the inheritance of Catholic Christianity? It is unlikely that any clear answer can be given, but it is none the less a question that needs to be pondered. Ideally, a council acceptable to both sides would be the soundest solution, but Erasmus was not oblivious to the harshness of the divisions in Western Christianity.

*****

156 Ibidem LB V 485E; he concludes: 'If we seek peace of mind, let us remain in the tabernacle of the Lord of hosts and stay in the unity of the Catholic church – "Jerusalem, which is built as a city founded upon itself."'
157 Erasmus is anxious to declare the antiquity of confession, since he had been attacked on this issue by Agostino Steuco when the latter dedicated his *In Psalmum 18 et 138 Interpretatio* (Lyons S. Gryphius 1533) to Pflug; see E. Rummel *Erasmus and his Catholic Critics* 2 vols (Nieuwkoop 1989) II 138–9.

Writing to Pflug in 1531, Erasmus already seemed less than sanguine about the power of a council to resolve the differences between the opposing camps. In a proposal that anticipates his ideas in the commentary on Psalm 83, he suggests a committee of a hundred or so godly and learned divines who might prepare the way for doctrinal reconciliation, carefully sifting opinions from matters of faith. He can only hope that, as in a well-structured play, the current turmoil can be turned to a happy ending by Christ the *choragus*, director of our comedy. At present to stand between the parties is to risk the fate of the hapless monk John, reported in the *Historia tripartita* of Cassiodorus, who attempted to separate two gladiators locked in combat and was cut down for his pains.[158] But until a council is summoned, one that can be regarded as truly ecumenical, discernment and charity must provide the basis for a better understanding of the church.

The complex semantic load of συγκατάβασις must have intrigued Erasmus, not least on account of its incarnational overtones: the descent of the sacred into the material order is of its nature a strategy of risk. In an angry disclaimer to Conradus Pellicanus that he had ever doubted the real presence in the Eucharist, Erasmus draws for support not only on the Scriptures and on the continuity of Christian practice over centuries but also on the way 'it accords wonderfully well with the ineffable love of God for all mankind that he should have wished those whom he redeemed with the body and blood of his Son to be nourished in some ineffable way by that same flesh and blood and to receive as a pledge the comfort of his mysterious presence, till he returns in glory to be seen by all.'[159] That 'ineffable love' has charged the material world with signs which are a means of access to grace, and of these the church is in a special sense the curator, instituted to safeguard their proper appreciation and use. Thus, while an institutional church is a necessary means to human transformation, there is a sense in which the church as a spiritual community cannot be confined to the visible institution. Although Erasmus deplored the violent antagonism between the churches, attacking each other like gladiators,[160] he must surely have seen

* * * * *

158 Allen Ep 2522. 'Ni fallor,' writes Erasmus, 'unless I am mistaken' (line 168); in fact the monk was called Telemachus and was stoned by the crowd, details that he had recalled accurately in Ep 1400:217–32, with the significant addition that the monk's death had led to abolition of the games. For Christ as *choragus* see P.G. Bietenholz *History and Biography in the Work of Erasmus of Rotterdam* (Geneva 1966) 26–8.
159 Ep 1637:39–44
160 Ep 1616:28

in the efforts at accommodation undertaken by men like Pflug an opportunity to reduce the discrepancy between the public face of the church and its spiritual character. Even were a council to settle the outstanding issues between the parties, it could never wholly resolve those tensions which are the inevitable accompaniment of incarnation.[161]

What emerges as a particularly suggestive feature of *De concordia* and *De puritate tabernaculi* is Erasmus' refusal to settle for either an institutional or a prophetic emphasis: what he aims at is rather a dynamic interplay between the two. As he allows in *De concordia*, 'there is a measure of truth in what some say, that the church is invisible,' yet this thoroughly Augustinian principle is qualified by his recognition of the impact which the visible church may have through eloquent preaching of God's word or the solemn performance of the rite of the mass; in all these shared actions the individual takes on a heightened dignity as a member of the ecclesial community.[162] Obviously the picture he gives here is of an ideal possibility, and it is characteristic that he gives priority to the public elucidation of Scripture, a function he associates especially with the bishop's role and which he describes in rhetorical terms as the *energia* of the Spirit at work on the hearers.[163] Both these actions – the preaching of the word and the performance of the liturgy – are to be seen as extensions of incarnation, vital consequences of that divine intervention in the human world which the tabernacle of the church exists to fulfil.

In the *Exposition of Psalm 85* this divine intervention is seen as the entire cycle of salvation, 'the day which the Lord made,' stretching from the creation to the day of judgment, throughout which the church unceasingly calls out for mercy. *Ecclesia* in this context has little to do with institutional forms, indeed it even precedes the light of the gospel: 'For although before the grace of Christ was revealed the gospel was in many ways hidden, no one who was pious was without the daylight of the gospel so far as was sufficient to that age.'[164] The word *pius* again conveys the idea of a proper alertness to the relations of creator with creature. Such piety is accessible to all those who

* * * * *

161 Cf the words of A.J. Festugière in the introduction to his translation of the *Enchiridion* (Paris 1971) 63: 'Or pour durer, tout mouvement spirituel doit devenir institution. C'est là le drame perpétuel du Christianisme. L'*Enchiridion* nous met en présence d'un des moments de ce drame.' This holds for Erasmus' ecclesiology as a whole.

162 LB V 477C–D. Cf *In psalmum 33* LB V 390B: 'The praise of the devout is praise of the whole church in common.'

163 The sense of the word here seems to be 'force of style'; in the *Ecclesiastes* skill in sacred oratory is rated as a gift of the Spirit (LB V 782F).

164 *In psalmum 85* LB V 525F

respond within the circumstance of their time to the inspiration of the Spirit, so that membership of the church can be described as potentially coexistent with human nature, taking in not only the sages of antiquity but primitive cultures as well: 'Peoples with such savage habits that you might wonder whether they are human beings or wild animals call on the name of the Lord and have experienced the abundance of his mercy.'[165] While Erasmus observes traditional caution over the salvation of pagans, there can be no doubt of his belief that grace was operative beyond the limits of the visible church; such a belief could only have profound consequences for his response to the divisions within Christendom.[166]

These issues are raised directly in the first verse of Psalm 14, that which opens *De puritate tabernaculi*, 'Lord, who will dwell in your tabernacle?' Basic to this, the last of the commentaries, is the theme of purification, that is, reanimation of the forms of piety; these forms should not be disregarded, but they must be cleansed from superstition and crowned with acceptable offerings. What are these offerings? 'A mind made pure through faith and innocence and prepared by love to treat everyone well.' The manifestation of the divine presence in history is conveyed through the concept of the tabernacle: first that constructed on Mount Sion to house the Ark of Moses, then that in the great temple built by Solomon on the same site, next to the palace of David. It was this cult of the temple which was displaced by the true David, Christ, when he identified the temple with his own body: 'Destroy this temple and I will restore it in three days.' The first part of the commentary therefore offers an anagogical reading of the psalm, one in which it is related to Christ and the heavenly life, before Erasmus switches to his more familiar tropological mode, 'which may perhaps be less exalted but is in my opinion more useful.' The common theme which links the two parts together is that of entry to the temple: this is not gained by ritual observances or by papal bulls but by purity of mind and deeds of charity.[167] The distinction between the two readings is, in fact, more formal than real – the shared idea lies in spiritual understanding of material signs, that is, of the tabernacle and those qualified to enter it. Understandably, it is

* * * * *

165 Ibidem LB V 529A; cf *Hyperaspistes* LB X 1529F.
166 'And perhaps the spirit of Christ is more widespread than we understand, and the company of saints includes many not in our calendar' (the colloquy *Convivium religiosum* CWE 39 192). For a succinct review of pertinent texts see M. O'Rourke Boyle *Christening Pagan Mysteries* (Toronto 1981) 86–7.
167 For the forms of piety see *De puritate tabernaculi* LB V 309E; the idea of the tabernacle 294C–E; the anagogical and tropological readings 301B.

in the moral reading that Erasmus adverts most directly to contemporary problems, stressing holiness as a process of growth consequent on faith and fruitful in good works. To walk without blemish means to walk within the tabernacle, since all actions, even those which seem virtuous, are defiled when performed outside it.[168] This passage has been taken as an untypically negative assessment of pagan virtue, but such a view seems out of keeping with that inclusive vision of the mystical church which emerges in the psalm commentaries. The issue appears rather to be one of spiritual adherence to the received consensus of Christian teaching: in contrast to those who walk without blemish, heretics and schismatics may perform all the works of virtue, but they have wandered from the holy mountain, the sanctified location on which the church is built. One can compare it to the blunt statement in *De concordia* that no one outside the church can see God, for outside the church no one has a pure mind.[169] In both these cases membership of the ecclesial community is not based on mere conformity to outward signs but on an attitude of mind: 'As long as you remain in charity with God and your neighbour, you remain in the company of the church.'[170] As an exponent of sacred rhetoric Erasmus allows for the place of subjectivity in religious experience; equally, he recognizes that the mystical body of Christ must be embodied objectively in time, however imperfect that embodiment may be. There is a visible church to which – in spite of all its faults and abuses – all Christians must adhere, and it is precisely to facilitate such adherence that doctrinal conformity should be restricted to those essential teachings defined by consensus over the centuries.[171] Erasmus never compromises his insistence on the unity of the church, but in the conditions of the 1530s he chooses to emphasize the spiritual membership which can transcend divisions within the visible church, even as it recognizes the possibility of grace outside it. The ideal would be for the visible and the spiritual communities to cohere, but that cannot happen until the advent of the mystical church in the heavenly Jerusalem, and in the meantime to be a heretic or a schismatic is to turn away wilfully from the presence of Christ implicit in the Christian community.

* * * * *

168 *De puritate tabernaculi* LB V 302A
169 *De concordia* LB V 492E; compare those penitents who while they may be *physically* outside the church are nevertheless within it in spirit (496A).
170 *In psalmum 22* LB V 337A; cf *In psalmum 4* 271 below.
171 For a clear statement of this position see Ep 1039:235–54, also J.K. McConica 'Erasmus and the Grammar of Consent' in *Scrinium Erasmianum* (n57 above) II 77–99.

At the close of *De puritate tabernaculi*, perhaps mindful of the layman Christoph Eschenfelder to whom he had dedicated it, Erasmus develops an elaborate comparison between the life of the faithful Christian and the temple rites of the Jews. It is as though the purification of outward forms of worship hinges on the hidden liturgy of the pure mind, so that the practice of Christ's precepts becomes an internal mode of sacrifice replacing the blood sacrifice of the old temple with the new rite of the temple of the Holy Spirit:

> Anything which used to be performed in the temple of Solomon in days of old or is performed nowadays, too, in the form of outward rituals, is accomplished spiritually within each of us; indeed it is accomplished all the more excellently and powerfully because it occurs spiritually, because it takes place within, in the most important part of a man, and because it occurs as a result of divine grace.[172]

It is fitting that this final work of exegesis should turn from the immediate occasions of religious conflict which had preoccupied Erasmus in *De concordia* to focus on those concerns which might reconcile Christians. Equally, it is fitting that this journey from the majestic ceremonial of Solomon's temple to the stillness of the spirit before God so aptly parallels the complex signification of the Psalms themselves, songs of the ancient Near East transformed by the prophetic perspective of the early church into means of personal encounter with Christ. Erasmus began and ended his writing on the Scriptures with treatments of the Psalms, and this underlines the central place they occupied in his ideas of divine intervention in history: to read them properly is to unravel a map of salvation and recognize the workings of grace through the medium of language. Above all, the act of reading the Psalms, of appropriating them subjectively, presupposes engagement with the broader controlling conventions of the church, understood as an interpretive community; the church as the mystical body establishes the terms which the individual activates in a personal encounter with Christ. The expositions display more vividly than any of his writings the rich implications of Erasmus' understanding of language as a medium in the human encounter with God.

* * * * *

172 *De puritate tabernaculi* LB V 310E

AN EXPOSITION OF THE FIRST PSALM, 'BLESSED THE MAN,' PRINCIPALLY ON THE TROPOLOGICAL LEVEL

Enarratio primi psalmi, 'Beatus vir,'
iuxta tropologiam potissimum

The *Enarratio primi psalmi* first appeared in September 1515 in an edition of Erasmus' *Lucubrationes* supervised by Nikolaus Gerbel (cf Epp 342–3) and printed by Matthias Schürer at Strasbourg; it was the only one of Erasmus' psalm commentaries not to appear first from the Froben presses at Basel. It was also one of the most frequently reprinted: between 1515 and 1525 it appeared no less than thirteen times, at first among the *Lucubrationes* (Schürer 1515, 1516, 1517, and 1519; Froben 1518 and 1519), then with the *Enchiridion* alone (Strasbourg 1522 and Venice 1523), and finally with other early psalm commentaries in four editions of 1524–5. Exceptionally, the second printing, probably an unauthorized one by Dirk Martens at Louvain in October 1515, appeared with the famous letters to and from Maarten van Dorp concerning the *Moria* (Epp 304 and 337). The *Enarratio* was also published in a German translation (1520) and in Spanish (1531).[1]

It was only in these translations that the *Enarratio* appeared as a separate work, and one might therefore suppose that it ranked fairly low in the hierarchy of Erasmus' writings. The dedicatory letter to Beatus Rhenanus reinforces this impression by claiming that the work was written while Erasmus' horses were recovering from a tiring journey, as a small but appropriate gift for Beatus, whose name just happened to coincide with the first word of the psalm. However, this scenario recalls suspiciously the self-deprecatory dedication of the *Moria* (Ep 222:1–12) and was, indeed, a superannuated device for preserving authorial modesty; moreover, Erasmus gave the *Enarratio* greater weight when he summoned it to his defence against Guillaume Budé's charge (Ep 403) that he spent too much of his energy on trivialities. In Ep 421:121–3 Erasmus associates the *Enarratio* with his projected commentary on St Paul and with his edition of Jerome; he describes it as a 'prelude,' and it is indeed the first work of scriptural exegesis from his pen, though it would shortly be followed by many more.[2]

Erasmus was perhaps inspired by the example of Jerome, on whom he had been working recently; Augustine and especially Hilary also provided many ideas and references.[3] None the less, Erasmus' commentary is by

* * * * *

1 For details, see ASD V-2 23–4 and CWE 3 77.
2 It does not seem likely that at this time Erasmus was considering writing a commentary on the whole Psalter, though such a project may have passed through his mind later; cf 148.
3 In his notes to the ASD edition, A. Godin detects the strong influence of Origen, but (for this psalm at least) this seems to come by way of Hilary, since Origen's commentary on it (PG 12 1085–1100) is very different in scope and intention. There can be no doubt, of course, of Origen's general influence on Erasmus' theology; cf A. Godin *Erasme lecteur d'Origène* (Geneva 1982) and Screech 19–26.

no means a traditional philological and theological exegesis. He expresses dissatisfaction with Jerome's concentration on the eschatological significance of the psalm (55) and several times scornfully rejects the vaporous quibblings of the medieval schoolmen; in the *Moria* he had jested about their ability to analyse *anything* in terms of the traditional 'four senses of Scripture': literal, allegorical, tropological, and anagogical.[4] In the title of the *Enarratio* Erasmus makes it plain that his exegesis will concern above all the tropological or moral meaning of the psalm;[5] only rarely does he deal with the allegorical sense (eg 37 and 51) and with the anagogical (49–50 and 60–1), and he usually points out in such cases that this is a departure from his preferred practice, and indeed frequently attributes these interpretations to his predecessors.

This concentration on the tropological sense, in pursuit of 'that reform of morality which is my principal aim' (11), helps to explain why the *Enarratio* was usually published with the *Enchiridion*,[6] that first formulation of the *philosophia Christi* with its practical counsels for living the Christian life on this earth. Its teaching is frequently echoed in the *Enarratio*, as it is in other works contemporary with the latter, in particular the *Adagia* of 1515 and the *Institutio principis christiani*.[7] It is interesting to see Erasmus apply the wisdom of the psalm to the same targets – tyrants, warmongers, foolish princes, treacherous diplomats, worldly bishops – that he was attacking elsewhere with the aid of Plato and Aristotle. It is another example of that cross-fertilization which means that the principal 'source' of Erasmus is often Erasmus himself.

It is obvious that Erasmus found in the language of the First Psalm an echo of his own practical Christian ethics. Not only does it recommend that the virtuous should 'meditate on the Lord's law,' which for Erasmus is an exhortation, in both Greek and Latin (28 and 30), to put God's commandments into practice; for him the psalm hinges upon a sustained contrast between the deeds in this world of 'the pious' and 'the impious.' This creates a

* * * * *

4 CWE 27 134; cf the definition of the four senses in the *Ecclesiastes* LB V 1035A. On Erasmus' general theological and literary principles in interpreting the psalms, see M.J. Heath 'Allegory, Rhetoric and Spirituality: Erasmus' Early Psalm Commentaries' *Acta Conventus Neo-Latini Torontonensis* ed A. Dalzell, C. Fantazzi and R. Schoeck (Binghamton, NY 1991) 363–70.

5 In the first editions; see ASD V-2 33:2–3n on later variations.

6 First published in 1503; it was included in the *Lucubrationes* with which the *Enarratio* appeared between 1515 and 1519.

7 CWE 27 199–288. In my notes to the text there I have pointed out many parallels with such adages as *Sileni Alcibiadis* and *Dulce bellum inexpertis*; in the present work I have confined myself to references to the *Institutio*.

small problem for the translator, since 'pious' nowadays has overtones of sanctimoniousness which are absent from Erasmus' *pius*, and impiety is now perhaps a milder term than Erasmus' (and Paul's) 'great and hopeless wickedness,' far deadlier than mere sin (61). It must therefore be kept in mind that 'piety' for Erasmus was an interior disposition born of that filial reverence which is the Christian's proper relation to God,[8] and that piety expresses itself not only in words but in deeds of charity towards one's fellows in every sphere of life – an attitude which informs so much of Erasmus' teaching in these years.

The text translated here is that established by A. Godin in ASD v-2 31–80, which is based on the first edition but includes a few additions made in 1518 and 1525; I have noted the most extensive of these. As well as marginal notes (which make up the bulk of the 'variants' in the ASD apparatus), the 1518 Froben edition adds Hebrew characters on the five occasions when Erasmus quotes a Hebrew word or phrase, and it occasionally polishes the style, for example substituting the more classical *edere* and *docere* for the cumbersome *manducare* and *erudire* of the first edition. But the text remained essentially unchanged through its many reprintings.

In the notes, the Psalms are cited according to both the Vulgate and the standard English numbering, but verses within them are given the English numbering alone (some Latin versions include headings as verses). Translations of Scripture are my own, since no English version consistently resembles the Latin. The reader will, however, recognize certain deliberate echoes, particularly of familiar passages of the Authorized Version. A 'working text' of the psalm follows this introductory note; I have translated the Latin version (based on Jerome's translation of the Septuagint) used by Erasmus and included within brackets the alternative readings which he considered in his exegesis.

MJH

* * * * *

8 Cf Boyle 69, and also 70 on the 'pious' reverence required in an exegete of the Scriptures; cf 8 below.

PSALM 1

1 Beatus vir qui non abiit in concilio impiorum, et in via peccatorum non stetit, et in cathedra pestilentiae non sedit.

2 Sed in lege Domini voluntas eius, et in lege eius meditabitur die ac nocte.

3 Et erit tamquam lignum quod plantatum est secus decursus aquarum, quod fructum suum dabit in tempore suo, et folium eius non defluet; et omnia quaecumque faciet prosperabuntur.

4 Non sic impii, non sic; sed tamquam pulvis quem proiicit ventus.

5 Non resurgunt impii in iudicio, neque peccatores in concilio iustorum.

6 Quoniam iustorum viam novit Dominus, et impiorum viam disperdet.

1 Blessed is the man who has not departed into [or 'walked in'] the council of the impious, and has not stood on the path of the sinners, and has not sat on the plague-seat.

2 But he takes delight in the law of the Lord, and he will meditate on his law day and night.

3 And he shall be like wood [or 'a tree'] planted beside the streams of the waters, which gives its fruit in its season, and its leaf shall not fall; and everything that he does shall prosper.

4 Not so the impious, not so; they are like the dust which the wind drives away.

5 The impious do not stand up again in the judgment, nor do sinners in the council of the righteous.

6 Because the Lord knows the path of the righteous and destroys the path of the impious.

ERASMUS OF ROTTERDAM TO BEATUS RHENANUS OF SÉLESTAT[1]

When I see, my dear Beatus, how ordinary and uneducated people keep their friendships in repair by sending and receiving small presents from time to time, it has seemed to me wrong that those who pursue the humanities should be found wanting in this form of friendly attention, and we especially who are linked by our devotion to studies in the closest possible relationship. And so the other day, when my horses were weary from a tiring journey and I was obliged to halt for a few days at Saint-Omer, I began, in order that the working-time might not be wholly wasted, to consider whether I could not get ready some modest gift for you. At that moment there came into my head a very sound precept of our favourite Seneca: one should take special pains to see that a present is appropriate to the recipient as well as worthy of the giver,[2] for thus things of small value in themselves become most precious, simply because they have been aptly chosen. And what could a theologian more properly send than a choice nosegay plucked in the flower-garden of the Scriptures? What present could be more fit for a Beatus than an actual working-plan for true beatitude, sketched by the pencil of the Holy Spirit? A heavenly name indeed it is, for it transcends the nature of mere man, so that the Greek poets used to ascribe this quality to the gods as their especial attribute, and call them *makares*, the blessed ones, *beati*. Not of course that the honour of such a distinguished name belongs to any mortal, unless he is so engrafted in Christ that he is already as it were transfigured and made one with him, and so deserves to be given a share in his immortality and in that splendid name. For nothing less deserves the name of true blessedness than those whom the foolish multitude calls blessed. It calls them blessed with as much warrant as it calls them divine; if in error, to its discredit, and if in flattery, to something worse. The name *Beatus*, blessed, recurs so often in the mysteries of Scripture, and never do we find it given to a rich man, never to monarchs, never to a Sardanapalus.[3] '*Beati*, blessed,' I find, 'are all they that fear the Lord, and walk in his ways.' 'Blessed,' I find, 'is the man unto whom the Lord imputeth no sin.' 'Blessed,' I find, 'is he that considereth the poor and needy.' 'Blessed,' I find, 'are those that are undefiled in the way, and walk in the law of the Lord.'[4] So many ranks of beatitude, of blessedness are there, and yet of those I name no more account is taken than of the Megarians in the old Greek

* * * * *

1 The dedicatory letter is Ep 327.
2 *De beneficiis* 1.12, 2.17
3 An Assyrian king proverbial for wealth and effeminacy; *Adagia* III vii 27
4 Pss 127/128:1, 31/32:2, 40/41:1, 118/119:1

proverb.[5] The first *Beatus* is he whom the fear of God restrains from doing wrong. Blessed again is he who has fallen into sin, but washes away the wrong with tears of repentance so that the merciful Lord does not impute to him what he has done. Blessed too is he who makes up the errors of his earlier life with works of piety and charity, for in the day of judgment the Lord will deliver him from evil. But more blessed is he who is kept free from all taint of sin by respect for the divine law; and most blessed of all the man whom it describes in this psalm, who not only is in the happy state of being untainted by sin, but lives continually according to the divine commandment in such a way that he himself always wears the flower of a blameless life, while contributing to others the lovely fruit of a high example and teaching that leads to salvation.

And so I send you yourself, a *Beatus* for a Beatus. What else could be more fitting – especially as you are blessed with a nature not prone to faults, and try hard to keep both life and reputation free from the stain of any fault? So hard indeed do you work at the best literature that, with Christ to prosper your admirable endeavours, you add not a little lustre and distinction to your native town, which, small as it is, is already famous as the mother of so many able men. There is good hope therefore that one day you will set the whole of Germany such an example as will show them all that your name Beatus was given you not by accident but by divine providence. And so this small present will not merely remind you of your Erasmus, but will set before you an example for yourself. If it please Almighty God, as we have hitherto been linked in the sweet companionship of common studies, so may we hereafter be thought worthy to enjoy together the true beatitude that lasts for ever. Farewell, best of friends.

Saint-Omer, 13 April 1515

* * * * *

5 The people of Megara were thought to be negligible by the rest of Greece; *Adagia* II i 79.

AN EXPOSITION OF THE FIRST PSALM, PRINCIPALLY ON THE TROPOLOGICAL LEVEL, BY DESIDERIUS ERASMUS OF ROTTERDAM, THEOLOGIAN

Divine wisdom is a very different thing from human wisdom, and similarly the language of the Holy Spirit is very different from that of the human heart. Nothing is richer than that heavenly eloquence, but it reveals its treasures only to a diligent, eager investigator whose curiosity, none the less, must be of such a kind that he treats all that he finds with love and respect. Accordingly, anyone setting out to expound the sacred psalms of the prophets must remember that he is not dealing with the hymns of Orpheus or Homer,[1] which relate to a pagan cult, but with the oracles of the Holy Spirit, designed to be a storehouse for the hidden treasures of its wisdom, accessible only to the pious inquirer. For this reason, no one must approach these mysteries unless he has been purified, and he must be not only pure, but also committed to God by, as it were, the sacrifice of prayer. To enjoy this heavenly music, the ears must be free from all obstruction; to be admitted to these well-concealed delights of the eternal godhead, a man must be intensely committed to God.

In the Hebrew text this psalm is ἀνεπίγραφος, that is, without a heading; some commentators also consider that it is not to be given a number like the rest, since it is included as a special case, taking precedence over the first psalm and acting as a sort of preface to the rest. St Augustine thinks (if in fact the beginning of the work in question can be attributed to him; my view is that it has been taken from some other writer and tacked on to his mutilated and headless book) that we should regard this psalm as being spoken by God in person, and that that is why the prophet dared not put a name at its head:

* * * * *

1 In Greek literature a 'hymn' was usually defined as a lyric poem addressed to a god. The so-called Homeric hymns are a collection by various hands, modelled on Homer's style and dating from the eighth to the sixth centuries BC. Orpheus was regarded as the founder of Greek poetry and author of another body of religious poems. On the preconditions for exegesis, see Boyle 70 and 75–7.

it might appear that something could take precedence over divine eloquence. Nor did he dare to make it the first, when perhaps it is not the first, but an exception.[2] Some commentators think it superfluous to call it the first when there is nothing in front of it.[3] St Jerome notes that this psalm and the next are treated as one by the Hebrews, since the one beginning 'Why did the nations rage?' is cited as the 'First Psalm' in the Acts of the Apostles.[4] Moreover, our psalm begins with 'bliss' and the other ends with 'bliss': 'Blessed are all those who put their trust in him.'[5] It is true that the Jews of our own time separate this latter one from the first, and call it the second, but they regard both as untitled. However, let us not worry unduly about the numbering.

As for the heading: what about the other psalms to which the prophet did not hesitate to give a heading, although some represent the Father's own words, and others the Son's? In fact, I cannot see anything here which obliges us to attribute this psalm to the divine voice itself, and it does not really matter much whether the words are spoken by God in person or by his prophet, whose voice God used as his instrument. St Hilary thinks that it cannot be ascribed to either Father or Son in person; this is clearly proved, he thinks, by the line 'he takes delight in the law of the Lord, and will meditate on his law, etc'; these words are inappropriate to the Father speaking of himself, and to the Son.[6]

Hilary certainly has a point, but there is nothing to prevent the whole psalm from being a description of the Son by his Father; St Augustine interprets it in this way,[7] taking 'the man' as a reference to Christ, who did not give way when Satan tempted him to sin, unlike the earthbound Adam of old,[8] and did not 'stand on the path of the sinners,' even if he did set foot on it when born as a man. He did not 'sit on the plague-seat,' since he scorned the kingdoms of this world, but in his budding innocence he brought sinners to God by his preaching and, finally, by his death, resurrection, and

* * * * *

2 Erasmus is quoting here an *Annotatio* on the First Psalm printed separately by Migne (PL 36 66); it is found in early printed editions of Augustine's works, but not in all manuscripts, and most commentators doubt its authenticity and distinguish it from the *Enarratio in psalmum 1* (PL 36 67–9).
3 Cf Jerome *Breviarium in psalmos* PL 26 823B. The attribution of this work to Jerome has been questioned by modern scholarship.
4 Acts 13:33, citing Ps 2:1
5 Ps 2:12; all these points are made by Jerome in the passage cited in n3 above.
6 *Tractatus in psalmum primum* 1 PL 9 248A
7 *Enarratio in psalmum 1* PL 36 67–9; Erasmus loosely paraphrases this text until the end of the paragraph.
8 Cf 1 Cor 15:47.

ascension he 'gave fruit in his season'; he will fulfil all his promises, so that none of his 'leaves' – his words – 'shall fall to the ground,' and his favour will cause the pious to 'prosper in everything that they do.' The impious, on the other hand, will be swept away, since they have not attached themselves to the solid rock that is Christ.[9] Those who have modelled themselves on Christ and fled from sin will enjoy immortality with him; those who have followed the devil and the old Adam, and embraced the world, will be condemned to eternal punishment. This is the gist of Augustine's interpretation.

On the other hand, Hilary thinks that the psalm cannot be applied to Christ in person,[10] and is persuaded particularly by the words near the beginning, 'he will meditate on his law day and night,' since Christ is himself the author of the law. Again, Hilary finds the following words inappropriate to Christ: 'He shall be like a tree that is planted.' First, it seems to him absurd to suggest that a mere tree could be more blessed than Christ: his reasoning is that the thing from which you draw your comparison must be exceptional, as you might say of a girl, 'she is as white as snow,' implying, of course, that snow is whiter than white. Second, 'he shall be' seems an incongruous way to speak of a being who existed before all time, 'the first-born of all creation,' and in whom and through whom all things were created.[11]

But, I might reply, when Christ calls himself a vine in the Gospel,[12] is there really any chance that a common vine will be more fruitful than Christ? Similarly when, in the guise of Wisdom, he compares himself to a terebinth or a palm,[13] are we really to worry that these objects may seem to take precedence over Christ? I think not, and certainly no more than when he is called a stone, a lamb, or a lion,[14] for it is a fact that even the most despised of objects are used as similes in the mystical writings to explain the workings of the divine nature. In any case, why should constant meditation on the divine law be inappropriate to him, who alone among men did not stray in any particular from God's commands and as a man observed the law which he had himself established as God? Are not these his very words in the Gospel: 'And I carry out exactly the commands my Father gave me'?[15] Paul

* * * * *

9 1 Cor 10:4
10 *Tractatus in psalmum primum* 3 PL 9 249A–C, followed until the end of the paragraph, except that the example of 'snow' is Erasmus' own
11 Col 1:15–16
12 John 15:1
13 Sir 24:16 and 14
14 For example in Matt 21:42, Luke 20:17, and Acts 4:11; John 1:29, Acts 8:32, and Rev 5:6; Rev 5:5
15 John 14:31

also bears witness to his obedience 'unto death, even death on the cross.'[16] If we can ascribe 'obedience' to him, why be afraid to speak of his 'meditation on the law'?

However, 'he shall be' must be applied, not to Christ's person or nature, which had no beginning, as they will have no end, but rather to his glorious resurrection and to his adoption of the faithful,[17] which certainly had a beginning in earthly time. Finally, since the faithful are like limbs,[18] and are as one with Christ, it happens sometimes that an attribute of the limbs is transferred to the head, for example when he says 'the confession of my sins is far from saving me';[19] similarly, a property of the head may be imparted to the limbs, as in 'I have said, you are gods; all of you are children of the most high.'[20] Thus it does not matter much whether these words are applied to Christ, in whom all pious people are contained, or to his limbs. I have said all this, not to refute Hilary's opinion, but to defend those who have interpreted the psalm differently.

I have decided to expound this psalm principally on the tropological level,[21] because this seems both more appropriate to it and also more conducive to that reform of morality which is my principal aim. It is not very enlightening to see the Jews twist this psalm to fit Josiah, the only secular king who did not 'depart into the council of the impious,' but obeyed God's law;[22] still less enlightening is Tertullian, who thinks that it should be applied to the Joseph who buried Jesus' body, or to those who do not flock to see the pagans' shows.[23]

It is worthwhile to observe for a moment how, despite its extreme brevity, this psalm deals with vital and universal themes. It begins by offering a great reward, bliss; it appeals to everyone to shun vice and turn to the pursuit of virtue, and by obeying divine law to be renewed, to flower again

* * * * *

16 Phil 2:8
17 Cf Rom 8:15 and 23 and Gal 4:5.
18 Cf Rom 12:4–5, 1 Cor 6:15, 12:12–27.
19 Ps 21/22:1; the sense is that Christ, assumed here to be speaking in person, is without sin, and in no need of salvation.
20 Ps 81/82:6
21 On Erasmus and the 'four senses' of Scripture, see Introduction xxix–xxx and the introductory note 3 and n4 above.
22 Erasmus is echoing Jerome's scorn for this historical interpretation; *Breviarium in psalmos* PL 26 815–16. On Josiah himself, see for example 2 Kings 22:2.
23 *De spectaculis* 3 PL 1 634A–B, but only on pagan shows. In fact, Erasmus is again quoting Jerome (PL 26 823B), who introduces Joseph of Arimathea (Matt 27:57–60, Mark 15:42–6, Luke 23:50–3, John 19:38–42) into a comment on Tertullian.

in Christ, in whom they are already engrafted through baptism. Second, it enhances the glorious destiny of the pious by contrasting it with the very different lot of the impious, even in this mortal life. Finally, it reveals the happiness which awaits the pious in the Last Judgment, and the punishment which awaits the impious. Now to begin, as best I can, a detailed exposition of the prophet's words.

'Blessed is the man': The psalm could not begin more auspiciously than with this forecast of bliss, something which all human beings seek: we were all equally made for it and aspire to it, since all men's efforts are directed towards achieving peace of mind; certainly the impulse is common to us all. But, in choosing our path, we are led astray by strange delusions, and most of humankind clutches at insubstantial phantoms, at the empty shadows of good things, instead of true and supreme good. What was it that preoccupied all the ancient schools of philosophy, what was the question that they so painstakingly discussed in all their books, if not this: 'Wherein lies the happiness of man?' I cannot but approve their enthusiasm and praise their efforts, since they worked so hard and searched so carefully; and I feel ashamed that certain Christians, drowning in pleasure and wealth, drunk with the lust for power, do not even ask themselves such an important question. I am appalled by their sloth and, equally, I am sorry for the philosophers who failed to find what they sought with such determination; they failed for the simple reason that they lacked the one and only teacher of true wisdom, the Spirit of Christ. In those days, the source of human happiness was hotly disputed among the various schools of philosophers: some said that it lay in virtue itself, others in the practice of virtue, or in the three categories of good things, or in learning, in indolence, in pleasure,[24] and so on and so forth; it would take a long time to list here all the different opinions, and even longer to refute them. To prove that they all missed the truth, it is perhaps sufficient to point out that they never reached agreement among themselves. But the ordinary people were still more misguided, and were not allowed even a fleeting glimpse of the truth about happiness; they measured it in terms of filthy lucre or sordid pleasure, of carefree extravagance or the wretchedly anxious exercise of power: in short, to each his own nonsense!

We should pity these pagans, on whom Christ had not bestowed this wisdom, and who could not attain it by reason or merit it by their lives; but much more should we weep for Christians of our own time, and in particular for the princes, who play the role of God on earth, for the priests, whom

* * * * *

24 Allusions to the theories of Plato, the Stoics, Aristotle, and the Epicureans; as Erasmus says, the source of happiness was a commonplace subject of philosophical discussion.

Christ singled out more particularly for his service, and for the bishops, who represent Christ himself among us: because all these seem to believe that happiness lies in much the same things as those unenlightened gentiles. Is there any explanation for the disorder and strife which fill our world except the desire of each of them to extend the frontiers of his tyranny, to increase his income, to impress others with his brilliance, to live at his ease, and do whatever he pleases?

For these reasons, everyone must listen, or at least we Christians must listen, the princes rouse themselves, and the bishops be attentive, to what the Spirit, which knows all and speaks nothing but the truth, tells us concerning true bliss through the mouth of the holy prophet. The philosophers squabble, the common people rave, and even Christians are blind – and yet all dream of bliss in some form. And so, right at the beginning, the heavenly teacher reveals the objective of true bliss, lays down the principles, and completely removes all possibility of error by declaring that the happiness of man resides in piety allied to purity of life. For what brings true peace of mind except the supreme good? And can anything be called the supreme good, is anything, in fact, completely good, except God himself? Since the human heart was made in God's image, it cannot be truly fulfilled by anything but him. Pile up as much wealth as you like, outdo Croesus, surpass Crassus,[25] your heart will desire something more. Plunge into pleasure, drown in delights, surpass Sardanapalus, outdo Epicurus,[26] your heart will still demand something more. Extend the bounds of your empire as far as you please, subdue the whole world, even; another world will be waiting for you to conquer.[27] In all other areas, either we do not achieve our ambitions because our desires are infinite, or else we are shamed by success because we have enjoyed what we should have shunned. There is a single pearl, one good thing, which brings peace to the human heart, and once you have tasted its sweetness (for it can be tasted in this life, if not to the full) you will at once be disgusted with everything that is so much admired by the wretched mass of humanity.[28]

But only piety will enable us to reach this goal, linking us with God in a wonderful way, so that we are made one with him. Conversely, impiety

* * * * *

25 A Lydian king and a Roman politician, both proverbial for wealth and thus put together in *Adagia* I vi 74A
26 An Assyrian king and the Athenian philosopher, both proverbially associated with materialism; see *Adagia* III vii 27.
27 An allusion to Alexander the Great's restless search for new worlds to conquer; Valerius Maximus 8.14 ext 2
28 Cf Matt 13:46 ('single pearl'); Ps 33/34:8, Heb 6:5, and 1 Pet 2:3 ('tasted its sweetness').

cuts the wicked off from God, and in such a way that, divorced from the
supreme good, they are made limbs of the devil. What good thing can anyone
lack, if he has Christ, the source of all goodness? Similarly, what good thing
can anyone possess if he is joined in this way to the father of all evil? Why
torment yourself, in vain? Why wear yourself out in useless struggle?

You may sigh, and say: 'Oh, I should be truly happy, if I could win my
case and grab that estate,' or '... if my soldiers could conquer that province,'
or '... if I could get myself appointed to that living.' You are listening to what
your emotions dictate; listen, instead, to what Christ's spirit dictates: 'They
called the people who possess such things blessed.'[29] What things? Why,
land, servants, power, all the things that the world esteems as the height of
good fortune. But who 'called them blessed'? At first, only the pagans, who
knew nothing of God, and not even all of them, just the more brutish, who
barely deserved to be called human. Why then are these same sentiments
heard among Christians? Why do we – even the clergy, even the monks, even
the bishops – pursue the same things, perhaps with even greater eagerness
than the pagans? It is clear enough how much we prize these shoddy goods,
seeing that we fight for them with any and every weapon, and leave no
stone unturned[30] to find them. Where did it come from, this pagan outlook
on Christianity, this worldly Christ who speaks not of heaven but of earth?
Let us banish from Christian mouths, and still more from Christian hearts,
the idea that human happiness depends on such things. If we are truly
Christians, that is, if we are guided by Christ's Spirit, let us agree with the
Spirit that 'blessed is the people whose God is the Lord.'[31]

For each individual, his god is the thing in which he places his greatest
expectation of bliss. If he will do and suffer anything for money, his god is
not the Lord, but Mammon;[32] if he is a slave to pleasure, his belly is his god;[33]
if he wrecks everything for the sake of power, the Lord is not his god: the
god he worships is called ambition. Thus, in this verse, it is not those who are
well-supplied with what ordinary people admire who are called 'blessed,'
but those who lead lives of purity, and have not 'departed into the council of
the impious' who pursue such things by fair means or foul.

'Blessed is the man, etc': The psalm uses the word 'man,' but does this
exclude woman from a share in bliss? Not at all. In the kingdom of heaven

* * * * *

29 Ps 143/144:15; as the quotation at the end of the paragraph makes clear, Erasmus
     regards this first half of the verse as an ironical statement (cf n31 below).
30 *Adagia* I iv 30
31 Ps 143/144:15; cf n29 above.
32 Cf Matt 6:24 and Luke 16:13.
33 Phil 3:19

sex and status count for nothing. In Christ there is no master or slave, no man
or woman, no rich or poor, but a new creature.[34] It is true that in mystical
writing the superior part of the mind, which the philosophers call reason and
Paul the spirit, is often described symbolically as 'man'; similarly, the word
'woman' describes the weaker part of our mind, which the philosophers call
instinct and Christians the flesh.[35] It is relevant to this that at the world's
beginning woman was ordered to obey her husband[36] and to follow him in
acts of worship, as she had led him by her example into sin. It is relevant
that Abraham's name was lengthened from Abram, but Sara's was shortened
from Sarai;[37] the Gospel text 'Go, call your husband'[38] makes the same point.
Clearly, it requires a true man to scorn all that is terrifying in this world,
to reject and trample underfoot all that is stimulating or tempting, and to
approach Christ along the narrow path[39] of virtue. Believe me, this is no
task for the soft or the unwarlike. If nothing can separate you from the love
of Christ, be it the glitter of gold, the snares of pleasure, the affection of
friends, disgrace in the eyes of men, or indeed the sword, hunger, death, life,
or angels:[40] then, clearly, you are a true man – even if you are a woman.

Therefore, 'blessed is the man who has not departed.' When we imitate
God, we draw nearer to him; when we do not, we drift away from him;
our inclinations are like feet that carry us towards him or away from him.
That explains why the prodigal son, at odds with his father, 'departed' into
a distant land.[41] In the same way, Adam hid himself from God's sight;[42]
not only did he 'depart' from God but, forgetting God's command, he drew
nearer to the serpent. In fact, the Greek text has, instead of 'departed,'
'walked' or 'entered' [οὐκ ἐπορεύθη].

'In the council of the impious, etc': Three terms require comment
here: 'impious,' 'sinner,' and 'plague-ridden.'[43] The first 'walks,' the second

* * * * *

34 Cf 2 Cor 5:17, Gal 3:28 and 6:15.
35 This recalls several passages in the *Enchiridion* (CWE 66 25, 47–8, 51) where
    woman (or Eve) is identified with the carnal part of man; on the spirit and the
    flesh, see especially Romans 8 and Galatians 5.
36 Cf Gen 3:16.
37 Gen 17:5 and 15
38 John 4:16
39 Matt 7:14
40 This passage is a conflation of Rom 8:35–8 and Rev 6:8.
41 Luke 15:13
42 Gen 3:8
43 Erasmus is here using a variant in the Greek text of the psalm which translates
    as 'the seat of the plague-ridden'; his normal reading of this phrase is 'the seat
    of the plague.'

'stands,' and the third 'sits on a seat,' despite the fact that normally we sit in council, rather than walk, and walk on a path rather than stand there; moreover, we usually associate a seat with rest, rather than plague. Impiety is committed against God, sin against anyone; therefore anyone who is impious must by definition be a sinner, but the reverse is not true. For example, a drunkard or a wastrel might respect his parents: 'he is guilty of sin, but he is not guilty of impiety,' to use Hilary's terms.[44] Hilary's view is that 'impious' describes those who hold false opinions about God, who deny, for example, that God exists, or that he created the world, or that he is beneficent and just. In fact, anyone who holds such opinions has also 'departed' from a natural way of reasoning, and entered 'the council of the impious,' since common sense tells us that there is a divinity who so miraculously created the world and who governs it so wisely. The 'impious' have no consistent doctrine but are tossed to and fro by various mistaken ideas,[45] and so they are aptly described as 'walking' rather than 'standing still.' Now, the first rule of piety is that our opinions about God must be worthy of him; this is ensured for us by the gift of faith, called the door to Christ, by which we stand, as Paul says,[46] just as we also stand on the solid rock which is Christ.[47] Meanwhile the impious are distracted by their different errors, as dreams distract the mind; often, too, their statements are self-contradictory; they do indeed hold a 'council,' but there, instead of 'sitting,' they 'walk' to and fro.

The adjective 'impious' is no less appropriate for those who, having stumbled into heresy, are not bound by any scriptural ordinance but are led this way and that by their fitful delusions; they define God, not according to his nature or the testimony of the sacred writings, but according to their own personal whims. Among those in particular who blundered about in this 'council' were the Gnostics, who held that God is made of the same substance as our souls.[48] The Arians paced up and down there, maintaining that Father,

* * * * *

44 *Tractatus in psalmum primum* 1 PL 9 251B; Erasmus uses Hilary's examples rather than his exact words; his subsequent discussion of the distinction between impiety and sin draws freely on this part of Hilary's treatise.
45 The phrase 'tossed to and fro by mistaken ideas' is a conflation of Eph 4:14 and Heb 13:9.
46 Cf for example Acts 14:27, 1 Cor 16:9 and 13, and 2 Cor 1:24.
47 1 Cor 10:4
48 Gnosticism, a widespread religious philosophy denounced as heretical early in the second century AD, was influenced by pagan models and taught that the 'pneumatics,' or Gnostics themselves, truly belonged to the divine rather than the human world, since they contained a divine spark directly descended from the 'pleroma,' from God himself.

Son, and Holy Spirit are not ὁμοούσιους (that is, of the same essence), but that the Father alone is the creator, that the Son was created by the Father, but not born of him, and that the Holy Spirit is the creature of a creature, that is, created by the Son.[49] The Valentinians are there, claiming that Christ did not have a human body but a celestial one, which he did not take from the Virgin, but brought with him from on high.[50] There, too, are those who rob him of his human soul,[51] who make him less important than the Father or superior to the Holy Spirit. Could anyone enumerate all the twists and turns of the paths into which these sects are unhappily led by their different errors, when once they have strayed from straightforward truth? If you press them in debate, they mutter, they dissemble, they make excuses, they look for a chance to slink away and, like Proteus, change themselves into a dozen different shapes.[52]

Happy the man, therefore, who has always taken his stand on Christ, always clung to the evidence of Holy Writ, always accepted the decrees of the church, and never 'walked in the council of the impious.' Paul also advises us to avoid them: 'Bad company is the ruin of a good character.'[53] The pious find it painful even to listen to the impious speaking of God; they think it sinful even to contemplate their ideas, let alone accept them. Not for nothing was the name of heretic so hateful to our forefathers, since from heresy springs, as from a fountain, everything that poisons our existence; our opinions give rise to all our actions. Suppose, for instance, that I were to attempt to twist the sacred writings to suit my own way of life and force them to excuse my faults when they ought to correct them; what hope should I have then of returning to my senses? What remedy is left if I turn the only possible cure into poison for myself?

But it is not enough merely to accept the church's decrees; I mean that correct beliefs are not enough, but must be supplemented by a way of life that corresponds to one's beliefs. If not, 'devils too believe, and tremble.'[54] Therefore the psalm adds the next step: 'And has not stood on the path of the

* * * * *

49 The anti-Trinitarian heresy of the followers of Arius was condemned at the Council of Nicea in 325, where the Greek term quoted by Erasmus was coined.
50 The Valentinians were a Gnostic sect of the second century from whose complex doctrine their enemies, such as Irenaeus and Tertullian, extracted the example cited by Erasmus.
51 Probably an allusion to the third-century Apollinarist heresy. Erasmus here lists the main issues of Christological debate in the early church.
52 The ancient sea-god eluded questioners by this means; cf *Adagia* II ii 74.
53 1 Cor 15:33
54 James 2:19

sinners.' How many Christians there are today who would rather lay their heads on the block than desert to the teachings of the heretics! Yet the same people serve Mammon,[55] cheat, swindle, perjure themselves, steal, wallow in degrading vices, and rush headlong into crime for ambition's sake. They deserve credit for turning away from the 'council of the impious,' but they also deserve blame, since they have not only 'stood on the path of the sinners,' but have even lain down there! To 'stand' is merely to linger, but to lie down is to be so bound by sin that Christ is needed to 'free the paralytic.'[56]

You will notice, reader, the aptness of the terms: we are forbidden to 'walk into' the council of the impious, because we must not even hear their impious ideas about God; anything which smacks of impiety must at once be rejected and spat out. But, to obtain bliss, it is enough not to have 'stood' on the path of the sinners since, whether we like it or not, all of us must at some time pass that way. Some natural impulse, a relic of Adam's sin, seems to propel us towards it. Even Paul feels the rule of sin in his body battling against the rule of conscience, and is driven to cry out: 'Wretch that I am, who will free me from this body of death?'[57] What then is to be expected of us lesser mortals?

However, those whom natural weakness propels towards that path may be quickly brought back if their thoughts are holy. If the disease of avarice perturbs your thoughts, think of Christ's poverty; if the temptations of the flesh disturb you, think of Christ's crucifixion. If it is ambition, think of Christ, rejected, despised, more like a worm than a man.[58] In this way, you will not only be uninfected by contact with sinners, but you will even profit from this natural inclination towards evil as it turns your thoughts towards goodness. Only, do not rush headlong along this path, do not even linger there for a moment. You must run in the paths of God's commandments,[59] but you must avoid taking the path of the sinners to the extent that you do not even set foot there. You must withdraw your foot at once and flee while there is time; the children of Babylon must be dashed against the stone while they are still young.[60] It should be noted also that 'stand' is used of someone who refuses quite deliberately to bow his head to the God whom he offends; instead, he stands erect, head high, and rejects God's

* * * * *

55 Cf n32 above.
56 Cf Matt 9:2–7, Mark 2:3–13, and Luke 5:18–26.
57 Rom 7:24
58 Cf Ps 21/22:6.
59 Cf Ps 118/119:32.
60 Cf Ps 136/137:9.

mercy. 'You too,' says Paul, 'have held up your heads and refused to grieve instead.'[61]

So, your beliefs are orthodox, you have not 'departed into the council of the impious.' You live honourably and behave virtuously or, in other words, you have not 'stood on the path of the sinners.' You are already a Christian in word and deed. What, then, remains? Why, the third injunction: 'Do not sit on the plague-seat.' The prophet seems to be warning Christians who are fighting God's battle not to involve themselves in worldly affairs;[62] therein lies danger even to upright men. One comes across people who believe all the right things about God, who shun vice, and yet who seem ashamed to be mere private citizens, to belong to the lower ranks, although that is the best way to preserve moral purity. They hanker after, or at all events accept, the offices of state, they become governors, sometimes indeed they put themselves forward for bishoprics.[63] 'What if they do?' someone will say. 'Do you condemn such public service? Does not all power come from God?[64] Can anything but good come from good? Why is the place where Moses and Peter sat, where, moreover, bishops sit today, why is this to be called the plague-seat?'

It is not the seat that is condemned, but the act of sitting in it. Plague is a disease whose unseen contagion can rapidly infect everyone; unless you are very careful, any public office, especially the more prestigious ones, will infect you in the same way. If an office has been obtained dishonestly, as is so frequently the case, the risk of infection is doubled from the start; anyone who pursues public office is unfit to govern and useless to the state.[65] Only people who are immune to the contagion must be dragged, against their will, to the seat of power. Even people of irreproachable character can be corrupted by ambition and the trappings of power, and even the best of intellects can go astray amid the storms of worldly affairs, and be diverted from the course of honour. For this reason Socrates, the best of the pagans,

* * * * *

61 Cf 1 Cor 5:2.

62 2 Tim 2:4

63 On Erasmus and the role of bishops generally, see for example the 1515 adage *Sileni Alcibiadis* (*Adagia* III iii 1), the *Institutio principis christiani* CWE 27 284–6 and nn15 and 24, and *Ecclesiastes* LB V 805–7. The particular relevance of the phrase here translated 'plague-seat' (*cathedra pestilentiae*) to bishops lies in the presence of the Latin word used to designate the bishop's throne (*cathedra*).

64 Cf Rom 13:1.

65 A theme of Plato's *Republic* (1.347C and 7.520D–521B) echoed with particular approval by Erasmus in the *Institutio principis christiani* CWE 27 222

considered that it was not a sign of wisdom to participate in official duties of state.[66]

We also know that true Christians among our forefathers were extraordinarily reluctant to accept even ecclesiastical office.[67] Those who were to be forced to become deacons had to be trapped or tricked into it; those who were considered worthy of episcopal office had to be raised to that dignity by being seized and forcibly[68] detained. Even today we hear pious men, if ever they are forced to take the bishop's throne, bewail their fate, abhor their enforced new role, and long to return to that peaceful and happy existence in which they lived for themselves and for Christ. Now if the bishop's throne, even when occupied by a man of good character, is still tainted by this infection, is it any wonder that the same applies when it is obtained by force, money, and all the other evil tricks, by fools, rogues, the miseducated, people empty of virtue and tainted with every kind of vice? Yet everywhere today we see bishops, not content with ecclesiastical position, taking on the roles of kings and satraps, causing universal bloodshed and slaughter in their tyrannical pursuit of power, revenue, and plunder; and the reverend fathers in Christ spend their lives doing nothing else. Such power is not a 'plague-seat' to those who have brought their own plague with them, but the danger of plague is doubled every time that a fool's depravity is dignified by the power of public office.

On such a seat sat Pilate,[69] who was otherwise an upright judge; but because he feared Caesar, he was infected by the plague-seat. Here sat the Scribes and Pharisees,[70] who observed the precepts of the law but, in their greed and ambition, exercised power for themselves, not for the people. Samuel sat in this seat for many years, and yet he remained free from infection; but he was an exception, having been brought up in God's temple from boyhood.[71]

If this exposition offends anyone, he must blame St Hilary,[72] not me, and I must admit that, while I find his interpretation very convincing, it seems to apply more to conditions in his time than in ours. For at that time,

* * * * *

66 See for example Plato *Apology* 31C–33A.
67 Cf a similar remark made by 'St Peter' in *Julius exclusus* CWE 27 176.
68 *obtorto collo*, literally 'having one's neck twisted,' and used to mean 'taken prisoner by violent means'; cf *Adagia* IV ix 50.
69 John 19:12–13
70 Cf Matt 23:2.
71 Cf 1 Sam 1–2.
72 *Tractatus in psalmum primum* 5 PL 9 252C–253A, citing the examples of Pilate and the Scribes and Pharisees

both private and public life were so confused by the interaction of the pagan and Christian worlds that it was extremely difficult to preserve one's moral purity as a Christian while continuing to fulfil one's public obligations. Mind you, even today the morals of Christians, and especially of princes, are so corrupt that, in such a climate, it is perhaps more difficult than ever to be an honest politician or a pious bishop.

Now someone will object: 'Where is all this leading? Do you want the episcopal thrones to be empty – since you say that a good man runs the risk of being infected by the plague, and that a bad one will bring the plague with him and double the dangers?' I do not think that we need really fear that any see will remain vacant, when we see so many candidates battling for each one, wherever it may be! I want them to be occupied, but not by a usurper; I want the newcomer to be a conscript; I want a candidate who is experienced and acceptable to all, and I want him sober and watchful, endowed with all the qualities listed by Paul.[73] I do not want an evildoer who brings the plague with him; I do not want an average man, liable to be corrupted by his good fortune. Now it may be that those who are immune to its poison do not in fact get to sit in this seat. It is rather those who covet public office, those who find satisfaction in that sort of thing. But someone who considers it a burden rather than an honour[74] will not take this seat; he recognizes its responsibilities rather than its rewards, which in any case he will despise. But if such a man should take up the post, yet still he 'has it as if he had it not,'[75] and holds at arm's length what other men rush to embrace.

If anyone does not accept the subtle differences between the expressions used in this verse, he must at least agree that the prophet indicated three stages by which a man may descend to the lowest depths of impiety. First, he 'departs into the council of the impious' whenever his mind gives way, however briefly, to the promptings of the demons, or his association and intimacy with dishonourable men gradually make him waver from his intention to pursue a blameless life; for not even the plague, passing from the sick to neighbouring bodies, spreads infection as quickly as the conversation of criminals corrupts their associates. However, salvation is still more remote for anyone who has made a habit of 'standing on the path of the sinners' and has become inured to sin because of the length of his stay there. Furthest of all from the hope of bliss are those who have also 'sat on the plague-seat,' whose conscience is now so utterly overthrown and obliterated

* * * * *

73 1 Tim 3:2–7 and Titus 1:7–9
74 The phrase 'a burden rather than an honour' is a pun on *oneratus* and *onoratus*.
75 Cf 1 Cor 7:29.

that they even expect praise for their foulest deeds, accepting the worst evil
as if it were the greatest good; their lives are tainted in every particular, and
all who come near them are infected, as if by a contagious disease, by their
pestilent example and pestilent words. They, of course, are so little ashamed
of their impious life that they 'glory in their wickedness and their power to
do evil.'[76] In the end these unfortunates are brought to such a point of madness that they are not afraid to scoff at the Holy Scriptures, knowing that
their whole way of life is utterly at variance[77] with them. They are not afraid
to inveigh scornfully against the simplicity of pious men, and indeed they do
not hesitate to insult Christ and to voice impious and heretical ideas.

   This interpretation certainly fits in with the term used, according to
Jerome, in the Hebrew original, וּבְמוֹשַׁב לֵצִים *uvmoshab laytzim*, meaning 'on
the seat of the mockers.'[78] Similarly, the blessed Jeremiah boasts that he did
not sit in the 'council of the scoffers,'[79] those who say such things as 'Get along
with you, bald-head, get along with you!'[80] and 'If he is the Son of God, let
him now descend from the cross.'[81] Compare the text in the Book of Wisdom:
'Those whom once we held in derision and thought their life madness.'[82] God
forbid that any who worship him should sink so low as to boast of their sins
instead of confessing them, and to delight in their misdeeds, laughing like
madmen, instead of washing them away with tears; and yet, all too often,
this is precisely what we are obliged to witness. To sum up, 'to depart into
the council of the impious' is a mark of human weakness, 'to stand on the
path of the sinners' shows corruption of the will, and 'to sit on the seat of the
scornful' is the result of hopeless wickedness and an incurable depravity.

   This interpretation is not inconsistent with that of Augustine (or whoever it was), for whom 'sitting on the plague-seat' refers to those who, abus-
ing the authority of their position, corrupt the minds of simple people with
pernicious teaching.[83] What greater plague could afflict Christianity than
that those who claim doctrinal authority should divert us from Christ by
their teaching? What hope is there for the people, if the salt itself has lost

* * * * *

76 Ps 51/52:1
77 Cf *Adagia* I ii 63, a forceful expression quoted here in Greek.
78 *Breviarium in psalmos* PL 26 823C, also giving the following reference to Jeremiah.
     The 1518 Froben edition was the first to add Hebrew characters here and on the
     four subsequent occasions when Hebrew is quoted in this work.
79 Jer 15:17
80 2 Kings 2:23
81 Matt 27:40 and 42
82 Wisd 5:3–4
83 *Enarratio in psalmum* 1 PL 36 67; on the authenticity of the treatise, see n2 above.

its savour?[84] Are not some priests doing just this when they envelop their credulous flock in ritual? The people are led (by the nose,[85] as it were) to depend on it, and thus they never grow towards the true teaching of Christ, but remain forever infants and children in Christ.[86] Is not the same true of those who, in pursuit of their own interests, and to protect their own power, force the Holy Scriptures to serve their human passions, and also of those who trap and burden the people with regulations redolent, not of Christ, or of the public interest, but of pure self-love?[87] Do we not observe, daily, that such regulations oppress the pious and the modest, strike down the weak, and deceive the simple? For we must also note in passing that the idea of 'plague' does not apply only to the corruption of the sitter, who is made worse by the success of his machinations, but even more to those infected by the insidious poison of this pestilent bishop or prince. Every vice carries infection with it, but there is no more comprehensive, more rapid, or more deadly way for impiety to spread among the mass of the people than through bad and foolish princes and bishops. In the final analysis, the worst of men must be the one who, if he were good, could be the most valuable of all, but who is in fact evil, to the great detriment of all. However, such is the ambition, the greed, the folly, the impiety of those (the bad ones I mean) who should be the teachers of piety, that they consider anyone who strives earnestly to be a true Christian to be virtually a heretic!

Thus, to think evil is to 'depart into the council of the impious,' to do evil is to 'stand on the path of the sinners,' and to teach evil is to 'sit on the plague-seat.' Some commentators also make the following division: the first step, they say, refers to Jews, the second to pagans, and the third to heretics;[88] however, I find this final interpretation more ingenious than convincing.

The objection could be raised here that if, as Paul says, God made all things prisoners to sin[89] and no one, not even a newborn babe, is free from

* * * * *

84 Cf Matt 5:13, Mark 9:50, and Luke 14:34.
85 *Adagia* II i 19
86 Cf 1 Cor 3:1. This sentence was recommended for deletion in the *Index expurgatorius* LB X 1820B.
87 Erasmus, who draws attention to the term by citing it in Greek here, had dealt fully with the dangers of *philautia* in the *Moria*; see CWE 27 89 and *Adagia* I iii 92.
88 Cf Jerome *Breviarium in psalmos* PL 26 823B.
89 Cf Gal 3:22 and Rom 11:32. The reference to those few exempted from original sin probably alludes to the often heated debate over the Immaculate Conception of Mary, a doctrine supported by the Franciscans and the Paris theological faculty but opposed by the Dominicans. The case in favour is argued by

guilt, then these words of praise can only be applied to Christ or, at best, to very few others, whom modern theology exempts from the general fate of mankind. I suppose that this explains why some commentators have chosen to apply these words to the person of Christ.[90] But as well as being personally free from all imperfection, Christ also helps those reborn in him to avoid sin: inasmuch as we are descended from Adam, we all sin; but inasmuch as we are reborn in Christ by baptism, we do not sin. Christ does not sin for the simple reason that he is akin to a Father without sin. Once all men were sinners, since they traced their descent to sinful Adam. By nature we are born inclined to wickedness, but by faith we are reborn of God and made new creatures, reflecting our new progenitor. Like John, when he wrote 'he who is from God does not sin,'[91] I am speaking of the sin which brings death. In general, anyone who commits a deadly sin at once forfeits his status as an adopted child[92] and, cut off from the body of Christ, is engrafted upon the body of Satan. Therefore our 'blessed man' does not sin, but the prophet's description of him applies only from the time when he is reborn in Christ.

'But he takes delight in the law of the Lord': The psalm has shown what must be avoided, pointing out the dangers, revealing the yawning chasm which awaits us unless we are quick to withdraw our foot as soon as we stumble. If avoiding impiety is the first step towards piety, it is also a large step towards it, and I am fairly sure that it is much the most difficult part of the struggle. The first step is to have avoided evil; the second is to be prepared to do good. Moral purity helps us to avoid sin; charity commands us to do good to all; forbearance teaches us to tolerate evil men. In these three qualities the foundation of perfect Christianity is laid.[93]

Christian wisdom is the same thing as true piety. It may be that 'the beginning of wisdom is the fear of the Lord,'[94] and indeed fear can keep us from sin, but perfect piety is not founded on it. The fear of punishment has done much to spread the ideal of purity, but to be perfect and blessed you must put on the 'charity which drives out fear.'[95] It is not enough to hate

* * * * *

Josse Clichtove *De puritate conceptionis beatae Mariae virginis* (Paris: Henricus Stephanus 1513).
90 Presumably St Augustine; see 9 and n7 above.
91 See 1 John 5:18 and 16.
92 Cf Rom 8:15 and Gal 4:5.
93 Literally 'the circle is completed'; *Adagia* II vi 86
94 Sir 1:14 and Ps 110/111:10
95 1 John 4:18

Satan and all his evil works, unless you also begin to love Christ and all his virtues. Now, obedience to his law is the clearest evidence of love for him, as he says himself in the Gospel: 'If you love me, keep my commandments.'[96] Therefore, 'he takes delight in the law of the Lord' – not in riches or power or sensual pleasures or all the other things which the wretched multitude endlessly pursues; on the contrary, this blessed man 'takes delight in the law of the Lord.'

By 'law' the psalm means all the Holy Scriptures; earnest study of them will assist greatly in keeping us from sin. To avoid finding pleasure in the sins of the flesh, take pleasure in the study of literature (of sacred literature, of course, since literature unconnected with Christ scarcely deserves the name). The one sure bulwark against all the assaults of the demons is that a man should be thoroughly and wholeheartedly imbued with the Scriptures.[97] In them the righteous man 'takes delight' each time that, scorning and rejecting all others, he gazes with wonder and love upon this one true pearl; as the Gospel says: 'Where your treasure lies, there will your heart be also.'[98] Here is another text which applies to him: 'He takes great delight in God's commandments.'[99] The human heart is naturally disposed towards love, and cannot remain empty of it; moreover, the lover himself becomes like the things he loves. If someone loves the Holy Scriptures, he is enraptured, changed, transfigured into God.[100]

The prophet speaks of 'delight': fear is banished, love enters in, and now nothing can be difficult or irksome. In the earlier stages there was fear, there was danger, there was strife; but this verse deals with someone willing and eager to 'run the race.'[101] Those who, as Horace puts it, 'hate sin because they dread a beating'[102] do not 'take delight in the law.' If someone hates sin, not because it always brings disaster with it, but because it is the opposite of that fair model of virtue whose love enraptures him, then such a person 'takes delight in the law of the Lord.' God's law is a spiritual law, and moreover 'where the spirit of the Lord is, there is liberty.'[103]

* * * * *

96 John 14:15
97 Perhaps an echo of the similar imagery in the *Enchiridion*, for example CWE 66 33 (where Ps 1:2 is quoted)
98 Matt 6:21
99 Ps 111/112:1
100 On this clearly ecstatic language, see ASD V-2 49:461n and Screech *passim*, especially 237–40.
101 Ps 18/19:5; editions subsequent to the first add 'of his commandments.'
102 *Epistles* 2.1.154
103 2 Cor 3:17

Christ's single law, the law of charity, is as follows: 'This is my commandment: that you love one another as I have loved you.'[104] Moses made innumerable laws on the rites of sacrifice, clean and unclean food, leprosy, dress, feast-days and ordinary days, fasting, prayer; philosophers and other leaders of men have made countless other laws. Christ says: 'I bring you one law only, which is that you love one another.'[105] If you obey this one law, you will need no other; if you disobey this one law, it will be useless for you to pile law upon law.

The psalm does not say merely 'in the law,' but 'in the law of the Lord'; not in the laws of princes, which are imbued with much falsehood and still more flattery and embody no more than worldly wisdom. They may perhaps bring you wealth and fame, but they cannot bring you bliss; moreover, they can be changed suddenly, like a doctor's prescription, to conform with the times or the prince's whim. Anyone who looks towards eternity and thirsts for heaven takes no delight in these; 'the law of the Lord is perfect and bestows wisdom on the simple.'[106] Even if men's laws are just, they are designed to check the behaviour of the uncouth mob, and so they must always be more or less uncouth and squalid themselves, when set beside the Lord's law. 'They who are of earth speak of earthly things; he who comes from heaven has brought a heavenly law.'[107] Men's laws may serve us for a time; Christ's law alone can bring us bliss.

I would venture[108] to add that our 'blessed man' does not take delight in the quibblings and specious reasoning of sophistical theologians or in the labyrinthine complexities of the *quaestiones*,[109] which produce noisy arguments but nothing conducive to piety, or in the decrees or constitutions of the popes as men.[110] Not that the pious man will despise them, especially if they

* * * * *

104 John 15:12
105 Cf John 13:34.
106 Ps 18/19:7
107 Cf John 3:31.
108 Erasmus' caution was justified: the next three paragraphs were recommended for deletion in the *Index expurgatorius* LB X 1820B. But Erasmus is simply repeating (albeit somewhat gratuitously in this context) attacks made elsewhere: on theologians, for example, in the *Moria* CWE 27 126–35 and 144–7 and on legislators and tyrants in the *Institutio principis christiani* CWE 27 264–73.
109 An allusion to the technical exercises of scholastic theology, a frequent target for Erasmus; cf for example Epp 337, 456, and 512.
110 Erasmus appears to distinguish here, as he does for example in the *Moria* and the *Julius exclusus*, between the ideal pastoral and spiritual role of the papacy and its actual functioning as a legal and administrative office. 'Constitutions' are papal regulations, often those concerned with administrative matters.

breathe a Christian and apostolic spirit, if they seem to be founded on that one law of charity, and aim only to improve the general well-being (measured by an increase in true piety, rather than in the things which ordinary people admire). But when constitutions of this kind have nothing more apostolic than their titles and deal only with obtaining, preserving, or increasing personal profit; when they savour of nothing but a certain kind of worldly wisdom – also found among pagan tyrants; when they achieve their aims by inspiring sheer terror and panic, rather than by showing a spirit of mercy and mildness: what do these endlessly proliferating laws do except entangle Christian liberty in a series of snares? In the end there is a danger that, as the Greek proverb puts it, the rope will break under too much strain.[111]

Good popes should therefore do their utmost to ensure that true charity is awoken in the minds of men, so that God's law, not man's, may flourish. What need of so many threats, chains – and constitutions – if the flames of holy charity burn brightly? Should it grow cold, still fear will be unable to extort anything sincere or lasting. Did not the ancient tyrants try everything? Did they not think up all kinds of laws to cow the people and bolster their power? None of them reigned for long. If your subjects are well disciplined, the minimum of laws will be enough, and all else will be settled according to the law of charity. But if they are undisciplined, there is nothing more useless than to multiply the number of laws; mankind's ingenuity when it comes to wrongdoing is such that, as soon as a law is introduced, criminal perversity will nearly always turn it against the state, greatly to its detriment. If something new has to be introduced, Christian princes should not make the sort of law which provokes sighs from the pious, muttering from the timid, and curses from the dishonest, but rather laws in which we can recognize the supreme mercifulness of Christ himself, and which aim to further any interest but the prince's own. I admit that the people have no right to make rash judgments on the princes' decrees; but, equally, it is the princes' duty, in framing their laws, to remember that the rest of humanity too is endowed with common sense, that it will be human beings, not cattle, who pass judgment on them, and that they are free men, not slaves.

Perhaps none of this is relevant, but it is surely desirable that there should be a single law, just as there is one God and one faith. It will be able to dictate what is to be done in every circumstance, for charity is nowhere idle. The 'blessed man' will not entirely despise other laws, but in this one alone will he 'take delight.'

* * * * *

111 *Adagia* I v 67

Some readers may ask why it should be said of our blessed man that he takes delight 'in the law of the Lord,' since the law is not imposed on the righteous; as Paul says: 'Those who have been redeemed through Christ by adoption as the children of God are now not under the law, but under grace.'[112] But to live 'under the law' and 'in the law' are two different things. The Jews were under the law; they were confined, fenced in, as it were, by the dictates of the law, and they obeyed it, out of fear not choice, as if it were a slavemaster. Christians live their lives 'in the law,' and choose to live according to the law because they are invited to do so by charity, not compelled by threats of punishment. Slaves are under the law, free men live by the law. The Jews, with their offerings of wheat cakes,[113] know only the stale and tasteless letter of the law, and are oppressed by the weight of it. But we hold the spirit of the law and, alert and unencumbered, are not dragged along but run, as the prophet says elsewhere: 'I have run along the path of your commandments, for you have lightened my heart.'[114] Superstitious observance of the letter burdens the heart, whereas the spirit and charity lighten it. Anyone who obeys the letter is in a constant state of anxiety and dares not eat ordinary food. The spiritual believer says: 'To the pure, all things are pure,'[115] or: 'Everything is permitted me, though not everything is good for me,'[116] or: 'I became all things to all men, that I might win them all.'[117]

Can you not see how far the spirit can reach? Accordingly, success depends to a large extent on your earnest desire to achieve your aims. But desire is not enough: you must also 'meditate,'[118] as you strive to adjust your character and your life to the rule of divine law. For in Latin 'to meditate' essentially means not 'to turn over in your mind' but 'to practise,' and to be fully prepared for action. If you speak and act in accordance with the precepts of charity, then in everything you say and do you are truly 'meditating on the Lord's law' and are doing so 'day and night,' that is, in good times and in bad.[119] In good times, do not take anything for granted, but give thanks

* * * * *

112 A paraphrase of Gal 4:4–5
113 Probably a reference to the offerings specified in Exod 29:2
114 Ps 118/119:32; English versions use the future tense here.
115 Titus 1:15
116 1 Cor 6:12 and 10:23
117 Cf 1 Cor 9:22.
118 Erasmus now passes to the second part of verse 2: 'and he will meditate on his law day and night.'
119 Augustine's interpretation; *Enarratio in psalmum 1* PL 36 67. The next interpretation ('without pause') is also found there, as well as in Jerome and Hilary.

instead; in bad times, be not downcast. In either case, our single law will stand you in good stead.

It might be preferable to interpret 'day and night' as 'assiduously, without pause'; if our whole life is directed towards the goal set by divine law,[120] then whatever we do, be it eating, drinking, or sleeping, we shall be 'meditating on the law,'[121] just as anyone whose whole life is directed towards Christ is following Paul's injunction to 'pray without ceasing.'[122] Naturally someone who is fickle and inconsistent, sometimes giving a little thought to Christ, but at other times turning towards the world, cannot be our 'blessed man.'

I do not think that the repetition here of the word 'law' is unnecessary, even though they are one and the same: 'in the law of the Lord' and 'on his law.' It helps us to understand that all the different things which contribute to a life of bliss must be sought from this one law. If you are undecided about something, seek its advice. If fortune turns against you, seek its help. If you wish to learn something, there is no better place to go. Lastly, all the benefits which the rest of humanity expects from all kinds of different sources can, in truth, only be fully obtained by meditation on the Holy Scriptures. So now, reader, tell me: was it a waste of time to say 'he takes delight in the law'? But anyone who makes the law conform to his own desires does not 'take delight in the law'; on the contrary, it is the person who desires nothing but what the law itself prescribes.

This strikes indirectly at certain theologians 'with unwashed hands and feet'[123] who do violence to the Holy Scriptures in their exegesis, bending them, reluctant and unwilling, to suit their own pleasure, as is their Lydian rule (as the saying goes).[124] Learned divines of this sort decide at the outset what they want, what is best for them, calculating according to their own inclinations; then, when they have made up their minds, they hunt for some scriptural text which they can force to support their conclusion by wringing its neck,[125] as the saying is. But justice demands that our inclinations be subordinated to divine law, rather than the other way about; the conclusions,

* * * * *

120 On the term 'goal' (*scopus*) used here, see Boyle 74–81.
121 Cf Jerome *Breviarium in psalmos* PL 26 823D.
122 1 Thess 5:17; see J. Trapman 'Erasmus' *Precationes*' in *Acta Conventus Neo-Latini Torontonensis* ed A. Dalzell, C. Fantazzi, and R.J. Schoeck (Binghamton, NY 1991) 769–79.
123 *Adagia* I ix 55, meaning rashly, presumptuously, or irreverently
124 *Adagia* II x 37; some later editions have 'Lesbian rule,' referring to a proverb in *Adagia* I v 93, but in any case both proverbs suggest habitually faulty and self-interested reasoning.
125 *Adagia* IV ix 50; cf n68 above.

too, should have been sought in the law, instead of the law being subverted by the promptings of human passion. The entire credit and authority of Holy Scripture are undermined if it is twisted to yield an unjustifiable interpretation.

Finally, when the psalm says 'he will meditate on his law,' it is warning us that the divine law must not be approached lightly. It is with good reason that the Greek text uses the word μελέται, meaning meditations or exercises:[126] indeed, complete concentration and thorough study are required here. Those who, day after day, mumble their way through psalms they don't understand are not 'meditating on the Lord's law' but 'beating thin air'[127] instead. Those who approach the mystic writings seeking ammunition for their frivolous debates are not 'meditating on the Lord's law.' Those who grow old among their niggling, inquisitive, and never-ending *quaestiones*[128] are not 'meditating on the Lord's law.' But someone who disregards everything else and approaches the fountain-head that is Holy Scripture, thirsting only to improve himself, to be transformed into Christ,[129] to drink in his Spirit, seeking high and low, yearning for the Spirit alone: such a person truly 'meditates on the law of the Lord.'

Again, anyone who gets no further than the outer shell of the law is not 'meditating on the law of the Lord.' An outer shell is usually tasteless and, far from being nourishing, it can be poisonous and even lethal, as Paul says.[130] You must therefore nibble away until you reach the centre, where at last you will discover true nourishment for the soul; eat and you shall be transfigured into the image of Christ. This is why we read elsewhere in the Psalms: 'Blessed are those who study God's testimony.'[131] The adjective is not applied to those who merely read God's law or memorize it; even the Pharisee remembered it correctly when he immediately replied: 'You shall love the Lord your God' etc.[132] Today, too, the Jews know their Law by heart, better almost than Christian theologians, and during the fast they carry round the five barley loaves.[133] But in the end the only 'blessed man' is

* * * * *

126 On the sense of this word (and its Socratic overtones) as used by Erasmus in the *Moria*, see Screech 81–3.
127 1 Cor 9:26
128 Cf n109 above.
129 Cf n100 above.
130 Cf 2 Cor 3:6 on the 'letter which kills.'
131 Ps 118/119:2
132 Luke 10:27
133 An allusion to the matzoh bread used at the time of Passover; probably also a reminiscence of the miracle of the loaves and fishes (John 6:4–14) to which

one who has gained admission to the secret mysteries of the Holy Spirit by devoted study.

To help us understand more fully how profitable the mystic writings can be, this passage also seems to advise us that the Holy Scriptures should be imbibed by constant meditation from childhood, that they should be implanted in us by frequent practice and frequent repetition so that we have them in our memory as well as at our fingertips. Then by comparing different texts we can easily arrive at the true meaning. At the moment, however, we waste much of our time on the ramblings of the sophists, on the works of Aristotle[134] or, worse still, on our own imaginings, to the extent that even the great theologians rarely find time to draw on the original sources; if a quotation from them is required, there is a great rush for indexes and canons.[135] Without skill in the three languages,[136] Holy Writ cannot be understood at all, but it can be understood without Aristotle's *Physics* and *Metaphysics*. We ignore the things we need and cling only to those which will hinder us, but anyone who wants truly to be a theologian must be familiar with the original sources.

However, it is not the prerogative only of theologians to 'meditate on the law of the Lord,' unless we believe that they alone can be called 'blessed.' Everyone who wants to be 'blessed' must 'meditate on the law of the Lord.' Ordinary people too should read the Lord's law, in any language;[137] even Scythians[138] should read and 'meditate on it' to the best of their ability. Everybody should study it as far as their understanding will allow; they should talk about, discuss it. As the man is, so is his talk,[139] or, rather, we

* * * * *

Erasmus alludes in a similar context (the intransigence of the Jews) in the *Enchiridion* CWE 66 84.

134 Erasmus often castigated theologians for their reliance on Aristotle rather than Scripture; see for example *Institutio principis christiani* CWE 27 225 and n81 and Ep 337:423–39 and 733–7.

135 A reference to the collections of ecclesiastical regulations which became known as 'canon law' and which, Erasmus suggests, have undermined the role of the original sources, the Scriptures

136 Latin, Greek, and Hebrew. Erasmus himself never learned Hebrew, as he admits elsewhere in this work (40). This sentence and the next were recommended for deletion in the *Index expurgatorius* LB X 1820B.

137 On the theme here, see M. O'Rourke Boyle 'Weavers, farmers, tailors, travellers, matrons, pimps, Turks, little women, and Other Theologians' in *Erasmus in English* 3 (1971) 1–7.

138 Proverbial for barbarity in the ancient world; their modern counterparts were the Turks, as Erasmus points out in *Adagia* IV ix 85; cf n292 below.

139 *Adagia* I vi 50

all become the sort of persons that our everyday talk makes us. If we are Christians, let our talk be of Christ. If we talk of nothing but the world, then inevitably we become worldly. At the moment, however, some people believe that great care must be taken to prevent the common people from having direct contact with Holy Writ, translated into the vernacular, claiming that they will understand nothing and will fall into heresy. As if Christ's teaching were the kind that may only be understood by a few theologians! On the contrary, no one was ever more unpretentious than Christ, and similarly no teaching was ever more accessible than his. Let the ploughman read it and he will find food for thought; let the scholar read it and he will learn something. Essentially you need piety rather than ingenuity to understand the Scriptures; the Spirit explains them, not Aristotle; grace, not reason; the breath of God, not syllogisms.

If an understanding of their mystical meaning depends on the help of the Holy Spirit (what Paul calls the gift of prophecy),[140] why do we cut off the great mass of Christians from a share in this gift? Cannot the Spirit of Christ be imparted to anyone he wishes? Indeed, on whom is it more likely to descend than the humble and the meek? – rather than on those who are made arrogant and bombastic by a false belief in their learning, who rely on the misguided theories of the sophists, or whose heads are swollen with the casuistry of Aristotle. Christ himself gave thanks to the Father for concealing the mysteries of heavenly wisdom from the wise and revealing them to the simple.[141] Believe me, the Holy Spirit has its own likes and dislikes. I am not at all convinced that it will honour with its communion someone who relies on vast amounts of profane learning, countless Aristotelian syllogisms, and the conclusions of the pagan philosophers – or rather, not on a knowledge of all this but on an entirely false belief in his learning – and who thus approaches the portals of the mystic writings full of irreverence and presumption. But I am afraid that in reality those who wish the people to have no contact with the Scriptures are moved less by the danger to the people than by their own self-esteem, because, of course, they want every question to be referred only to them, as if they were the oracle: 'What is written on this subject?' 'This.' 'What does it mean?' 'Interpret it this way, take it this way, say this ...' This is treating people like dumb animals. Perhaps some are also motivated by the realization that Holy Scripture does not exactly tally with the lives they lead, and so they prefer to 'repeal' it,[142] or at least to ignore it, in case

* * * * *

140 Cf 1 Cor 12:10 and 13:2.
141 Matt 11:25 and Luke 10:21
142 Aptly, Erasmus uses the legal term *antiquari*.

they get it thrown back in their faces. They distract the people with little tales of everyday life which they have carefully concocted for their own purposes.[143]

What, then, is to be done? The people must hear from truly devout teachers, that is, the bishops, as often as possible. When it is not possible, they must 'meditate on the Lord's law,' as far as they can, by reading and discussing it. Second, the bishops, by constant meditation on the divine law, must equip themselves to answer all questions by reference to the Scriptures.

'And he shall be like wood': Up to this point the psalm has described the qualities of the 'blessed man'; now it describes his reward. First it described the preparations; now it describes the fruits. He has avoided 'the council of the impious'; he has not 'stood on the path of the sinners,' however attractive it seemed outwardly; he has spurned the 'plague-seat'; he has schooled himself in the divine law with unwearying diligence, not merely paying it lip-service, but enacting it in the purity of his life. What, then, is his reward? 'And he shall be like wood planted beside the streams of the waters.' The psalm uses 'wood' instead of 'tree' in a figure called synecdoche by the rhetoricians – like saying 'steel' instead of 'sword.' If we apply this line to the person of Christ,[144] the meaning will be as follows: the Son of God will assume a human body and, descending from heaven, will be planted on earth, beside the streams of the waters; not in an arid desert, but beside the fertile waters of the Holy Spirit and of eternal wisdom. A Gospel text confirms that the waters may be interpreted as the Spirit: 'Out of his belly shall flow rivers of living water. This he said of the Spirit, which was to be received by those who believe in him.'[145] Similarly, we find in another psalm: 'The streams of the river fertilize and gladden the city of God.'[146] A tree cannot bear fruit, or remain fertile and evergreen, unless its roots are watered and fed by such streams of water.

Some[147] interpret 'the streams of the waters' as the people, because elsewhere we read that 'the peoples are as many as the waters,'[148] either because

* * * * *

143 For confirmation of this charge see the accounts of the style and technique of contemporary sermons in A.J. Krailsheimer *Rabelais and the Franciscans* (Oxford 1963) 61–79 and J.W. Blench *Preaching in England in the Late Fifteenth and Sixteenth Centuries* (Oxford 1964).

144 As do Hilary (PL 9 255) and Augustine (PL 36 68), though Erasmus does not follow their exegesis in detail.

145 John 7:38–9

146 Ps 45/46:4; the two verbs translate the punning *laetificat*.

147 Augustine *Enarratio in psalmum 1* PL 36 68

148 Rev 17:15

they are always falling downwards – into sin, I mean – or because they are constantly being rolled away towards death. In this reading, Christ absorbed these peoples, who were sinking into sin, into his roots, and passed them through himself so that they might burst forth as fruit, the congregations of the faithful, which they did 'in their season.' In other words, when by his death Christ had overthrown the principalities and powers[149] and handed over the kingdom to his Father,[150] and by his resurrection and ascension had added fresh lustre to his glory, then the heavenly Spirit was sent with new gifts to arm the faithful against worldly wisdom and worldly power. This was the fruit of that wondrous tree: that many thousands should be summoned from this world and, through Christ, be made the children of God.[151]

Moreover, none of its leaves has fallen, because 'although heaven and earth shall pass away, his words shall not pass away until all these things come to pass.'[152] Isaiah also says: 'The word of the Lord endures for ever.'[153] The words of kings often prove false, and 'all men are liars,'[154] either because they change their opinions, or sometimes because they cannot fulfil their promises. But the mind of God is unchanging, and since he alone is all-powerful, there is nothing so difficult that he cannot do it with ease whenever he wishes.

This is not all, for 'everything that he has said or done shall prosper,' or, as Hilary reads it, 'shall be well directed':[155] the Greek text reads $\kappa\alpha\tau$-$\epsilon\nu o\delta\omega\theta\dot{\eta}\sigma\epsilon\tau\alpha\iota$, meaning something like 'shall complete a successful journey.' Christ did not fail to accomplish all that he had promised. He died, rose again, ascended, and sent down his advocate.[156] He succeeded in all this, and there is no doubt that he will also keep his promises concerning the Last Judgment, the rewarding of the pious and the punishment of the impious.

To the literal-minded, it may possibly seem rather demeaning to compare Christ to a tree, since we commonly call stupid people, who are barely human at all, 'wooden-headed' or 'blockheads.' But in the mystic writings the tree as a symbol enjoys great prestige. In paradise is planted 'every tree that is pleasant to see and fit to be used. In the middle of paradise stands the

* * * * *

149 Cf Eph 6:12.
150 Cf 1 Cor 15:24.
151 Cf John 1:12.
152 Adapted from Matt 24:32–5, Mark 13:28–31, or Luke 21:29–33
153 Isa 40:8 and 1 Pet 1:25
154 Ps 115/116:11
155 *Tractatus in psalmum primum* 13 PL 9 258A
156 Or 'paraclete'; cf for example John 14:16, a prophecy of the descent of the Holy Spirit at Pentecost.

tree of life, and the tree of the knowledge of good and evil.'[157] Its root is watered by that prolific river which divides into four streams and waters the whole face of the earth.[158] There are many handsome trees which produce healthy and useful fruit, but there is only one tree of life, planted, not beyond the streams of the waters, like the rest, but 'beside the streams,' that is, close to the source and fountain-head of all the streams of heavenly wisdom.

What exactly is this tree of paradise? Solomon interprets it as eternal Wisdom (which is Christ himself): 'It is a tree of life to all who take hold of it.'[159] Moreover, all the other trees receive their foliage and their fruit from this one. John, the witness of mysteries, saw this tree in his apocalypse: 'He showed me a river, shining like crystal with living water, proceeding from the throne of God and the Lamb, in the middle of the city street; and on each side of the river was the tree of life, which produced fruit twelve times, bearing fruit every month, and the leaves of the tree are for the healing of the gentiles.'[160] If we take this literally, how can one tree stand on both sides of a river, unless perhaps it is so broad that its roots stretch to both banks? In fact this one tree symbolizes the one Christ. There is but one Son, there is but one Wisdom; the wisdom of this world is many-sided, but divine Wisdom is unique in its simplicity. Again, Christ's mystical assumption of a human body has been compared to the life of a tree: he was 'planted' by being born of the virgin, 'watered' by being filled with divine grace, and 'bore fruit' in bringing hope of immortality to the faithful throng by his glorious resurrection.

Divine Wisdom is compared to a tree in another book: in one verse to a cedar of Lebanon, in another to a terebinth stretching out its branches, and in a third, to a tall palm in Engedi.[161] Every tree springs from the earth, growing from a tiny seed to a great size; it needs to be watered but gives back in fruit what its roots have received. It performs many services for mankind: we may lean against its trunk, or feast our eyes on its beauty; its spreading branches and foliage cool the summer heat and provide shade for the weary; its fruit sustains and nourishes us.

Every one of these qualities is also wonderfully appropriate to Christ. Indeed, in the Gospel he calls himself the vine, his Father the husbandman,

* * * * *

157 Gen 2:9
158 Cf Gen 2:10–14.
159 Prov 3:18
160 Rev 22:1–2
161 Sir 24:13–16 (Vulg 17–22)

and his disciples the branches.[162] Again, when the Jews falsely alleged that he was casting out demons in the name of Beelzebub, he called himself a tree, saying: 'Either call the tree good, and its fruit good, or call the tree bad and its fruit bad. For the tree is known by its fruit.'[163] They admitted that casting out demons was the best of 'good fruits,' and yet they attributed his power to Beelzebub, whose fruit must be thoroughly bad, since he himself is thoroughly evil.

Again, while carrying the cross, he used the tree as a metaphor to underline his innocence: 'If they do such things to a green tree, what will be done to a dry tree?'[164] A dried-up tree, already withered by vice and deprived of the sap of divine grace, is neither agreeably shady nor pleasant in appearance nor useful in providing fruit; it is therefore destined for the fire. Mind you, Christ was not a forest tree, springing up accidentally in no particular position; he was planted by the Father – and according to the Gospel any tree not planted by him shall be rooted up and sent to the fire[165] – he was planted in paradise beside the spring which is the source of all heavenly gifts.

The words 'gives its fruit' are not chosen at random either, though we read that other trees 'produce' fruit rather than give it: 'A good tree cannot produce bad fruit,'[166] and in Isaiah: 'I expected it to produce grapes, and it produced wild grapes.'[167] But this tree 'gave' its fruit, it did not merely produce it. Other trees' fruit falls off, is shaken down, or is picked; in Christ's case, nothing happened by chance or by necessity; everything was decided and managed by him. He is a tree guided by reason;[168] he gives his fruit to those he chooses, in the way he chooses, and 'in his season,' that is, at the time which he himself prescribes. 'In his season' he taught of the kingdom; 'in his season,' and of his own free will, he chose to be taken, judged, and killed. By his own decision he rose again, descended to hell, ascended to heaven, and sent the Holy Spirit, through which so many congregations of the faithful became established throughout the world.

* * * * *

162 Cf John 15:1 and 5.
163 Matt 12:33
164 Luke 23:31
165 Cf Matt 3:10 and John 15:6.
166 Matt 7:18
167 Isa 5:4; both these quotations are used to make the same point in Hilary *Tractatus in psalmum primum* 10 PL 9 256B.
168 *rationalis*, a term used by Hilary, *Tractatus in psalmum primum* 10 PL 9 255A, whom Erasmus follows particularly closely here. Hilary was probably influenced by a similar interpretation in Origen PG 12 1089A.

It has to be explained how we can apply to the person of Christ the phrase about 'meditating on the Lord's law day and night,' after which he received the reward for his honest labours, as it were, in the metaphor of the fruitful tree; perhaps we should accept that Christ 'meditated on the Lord's law' when, as we read in Luke, he 'increased in age, grace, and wisdom in the eyes of God and men.'[169] If 'meditating on the law' means obeying the law scrupulously, then no one is more worthy than Christ to receive this eulogy since he, alone among men, never deviated from the Lord's law.

As a tree of the kind we have described, not only does Christ not produce bitter or tainted fruit, but he who bore them has offered to all his saving fruits, so imperishable that from them 'not a single leaf shall fall,' that is, not a single word from him has been, or ever shall be, spoken in vain. The shade of his evergreen leaves fosters our hopes and refreshes our spirits when they droop in the sweltering heat of the world. We may be sure that all the other things which he has done will bring a happy outcome to all those who remain faithful to him.

One might add the following allegorical interpretation:[170] it would not be far-fetched to interpret 'the streams of the waters' as that holy river by which we are reborn in Christ, for through its water we are translated into him, so that we too become a fruitful and evergreen tree.

To return to the tropological sense, it might occur to some dullards that someone who has forbidden himself all the pleasures of this life, scorned public office, suppressed all his instincts, overcome nature itself by his religious way of life, and taken the unpopular course of devoting himself single-mindedly to 'meditation' on the divine law: that such a person is leading a somewhat disagreeable life, and is not so much a man as the empty shell of a man, as it were, useless to himself and to others. Even today we hear some people talk like this against those who practise the Christian life: 'The dreamer! what does he do? what does he know? what can he do? what use is he?' But hear what bliss this despised being enjoys, and what a reward he has, such as the world cannot grant to its followers. While others, who have devoted themselves to the worldly and the ephemeral, rotted by vice and worn out by their anxieties about worthless trash, are now not only useless but dangerous, and ready for the eternal fire, this 'blessed man' of mine, like a tree planted in a well-watered spot beside the river, shall constantly blossom forth with the joyful strength that is derived from a pure conscience

* * * * *

169 Luke 2:52
170 On the different levels of interpretation, see the Introduction xxiv–xxx and the introductory note 3 above.

and a spotless reputation, and shall daily grow stronger and better through potent infusions of heavenly grace, until he shall come 'to perfect manhood, measured by the full stature of Christ.'[171]

In addition, I do not think that he is called 'wood' instead of tree for no reason; it is to make us understand that here praise is not being given to those short-lived plants, the intentions of the irresolute, which are destroyed as soon as an icy blast of temptation strikes them, or to the 'reed shaken by the wind,'[172] or to the bush bending in every direction and hugging the ground, but to a solid and firm decision to lead a life of piety, established on such deeply embedded roots that not even the fear of death can drag him down from the sublimity of his thoughts. Similar symbolism explains why, in Hebrew retreats, palm groves are dedicated to the martyrs; this tree is always green, it is the only one which springs back into place when weighted down, and it produces by far the most succulent of all fruit.[173]

But this tree is not just any tree, nor does it grow by accident, but is planted. By whom? By the Father, the husbandman,[174] of course, who, unless he has summoned them, allows no one to come to Christ;[175] in short, the tree is planted by the one who planted Christ himself, in whom, according to Paul, we are ourselves implanted.[176] In fact, as Jerome noted, the Septuagint translated the Hebrew שָׁתוּל shathul as πεφυτευμένον, meaning 'planted,' but Aquila translated it as 'transplanted,'[177] which indeed is thoroughly appropriate either to Christ, sent down from heaven to earth, or to us, when we are translated through Christ into a new kind of life.[178] We are 'transplanted' from paganism to the faith, from Judaism to the gospel, from the letter to the spirit, from enslavement under the Law to the freedom of grace, from this world to the kingdom of heaven, from guilt to innocence, from Egypt to a land flowing with milk and honey,[179] from turmoil

* * * * *

171 Eph 4:13
172 Matt 11:7 and Luke 7:24
173 Perhaps an allusion to the Feast of Tabernacles, with its custom (Lev 23:40–3) of making 'booths' or 'arbours' of palm boughs in commemoration of the exodus. On the strength of the palm tree see *Adagia* I iii 4, *Parabolae* CWE 23 263, and *De ratione studii* CWE 24 677.
174 Cf John 15:1.
175 Cf John 6:44.
176 Rom 6:5
177 Cf Jerome *Breviarium in psalmos* PL 26 823D; Aquila made a literal Greek version of the Old Testament in the second century AD.
178 Cf Rom 6:4.
179 Exod 3:8, 17, and frequently in the Old Testament

to peace; we are transported from secular distractions to the pursuit of holiness.

What was badly planted in Adam is profitably transplanted in Christ; what was fruitless in nature begins to be fruitful through grace. Trees are improved by being transplanted to new soil, and under cultivation they are trained to shake off the wildness of nature and produce sweeter fruit. Was not Paul a tree profitably transplanted from persecutor to apostle?[180] Was not Cyprian a tree well transplanted from Magus to martyr?[181] Was not Matthew a tree transplanted from tax-gatherer to apostle?[182] And Ambrose, from pagan judge to saintly bishop?[183] And Augustine, from windy rhetorician to Doctor of the church?[184] And Francis, from greedy tradesman to advocate of poverty?[185] And were not countless others most profitably transplanted, like them, into Christ?

'Beside the streams of the waters': Transplanted, I repeat, not into the rocky soil of ambition and arrogance, the shifting and ever-thirsty sands of avarice, the muddy soil of lust, or the marshes of idleness, but to a place beside the waters – waters which are not sluggish, but swift-moving and lively, flowing through the lower plains and valleys, bringing a special richness and fertility to the soil and the plants; everything this soil produces is nourished and propagated by this special secret ingredient of the waters.

Fruit trees in particular require a great deal of moisture. Grammarians consider that the word 'fruits' [poma] comes from 'drink' [potus],[186] because they absorb such large amounts of liquid. When the root has taken in this liquid from all around, it transmits it through deeply hidden channels to the whole tree, until the leaves burst forth, then the flowers with their promise

* * * * *

180 Acts 9; see also 1 Tim 1:13.
181 Bishop of Carthage, martyred in 258; before his conversion in 246 he had been a rhetorician, according to his own account, but a tradition going back to Gregory of Nazianzus (Oratio 24 PG 35 1177C) asserted that he had been a Magus. Erasmus was to edit his works in 1520.
182 Cf Matt 9:9.
183 Coming from a patrician Roman family, Ambrose trained as an advocate and rose to be governor of Liguria; he was baptized and consecrated bishop of Milan in 374.
184 Augustine gives an account in Confessions 3–5 of his early career as student, Manichean, and teacher of rhetoric before his conversion in 386–7.
185 St Francis of Assisi, whose father was a wealthy textile merchant; the young Francis had a reputation for wealth and love of life rather than for greed. He was converted in 1205–6.
186 A false etymology, suggested by Varro De re rustica 1.31.5; cf ASD V-2 61:818n. The true etymology is uncertain.

of fruit, and finally the fruit itself, as healthful as it is tasty. The sight of the sturdy trunk, impervious even to a gale, the spreading branches, the lovely green foliage adorning the tree, the colours of its scented flowers, and the weight of its delicious crop of fruit: all this splendour,[187] all this wealth, all is provided by the root alone, watered by this hidden moisture. Nothing is more deeply hidden than the workings of men's minds, yet it is clear that all the qualities we see in pious men gush out, as it were, from this source; but the root must be watered for many years by an outpouring of divine grace.

Those who know Hebrew say that the word is not 'streams,' but פַּלְגֵי *palge*, which they translate *pelagus*, meaning more or less a gulf, an expanse of very deep water. And indeed it often happens that our earthly trees are suffocated by an excessive intake of water. Not so the rational tree described by the prophet;[188] the more it is filled and bathed by that heavenly river which 'gladdens the city of God,'[189] the more fertile and fruitful it becomes. The whole river flooded into Christ, and as a result he produced a mass of blossom and a huge crop of fruit. The apostle Paul had drunk deeply of it, and for that reason this one man produced more fruit than several other apostles put together; the gifts of the Spirit may be bestowed in different proportions, and thus its fruits too will differ. But all who long to be living trees in Christ, growing, flowering, fruitful, must drink from this source. This liquid is not imbibed from the writings of Plato and Aristotle or from the books of orators and poets; it must be drawn from that fountain which John saw flowing from the throne of God and the Lamb.[190]

I notice that some commentators interpret the tree as the cross of Christ and the river as baptism, because the church lives and grows strong through his holy death and the mystical ceremony of washing, and blossoms with countless gifts from heaven. Hence the graceful hymn sung by the church's choir in mystic praise of the cross: 'The cross alone is steadfast, the one noble tree; no forest can boast its like, in leaf, in flower, in bud.'[191] It is a tree which has brought us so much: Christian churches throughout the world, hosts of martyrs, throngs of monks, choirs of virgins, squadrons of confessors; so

* * * * *

187 The phrase 'all this splendour,' which was added after the first edition, is omitted by ASD, but is a help to the articulation here.
188 Cf n168 above.
189 Ps 45/46:4; cf n146 above.
190 Cf Rev 22:1.
191 From the hymn 'Pange, lingua, gloriosi' by Venantius Fortunatus (c 535–c 600), incorporated in the liturgy for Maundy Thursday

many sacraments, so many divine gifts. However, if you interpret the tree as Christ himself dying on the cross, and the streams of waters as baptism, then you are saying that the waters do not feed the tree, but the opposite.

'Which gives its fruit in its season': Of course, no tree could possibly be barren when planted by such a husbandman,[192] and positioned and watered in the way I have described. True piety is never fruitless: it bursts forth eventually and shares its goodness with others, either by sowing Christ in the hearts of the faithful and the faithless through holy preaching, or by inspiring them to the pursuit of holiness by the sweet fragrance of its life. Paul, in his letter to the Romans, was propagating this sort of fruit: 'That I might have some fruit among you also, as I have in the rest of the world.'[193] He also mentions the idea of exemplary living: 'We are a sweet fragrance to God in every place.'[194] Jesus was hungry for the same fruit when he said to the apostles: 'I have other food to eat, of which you know nothing.'[195] The mystic bride was longing for this fruit when she said in her wedding-song: 'I shall go up to the palm tree and pluck its fruit.'[196]

This tree does not merely produce fruit, but gives it away, for true charity places itself completely at the disposal of others, and serves their interests, not its own. The miser makes profit for himself, the place-seeker makes plans for himself, the lecher makes pleasures for himself; every sinner produces fruit for himself alone, if indeed he produces anything at all. But for this tree of ours, to produce is to give and, what is more, it will give a special kind of fruit. There are poisonous trees, and a taste of their fruit brings death: certain varieties of sorb tree, for example. Again, there are some trees which vaingloriously pretend to be what they are not; but this tree 'will give its fruit,' that is, its true, natural fruit, whose taste and smell recall the nourishing liquid in its roots. If the tree is of the earth, it bears earthly fruit; if, on the contrary, it is spiritual, it bears a spiritual crop.

Shall I list the various trees and their equally varied fruits? 'The fruits of the Spirit,' says Paul, 'are joy, peace, patience, kindness, goodness, for-bearance, gentleness, faith, restraint, continence, chastity.' On the opposite side, the fruits of the bad tree: 'But the works of the flesh are obvious: fornication, impurity, immodesty, lust, idolatry, witchcraft, enmity, quar-rels, rivalry, anger, brawling, dissension, party strife, murder, drunkenness,

* * * * *

192 John 15:1
193 Rom 1:13
194 2 Cor 2:14–15
195 John 4:32
196 Song of Sol 7:8

gluttony, and the like.'[197] It sounds a most prolific tree – but its fruit is deadly. 'The tree is known by its fruit,'[198] good or bad. If thoughts are like the root, then deeds are like the fruits of a tree. If your mind has been corrupted by perverse opinions and evil desires, you will speak and act in the way described by Paul. Your heart is the root of this tree; 'from the heart spring wicked thoughts, theft, murder, blasphemy.'[199] Whatever an impious person says or does must be dangerous, infectious, poisonous; it is very hard to have dealings with evil and avoid contamination. Conversely, the bearing, appearance, speech, and actions of pious people produce healthy fruit, so that anyone who associates with them is bound to improve from day to day, unless he is an utterly hopeless case.

So the tree will 'give fruit,' but in that it is no different from the bad tree. It will, however, 'give its own fruit,' that is, special fruit, and it will give the fruit 'in its season,' not when it decides to do so, but when God deems it appropriate. Some have given their fruit early, some later. In some cases, holiness shone out already in childhood games; in others, such as Paul the Hermit,[200] only death revealed their piety in all its splendour. The first step is to burn with an inner fire, the next is for it to shine forth and set others afire. The first step is to take in moisture, the next is to produce buds; your task is to ensure that your tree is well watered, that it grows green with plentiful moisture. Do not worry about the fruit; it will burst forth in its season, when God thinks fit. His warmth will bring on the fruit, just as his moisture has fed the roots.

Thus far everything in the psalm has applied very aptly to all the pious people who follow Christ's example and shun the world's pollutions, who 'meditate on the law of the Lord' with all their heart, in order to learn his will and to do the things which divine law commands, not those which human passions dictate, who are watered by the secret gifts of divine grace, grow strong in purity, produce buds by their delight in charity, flower in anticipation of their good deeds, and finally bear fruit, to the glory of God and for the salvation of their fellow man; they have now overcome Satan and, rich and fertile in Christ, they enjoy the fruits of their good works, endlessly happy in the joyful knowledge of their goodness. Yet all this seems to me

* * * * *

197 See Gal 5:19–23 for these contrasting lists; not all their elements are in the English versions, but the Vulgate contains them all.
198 Matt 12:33; cf Luke 6:44.
199 Cf Matt 15:19.
200 Paul of Thebes (fl c 300), often considered the first hermit, whose biography was written by Jerome (PL 23 17–30)

to apply still more clearly to a Doctor of the church, that is, to a bishop. For, according to Paul, it is the special duty, the first duty, of the bishops to teach the Christian people:[201] to teach, not Plato, or Aristotle, or the subtleties of scholastic disputation, but the doctrine of Christ, the unique teaching of the uniquely simple being.[202] It is therefore all the more remarkable that today some bishops shuffle off this most splendid of their duties to other people, whom they actually hold in scorn and derision and call 'brothers' – as an insult. Not content with this, they delegate their second important duty, the administration of the sacraments, to obscure hirelings, one might almost say pseudo-bishops; they keep for themselves only the most sordid of their duties, litigation and money matters, which ought to be entrusted to the dregs, as it were, but which they seem to consider the only tasks worthy of a mighty bishop.

Let us see, then, in what colours the prophet paints the teacher of Christ: that blessed man, he says, who is 'mine and undefiled,'[203] whom God has appointed to school the people, must first be uninfected by any dangerous and unhealthy opinions, and thus has not 'departed into the council of the impious.' Who will teach well if he has learned badly? Second, he must be far removed from any contact with sinfulness and so completely blameless that he is a stranger to any semblance of wickedness; in other words, a man of such spotless character that rumour itself would be ashamed to invent a criminal charge against him. Otherwise, what words will he use, in the end, to reproach others with their sins, if he himself is guilty of sin? How can a man persuade others to pursue holiness, if they see that his life is at odds with holiness? In addition, he should be untrammelled and unimpeded by secular offices and involvement in worldly affairs. If it is true that 'divine wisdom will not enter into the wicked soul,'[204] neither will it into one that is preoccupied. The heavenly Spirit seeks a lodging that is not only pure, but also free from all sordid concerns.

What then is our conclusion? It is that, unconcerned with the foolish opinions of the common herd, free from heretical dogma, free from any intellectual or moral defect, free from all desire for worldly honours, free from all concern for material interests, he should immerse himself day and

* * * * *

201 See Titus 1:9 and 1 Tim 3:2.
202 Erasmus uses the technical term *simplicissimus*; see Screech 94–5 on his frequent use of the term to describe the nature of God as uniquely single, uncompounded, and unmixed.
203 Song of Sol 6:9
204 Wisd 1:4

night in the law of the Lord, in other words, in the Holy Scriptures. Let him
drink deeply of them, let him learn them by heart – and not merely learn
them, but 'meditate' on them, that is, apply them to his mental attitudes, his
feelings, his morals, and his life.[205] Let him study at length in them what
he will subsequently teach. What will be the result? If he has done all this,
this teacher of mine, says the psalm, 'will be like a tree planted beside the
streams of the waters, because he will give in his season the fruit' of salutary
doctrine. He will be a tree that will not bend to the buffets of fortune, a
living tree, a tree watered by the abundant stream of heavenly grace, forever
standing by the sacred river of Scripture. Ezekiel entered this river long ago,
and was amazed to find that it could not be crossed;[206] it is immeasurably
deep, and no mind of man can reach to the bottom. You must be satisfied to
drink from it as much as is permitted.

What is the final destiny of this wondrous tree? First, in its fresh green
innocence it will show that it is a living tree. Then, as it grows in Christ
gradually and silently, it unfolds charity's branches, bursts into bud, and
begins to hint at the fruits which are to come. Soon, blossoming with flowers,
it provides clearer grounds for hope. Immediately afterwards the whole tree
is clothed in the foliage of heavenly words. Finally, it bears fruit. In this case
the verdant leaves do not hold out to onlookers a mere vain hope of fruit, as
did the fig tree which Jesus cursed in the Gospel:[207] its leaves attracted him
when he was hungry, but it gave him no fruit. Certain teachers are like this
fig tree: they speak of holiness, they use its name and go through the motions
of holiness, but they are strangers to the fruit of true holiness. They have 'sat
on the throne of Moses: do what they say, but do not do what they do.'[208]
Their mouths preach holiness, their lives preach the opposite. Hearing their
titles, looking at their dress, listening to their talk, you would expect some
new fruit of holiness; but if you examine their lives, you realize that you
have been duped,[209] and, as the Greek proverb says, 'looking for treasure,
you have stumbled across coal.'[210]

Christ is particularly angered by such trees, since they make an outward
show of holiness, but are strangers to works of holiness: they preach against
stealing, and yet they steal; they preach against adultery, and yet they

* * * * *

205 On this practical sense of *meditari*, see n126 above and Introduction xxx.
206 Ezek 47:5
207 Matt 21:19 and Mark 11:13
208 Matt 23:2–3
209 *Adagia* I v 49: *Dare verba*, literally 'to give (mere) words'
210 *Adagia* I ix 30

commit adultery; they abhor idols, and yet they commit sacrilege.[211] The fig tree promised Christ the sweetest of fruit, the most pleasant by far, as he gazed on it from a distance; when he looked more closely, it had deceived him. He did not curse the briars, from which no one expects fruit; he did not curse the willow, which promises no fruit, being barren by nature. He cursed the fig tree, whose luxuriant foliage and very name held out hope of fruit, indeed of the sweetest of fruits. Hearing the title 'bishop,' it is as if I heard the word 'fig'; I see the bishop's vestments, his foliage, as it were, and I run to pick the fruit. But what do I find? Something very different from what was promised by his title and trappings. I find a gambler, I find a fornicator, I find a drunkard, I find an extortioner, I find a warmonger and a satrap. Can you imagine how Christ's anger flares up, when he is deceived in this way? Paul calls them 'whitewashed walls,' and Christ 'whited sepulchres, sparkling on the outside, corrupted by sin within.'[212] Thus everything to do with ritual and outward displays of holiness is no more than foliage.

If you prefer to interpret the foliage as the teaching of holiness, you may well encounter some bishops who, stripped of leaves just like withered trees, retain only the titles of the ancient bishops, as though under some curse. If they are discussing hunting, riding, war, or property, they are wonderfully eloquent; if the subject is Christ, however, they seem to be suddenly transported to an unfamiliar world.

But let us return to our own 'tree,' who 'gives his fruit,' in other words, who studies Holy Writ, not just for himself, but to share willingly with others; he gives, but he does not squander it. He is distributing the divine word; he knows to whom, when, and how to speak. One person needs consolation, another exhortation, another a reprimand, another a friendly warning, yet another instruction; he distributes the gift of the divine word to each according to his apparent need – that, truly, is giving.

Now, he gives both 'his own fruit' and also 'in its season.' What is 'his own' fruit? What do we have that we have not been given?[213] How can it be ours, when it depends on the generosity of another? Here the psalm is calling 'our own,' not things for which we alone are responsible, but rather things which do not belong to anyone else. We put to use the virtues we have received from God in such a way that they are none the less our own. Someone who recites to the people words which he does not love or obey himself is not giving 'his own' fruit; such teaching does not belong to him;

* * * * *

211 Cf Rom 2:21–2.
212 Respectively Acts 23:3 and Matt 23:27, also brought together in *Adagia* III vi 23
213 Cf 1 Cor 4:7.

rather, being barren himself, he acts like a canal and transmits it to more fertile soil. That fruit did not come from your roots; you offer me figs not grown on your branches but picked elsewhere. Anyone who cares deeply for the things he teaches and whose appearance and character also reflect what he preaches, such a one, truly, 'gives his own fruit.' Anyone who transmits to others by his words the flame which has been kindled in his heart 'gives his own fruit.'

Perhaps this passage has some relevance for certain priests, who busily recite sacred psalms which they do not understand,[214] either through lack of attention or lack of education. These, of course, are merely showing off their leaves, being barren of fruit. Did not Paul point out the same thing very clearly in Corinthians? 'For if I pray in this tongue,' he says, 'the spirit within me prays, but my understanding is without fruit.'[215] Anyone who does not merely read out the sacred words, but also expounds them to the faithful – or even to the faithless – in the form of teaching, exhortation, or consolation, 'gives his own fruit.'

That vine of which God complained through the prophet did not 'give its own fruit': 'I expected it to produce grapes, but it produced wild grapes.'[216] The proper fruit of a man is to deserve well of all his fellows, since he is not born for himself,[217] but for his country and his friends. When I hear the word 'man,' that is, a civilized animal, together with the adjective 'Christian,' I expect to find some good deed among the vine-leaves, I expect to find acts of holiness. But when I see instead a traitor,[218] a warmonger, a slanderer, a swindler, then I have found not grapes, but wild grapes.

None the less, the leaves of our tree are not superfluous; in Revelation John wrote that they were provided 'for the healing of the gentiles.'[219] They offered welcome shade to the one who said: 'I sat beneath the shade of him whom I desired, and his fruit was sweet to my taste.'[220] The leaves clothe and shield the fruit, protecting it from both sun and rain.

Obviously it is very foolish of certain blockheads to ignore this careful use of language: 'What do the words matter,' they say, 'if the meaning is

* * * * *

214 Cf *Enchiridion* CWE 66 35.
215 1 Cor 14:14
216 Isa 5:2 and 4
217 A commonplace deriving from Plato's ninth epistle (358A); cf *Adagia* IV vi 81.
218 The Latin is *quadruplator*, literally a paid informer in ancient Rome, but a term synonymous with treachery.
219 Rev 22:2
220 Song of Sol 2:3

clear enough?' First of all, how can you understand an idea unless you know exactly what the words mean? Second, if languages are to be studied at all, is it not much easier to learn one or two[221] thoroughly and correctly than to learn a lot of ways of making grammatical errors? Correct language is simple and can be learned properly in a few years, whereas the sloppy use of language creates a thousand extra difficulties. Finally, it is extremely important to use the right sort of words to convey a useful idea; some words are more impressive than others, some more meaningful, some more impassioned, some more pleasant. No less important is a knowledge of the rhetorical figures associated with words and phrases. This is easy to see: when ideas which our forefathers expounded in the most majestic and glorious language, producing a wonderful effect on their audience's minds, are expounded in Scotist language,[222] they lose their vitality, fall flat, become mean and worthless; you would not believe they were the same ideas.

An example, perhaps? The following is to hand: 'Peter sits in Antioch and Rome, Paul converts Greece.' Was not a great deal of grace as well as dignity added to this sentence when it was embellished by figures of speech, as follows: 'To thee, Peter, Antiochus and Remus yield a royal throne; thou, Paul, hast assailed the tyranny of Alexandrian Greece'?[223] On the other hand, such ideas just seem thoroughly unsatisfactory when couched, or rather muffled up, in terms that are barbaric, shabby, artificial, in short quite monstrous.

I have not said this because I want my Doctor of the church to frolic among the flowers of rhetoric;[224] I am not asking him to use extravagant embellishment, but on the other hand I cannot abide shoddy language. I would not want Christ's teaching to be corrupted by meretricious eloquence, but equally I would not want it to be disfigured by tawdry words and images. This Doctor of mine will therefore give the best of leaves as well as the best of fruit, so that he can say with the prophet: 'The Lord has given me an educated tongue, that I may lift up the fallen with words.'[225] He will also

* * * * *

221 Cf n136 above.
222 Duns Scotus (c 1264–1308), the 'subtle doctor,' and his followers were notorious for the technical intricacy of their language; cf n109 above. The 1525 Basel edition replaced 'Scotist' by 'more modern' ('recentiores').
223 Erasmus quotes from a sequence 'In natale apostolorum' by the ninth-century monk of St Gall, Notker Balbulus; see *Notkeri poetae liber ymnorum* ed W. von den Steinen (Bern and Munich 1960) 78.
224 On Erasmus' frequent pleas that appropriate verbal tools be used in exegesis, see Boyle 55 and 73.
225 Isa 50:4

say, with Jeremiah: 'The Lord has put his words in my mouth, that I may uproot and pull down, destroy and demolish, build and plant.'[226]

However, he will also give fruit 'in his season.' Some people embark on the task of teaching before the time is right, and try to teach others what they have not yet learned themselves. In fact, premature fruit is often evidence that a tree is soon to die. Our tree, therefore, will finally take up his role as teacher, adviser, and critic only when he has drunk in the moisture of divine grace for a long while, has grown gradually stronger by imperceptible stages, and has been hardened by the slowness of his growth; he will have been summoned like Aaron,[227] and prepared in every way for his wonderful mission. He will not push himself forward, as some do when they try to present themselves as teachers although they never have been pupils; they claim authority over others before they have even learned to obey; they want to shine before they are even warm, and to inflame others when they are themselves cold.

'And its leaf shall not fall': The leaves of most trees fall in winter, though the trees themselves do not die completely. The leaves never fall from some, such as the palm and the blackthorn, not forgetting the laurel. A few have perennial leaves, and indeed perennial fruit, such as the orange tree.[228] But our tree, according to John's prophecy, bears fruit twelve times or, in other words, every month,[229] and indeed, far from losing its leaves, not a single one falls to the ground. For the singular 'leaf' is used in the psalm, either by hypallage for 'leaves' or for emphasis,[230] as one might say 'not even one leaf'; compare the Gospel text: 'Not even one hair of your head shall perish.'[231] It is wrong for a Christian teacher to utter even one word that is stupid, false, or useless. Let him never fall silent, let his voice ring out continually like Aaron's,[232] but let all his words teach holiness, and his voice sing of Christ, not the world.

Now, who are the ones whose leaves repeatedly fall to the ground? Those who sometimes speak out and dare to confess Christ, but then, fearing

* * * * *

226 An adaptation of Jer 1:9–10
227 Cf Heb 5:4 and Exod 28.
228 Or 'Median apple tree,' a species of citrus tree described in Pliny *Naturalis historia* 12.15–16
229 Rev 22:2
230 'Emphasis' is in Greek in the text to convey that it is being used as a rhetorical term. Hypallage is normally defined as a figure in which two elements are reversed or interchanged (Quintilian 8.6.23); Erasmus is using the term loosely to suggest an unexpected grammatical form.
231 Luke 21:18
232 Cf n227 above and Exod 4:14 and 16.

to offend the prince and lose their position, very quickly either suppress Christ's words altogether, or water them down to suit mere mortals. One might perhaps prefer to apply this image to all those who do not follow Christ wholeheartedly, but share themselves out, as it were, between God and the world, so that at one moment they grow leaves, as if the warm and gentle wind[233] of the godhead were blowing on them, but the next moment, on the contrary, they sicken and die back, as it were, torn asunder by worldly cares or buffeted by storms of misfortune. But anyone who has stoutly renounced all that and devoted his thoughts entirely to Christ is like a palm tree, which cannot be harmed by any assault. Calumniators may roar, like so many blustering winds; evil men may buffet him, like winter storms: they can make no impression on the living strength of his virtue and, so far from dying, he loses not a single leaf.

Some commentators prefer to interpret the fruit of the tree here as his reward, rather than his works,[234] and the Holy Scriptures do indeed use the word 'fruit' in both senses. Christ calls the actual deeds 'fruit,' when he says: 'By their fruits shall you know them.'[235] But when Paul writes: 'What fruit, then, did you have from things which now make you ashamed?'[236] he is obviously using 'fruit' to mean a reward. However, sometimes the same deeds are both works *and* reward. Paul meant this, when he wrote to the Romans about people who scorned God and were abandoned by him to their own depraved instincts, so that men burned with filthy lust for men, and women for women, 'receiving a fitting recompense in their own persons.'[237] He calls their disgusting deeds their recompense, but there are such deeds as earn their specific rewards as well. These are the rewards given by God to those who know but scorn him: their reward will be the eternal fire, as Origen[238] neatly observed. The same is true of pious deeds as of sinful ones: certain works are so heavenly that they may rightly be called the reward for others.

I am aware that some commentators apply this passage, not to happiness in this life, but to future rewards; if we 'meditate on the law,' refraining from sin in this world, we may be clothed in everlasting verdure at the resurrection when, with all the miseries of this life ended, we may enjoy

* * * * *

233 In the Latin *Favonius*, the zephyr or west wind which blows in spring; the 'blustering winds' below are *Aquilones*, north winds.
234 Hilary *Tractatus in psalmum primum* 10 PL 9 256C
235 Matt 7:16 and 20
236 Rom 6:21
237 Rom 1:27
238 *Commentarius in epistolam ad Romanos* PG 14 884A

perpetual happiness with him upon whom we are engrafted by baptism and by the practice of piety. But the prophet's words, 'Eye has not seen, nor ear heard, nor man's heart conceived the things which you have prepared, O God, for those that love you,'[239] refer not only to the glory of immortality, but also to the happiness in this life which godly men receive like a down payment, as it were, or a pledge, for the immortality to come. Similarly, this passage in the psalm can also be applied to the calm and fruitful earthly life of the devout.

On this earth, too, purity has its springtime, its flowering, its fruit; the youth of the devout will be renewed, like the eagle's,[240] and they will blossom like the lily[241] in the sight of the Lord. Moreover, 'the righteous shall flourish like the palm tree.'[242] All this is ensured by upright conduct, pure and innocent thoughts, calmness of mind and, as Solomon says, a 'continual feast,'[243] so that even the body, as it approaches the end of life, retains a constant glow of health, as if it were already preparing itself, in the here and now, to be what it will shortly become, namely spiritual, heavenly, free from all decay, corruption, and age. The Holy Spirit, inhabiting our spirit, overflows into it and, being the more powerful, changes our spirit into itself, as it were; similarly this transformed spirit of ours overflows into the body, its present lodging, and, as far as is possible, changes the body into itself. This explains that youthful old age which we observe in some spinsters and which St Jerome marvels at in Paul of Concordia, whom a kind of youthful freshness seemed to make evergreen.[244] It explains too the animation which shines in the eyes of those whose thoughts are pure. Sin, rather than nature, is largely responsible for old age and illness. In case anyone finds this too extraordinary, remember that we see this bodily condition persisting in the saints even when they are dead.

I have described much of the happiness enjoyed by our 'blessed man,' but now hear how the psalm describes its culmination: 'And everything that he does shall prosper.' It is clear that these words apply to the circumstances of this life, even though Jerome disagrees, thinking that they cannot be applied to any of the saints in this earthly life.[245] But what shall we be doing

* * * * *

239 1 Cor 2:9, based on Isa 64:4
240 Cf Ps 102/103:5.
241 Cf Hos 14:5.
242 Ps 91/92:12
243 Prov 15:15
244 See Jerome's eulogy of this pious centenarian in Epistle 10 (21) PL 22 343–4.
245 *Breviarium in psalmos* PL 26 824C

in heaven that will need to 'prosper'? In addition, to touch for a moment on the allegorical sense, did not our first mother Eve's wilfulness turn out most unhappily for us? And, similarly, father Adam's indulgence of her? Did not all the serpent's promises lead to disaster? But, on the contrary, everything done by Christ led to a joyful conclusion: joyful birth, joyful labours, joyful teaching, joyful death, joyful resurrection, joyful ascension; then the joyful descent of the Holy Spirit, the joyful union of the churches, the joyful sacrifice of the martyrs. The Last Judgment of the world, too, will be joyful for the pious.

In the same way, what ill fortune can befall those who are with Christ at present? Whatever they do, they have God as their guide, God as their sponsor: 'I was with you,' he says, 'in all things, wherever you went.'[246] 'And I am with you,' he says, 'in tribulation.'[247] How could anything undertaken with God's guidance fail to prosper?

To underline just how confident our blessed man can be: with God's aid, evil itself becomes an extra measure of good fortune. Whatever an impious man does is impious; in other circumstances his deeds might be works of piety, but the omens are against him. Anything that happens to an impious man, whether happy or sad, merely adds to the sum of impiety. On the other hand, whatever befalls a pious man is turned into a gain for piety, even, I would venture to say, if on occasion he happens to lapse into sinfulness; God's hidden plan sometimes permits even this to befall his chosen ones, to ensure, of course, that, once reformed, they love him more warmly, keep watch more carefully, forgive others more readily, and give help more attentively.

In short, as Paul says, 'charity does no wrong,'[248] to the extent that even when it does wrong it is not wrong. Small wonder, then, that everything else prospers, when even the one thing that can make a Christian unhappy results in happiness. If something turns out well for a good man, he gives thanks and shows kindness to others. If it turns out badly, he shows his self-possession and turns his thoughts towards the life to come. An impious man is made more arrogant by good fortune, more inclined towards vile pleasures, and, when shattered by ill fortune, is plunged into despair, whereas 'all things work together for good for those who love God.'[249]

What could not be joyful to someone living a life of holiness, when even death itself, the unhappiest of all events, is to him the most welcome of

* * * * *

246 2 Sam 7:9
247 Ps 90/91:15
248 Cf 1 Cor 13:4 in the Vulgate: 'Caritas . . . non agit perperam.'
249 Rom 8:28

all, and indeed desirable above all else? But 'everything shall prosper,' or, as Hilary translates, 'everything shall be well directed.'[250] By whom? By none other than God who, since he is supremely good, can change even the worst of evil into supreme good for his own people. Nowhere is he closer or more helpful than amid the trials and storms of this world. When the attacks of our tormentor are at their most violent and cruel, his heavenly balm brings us the most soothing of relief.

'Not so the impious, not so': Up to this point the psalm has presented an ideal portrait of the blessed man, an ideal towards which we must strive. Now, to instruct us more fully, it traces the very different portrait of the impious. It is the duty of a good teacher not only to teach what is right, but also to warn against what is wrong; to show not merely what must be imitated, but also what must be avoided. If, for instance, one were to describe the ideal of a good prince, one would set against it the image of the tyrant,[251] thus applying twin spurs to the pupil's mind: inspired by the portrayal of honour, he will recoil from its opposite. In fact, it often happens that we are more deeply influenced by a well-constructed representation of wickedness than by honour itself, just as some people are more powerfully affected by the fear of disgrace than by a desire for glory.

'Not so the impious, not so': This repetition is not found in the Septuagint or in the Hebrew, but merely: 'Not so the impious.' Jerome says that he found this reading in only one book, the *Hexapla* of Origen, in the imperial library.[252] It seems to be a useful interpolation by some unknown scribe seeking to emphasize[253] the immense distance between the pious and the impious. What possible resemblance is there, indeed, between the sort of tree which has just been described, and 'the dust which the wind drives away'?[254]

Where now[255] are those who gaze up at kings, and imagine that they enjoy a happiness beyond human experience? Where are those who gape at the rich men of our age, wallowing in wealth and pleasure? Where are those who envy the men in power and the ostentatious style in which they

* * * * *

250 *Tractatus in psalmum primum* 13 PL 9 258A; cf 34 above.
251 As Erasmus does at length in the contemporary *Institutio principis christiani* CWE 27 223–31
252 *Breviarium in psalmos* PL 26 824D
253 The word 'emphasize' is in Greek in Erasmus' text, to denote a rhetorical device. Cf n230 above.
254 Ps 1:4
255 A rhetorical commonplace on the ephemerality of this world, dating back at least to Isaiah 33:18; cf E. Gilson 'De la Bible à François Villon' in *Les idées et les lettres* 2nd ed (Paris 1955) 9–38.

live? They think themselves demigods; the people worship them as if they
were divine. Some people applaud them and congratulate them on their
apparent good fortune; others envy them. So much for popular opinion: now
hear the verdict of a true judge. He compares all their good fortune to the
merest dust; they have abandoned Christ and, failing to entrust their lives
to the real and the eternal, have put their trust in 'things of nothing,' as the
Scriptures put it,[256] and have based their happiness on false values, unstable,
frail, ephemeral; such people, it is clear, are the furthest of all from the image
of our tree, and instead are as dry as dust, since they are not imbued with the
moisture of the Holy Spirit, and are not only sterile and infertile themselves,
but are also dangerous and infectious to others, causing trouble for those
who walk the paths of holiness. They molest, harass, and insult the pious, as
though the latter were an affront to their eyes.

What is more worthless than dust? what more despicable? what is
nearer to nothing? And yet, as if it were not enough to call them dust, the
psalm adds: 'Which the wind drives away.' Nothing is more contemptible
than dung, and yet a use is found for it, as manure for the fields. But what is
the value, what the use, of dust flying through the air?

Here again it seems that the Greek translators have added some words
of their own, which they do occasionally elsewhere, as in the psalm 'God,
my God, look upon me. Why have you forsaken me?'[257] Here they have
added the words 'look upon me,' which are not in the Hebrew, although
it does not make much difference to the meaning. More important here is
that the Hebrew word מוֹץ‎ *kamotz*, which the Septuagint translates as χνοῦν,
that is, 'dust,' is alleged by some to mean, in Hebrew, something more like
'floor-sweepings' or 'husks'[258] than 'dust,' that is, some utterly worthless
substance which flies out from the chaff or the husks when they are beaten,
and is carried away through the air.[259] In any case, either reading is entirely
appropriate. If one reads 'dust' it corresponds to God's threat against the
wicked: 'I shall crush them like dust before the wind, I shall destroy them
like mud in the streets.'[260] If one prefers 'husks' or something similar, it fits

* * * * *

256 For example Isa 29:21 and 41:12 and Jer 14:14
257 Ps 21/22:1
258 The latter are indeed closer to the meaning of the Hebrew, but the Greek term
is also a more general one than Erasmus suggests, denoting any light porous
substance. As usual in this work, Hebrew characters were added in the Basel
edition of 1518.
259 The definition 'that is ... the air' was added to the text in the Basel edition of
1518.
260 Ps 17/18:42; cf 2 Sam 22:43.

in better with the simile of the fruitful tree, for what is emptier than a husk, what more barren, more contemptible?

Although, as I have said, these words can be applied to the future punishment of the wicked, I prefer to apply them to this life. When no thought is given to the life everlasting, when a heart is 'swept bare'[261] by a passion for the ephemeral, rather than being fixed on that solid rock, Christ,[262] then it will not only waste away, consumed by the utterly futile concerns of this life, but it will also be torn asunder by conflicting desires: as, indeed, the winds change from hour to hour, and are often at war with one another. Like a husk driven by the winds, anyone inclined to impiety is exposed to worldly desires; first he covets one thing, then another; by turns he loves and hates, he favours and envies, he fears and hopes, he exults and despairs. He is at odds with himself in a ferment of indecision: lust suggests one course, greed another; hatred calls him one way, ambition pulls him another; love decrees one thing, shame dictates another; finally, in the general ebb and flow of human affairs, he can change in an instant and there is no consistency or calm in him for a moment; to sum up, how else could such a person be described than as a husk at the mercy of the winds?

Does not this image seem to fit certain foolish princes, whose rapid shifts of policy shake the very earth? At one moment they are locked in armed conflict, at the next they are cemented to one another by marriage alliances.[263] War at one moment, peace treaties the next – but they will not last long. For a time things are patched up, but soon they will fall apart in the absence of any settled policy, which can only be achieved if they have Christ as their goal. But they twist and turn, from one course to another, never holding steady; they do not escape misfortune, they merely change its form. Anyone inclined to piety directs his attention towards a single purpose, measures everything by reference to it, clings to it, for if the inescapable demands of human existence cause pious men a certain anxiety, they have caverns in which to shelter, they have clefts in the rock where they may rest.[264] The impious have nothing to stand on or, as you might say, they are floundering in the water.[265]

* * * * *

261 Erasmus quotes in Greek an emphatic phrase applied usually to a plundered country; cf *Adagia* III vii 32.
262 Cf 1 Cor 10:4.
263 Cf the chapter on this subject in the *Institutio principis christiani* CWE 27 277–9 (chapter 9).
264 Cf Song of Sol 2:14.
265 Cf *Adagia* I iv 100.

We have looked at the very different way of life of the pious and the impious; let us now contemplate their quite dissimilar ends. On this point the psalm says: 'The impious do not stand up again in the judgment, nor do sinners in the council of the righteous.' I am aware that others relate this text to the Last Judgment of the world,[266] but, leaving that view aside for a moment, I shall set out my ideas on a humbler level of interpretation, and come later to that loftier theme.[267]

A little earlier the psalm had called the 'fruit' of the good tree the process whereby, having 'meditated on the Lord's law' at some length, a pious man would afterwards engage in public duties and apply to the public service everything that he had learned in private; this does not happen to the impious, although it is the height of their ambition. What place is there in the administration of public affairs for the impious, who are a prey to every vice and have not learned wisdom from the Lord's law? Two particular qualities are required in a public official: anyone who punishes others' crimes must be free from crime himself, and wise enough to be able to decide wherein lies the public interest.[268] Therefore they do not 'stand up' (this is the correct Hebrew reading, rather than 'stand up again': the word is יָקֻמוּ *iakumu*)[269] 'in the judgment' – it was their custom to stand up to speak in council. Thus the words 'they do not stand up in the judgment' may be taken to mean 'they have no place in the judgment.'

'Nor do sinners in the council of the righteous': As you see, the same idea is repeated with just a slight change in the wording. If you examine the Holy Scriptures, you will often come across a similar flexibility of expression: sometimes the same idea is expressed in different words, sometimes a related idea, sometimes an opposite one. Similar techniques are a feature of the pagan poets' rustic verses. Here is an example of the repetition of the same idea: 'The mouth of the righteous shall speak of wisdom, and his tongue shall talk of judgment.'[270] Similarly: 'Her feet go down to death, and her steps take her down to hell.'[271] Related ideas: 'Obey, my son, your father's instructions,

* * * * *

266 Notably Jerome in *Breviarium in psalmos* PL 26 819–20
267 As so often, Erasmus deals principally with the tropological or moral sense, generally considered 'humbler' than the sublime eschatological or anagogical level of interpretation; see the introductory note 3 above.
268 This echoes the chapter on magistrates and their duties in the *Institutio principis christiani* CWE 27 273–5 (chapter 7).
269 Hebrew characters were added in the Basel edition of 1518. Erasmus is correct about the meaning, though the Hebrew is in fact in the future tense.
270 Ps 36/37:30. The preceding allusion is probably to the style of Virgil's *Eclogues*.
271 Prov 5:5

and do not reject your mother's teaching.'[272] Antithetical ideas (a technique mentioned also by Quintilian):[273] 'A clever man acts always with wisdom, but the stupid parades his folly.'[274] If you leaf through Solomon's proverbs, the wise sayings of Ecclesiasticus and Ecclesiastes, the Psalms, the Songs, in fact all the places in the Old and New Testaments where the Holy Spirit speaks in its characteristic poetic manner, you will find that almost all these passages ring the changes on these three devices; but the most common is the one which expresses the same idea in different words. For this reason it is perhaps not so important to examine with scrupulous exactitude the difference between words which convey the same meaning.

The Spirit now calls 'sinners' those whom it had previously called 'impious'; whereas earlier it said 'in the judgment,' it now says 'in the council of the righteous.' It was a Hebrew custom to refer the most important decisions to a council similar to the assemblies of the Amphictyons and the Areopagites in Greece.[275] Therefore the 'impious' do not stand up in the council of the righteous either, or in public life at all, since it requires men of honour and integrity, and indeed not only integrity but wisdom too, and long experience of 'the Lord's law,' which alone brings true 'wisdom to the simple.'[276]

Do you require more proof that what is here denied to the impious is elsewhere granted to the righteous? 'In the midst of the church,' says the Spirit, 'she has opened her mouth';[277] and again: 'In the midst of the people she shall be exalted.'[278] And again, speaking of Moses: 'He made him glorious in the sight of kings, and gave him a commandment for his people';[279] there are countless similar examples. It is clear from them that wise and upright men have a duty to attend distinguished public assemblies, from which the wicked and foolish are to be banned, since they are neither capable of giving advice, being fools, nor willing to do so, being demoralized by their sensual appetites.

It may happen occasionally that an impious man enters the 'council of the righteous,' but he does not 'stand up' because he will not be given a

* * * * *

272 Prov 1:8 and cf 6:20.
273 Quintilian 5.10.73
274 Prov 13:16
275 Respectively, councillors delegated by the various states to debate matters of common interest and members of the highest judicial court of Athens, which sat on the Areopagus hill
276 Ps 18/19:7
277 Sir 24:2; the usual reading is 'she shall open.'
278 Sir 24:1
279 Sir 45:3

hearing. Pagan historians tell us that when some disreputable character had included in a speech an important and politically sound point, the presiding magistrate gave orders that the same idea should be put forward by someone else with a better reputation; they were convinced that a bad man should not be heard in council because even if he said something very valuable, it would be rejected because of the speaker's notoriety. Is not the Holy Spirit angered by something similar in another psalm? 'But God said to the sinner: "What right have you to tell of my judgments, or to take my covenant in your mouth?"'[280] What is pure must be discussed only by the pure, what is holy by the holy. Is it not unseemly that a man can overlook his own squalid vices and preach the gospel's doctrine to the people? In the Gospels, Christ refuses to listen to praise of himself, however truthful, from a devil. 'Be silent, spirit,' he says.[281]

We should discuss briefly whether this verse goes with the preceding one, or the following one, or indeed with both. If we ask: 'Why do the impious not stand up in the judgment, in which the pious are seated?' and we answer: 'Because the latter are fruitful trees and the former useless dust or husks,' then this verse goes with the preceding ones. But if we ask: 'Why do they not stand up in the judgment, although the pious do?' the answer is: 'Because the Lord knows the path of the righteous and destroys the path of the impious.'[282] God 'knows,' that is, approves, the councils of the pious. Since they are founded on his law, God acknowledges and approves them, and thus they do not perish, because they rest upon truth; they turn out well because, naturally, God protects them. But the councils of the impious originate in foolishness or depraved passions, and are thus not approved by God; they do not turn out well, and indeed they are destroyed because, naturally, God disapproves.

The impious do indeed have their councils, which our blessed man does not deign to enter. The pious too have their councils, in which the impious are not given a hearing. They have nothing at all in common: the pious look towards Christ and heaven, the impious towards the world and this earth. The pious consider only the dictates of Christ's law, the impious only the dictates of ambition, avarice, and gluttony. How, then, could there be any common ground for debate or voting between two groups whose whole way of life is so 'diametrically opposed,'[283] as the saying goes? Whatever is right is also

* * * * *

280 Ps 49/50:16
281 Mark 1:25
282 Ps 1:6
283 *Adagia* I x 45, quoted in Greek here

uncomplicated, and good men easily agree on it. But the errors of those who stray from the right path are many and various: hence the senseless disputes and conflicting votes in the councils of the wicked; and it often happens that when, after enormous efforts, they have made some decision which is supposed to last for all time, it is overturned before it has even been tried. Human plans are ephemeral; only the divine plan remains for all eternity.

Just as the impious have a kind of council, so too they have a kind of wisdom, but it is the wisdom of the sensual world, which James calls 'demonic.'[284] What threat does God utter against it, through the prophet? 'I will destroy,' he says, 'the wisdom of the wise, I will reprove the prudence of the prudent.'[285] How strenuously the Romans fought, long ago, to ensure that their empire should last for ever! How much trouble, how much toil, how much bloodshed went into their efforts! But today, as we see, that empire has disappeared, so completely that there is scarcely a true Roman to be found: God laughed to scorn the plans of the impious.

Do we not witness similar events in the councils of princes today? How ostentatiously the whole thing is usually carried out! Swarms of distinguished noblemen and doctors of laws look on, full of assurance, as the business is conducted with all due ceremony; the decisions are confirmed in a thousand documents. One would say that the treaty was already destined to last for ever. But it is not unusual for that very treaty rapidly to cause a mighty war.[286] Why? Because, of course, the affair was handled by the council of the foolish and impious. The bishop has signed, the emperor has signed, the nobles have signed – but God has not signed.

God forbid that anything smacking of worldliness and alien to Christ's counsel should ever be agreed in the councils of the popes too. The desires of the flesh have no place in this spiritual council; fleshly desire is the worst of all counsellors, and belongs in the council of the impious. Only the advice that the Spirit has given is everlasting.

Paul's wise tutor Gamaliel understood this: 'Leave them alone,' he said. 'If this plan or its execution is of human origin, it will be wrecked; but if it is from God, you can never wreck it.'[287] Theudas' plans were wrecked, Judas' plans were wrecked.[288] But what of the apostles' plans? How many

*****

284 James 3:15
285 Isa 29:14, quoted in 1 Cor 1:19, the version used by Erasmus here
286 Another passage recalling a chapter of the *Institutio principis christiani*; see CWE 27 275–7, on treaties.
287 Acts 5:38–9
288 Acts 5:36–7

high priests, how many kings, how many governors tried to suppress them, by imprisonment, torture, death – and indeed all the most painful forms of death. But they had little success, and in fact their cruelty enhanced the glory of the gospel. Nothing can last for ever, unless it has the approval of him who has no ending. The builders of the tower of Babel set their sights on immortality, but God wrecked that particular 'council of the impious' by confusing their language.[289] How many kings had similar ambitions when they built those extraordinary pyramids? God mocked their plans as well.

Only the pious achieve all that they desire, since they hasten towards their goal on the 'path which God knows'; he walks before them, the author and the sponsor of everything that is done. The impious, because they are struggling towards their objectives along a path which God does not recognize, are thwarted in their desires, since their efforts incur God's disapproval and wrath. For it is hard to 'kick against the pricks,' as Paul heard when, still a member of the 'council of sinners,' he continued to persecute Christians.[290]

Another level of interpretation yields a similar meaning: let us imagine (and indeed they exist) two councils, as if composed of two peoples who disagree on many points, the pious and the impious. The former is descended from Jacob, the latter from Esau, whom God hated[291] and whose descendants differ little from their ancestor, since they persecute the righteous, that is, true Christians, with a hatred that is worse than mere hostility. But God, the unshakeable defender of his little flock, overpowers and drives them back, and destroys them so utterly that they will never rise again or prevail against the elect, however fiercely they attack, maim, and slaughter.

All this applies not only to pagans and Christians, but still more to those who are Christians in name only – since their deeds are pagan – and those who are truly Christian. If we Christians are no less avid for gold than the Turks,[292] if we are prepared to sweat, lie, swindle, slander, fight, and kill just for gold, if we will struggle with no less frenzy than they to obtain and keep worldly wealth, if we are no less – indeed more – addicted to shameful pleasures than they, if all the desires of the flesh hold sway among us more

* * * * *

289 Gen 11:1–9
290 Acts 26:14 (and 9:5)
291 Cf Rom 9:13.
292 Erasmus frequently reproached Christians for being no better, and in many cases worse, than the Turks, widely regarded as the new barbarians: see for example Ep 858:78–110, *Institutio principis christiani* CWE 27 286–7, and *De bello Turcico*.

than among them, what, I ask you, remains to distinguish Christians from Turks except the name itself and a few minor rituals?

Moreover, the Turks' hatred for the name of Christian is mild compared with that of bad Christians for the true Christian. If they discover that someone is a true Christian, an opponent of all their works, they plot against him, persecute him, get him out of the way, and, if they can, utterly destroy him. But the flesh cannot extinguish the Spirit of God. Just as the impious themselves are husks, reduced to virtually nothing since they have cut themselves off from him who says: 'I am that I am,'[293] so too are their plans brought to nothing. A tree that is pruned grows all the more vigorously and gives more abundant fruit. Virtue that is oppressed shines all the brighter. But an impious man, like the dust blown in the wind, is utterly destroyed, beyond hope of redemption, and is not only compelled by death to relinquish all that he has laboured so long to acquire, but is also excluded from the company of the blessed souls in the world to come.

For they too will rise again, since it is written: 'Indeed, we shall all rise again';[294] but they will not rise up into life, or be among the sheep, that is, 'in the judgment of the righteous' (I think that the genitive 'of the righteous' applies to both parts), but among the goats.[295] On that day 'the righteous shall stand up with great assurance.'[296] On the other hand, the impious will confess their madness, finding no cause to object to God's manifest justice, and with belated tears they will regret the worthless plans they made. But God will not even acknowledge their presence, since they refused to acknowledge him on earth.

Blessed are those whom God consents to recognize. He acknowledged the faithful Abraham: 'Now I know you because you fear the Lord.'[297] He refused to see Adam the sinner and asked, as if of a stranger: 'Adam, where are you?'[298] In Luke's Gospel, the sinners who say: 'Lord, Lord, let us in!' get the reply 'I do not know where you come from.' And when they insist: 'We have eaten and drunk in your presence, and you have taught in our streets,' the reply is 'I do not know where you come from; leave me, all you workers

* * * * *

293 Exod 3:14
294 1 Cor 15:51, though the English versions are rather different
295 Cf Matt 25:33. The parenthesis suggests that Ps 1:5 should read 'in the judgment of the righteous . . . in the council of the righteous.'
296 Wisd 5:1
297 Gen 22:12
298 Gen 3:9; both these examples are cited in this context by Hilary *Tractatus in primum psalmum* 19 PL 9 261A.

of iniquity. Then there shall be a weeping and a grinding of teeth, when you see Abraham, Isaac, Jacob, and all the prophets in the kingdom of God, while you are thrown out of doors.'[299] In Matthew, the foolish virgins get the reply 'I do not know you,'[300] and similarly Paul says: 'He who ignores this shall be ignored.'[301] Moreover, the Lord knows the paths which are to the right; he does not know those to the left. Why not? Because he, whose very nature it is to be straight, does not know the crooked. To see and to know are the same thing for God. He refused to see Adam when he was there, and he had seen Nathaniel before he arrived under the fig tree.[302]

Perhaps someone will wish to examine more closely the words 'the impious do not stand up in the judgment' in the light of the earlier distinction between the impious[303] and the sinners. According to Christ's words, 'anyone who has not believed is already judged,'[304] like a man whose sins are so evident that they precede him to his judgment, as Paul wrote.[305] He calls impiety great and hopeless wickedness. What need is there to judge those whose lives already clearly proclaim their guilt? However, sinners do indeed 'stand up in council,' but not in the 'council of the righteous'; and they will in fact be judged, but among the impious. Therefore the pious will not be judged, since their salvation is certain; nor will the impious, since their damnation is certain.

However, it is usual to discuss doubtful cases in councils and courts of law. Judgment has already been given against the impious, judgment is superfluous in the case of the pious. Therefore only the sinners need be examined. Whom does the psalm mean by 'sinners'? Presumably those who are a mixture of good and bad, who are pious in their beliefs and their words, but are impious in their deeds, like so many ordinary Christians today. They confess Christ, sing his praises, go to church. But their entire way of life conflicts with Christ's teaching. If you ask them whether they believe the Gospels: 'How dare you!'[306] they cry, 'Of course we do!' 'Why then do you

* * * * *

299 Luke 13:25–8
300 Matt 25:12
301 1 Cor 14:38
302 Cf John 1:45–51.
303 All the texts, including ASD, read 'the pious' here, but this seems to require emendation in the context. Erasmus is referring to a passage in the commentary on verse 1, 15–16 above.
304 John 3:18
305 1 Tim 5:24
306 *bona verba*, literally 'words of good omen,' an expression used ironically by Terence (*Andria* 204) and a favourite of Erasmus; cf CWE 28 176 n72 (page 499).

not live according to the Gospels?' Now they are struck dumb. If you ask them if they believe that we shall be resurrected, they reply that they believe it with all their hearts, and yet their way of life suggests that they do not expect any life after this one. They know what is good, but, corrupted by their passions, they drift into evil.

It is these dubious creatures, an amalgam, as it were, of pagan and Christian, who will come into the council, as the psalm says, not to be saved along with the pious, but to be joined to the impious and, in cases which were previously in doubt, the debate will establish clearly to which group they belong; they must be judged, not by their titles or their performance of ritual, but by their acts of piety. I hear someone called a Christian, I see him baptized, I hear him confessing, I see him praying, I see him taking the sacraments. But I also see deeds which have little to do with any of this. I dare not call him a gentile,[307] yet I cannot call him a Christian.

Perhaps the Lord does not want us to pronounce judgment on such people; they may be reserved for his courtroom, reserved for him to judge. If a man were seen prophesying, preaching the gospel, performing miracles, casting out devils, who would dare to judge him impious? And yet, in the Gospel, our judge does reject some people like this and orders them to be cast into the eternal fire.[308] This then is a judgment like that which Christ pronounces in John: 'For a light came into the world, and men preferred darkness to light.'[309] The sinners have seen the light of Christ through faith but have preferred to cling to their darkness; they love Christ up to a point but have a greater love and desire for all those things which cut them off from the teaching of Christ. 'I do not want to hurt anyone,' they say – but public acclaim is sweet. 'I do not want to cheat anyone' – but greed triumphs. 'I want to suffer with Christ, that I may share his kingdom' – but pleasure calls. 'I do not want to fight wars' – but there is no other way to extend his kingdom. People like this do indeed 'rise up in council,' but not in the council of the saints.

One more note: the psalm did not say that the impious would be destroyed, but rather 'the path of the impious'; they themselves will survive the punishment, but will be thwarted of their desires; they will not obtain what they turned everything upside down to achieve, and, in fact, completely the opposite will happen. Therefore, if we wish to acquire that most blessed title of 'blessed man' let us ensure that it is not only in our confessions and

* * * * *

307 The 1525 edition replaces 'a gentile' with 'a pagan.'
308 See Matt 7:22–3 for an apt example; the punishment is an echo of Matt 25:41.
309 John 3:19

our acts of worship, but also in our lives and our deeds, that we reflect the only source of bliss, Christ, to whom be praise and glory without end. Amen.

POSTSCRIPT

Here, my Beatus Rhenanus, is my little present, more than somewhat improvised, and not perhaps what you deserved, but rather what I was able to prepare in the time at my disposal. But – are you listening? – do not think that I shall let you take it away scot-free. It may be a virtue in others not to remember the kindness they have done, but here the rule is that one asks for one's gifts to be given back, with interest, as it were, and it is a fine thing to send back what one has received with a whole pile of interest – especially when the recipient gets more, but the donor is left with no less. Therefore I fully expect that Beatus shall be to Erasmus what Glaucus was to Diomedes in Homer.[310] The more blessed you are, the easier it is for you to produce important work. Lesser men like me make such gifts as we can, not so much for the sake of giving as to elicit a gift in return. Farewell, and make greater efforts each day to live up to your name.

* * * * *

310 Glaucus was proverbially the epitome of generous friendship (*Adagia* I ii 1); in *Iliad* 6.234–6 he exchanges his golden armour for Diomedes' bronze armour.

A COMMENTARY ON THE SECOND PSALM, 'WHY DID THE NATIONS RAGE?'

Commentarius in psalmum 2,
'Quare fremuerunt gentes?'

The *Commentarius in psalmum* 2 first appeared in September 1522 as an appendix to Erasmus' edition of the psalm commentaries of Arnobius; like all Erasmus' subsequent writings on the Psalms, it was published by Froben at Basel. The same material was printed twice more in the same year, at Cologne and Strasbourg; subsequently, Erasmus' commentary alone was republished with his exposition of the First Psalm at Cologne and Antwerp in 1524, and finally the Froben press issued two further editions, the one undated and the other dated 1525, in volumes containing Erasmus' expositions of Psalms 1–4. Of all these editions, only the 1525 Froben was (possibly) revised by Erasmus.

The gap between the appearance in 1515 of Erasmus' exposition of the First Psalm and that of his commentary on the Second Psalm may be explained by the simple fact that Erasmus was extremely busy in the intervening years;[1] moreover, it is by no means certain that in 1515 Erasmus had any intention of writing a commentary on the entire Psalter. However, a passage near the end of the present work (144) does suggest that such a project was now in his mind, and this impression is reinforced by the brief – and tantalizingly vague – note to the reader, signed by Froben but possibly the work of Erasmus himself,[2] which does duty as a dedicatory letter:

> Erasmus of Rotterdam was induced by the earnest entreaties of certain eminent persons to attempt to complete the commentaries on the Psalter which he had begun a few years before. He intended to give me a number of psalms, the fruits of this enterprise, but he was frustrated in his intentions partly by poor health and partly by the dishonesty of certain tricksters. However, to avoid losing the little that is ready, I have added this treatise as a kind of extension to Arnobius' commentaries. Erasmus also thought it worthwhile to publish this specimen, as it were, to test the reactions of scholars before going on to greater things; it is important to satisfy your audience. Profit from the book, reader, and support us in our labours.

This text implies that the commentary on the Second Psalm is a continuation of Erasmus' earlier work, but it is in fact very different in character and intention. In 1515 he expounded the First Psalm 'principally on the tropological level' as a contribution to that pursuit of moral reform which was then his major concern,[3] but his commentary on the Second Psalm concentrates on the allegorical level of interpretation, which, according to tradition,

* * * * *

1 For more ingenious explanations, see ASD V-2 4–5 and 84–5.
2 See Allen V 100 and ASD V-2 4.
3 See 11 above.

elucidated the religious lesson; Erasmus considers Psalm 2 as, above all, a prophecy of the passion and triumph of Christ. The punishments threatened in the last four verses of the psalm inspire a passage (134–8) in the moralizing vein of 1515, but this is an exception; the messianic prophecy of the Old Testament draws Erasmus ineluctably towards its fulfilment in the New.[4]

It is also noticeable that Erasmus allots little space to a literal interpretation of either the First or Second Psalm. In the present work (79–80) he rejects the rabbinical tradition of historical exegesis, which he knew from the fourteenth-century commentary of Nicholas of Lyra; Erasmus generally neglects the medieval tradition of exegesis in favour of the great patristic commentators. Not unnaturally, he warmly recommends Arnobius (144), and he alludes to Cassiodorus (93), but the great majority of his references are to Augustine, Jerome (the most useful on linguistic questions, of course), and above all to Hilary: Erasmus was to publish his edition of Hilary in January 1523, and it is clear that he was already immersed in the task. But, however much it may owe to these revered predecessors, Erasmus' commentary on the Second Psalm is, remarkably, many times longer than any of theirs, and is probably the most detailed allegorical exposition of the psalm ever made. Erasmus' devotion to Christ and to the *philosophia Christi* could not be more explicit.

As usual, the Latin text of the psalm used by Erasmus presents certain ambiguities which cannot always be conveyed exactly in English. In the first verse the verb *fremere*, which I normally render 'to rage,' has overtones of frenzy, madness, and wildness for which there is no single adequate English verb, and in the same line *gentes* can stand both for 'nations,' meaning the tribes of the whole world, and for 'gentiles.' 'The peoples' with whom they are associated in this verse *meditati sunt inania*; as Erasmus had explained in his exposition of the First Psalm, the verb could mean both to 'meditate' and to 'practise':[5] to 'plot vain things' and to 'carry through' their empty or futile plots. In the second verse the word *principes* is translated 'leaders' in most contexts, since Erasmus usually applies the term here to the Jewish rabbis and elders, but the word also means 'princes,' and on occasion Erasmus applies it to those eminent contemporaries who had so often been the butt of his satire. Other doubts and obscurities in the text of the psalm are discussed by Erasmus himself in the course of his commentary.

The text translated here is that established by S. Dresden in ASD V-2 96–158, which includes the few additions made to the text in the 1525 Froben

* * * * *

4 See Boyle 90 on Erasmus' advice that the exegete 'refer everything to Christ.'
5 See 28 above.

edition; these are pointed out in my notes. A manuscript preserved in the Royal Library at Copenhagen contains a preliminary draft of the commentary in Erasmus' own hand;[6] although this is of undoubted interest in showing Erasmus at work, its variants, recorded in the critical apparatus in ASD, are too numerous to be dealt with here; in any case, the printed text is an expansion rather than a revision of this early draft. In translating Scripture, in referring to the Psalms, and in providing a 'working text' of Psalm 2, I have followed the principles described in my introductory note to the exposition of the First Psalm (4).

MJH

* * * * *

6 See C. Reedijk 'Three Erasmus Autographs in the Royal Library at Copenhagen' in *Studia bibliographica in honorem Herman de La Fontaine Verwey* (Amsterdam 1966) 341 and ASD V-2 91–2.

PSALM 2

1 Quare fremuerunt gentes, et populi meditati sunt inania?

2 Adstiterunt reges terrae et principes convenerunt in unum adversus Dominum et adversus Christum eius.

3 Disrumpamus vincula eorum, proiiciamus a nobis iugum ipsorum.

4 Qui habitat in coelis irridebit eos, et Dominus subsannabit illos.

5 Tunc loquetur ad eos in ira sua et in furore suo conturbabit eos.

6 Ego ordinavi [unxi] regem meum super Sion montem sanctum meum, prae-
dicans praeceptum eius [meum. Annunciabo Dei praeceptum].

7 Dominus dixit ad me: 'Filius meus es tu, ego hodie genui te.

8 Postula a me, et dabo tibi gentes haereditatem tuam, et possessionem tuam
terminos terrae.

9 Reges eos in virga ferrea; tamquam vas figuli confringes eos.'

10 Et nunc, reges, intelligite; erudimini qui iudicatis terram.

11 Servite Domino in timore, et exsultate cum tremore.

12 Apprehendite disciplinam, ne forte irascatur Dominus, et pereatis de via
iusta. Beati omnes qui confidunt in eo.

1 Why did the nations [or 'gentiles'] rage, and the peoples carry through their
futile plots?

2 The kings of the earth stood ready, and the leaders conspired together against
the Lord and against the Lord's anointed [or 'Christ'].

3 Let us break their fetters, let us throw off their yoke from us.

4 He who dwells in heaven will laugh at them, and the Lord will laugh them
to scorn.

5 Then he will speak to them in his wrath, and in his fury he will confound
them.

6 I have enthroned [or 'anointed'] my king on my holy mountain of Zion,
announcing God's decree [or 'Zion. I will proclaim God's decree'].

7 The Lord said to me: 'You are my son, this day I have begotten you.

8 Ask it of me, and I will give you the nations as your inheritance and the ends
of the earth as your possession.

9 You shall rule them with an iron rod; you shall break them like a pot of clay.'

10 And now, you kings, understand; learn your lesson, you judges of the earth.

11 Serve the Lord with fear, and rejoice with trembling.

12 Grasp this instruction, lest the Lord be angry and you are struck down from the righteous path. Blessed are all those who put their trust in him.

A COMMENTARY ON THE SECOND PSALM, 'WHY DID THE NATIONS RAGE?'

Before I embark on an exposition of this psalm, it will perhaps be useful, and at the same time not disagreeable to the diligent reader, to have a few words of introduction: first, on the position of the psalm, second, on its heading, and, finally, on its subject.

The Hebrews place the Psalms in a particular order which is said to have been assigned to them by Esdras,[1] who performed the same service for the Hebrews' mystic hymns as Aristarchus did for Homer's poetry.[2] The order is the same in Hebrew and in the Septuagint, but it is not at all clear what principle Esdras followed in establishing it; it is obvious that it was not according to chronology or to the status of the authors, nor did he follow the sequence of the incidents or subjects described. Again, he did not divide them into individual poems or books, since it is clear from the apostles' quotations that the psalms, or hymns (as the Hebrews call them), constitute a single book. But it is said, and this seems likely, that the translators of the Septuagint attached a number to each psalm to avoid any further confusion over the order established by Esdras.[3] You will say to me, dear reader, 'If that is the case, where is the problem? Why broach the subject?' But listen: although it is beyond dispute that the psalm 'Blessed the man' is placed first in the Hebrew, Greek, and Latin texts, yet the psalm which we have undertaken to expound here is named as the first. For instance, it is quoted by St Paul in the Acts of the Apostles, chapter 13: 'And we give you the news that God has fulfilled to your sons the promise he made to our fathers, by

*****

1 After the return from Babylon, according to 'ancient traditions' mentioned by Hilary *Prologus in librum psalmorum* 8 PL 9 238A

2 The most famous literary critic of the ancient world, proverbial for his severity (*Adagia* I v 57), Aristarchus was the author of a detailed revision of Homer.

3 Hilary *Prologus in librum psalmorum* 9 PL 9 238B. The Septuagint version of the Old Testament and Apocrypha was made, traditionally, by seventy-two Egyptian Jews in about 270 BC.

raising Jesus from the dead, as indeed it was written in the First Psalm.'[4] Although the passage has now been amended in our texts, and 'First' changed to 'Second,' this has been done in the teeth of unanimous opposition from all those who have published commentaries on the Psalms. There is a certain unholy presumption about trying to patch up the text like this whenever there is something we do not understand or do not like in the Holy Scriptures. That is why the orthodox Fathers, who did not allow themselves to take such liberties with texts whose authority should be entirely unassailable, tried different ways of interpreting the passage so that the apostle's quotation should not conflict with the evidence. For example, St Hilary talks a lot about the seventy elders, to whom Moses passed on orally certain mysteries of the Law, and he seems to conclude from this that we must accept that the translators of the Septuagint, not unfamiliar with those mysteries, were not unaware that this psalm had been called the first, as they arranged in order and divided into individual poems all the Hebrew psalms, which at the time were still in a state of disorder and confusion.[5] Now in the passage quoted, Paul, 'a Hebrew of the Hebrews,'[6] debating with the Hebrews in their own synagogue, preferred to give his quotation extra weight by following the Hebrew order rather than the Septuagint's. But although Paul was permitted to do this at the time for a particular reason, Hilary does not consider that this gives us the right to reject the authority of the translators of the Septuagint, who decided that this psalm should be the second rather than the first.

It is not worth agonizing over a matter which is indeed of little importance as far as our worship and our attitude towards God are concerned. However, with due respect to an eminent predecessor, let me raise a few points: granted that as much authority is allowed to the translators of the Septuagint as Hilary thinks proper – though St Jerome is not afraid to overrule them from time to time, and indeed the versions in general use today in the Catholic church differ on many points from their version – even so, is it likely that in Hilary's time the psalms were still not numbered and placed in

* * * * *

4 Acts 13:32–3; modern versions maintain the change to 'Second.'

5 *Tractatus in 2 psalmum* 2–4 PL 9 262B–265A. Hilary's point here, which is none too clear in Erasmus' account of it, is that an oral tradition among the rabbis held that this psalm was part of the first, but that the translators of the Septuagint version, though aware of this tradition, preferred to tidy up the order and split what had previously been the First Psalm into two. On the 'seventy elders' see Num 11:16–25.

6 Phil 3:5

order in the Hebrew version? Jerome nowhere mentions this as a problem, not even when correcting the Septuagint version in the light of the true Hebrew text. If it had been a problem, surely he would either have restored the true Hebrew order, or complained that there was no order in the Hebrew. But supposing for a moment that there was either a vague and uncertain order, or none at all, in the Hebrew, how could Paul call it the first, if it had no number? That would be no less absurd than to describe as 'first' any one out of a pile of beans completely indistinguishable from one another. Moreover, if the translators of the Septuagint did arrange and number the psalms on the basis of their privileged knowledge of the Law, is it reasonable to suppose that this was hidden from Paul, who was most learned in the Law? And if it was not hidden from him, why did he not follow such an order, based on abstruse knowledge of the Law, especially since at the time he was speaking to the Hebrew people, with the rulers of the synagogue as authorities and witnesses?

For these reasons, I would rather subscribe to the opinion of those who suspect that this psalm does not follow the preceding one, but is continuous with it:[7] that is, it is not the second, but the same. Their argument runs as follows: if it cannot be called the first, being preceded by another, then either the heading is wrong, or it must be the same as its predecessor. But the heading, which is given all the weight of the apostle Paul's authority by Luke, cannot be erroneous; it follows, therefore, that it is as one with the preceding psalm. Moreover, the subject of the two psalms gives some support to this hypothesis.[8] The former describes that blessed man who, departing from the council of the impious, relying on righteousness alone, and enjoying God's favour in everything he does, is led to real and everlasting bliss, while on the other hand the council of the impious is destroyed, simply because God knows the path of the righteous and does not recognize the council of the wicked; and thus they perish, because, reliant upon their human powers, they are deprived of divine favour. Moreover, although human efforts cannot prevail against God's decree, yet the impious, conspiring together in wicked harmony, are not afraid to put all their wealth, strength, wit, and ingenuity into a tenacious struggle against God. The prophet cries out in amazement at this: 'Why did the nations rage?' For some commentators, another detail lends support to this theory: the beginning of the earlier psalm harmonizes with

* * * * *

7 This opinion is cited by Hilary (cf n5 above), but Erasmus is clearly following Jerome here; *Breviarium in psalmos* PL 26 823B.

8 There follows a résumé of the First Psalm, which Erasmus had expounded in 1515; see 8–63 above.

the end of the later one.[9] 'Blessed the man' begins, auspiciously, with bliss; this second one ends with the sentence: 'Blessed are all those who put their trust in him.' This is a poetic device, not unknown even today to teachers of rhetoric, in which the idea with which you began is repeated at the end.

More subtle is the opinion of St Augustine, or whoever it was,[10] that the First Psalm is an exception, and is not numbered with the rest because of its special authority and dignity; since he attributes the words of this psalm to God the Father, he thinks that it would be unseemly for any human name to be placed before them, as if being given precedence over the divine authority. Moreover, he says, it is not even appropriate to give it a number; if it were to be labelled 'the First,' it might seem to stand before all the others merely because of its position and number, rather than because of the grandeur of the speaker and the subject; his argument is that something so entirely exceptional and outstanding is set apart so far that it should not even be numbered with the rest. Now, this argument would be more convincing if it were entirely certain that the First Psalm is spoken in the person of the Father, not of the prophet, and also that this is a characteristic exclusive to this psalm, and not one shared with a number of others.

It is similarly very subtle of Jerome – or perhaps it was someone else – to say that it is unnecessary, and pleonastic, to call the psalm the first when no other precedes it: it is obvious that it is the first.[11] It is strange, however, that we are never bothered by the same 'pleonasm' in other books or in their chapters: we write 'first' on the first book, and we put its number on the first chapter. And anyway, while it may be unnecessary to call something 'first' when there is nothing in front of it, it is certainly much more awkward to call it 'first' when there *is* something in front of it!

In conclusion – and I would not want to impose my opinion on anyone else – it seems to me that those commentators come closest to a semblance of the truth who say that the First Psalm is not so much a psalm in itself as a preface to the whole Book of Psalms; we all know how scholars often preface their books with a poem commending their work to the reader and

* * * * *

9 Erasmus makes the same point in his commentary on the First Psalm; see 9 above.
10 As at the beginning of his commentary on the First Psalm (8–9), Erasmus is quoting an *Annotatio* on the First Psalm (PL 36 65–6) which is attributed to St Augustine in the early printed editions of his works but which is not found in all manuscripts.
11 Jerome *Breviarium in psalmos* PL 26 823B. Erasmus also casts doubt on the authenticity of this work in his commentary on Ps 33 (LB V 377B and 396C). The treatise is now considered largely apocryphal.

encouraging him to drink in the contents of the book with greater enthusiasm and attention. It would not even be stretching the facts too far to attribute this preface to Esdras,[12] who not only collected psalms written by various hands, but is also believed to have composed some himself, and added some of the headings, for reasons as yet imperfectly understood.

So much for the number; now a few words about the heading. Most of the psalms are marked by some kind of heading; like new stars they light our path as we approach the threshold of the mystical meaning; they act as a key,[13] as it were, and unlock the outer door leading to the hall, from which we then proceed towards the inner rooms. Sometimes the inscription indicates the form of the poem,[14] describing it, for example, as a psalm, or a canticle, or a canticle of a psalm, or conversely a psalm of a canticle;[15] there is, finally, the diapsalm, a notation inserted in the middle of a psalm to indicate a change in the structure of the poem and in the rhythm: all this can be dealt with more conveniently elsewhere.

Sometimes the heading indicates the importance of the subject, for example when it starts with εἰς τέλος, that is, 'towards an end,' which Jerome translates, from the true Hebrew text, as 'to the victor.'[16] Since everything else leads up to an end, and it is not possible to go beyond it, the reader is alerted by this heading to prepare his mind, by clearing and cleansing it, to receive some notable and flawless conception of the sublime. Sometimes a heading indicates the season, for example the headings 'for the wine-press' or 'on the fourth sabbath';[17] sometimes it mentions a historical incident, the basis for the allegory, such as 'Jeduthun, for the victory.'[18] Sometimes the names of persons are supplied, not to indicate the author, but to remind the reader of the historical circumstances, for instance when Absalom, Saul,

* * * * *

12 See n1 above.
13 This function of the heading, and the metaphor itself, were apparently found in Hebrew sources by Origen and repeated by Hilary and Jerome; cf PL 26 824A and note.
14 The following remarks on the musical and metrical form are inspired by Hilary *Prologus in librum psalmorum* 17–23 PL 9 243–6. Erasmus deals with these matters at greater length, though still following Hilary, at 81 below.
15 Cf for example Pss 64–67/65–68.
16 In his *Psalterium iuxta Hebraeos* (see Introduction xxi); the Hebrew expression in fact means 'Dedication.' Erasmus' interpretation is probably based on Hilary *Prologus in librum psalmorum* 18 PL 9 243–4.
17 For example Pss 8, 80, 83, and 93 in the Vulgate; the English versions often have very different headings, if any at all.
18 Pss 38/39, 61/62, and 76/77; Jeduthun was one of the chief musicians of David.

or Solomon figure in the heading. Sometimes the heading includes several
things at once, such as that of Psalm 51: 'Towards an end, the understanding
of David, after Doeg the Edomite came to him and then told Saul, and said
to him: "David has come to the house of Abimelech." '[19]

In addition, a number of psalms are ἀνεπίγραφοι, that is, preceded by
no heading to indicate the author, the season, the subject, the history, or the
form of the prophecy or poem. Hilary gives this ruling on them: whenever
we meet a psalm which does not bear the author's name in the heading, we
may ascribe it to the author whose name appeared in the previous heading,
and continue until we reach a later psalm bearing the name of a different
author.[20] I am not sure that this is a true or comprehensive rule, especially
since the name supplied sometimes refers to the subject, not to the author, as
I said a little earlier. Certainly it does not apply to the Second Psalm, since
the preceding psalm has no heading according to early interpreters, with
whom the true Hebrew text agrees. In a number of modern texts, however,
it is given the following heading: 'A song of David the prophet and king,'
despite the fact that Augustine declares that this one alone does not have
a heading.[21] This assertion is certainly far from true if it has one; and if it
has not, then it is not the only one. But, even though the psalm in question
here is not preceded by a heading, its author can lay claim to his own on the
evidence of Luke, who writes as follows in the Acts of the Apostles: 'Lord,
you are he who made heaven and earth and sea and all that are in them, who
through the mouth of our father David, your holy servant, said: "Why did
the nations rage?" '[22]

I do not think it right to try to avoid the problem, like Nicholas of Lyra,[23]
who makes excuses for Jerome by saying that, in a letter to Paulinus, Jerome
ascribed the First Psalm to David on the authority of Esdras, believing that

* * * * *

19 For example Pss 3, 17/18 and 71/72; Ps 51/52
20 *Prologus in librum psalmorum* 3 PL 9 234A
21 *In primum psalmum annotatio* PL 36 66; on the authenticity of this work, see n10
    above. Erasmus quotes the heading given to Ps 1 in Greek and translates it.
22 Acts 4:24–5
23 A Franciscan scholar (c 1270–1340) who, unusually, knew Hebrew and wrote
    a well-informed commentary on the entire Bible; it was the first commentary
    to be printed and was very popular in Erasmus' day. This remark, by which
    he tries to explain an apparent mistake by Jerome, and the following one on
    Augustine are made at the beginning of his *Postilla super psalterium*, which was
    often printed separately; see the edition of Paris (U. Gering 1483) sig a vi verso.
    Jerome's letter to Paulinus is Ep 53; in it Jerome states almost casually that
    'David' compared the righteous man to a tree in the First Psalm (PL 22 542).

the latter had written 'First Psalm' when in fact he had written 'the Book of Psalms, whose author is in part David'; but in my opinion the evidence of Luke is too strong to permit this evasion. I am still more puzzled as to why Lyra should have written that Augustine made the mistake of saying that all the psalms were written by David alone. In fact, in the commentaries which bear Augustine's name, the following words appear, which plainly refute Lyra's contention: 'Not all the psalms were pronounced by David, for David himself chose from among all the people four chief musicians, men purified by the Holy Spirit, named Asaph, Heman, Ethan, and Jeduthun,[24] so that if the divine spirit should enter any of them, he would sing a hymn to God. David therefore recited only nine psalms in his own voice; the rest were spoken by those four chief musicians, according to the wording of the headings.'[25] So far I have been quoting Augustine's own words. Should someone argue that Augustine says here that the psalms were 'pronounced,' that is, performed in public, rather than 'composed,' another doubt surfaces, as to whether the heading 'for David' refers to the author or the performer, especially since the name of the author should have been written in the genitive case, $\tau o \hat{v}$ $\Delta \alpha \beta \hat{\imath} \delta$. If this heading denotes the performer, then more than nine were written 'for David,' even in the Hebrew. If it denotes sometimes the author, sometimes the performer, this distinction requires investigation. Hilary suggests, and Augustine declares (in the *City of God*, book 17, chapter 14) that some commentators were of the opinion that whenever a name appeared in the genitive, for example $\tau o \hat{v}$ $\Delta \alpha \beta \hat{\imath} \delta$, that is, 'of David,' the author is meant; whenever it is $\tau \hat{\omega}$ $\Delta \alpha \beta \hat{\imath} \delta$, that is, 'for David,' it does not denote the author, but that the psalm contains some allusion to David.[26] But Psalm 109 refutes this view. Although its title reads 'for David,' in the Gospel Christ himself attributed its prophecy to David, in Matthew chapter 22: 'How then,' he says, 'can David, speaking in the spirit, call him Lord, saying: "The Lord has said to my Lord, sit at my right hand"?'[27]

In fact, Augustine had not asserted here what Lyra understands him to say. Augustine actually says: 'Almost all his prophecy is in psalms'; he had been talking about David's great skill in music, and his delight in the making of mystical and spiritual music, and he then added that 'almost all his prophecy is in psalms,' that is, in hymns set to music, whereas the rest

*****

24 *In primum psalmum annotatio* PL 36 65; see n10 above.
25 See 1 Chron 15:17 and 16:41.
26 Hilary *Prologus in librum psalmorum* 1 PL 9 233A and Augustine *De civitate Dei* 17.14 PL 41 547
27 Matt 22:43–4, quoting Ps 109/110:1

of the prophets produced their revelations in prose. A little later, Augustine says: 'Those who attribute all one hundred and fifty psalms to his hand seem to me to be more reliable judges.' In the first place, Augustine is repeating someone else's opinion, and someone who is the overall author of a book is not necessarily the author of each individual part. However, this too can be discussed more conveniently elsewhere. For the moment, I have mentioned all this only to establish that, among the oldest authorities, this psalm lacked any heading whatsoever, but that its author is conclusively revealed in the Acts of the Apostles. In the Gallican Psalter[28] it has the heading 'Towards an end; a psalm of David.' Whoever added 'Towards an end,' inspired by the content itself, was seeking to draw attention to the importance of the theme. Let us now say a few words about that.

In many psalms the theme is twofold: the historical, which underlies it like the foundations of a building, and the allegorical, or anagogical, which, beneath the cloak of historical events, conceals, or rather reveals, the gospel story, instruction in true piety, or an image of eternal bliss. There is almost no passage of Scripture which cannot be interpreted in the tropological sense.

To clarify this point, let me bring forward a single instructive example. The heading of Psalm 143 is 'For David against Goliath.' There can be no doubt that this psalm is a song of praise to God, with whose aid David, a defenceless and despised shepherd-boy, struck down with his slingshot that boastful giant Goliath, and cut off his head with his own sword.[29] But this historical sense does not in any way obstruct the allegorical; on the contrary, it ensures that the rays of mystical knowledge, as if caught in a mirror, shine all the more brightly and clearly before our mind's eye. Remember the story of how David, relying on heavenly aid alone, finished off his enemy, the Philistine who gloried in his own strength and spear, and by his unhoped-for victory freed his people from shame; you will surely see with greater clarity and satisfaction of mind how Christ, our David, overthrew the boastful prince of this world, and his uncircumcised people with him, not with the weapons of this world, but by a new method; and how by this unprecedented act he gave courage to his people, to whom he says in the Gospel: 'Be of good cheer, I have conquered the world.'[30] After feasting our eyes on this divine spectacle, we turn them inward, and realize that we must follow his example

* * * * *

28 St Jerome's revision of the Latin Psalter, so called because it was adopted first in Gaul, where an independent liturgy throve in the early centuries of the Christian era; see Introduction xxi.
29 Ps 143/144; cf 1 Sam 17.
30 John 16:33

and fight against the passions of this world, which struggle in our bodies against God's law.

Let us now see whether there lies beneath this psalm too a historical meaning on which the allegory may rest; the evidence of the apostle Paul and of Luke in the Acts of the Apostles confirms that the whole psalm is a prophecy of Christ.[31] These are Paul's words in chapter 13: 'And we give you the news that God has fulfilled to your sons the promise he made to our fathers, by raising Jesus from the dead, as indeed it was written in the First Psalm: "You are my son; this day I have begotten you."' Again, in chapter 4 of the same work, the congregation of Christians prays as follows: 'O Lord, who made heaven and earth, and all that is in them, you have said, through the Holy Spirit in the mouth of our father David, your servant: "Why did the nations rage and the peoples carry through their futile plots? The kings of the earth stood ready, and the leaders conspired together against the Lord and against his anointed." And indeed they did conspire together in the city against your holy child[32] Jesus, whom you anointed; Herod and Pontius Pilate, with the gentiles and the peoples of Israel, conspired to do what your hand and your counsel decreed should be done.' Paul says the same in his letter to the Hebrews, taking this psalm as evidence to prove that Christ is greater than the angels: 'Did God ever say to an angel: "You are my son; this day I have begotten you"?'[33]

It is therefore clear that this psalm is a prophecy of Christ, as indeed are many others, which are quoted by the apostles in various places as prophecies of the gospel story. Christ makes it even clearer in Luke's Gospel, in speaking of all the psalms: 'This is what I told you, while I was still among you: that everything must be fulfilled which is written of me in the law of Moses, in the prophets, and in the psalms.'[34] However, it cannot be established from the heading whether this psalm could apply, in the historical sense, to someone other than Christ. Rabbi Solomon[35] admits that it was usually interpreted by the old Hebrew scholars as referring to the King-Messiah, but none the less

* * * * *

31 Respectively Acts 13:32–3 and 4:24–7
32 *puerum*. In his note on Acts 4:27 (*vere in civitate ista*) *Annotationes in Novum Testamentum* LB VI 452–3, Erasmus discusses Valla's objection to this translation of παῖδα, with its suggestion of 'slave' as well as 'boy'; Erasmus replaces it in the *Novum Testamentum* by the less ambiguous *filium* 'son.' See also CWE 50 36 nn50 and 52 (pages 191–2).
33 Heb 1:5
34 Luke 24:44
35 An eleventh-century exegete of the Old Testament, quoted here by way of Nicholas of Lyra *Postilla super psalterium* (n23 above) sig a viii

he applies it to the story told in the Second Book of Samuel, chapter 5. King David had begun to rule the whole nation of Israel, and all the tribes had submitted of their own accord; he had been anointed once more, and had now decided to transfer his throne from Hebron to mount Zion, occupied at the time by the Jebusites. But his neighbours the Philistines organized a general conspiracy to eject him from his kingdom, afraid that he might become too powerful and one day might turn to destroy them. I do not disapprove entirely of looking at what Hebrew commentators have to say, especially the older ones, but I do not think that they have very much to offer, since I observe that their commentaries are pretty well stuffed with vapourings and old wives' tales, not to mention their desire to discredit our interpretations, and their hatred of Christ. So I shall not waste any time in considering how individual parts of the psalm may be applied to history; let us investigate instead the extent to which it applies to our David, that is, Jesus Christ, about whom it was unquestionably written.

In fact this one psalm embraces not merely a part of the gospel story, but the whole subject of the redemption of mankind: how the Son of God assumed a human body; how, overflowing with heavenly grace, he used the gospel teaching as a torch to dissipate the darkness of Moses' law, to lighten the yoke of ritual, to undermine the ungodly cults of the gentiles, and to overthrow the haughty pride of the philosophers; how he accomplished all this, not with the weapons of this world, but by a new and unprecedented application of that divine wisdom against which all mankind's ingenuity struggles in vain. The whole world conspired together to attack the gospel with all its might, but he turned all the scheming of Pharisees, high priests, kings, and princes into an ornament and a testimony of his victory, thwarting human cunning with heavenly wisdom, conquering godless violence by invincible gentleness, and by his death abolishing death's tyranny. In descending to hell, he opened up the kingdom of heaven, and in plumbing the depths of humiliation he rose to the heights of glory; and at the same time he showed us all the path by which we may overcome the prince of this world: distrustful of our own resources, we must rely entirely on Christ, as he relied entirely on the Father. Even princes and high priests,[36] whose influence towers above the rest, must fear to offend against Jesus Christ, the ruler of all, and must not dare to ignore his laws, ever mindful of the eternal judgment whose sentence no man, however humble, however mighty, can escape. So much for a summary of the theme.

* * * * *

36 Although echoing the list of Christ's own foes a few lines earlier, Erasmus' selection from it of *principes* and *pontifices* (which sometimes means 'popes') recalls the subjects of much of his contemporary satire and admonition.

Now, with Christ to inspire us, let us examine the individual verses, after saying a few words on the key to the psalm.[37] It often happens in passages of mystical writing, but particularly in the Psalms, that there is confusion over the identity of the speaker; and yet it is not unusual for the mystical meaning to depend on an awareness of his identity. St Jerome thinks that the first four verses (he divides both the first two verses into two because they contain an antiphonal pair) are spoken either by an angel or by the prophet, who asks in astonishment why humanity has risen up so recklessly against the Son of God; only the fifth verse [ie verse 3], 'Let us break their fetters etc,' should be attributed to the Father.[38] Hilary thinks differently, and attributes the first verses to God the Father as well. He was brought to this conclusion by the evidence of Luke, who seems to ascribe these words to the Father when he describes the congregation addressing God as follows: 'You have said, in the mouth of our father David, your holy servant, etc.'[39] Hilary adds the further argument that the fifth verse [ie verse 3] is separated from the first four by a diapsalm,[40] which seems to indicate a change of speaker; but he does not seem very convinced by this argument, adding that in the Hebrew texts no diapsalm is marked; and even if it were written down, it would not necessarily signify a change of speaker, because it sometimes indicates a change of rhythm. However, there was really no question in Acts of identifying the speaker of the prophecy, because anything the prophetic bards say, in whatever guise, may be considered an utterance of God spoken in their voices. Moreover, if these words are to be attributed to the Father, they are difficult to reconcile with the next phrase, 'Against the Lord, and against his anointed,' which would sound as if he were speaking of someone other than himself.

So on this point I disagree with Hilary, although I do not entirely concur with Jerome; what is the point of bringing in an imaginary angel here, when the whole discourse fits the prophet David like a glove?[41] Inspired by the heavenly Spirit, he could already perceive with his inner eye what was

* * * * *

37 See n13 above.
38 *Breviarium in psalmos* PL 26 825C–D
39 *Tractatus in 2 psalmum* 8 PL 9 266B, quoting Luke in Acts 4:25
40 See n39; but it is in his *Prologus in librum psalmorum* 23 PL 9 246B–C that Hilary suggests that *diapsalma* may be a musical notation. In the Septuagint text it stands for the Hebrew interjection *Selah*, which is generally thought to indicate a change of rhythm or perhaps a musical interlude.
41 *Adagia* I v 90: *Ad amussim*, literally 'according to the carpenter's rule'

done in Christ centuries later. Besides, the abrupt beginning of the speech is consistent with a visitation from the godhead, and the figure itself serves to emphasize his indignation. Could there be a more insane rage than this conspiracy between kings, leaders, and peoples to bring about the downfall of a man who had come to save them all? Moreover, he had come on a mission from God the Father, against whose design reckless humans struggle in vain. He had come, the man promised so often in the oracles of the prophets, the man promised to both peoples, Jews and gentiles, but especially to the Jews, the man foreshadowed so often and awaited so long. It could not be more clearly stated than in the worshippers' words: 'Come, O Lord, do not delay; relieve the sins of your people Israel.'[42]

He was the promised one, mild and gentle, generous to all, the saviour of all, freely taking upon himself the sins of all the world and lifting the harsh yoke of Moses' law; offering through evangelical faith and grace to the people of every nation, kings and commoners, scholars and simpletons, slaves and free men, the status of God's children and the bliss of life everlasting. Finally, it was not a judge or an avenger that was promised, but a redeemer, a liberator, a saviour. What is more loathsome than sin? He freely took it away. What is fairer, what is lovelier than innocence? He lavished it on us from his own treasury. What could be a greater honour than to be adopted into the company of God's children? No one is disqualified from the honour. What could be heavier than the unbearable yoke of Moses' law? He lifted it from our shoulders. What is sweeter than liberty? He conferred it on us. What is more desirable than heavenly immortality? He gives us an absolute guarantee of it. We had been promised someone so remarkable that all the nations of the earth should, by rights, have opened their arms to him, and when he arrived, he was all that had been promised. Wealth often creates envy; he neither had nor wanted riches. Power often causes hatred; he declared that he wanted nothing to do with the kingdoms of this world.[43] The least show of kindness can win men's gratitude; he spared no effort to help everyone, swiftly and without asking a reward: he fed the hungry, cured the sick, restored the crippled and the weak; he gave eyes to the blind, ears to the deaf, tongues to the dumb; and in his wholesome teaching, gently and patiently, he showed all men the path to eternal bliss.

Thus the prophet has every reason to be astonished that the gentiles should rebel, the peoples conspire, the kings rise, and the leaders take arms against a man like this, so full of loving kindness. They all conspire to destroy

* * * * *

42 A verse from the Gradual in the liturgy for the fourth Sunday in Advent
43 Cf Matt 4:8–10.

a single man, who had come, alone, to save them all; they unite to direct all their plots against him, who gave his whole being for them all. Why this frenzy? Why this mad conspiracy? because, of course, there was no common ground between the world and Christ. And so the world turned from him, as from a man summoning them to leave all that the stubborn children of that age held dear.

Did not that proud and godless world shudder at the very birth of Christ? As soon as it was known, by the Magi's sign, that the Messiah was born, and while it was still not much more than a rumour, what does Matthew's story tell us? that King Herod was much disturbed, and all Jerusalem with him. He summons the scribes, and asks where the Messiah is to be born; he asks the Magi at what hour they had seen the star, the sign which had summoned them; craftily, the king requests the Magi to produce the child; next he unleashes his fury on the blameless infants.[44]

Later, when Christ began to win fame by performing miracles, to dispel the shadows of the Pharisees' teaching with his heavenly doctrine, and to strike some tiny sparks, as it were, of his divine nature, how often did the people rage against him, running to pick up stones, or taking him to the brow of the hill to fling him headlong?[45] How often did the Pharisees, Sadducees, and Herodians attack him, trying to ensnare him by their captious questioning? How often did the Scribes and Pharisees hold clandestine meetings, plotting to lay hands on Jesus? – and they would have seized him, had they not feared the crowds. The Pharisees sent accomplices to attack him as he taught in the temple.[46] Soon afterwards the people were riven by dissent over him, some saying 'He is a good man,' and others the opposite; some claimed that he was one of the prophets, restored to life, while others supposed that he was the Messiah. Finally even Herod the Tetrarch, whose father had murdered the children at Bethlehem, and who was hostile to Jesus because of what rumour had told him, looked for a chance to kill him.[47] Now, when the ever-increasing malice and hatred of the Pharisees have suggested a sure method of killing Jesus, once more the Scribes, Pharisees, and elders of the people scurry into council. The influence of the high priests, Annas and Caiaphas, is brought to bear, and this unholy work is discussed in their holy temple. The governor's authority is made to minister to the ravings of the Jews, and a meeting takes place in

* * * * *

44 Matt 2:3–16
45 Cf John 8:59 and 10:31, Luke 4:29.
46 Cf Luke 20:19–20 and, on the Herodians, Matt 22:16.
47 See Mark 6:14–15 and Luke 9:7–9, 13:31, and 23:8–12; cf John 7:32–43.

his palace, which involves not merely Scribes and Pharisees, but the whole people.[48]

Since the gospel story so vividly describes for us these disturbances among all classes, these conspiracies, these meetings, it is fitting that the prophet's mind should be astonished when he foresees these events (which we can read about and believe, that is, we can see them with the eyes of faith), and thus he says: 'Why did the nations rage?' Some commentators apply this phrase particularly to the governor Pilate's guard, which, we read, gathered in the hall of the palace to make sport of the condemned Jesus.[49] They apply the next clause, 'and the peoples carry through their futile plots,' to the Jewish people, made up of people from various nations who had flocked to Jerusalem at that time for the religious festival. The governor's soldiers, unattached to any religion, made violent and stupid by their very way of life, lose all sense of discipline and 'rage,' using every kind of mockery to vent their fury on the Lord, the fountain-head of all glory. The Jews are 'carrying through futile plots' when, in their perverse enthusiasm for the Law, they vainly persecute the man whom the Law itself had promised and marked out: 'It is necessary,' it says, 'that one man should die for the people.'[50] They avoid defiling one festival,[51] but unwittingly create a new one. Similarly, Paul 'carried through futile plots' at the time when, in his zeal for the Law, he unleashed his fury against the Lord's disciples. Even today the Jews 'carry through futile plots' by clinging stubbornly to their circumcision, their sabbath, their ablutions and dietary restrictions, and by spurning the gospel teaching, through which they could truly win salvation.

Moreover, as if the people's fury were not enough to destroy one innocent man, there were present, more or less as the instigators of the disturbances, the 'kings of the earth,' meaning, presumably, Herod and Pilate; this is the view of the congregation in Luke's Acts of the Apostles.[52] Now this Herod was tetrarch of Galilee, as Matthew tells us in chapter 14;[53] moreover, St Jerome calls him a king in his commentary,[54] and Mark also

* * * * *

48 Cf Matt 27:1–25.

49 The word *gentes*, which I normally render 'nations,' can also mean 'gentiles,' which would give rise to the interpretation here, found in Hilary *Tractatus in 2 psalmum* 6 PL 9 265C. Pilate's soldiers appear in Matt 27:27, Mark 15:16, and John 19:2.

50 John 11:50 and 18:14

51 The Passover; cf Matt 26:5. The 'new festival' is of course Easter.

52 Acts 4:27

53 Matt 14:1

54 *Breviarium in psalmos* PL 26 825C

gives him the title of king in chapter 6.[55] Pilate of course was not a king, but the governor of Judea; but by virtue of his office he was Caesar, since he represented him in that province, and in fact the Jewish people, making their unholy clamour in the governor's palace, acknowledged Caesar as a king, shouting: 'We have no king but Caesar.'[56] Some commentators suggest that there is a hypallage of number here,[57] when they are called 'kings' although only one of them was in fact a king, but it would be a rather feeble figure to describe as kings everyone employed in the public service, especially since the psalm says 'kings of the earth.' No, the prophet's use of the plural is exactly right for a group whose numbers are in fact always on the increase; it describes not only those who condemned Christ at that particular time, but also those who, before Christ's coming, persecuted him in his prophets, those who later persecuted him in his apostles, and also the ones who today persecute him in those who preach the pure truth of the gospel.

'And the leaders conspired together' presumably refers to the Scribes and Pharisees, with the elders of the people. They were divided among themselves by sectarianism, and distrusted one another out of personal animosity (there is never harmony among the greedy, the proud, and the envious), but they united against Jesus and met together in the house of Caiaphas. Similarly, those 'kings,' Herod and Pilate, were previously at odds, but agreed on the death of the Lord, and thereafter struck up a friendship.[58] Such are the unholy alliances made by those who agree on nothing except attacking the innocent. Hilary remarks, in addition, that Herod and Pilate are described as 'the kings of the earth' because they used their earthly prerogatives to strike against a man proclaiming the kingdom of heaven. However, he says, the high priests, Scribes, Pharisees, and elders are called only 'leaders,' not 'leaders of the earth' or 'leaders of the priesthood,' because they had lost their temporal power when the government was transferred to Herod and Caesar, and they did not deserve the title 'leaders of the priesthood' or 'of the people' since they had hatched an impious plot against the source of all priesthood, the Lord Jesus.[59]

* * * * *

55 Mark 6:14; Matthew (14:9) also calls him a king.
56 John 19:15
57 See *In psalmum 1* 48 n230; Erasmus is using this rhetorical term rather loosely. Cicero *Orator* 27.93 says that hypallage is very close to synecdoche, which can certainly involve changes of number, according to both Quintilian 8.6.28 and Erasmus *De copia* CWE 24 341.
58 Cf Matt 26:3 and Luke 23:12.
59 *Tractatus in 2 psalmum* 8 PL 9 266A–B

While I admit that all this is cleverly argued, I am more satisfied with the simpler explanation that both parts of the verses refer to the same thing: 'Why did the nations rage?' refers to the people of Israel, and then the second clause, 'and the peoples carry through their futile plots,' echoes (as it were) and underlines the idea. Similarly, 'the kings of the earth stood ready' refers to Herod and Pilate, and then a similar phrase is tacked on to it: 'and the leaders conspired together.'

Anyone who thinks that I am making all this up myself should know, first of all, that Augustine perceives the same technique at work in the later verse, 'He who dwells in heaven will laugh at them, and the Lord will laugh them to scorn': 'The idea is repeated,' says Augustine, 'when the phrase "who dwells in heaven" is replaced by "Lord," and the phrase "will laugh at them" is replaced by "will laugh them to scorn." '[60] Second, it is well known that this technique is very common in the prophetic writings, when the idea conveyed in the first part of the verse is repeated in the second part in different words, or else is reinforced by a similar idea, or is answered by a contrasting one.[61] An example of the first type would be 'The righteous man utters words of wisdom,' which is followed by 'and his tongue speaks of justice.' The second type: 'The righteous man will flourish like a palm tree,' followed by the similar notion 'and he will spread like a cedar of Lebanon.' The third type: 'He has filled the hungry with good things,' which is underlined by the antithesis 'and has sent the rich away empty.'[62] Not only does the very frequent recurrence of this rhetorical device in the mystical hymns support my case, but also the authority of Luke, in whose book the congregation interprets the passage as follows: 'And indeed they did conspire together in the city against your holy child[63] Jesus, whom you anointed: Herod, and Pontius Pilate, and the people of Israel.'[64] Here the repetition 'the kings of the earth and the leaders' is reduced to a single statement about Herod and Pilate. Similarly, the repetition 'Why did the nations rage and the peoples carry through their futile plots?' is interpreted here simply as a reference to the 'people of Israel,' which includes the high priests, Pharisees, Scribes, and elders.

It must have been a truly terrible conspiracy, conceived in such a ferment of violence and with such unanimity by princes and peoples, pooling

* * * * *

60 *Enarratio in psalmum* 2 PL 36 70
61 Cf the similar discussion in the exposition of Ps 1 55–6 above.
62 The examples are taken from Pss 36/37:30, 91/92:12, and 106/107:9 (quoted in Luke 1:53).
63 *puerum*. See n32 above.
64 Acts 4:27

all their ideas, all their wealth and strength, all their influence and power, all the cunning and duplicity they could muster – against a single man. Had it been done against some mighty enemy of the state, there would be no cause for wonder or indignation. But let us just see how vile and how demented this conspiracy really was: the nations flock together, the peoples hatch their plots, the kings stand ready, the leaders conspire – against whom? What impiety! 'Against the Lord, and against the Lord's anointed.' The kings, however mighty or rich, the leaders, however great their power, the whole human race, however numerous: what are they all but transient, insubstantial creatures when compared to God, who is eternal, without beginning and without end, who with a nod has made and governs all things in heaven and on earth, and who can also, if it pleases him, destroy all things with a nod. It is madness for these weaklings to conspire against the Omnipotent, but it is also a mark of ingratitude and impiety to conspire against a being to whose goodness they owe their very existence, their lives, their thoughts, and all their powers of body and mind. Even if he had shown them no fresh kindness, had they not already plumbed the depths of ingratitude? But then God saw that all humanity was held in bondage, as wretched as it was degrading, by the devil, and walked in the darkest shadows of ignorance, worshipping idols, worshipping infamy, rushing headlong towards eternal doom; in his compassion for us, he sent his only Son, not armed with weapons and inspiring dread, but anointed with grace and inspiring love by his goodness and gentleness; his death was to reconcile us to him, his teaching was to lighten our darkness, his guidance was to reveal the path to immortal life. And yet, in their blindness, or rather their impiety, the princes and the peoples conspired against him!

You will notice, reader, that the technique I have just explained is also used in this verse: 'against the Lord' refers to the Father; 'against his anointed' relates to the Son. 'The Father was in the Son,' as the apostle Paul writes, 'reconciling the world to himself.'[65] Thus, if you oppose the Son, you oppose the Father too; if you acknowledge the Father, you must also acknowledge the Son. But the devil was in the princes and the peoples of the world, waging his hopeless war against God's plan. It is nothing new for the devil to rebel against his God, since, as soon as he was made, he raised a revolt against him. He fought the battle in person in heaven, and continued it afterwards on earth through his limbs. They are the 'kings of the earth,' and they relish only the things of earth; the things of heaven they detest.

*****

65 2 Cor 5:19

The word rendered 'Christ' in Greek, and 'anointed' in Latin, is 'Messiah' in the Hebrew, the name which the Jews reserved to designate that peerless prophet who was predicted and promised by the other prophets as the salvation of all the nations. Among the Hebrews, anointing was not only for kings, but also for priests, just as today it is given to all Christians, whom Peter calls 'a royal priesthood,'[66] because through our Messiah we have been adopted and share the rights and the fellowship of God's children.[67]

The word 'anointed' befits Christ in three different ways. First, as a priest, since he was that matchless priest after the order of Melchizedek,[68] who by the sacrifice of his sacred body soothed the Father's anger against us, and who with his most holy blood washed away all the sins of those who believe in him. Second, as a king: 'To me is given,' he says, 'all power in heaven and on earth.'[69] He was undoubtedly the promised Holy of Holies,[70] who abolished the Jews' powers of anointing, since they now possess neither priesthood nor kingdom. Third, the term 'anointed' befits him because of the full store of divine grace which 'dwelt in him bodily,' as the apostle Paul says.[71] John the Evangelist also testifies to this: 'Whose glory we saw, full of grace and truth ... from whose full store we have all received [grace].'[72] He is the anointed one of whom the Spirit speaks in the psalm: 'Grace is poured into your lips ... for God, your God, has anointed you above your fellows with oil, the token of joy.'[73] One day he shall come to 'judge the living and the dead,'[74] 'in the glory of his Father, with legions of angels,'[75] awesome not only to the impious, but even to the righteous, on that fearsome day when the heavens shall be moved and 'it will be hard for the righteous man to be saved,' as the apostle Peter writes,[76] and least of all will the sinner be able to stand up. But in the meantime the Lord's anointed came, mild, kindly, understanding, generous, friendly, gentle, a saviour not an avenger, a mediator not a judge, ready to serve all without exception, although he seemed more willing to welcome the humble. Isaiah

* * * * *

66 1 Pet 2:9
67 Cf for example Rom 8:15, Gal 4:5.
68 Ps 109/110:4; and for the argument here, cf Heb 5:1–10 and chapter 7 passim.
69 Matt 28:18
70 See Hebrews 9 for the argument here.
71 Col 2:9
72 John 1:14–16
73 Ps 44/45:2 and 7
74 2 Tim 4:1; cf Acts 10:42.
75 Matt 16:27
76 1 Pet 4:18

first made the prophecy which Christ quotes in Luke, saying that the oracle concerns himself: 'The Spirit of the Lord is upon me, because he has anointed me. He sent me to preach the gospel to the poor, to heal the contrite of heart, to proclaim deliverance to prisoners and new sight to the blind, to set free those that are brought low, to announce the year of the Lord's favour and the day of retribution.'[77] Who would not love a Christ of this kind? Who would not welcome, embrace, and kiss him at his arrival? And yet the world turned its back on just such a man; the blind fled from the light, the slaves from their redeemer, the sick from the physician, the dead from life.

It should also be noted that the prophet, in naming the Father, called him simply 'Lord,' to show that he is the Lord of all, whereas he qualified 'kings' with 'of the earth'; but he did not simply call the Son 'Christ' but 'his Christ,' intending no doubt to emphasize his status as the only being to have been specially anointed by God. This world too has its anointed, kings and priests; many of them are anointed outwardly, but their hearts are untouched by the oil. Men anoint the head, then the shoulder, the breastbone, and the chest, right down to the navel even, but it is futile for one man to anoint another's body unless the heavenly Spirit has anointed his heart. Thus we often see princes who have been anointed time and again, but who are none the less intolerable to the people in their cruelty, ambition, and greed.

God has his anointed, whom he does not wish to be harmed by those whom the world has anointed. These are his words in Asaph's song: 'He allowed no man to speak ill of them, but admonished kings for their sake: "Do not touch my anointed, and do my prophets no harm." '[78] Anyone whose heart is illumined by the light of faith, believing things not seen, hoping for things which are not in evidence,[79] is a prophet, and has been anointed. The apostle John states this in his letter: 'You have an anointing from the holy one, and know all things.'[80] But just as this anointing is given to us freely by God's goodness, so, all too often, it is lost by our own wickedness. Therefore he adds later: 'Be sure that the anointing which you have received from him remains with you.'[81] Again, Paul, writing to the Corinthians, teaches that this anointing does not touch us all in the same way or in equal measure, but that it is distributed to different people in different ways, in proportion to their

* * * * *

77 Isa 61:1–2 and Luke 4:18–19
78 1 Chron 16:21–2; cf Ps 104 / 105:14–15.
79 Cf Heb 11:1, the classic Pauline definition of faith.
80 1 John 2:20
81 1 John 2:27, an admonition in the Vulgate, but not in the English versions

faith.[82] Jesus, however, is described as the Lord's anointed in a unique way, and he alone bears the name of Christ among us, because God did not imbue him merely with a few drops of grace, but poured out as much on him as has ever been, or ever could be, bestowed on the rest of humanity. 'Christ' is a title pertaining to his human nature; he is called 'the anointed' only in so far as he was a man. By a similar distinction we too are called the children of God, but since he was, in a unique way, the Son of God, the Father's voice gave appropriate expression to this fact: 'This is my beloved Son, in whom I am well pleased.'[83] At that moment the shape of a dove appeared, alighting on his sacred head, proving to all that this was the true Messiah, whom God had anointed with all the fullness of his grace, and from whose full store we might all receive it. The full store of divine grace dwelling bodily in him is inexhaustible.[84]

For all these reasons, is not the prophet justifiably astonished to see the kings and peoples strain every nerve to concert their plans against the omnipotent God, against whom no power and no plan can succeed, and against his Christ, whose enemy is also the Father's? None the less, the Old Testament more than once predicts in prophecies and foretells in images the frenzy which was to break out in the world against Christ. Here is Christ himself, in the person of Jeremiah, speaking to the Father through the prophet's lips: 'But you, Lord, have shown it to me, and I did not realize it. You showed me their plans and I, like a lamb carried unresisting to the slaughter, did not know what plots they hatched against me: "Let us mix wood with his bread, and let his name be remembered no more."' He speaks of plans, he speaks of plots, a word implying unanimous approval among the conspirators; he even speaks of the manner of his death: 'Let us mix wood with his bread' – let us fix his body upon a cross.[85] It is further revealed here that the apostles will be persecuted to prevent them preaching his name; this is conveyed by the words: 'Let his name be remembered no more.'

* * * * *

82 1 Cor 12:1–11
83 Matt 3:17, Mark 1:10–11, and Luke 3:22
84 There are echoes here of both John 1:16 and Col 2:9.
85 Jer 11:18–19; most versions omit the negative in the first sentence. The phrase here translated 'let us mix wood with his bread' is an obscure one, meaning in Hebrew 'let us destroy the stalk with his bread' (Authorized Version marginal note), but translated in the English versions by references to trees and their fruit or sap. As Erasmus had pointed out in his exposition of Ps 1 (33 above), *lignum* 'wood' was a frequent synecdoche for tree, whence the association with the cross here; bread is a common symbol for physical life.

Another example: when we read chapter 2 of the Book of Wisdom,[86] do we not seem to hear the Pharisees, the Scribes, Annas, Caiaphas, the philosophers, in short, all those who are in love with this world, conspiring against Christ? 'Let us encircle the righteous man,' they say, 'since he is harmful to us, opposing our works, accusing us of formalism, and pointing out in public the faults in our teaching. He claims to know God, he calls himself the Son of God. He has become a living reproach to all our ideas, and the very sight of him is too much for us to bear, because his life is so different and his ways are not ours; he regards us as so much dross. He avoids our ways as if they were unclean and proclaims the final justification of the righteous; he even boasts that God is his Father.' And then: 'Let us condemn him to the most ignominious death.'

The world's conspiracy against the Lord Jesus had already been rehearsed, long before, in that prophetic symbol, the brothers' conspiracy against Joseph, related in chapter 36 of Genesis: 'They saw him in the distance, and before he reached them they made a plan to kill him, saying to one another: "Here comes the dreamer; come, let us kill him and throw him into this disused pit. We can say that a wild animal devoured him." '[87] The brothers accused him of terrible crimes, and the Pharisees charged Christ with blasphemy, saying that he had made a pact with Beelzebub the prince of demons.[88] Joseph's brothers were divided in counsel,[89] but united in evildoing; similarly, some of the Pharisees said: 'Not on the feast-day, or there may be rioting among the people,' and 'Let us deliver him to Pilate, so that we do not appear responsible for his murder.'[90]

The Lord Jesus himself admirably described this conspiracy against him in the Gospel parable in which the tenants ill-treated the servants sent to them one after another, and even killed some of them; finally they conspired against the son as well, saying: 'This is the heir; come, let us kill him, and the inheritance will be ours!'[91] Again, in another parable, the conspirators sent a deputation after him, saying: 'We do not want this man to reign over us.'[92] But all these efforts merely served to illustrate the wisdom and goodness of the divine plan, and showed that the plotters were worthy of their doom, since

* * * * *

86 Wisd 2:12–16 and 20
87 In fact Gen 37:18–20
88 Cf Matt 12:24, Mark 3:22, and Luke 11:15.
89 Cf Gen 37:21 and 26 (Reuben and Judah).
90 Cf Matt 26:5 and Mark 14:2.
91 Matt 21:33–9
92 See Luke 19:14.

they had conspired so obstinately against the source of all salvation. But, dear brothers, if we are truly the limbs of Christ, let us not dabble in such impious schemes, but embrace the Lord's anointed with heartfelt devotion and say with the prophet David, cursing, or rather pitying, the stubborn blindness of the Jews: 'Why did the nations rage, and the peoples carry through their futile plots? The kings of the earth stood ready, and the leaders conspired together against the Lord and against his anointed.'

However, we may also cry aloud, with all Christ's disciples: 'Let us break their fetters, let us throw off their yoke from us.' The patristic writers do not really agree on the identity of the speaker in this verse. Tertullian, who was unquestionably a great authority on the Holy Scriptures, repeatedly cites this verse as referring to those Jews and gentiles who became believers and, re-joicing in the freedom of the gospel, kept trying to shake off the burden of the Law.[93] Arnobius supports him: 'The nations,' he says, 'rage against Christ be-cause he put an end to idolatry . . . The peoples, that is, the Jews, carry through futile plots in their meticulous attention to dietary restrictions and the sabbath festival: the fetters of both need to be broken.'[94] Hilary's view is little different from theirs:[95] he applies these words to the apostles, who 'broke the fetters' of the gentiles, shackled by their sins, when they sprinkled them with water and set them free once and for all, through faith in Christ and the grace of the gospel, from all their past misdeeds; they 'threw off the yoke' of the Jews when they taught that the rituals of Moses' law are to be ignored: circumcision, the sabbath, the new moon festivals, ablutions, dietary restrictions, sacrifices, and all the rest which, as Peter says in the Acts, they could not bear themselves, and neither could their fathers;[96] all these things were like a darkness which had to be dissipated by the coruscating light of the gospel. Again, Jerome does not disagree substantially:[97] he considers that these words are spoken by the Lord Jesus, insisting that all the gentile peoples who believed that they were sprung from the Jews should break the fetters of formalism, throw off the heavy bur-den of the Law, and follow him, since his 'yoke is easy and his burden is light.'[98]

Only Augustine mentions a different view, though in such a way that it seems to be his own:[99] he thinks that this verse may be more aptly applied to

* * * * *

93 *Adversus Marcionem* 1.21, 3.22, 5.3, and 5.4 PL 2 269–70, 352, 474, and 478
94 *Commentarii in psalmos* PL 53 329B–C
95 *Tractatus in 2 psalmum* 9 PL 9 266C–267A
96 Cf Acts 15:10.
97 *Breviarium in psalmos* PL 26 825D
98 Matt 11:30
99 *Enarratio in psalmum 2* PL 36 70

those whom the prophet has just described as raging and making futile plots, because this is the language of impiety, corresponding to their thoughts: 'Let us break their fetters and throw off their yoke from us'; we should understand, he says, that they are like people saying to God: 'Go away, we do not want to know your ways!'[100] Their prototypes are the Gadarenes, who asked Christ to leave their shores,[101] and the people in the parable who said: 'We do not want this man to reign over us.'[102] The world refuses the gospel's yoke, preferring to bear the devil's ruthless yoke rather than submit to the gentle yoke of God and his anointed. Cassiodorus follows only this interpretation,[103] although Augustine places it in front of others in such a way that he does not disallow different ones.

For me, the most satisfying interpretation is the only one which obviously found favour with all the earliest commentators. It is clear enough from Old Testament history that the Hebrews were a rebellious and stiff-necked people, and as a result an onerous and inflexible law was imposed on them; since they were incapable of filial obedience to God's commandments, they were, like wayward slaves, to be forced to refrain from wrongdoing and compelled to do their duty by the harshness of the Law, by shackles and the yoke, as it were. Hence circumcision, dietary restrictions, the observance of the new moon, ablutions, fasting, formal prayers, and sacrifices; they could not turn round without encountering a statute of the Law, which fenced them in, as it were, and prevented them from living according to their own judgment. That is why Paul calls this law a law 'of slavery.'[104] And some orthodox writers relate to this the words of Ezekiel, chapter 20: 'And I gave them statutes that were not good statutes, and laws by which they could not win life.'[105] He calls it a harsh yoke of slavery, not a good one.

Someone may ask why, if God knew that the people would not observe his law, he burdened them with so many statutes and observances. No doubt, as Paul[106] says, the Law was intended to show them that they were sick, so that, once they realized their sinfulness, they would begin to desire a cure. Moreover, if you read the Acts of the Apostles and the Pauline Epistles, you will quickly discover how earnestly those Jews who had embraced the

* * * * *

100 Job 21:14
101 Cf Matt 8:34, Mark 5:17, and Luke 8:37.
102 Luke 19:14
103 *Expositio in psalmum secundum* PL 70 37B
104 Cf Gal 5:1, for example, 'the yoke of slavery.'
105 Ezek 20:25
106 Cf Rom 3:20 and 7:7.

gospel's teaching tried to impose this burden, not only on those whom Christ
had released from Judaism, but even on the gentiles, who had been exempt
from the impositions of Moses' law. This was widely practised by the 'false
apostles,'[107] who intertwined Christ and the Law, as if he alone were not
enough to bring salvation to all. First, they forced the Romans into Judaism;
they forced the Galatians back to it.[108] They sought to impose this yoke of
slavery on all the rest, who had believed in Christ as the source of freedom,
by ordering them to be circumcised (in order to triumph over their flesh),
and saying: 'Taste not, touch not, handle not!'[109]

Paul, that doughty defender of evangelical liberty, opposed them strenuously at every opportunity; he was not afraid to stand up even to Peter
in person,[110] because he considered that certain gentile converts to Christianity were being endangered by his example. To cut a long story short,
some Jews were so tenacious in their constant efforts to impose the yoke of
Moses' law on the gentiles that a meeting, crowded with both peoples, was
held to discuss this very question, at which Peter and James were among
the leading speakers. But there were certain sects of Pharisees whose principal aim was to continue this tradition, a faction apparently still more su-
perstitiously attached to the Law, for we read in the Acts of the Apostles,
chapter 15: 'But some of the Pharisee party who had become believers stood
up and said: "It is essential that they be circumcised, and above all that
they keep Moses' law." '[111] Presumably these were the same men mentioned
a little earlier: 'And certain men came down from Judaea and taught the
brothers that anyone not circumcised in accordance with Mosaic practice
could not be saved. This caused fierce dissension between them and Paul
and Barnabas, and so it was decided that Paul and Barnabas and some of
their opponents should go up to Jerusalem to discuss this problem with the
apostles and elders.'[112] There, Peter addressed them as follows: 'Brothers,
you know that in the early days God chose among us and decided that it
should be through my mouth that the gentiles should hear and believe the
word of the gospel. And God, who knows men's hearts, showed his approval of them by giving the Holy Spirit to them, as he did to us, and made
no distinction between them and us, purifying their hearts by faith. Why,

* * * * *

107 Cf 2 Cor 11:13.
108 Rom 2:17–29 and Gal 2–5
109 Col 2:21; on circumcision, cf Acts 15:1.
110 Gal 2:11
111 Acts 15:5
112 Acts 15:1–3

then, do you now challenge God by imposing on the necks of his followers the yoke which neither we nor our fathers could bear? On the contrary,
we believe that we are saved by the grace of our Lord Jesus Christ, and
so are they.'[113] When we listen to Peter's words, 'Why do you now challenge God by imposing a yoke, etc,' do they not convey clearly enough all
that disgust with Mosaic slavery which also seems to be felt by those who
say in the psalm: 'Let us break their fetters and throw off their yoke from
us'? James' speech, which followed, was not very different: 'My judgment
therefore is that we should not harass those of the gentiles who are turning
to God.'[114]

Furthermore, it was foretold (as the apostle Paul tells us) that when the
Jews had been rejected for their refusal to believe, the gentiles would be
received into the grace of the gospel, and it was also foretold that the carnal
rituals of the Law would be replaced by a spiritual pursuit of holiness, that
circumcision of the body would be replaced by circumcision of the heart.[115]
These are the Lord's words in Jeremiah: 'Break up your fallow ground, do
not sow among thorns; circumcise yourselves to the Lord and take away the
foreskins of your hearts, O men of Judah and dwellers in Jerusalem.'[116] He
also spoke of what the prophet calls 'fallow ground' in the Gospel, when he
said that new wine must not be put in old bottles.[117] Paul agrees with both,
saying that a man is not a Jew when a small piece of skin has been cut from
his body, but rather when his mind has been thoroughly purged of all the
gross passions which make war on the spirit.[118]

Already, in the time of Isaiah, God was displeased with all the old
rituals, the fasting, the sacrifices, the keeping of the sabbath, the feasts.[119]
Why was he displeased? Because they were all rituals of the flesh, and the
Father holds dear those worshippers who worship him in the spirit. God is
Spirit,[120] and he takes delight in spiritual worship. Human weakness made it
inevitable that the things of the flesh should take priority at first, but in such
a way that we should progress through the flesh towards the spirit. Why else
does the Lord say in Genesis: 'My Spirit shall not remain in man for ever'?

*****

113 Acts 15:7–11
114 Acts 15:19
115 Cf Rom 2 and 11, for example; the expression 'circumcision of the heart' occurs
     in Rom 2:29.
116 Jer 4:3–4
117 Matt 9:17, Mark 2:22, and Luke 5:37
118 Cf Rom 2:28–9.
119 Isa 1:13–14
120 John 4:24; the previous sentence echoes the preceding verse in John.

Why will it not remain? 'Because he is flesh,' he says.[121] God does not reject the substance of the flesh which he made, since he made nothing which was not good, but he detests the gross passions of the flesh.

In the course of its history, the world passed through a sort of universal childhood, so to speak, and its tutor then was Moses' law. Each of us, too, goes through a sort of childhood in Christ,[122] and the church thus has certain rituals of its own which cater for the weakness of youth until, growing up in the faith and charity of the gospel, we acquire sufficient strength. God tolerates the life of the flesh for a while, if it is gradually dissolved into the spirit, but he does not tolerate it for ever. Perpetual childhood is unnatural. We take delight in our own children's tender years, and lavish loving care upon them, but we would be horrified by such a 'prodigy' as a thirty-year old child! For as long as reason does not assert its power in us, we are little different from the beasts, and as long as we are in that state, we deserve to be treated like brute beasts. Oxen are led by the rope, bulls are controlled by the yoke, horses and mules are guided by the reins, asses are led by the halter, bullocks are led by the nose; since they do not change their nature, and are born to serve, they are burdened with the yoke for ever. But the yoke is applied to human beings only temporarily, until the power of reason unfolds itself, until the flame of gospel love shines in them.

Christ foretold, through his prophets, that the light of the gospel would banish the darkness of Moses' law,[123] and that the freedom and grace of the gospel would necessarily lift the yoke of petty carnal observances; none the less, in order to win over all kinds of men, he himself did indeed observe the statutes of the Law. At the same time, he did hint that the Law should sometimes be dispensed with: for example, on more than one occasion he performed acts of healing on the sabbath,[124] he defended his disciples against the Pharisees' accusation that they had plucked ears of corn on the sabbath and publicly proclaimed that the Son of Man is Lord even over the sabbath;[125] he told them to go and learn the meaning of the words 'I require mercy, not sacrifices,'[126] and he condemned over-zealous adherence to those ephemeral

* * * * *

121 Gen 6:3; a variant in the 1525 Basel edition reads 'in those men,' but the original reading is that found in the Vulgate and, for example, the New English Bible.
122 Cf 1 Cor 3:1 and Heb 5:12–14.
123 Cf Isa 9:2 and Matt 4:16.
124 Eg Luke 6:10, 13:12 and 14:4
125 Matt 12:1–8, Mark 2:23–8, and Luke 6:1–5
126 Hos 6:6, quoted in Matt 9:13; see also Matt 12:7.

institutions, intended as mere shadows of spiritual truth, which were used as an excuse for neglecting everything which is for ever holy by its very nature.

The apostles made the most of this freedom; following their teacher's example over the plucking of the corn, they ignored the sabbath and refused to fast (Christ himself having spoken in their defence on this matter), they dared to sit at table with tax-gatherers and sinners,[127] and they ignored the Pharisees' footling rules, which Christ also condemned,[128] about the washing of pots and copper bowls, about washing the hands before eating, and washing the whole body on returning from the marketplace. Of course they were still untutored, still permeated by Judaism, so that Christ called them νήπιους 'babes';[129] but like the bridegroom's friends[130] they made merry, so to speak, whenever they had a taste of gospel freedom. This was the cause of all the Pharisees' rage, the reason why they flocked to the wicked council held by Annas and Caiaphas.[131]

Jesus' disciples did not yet dare, however, to proclaim openly the gospel message 'Let us break their fetters and throw off their yoke from us.' They had not yet been visited by the fiery Spirit which would shatter all those petty, futile, and superstitious observances, the sabbath, the new moon, the ablutions, the fasting, the special food, the distinction between clean and unclean. They became more daring when intoxicated by the new wine of heaven.[132] Once Peter had learned that nothing which God has made holy can be called profane, that God is no respecter of persons, and that all are considered equal in the gospel faith, he was not afraid to meet Cornelius, he was not afraid to lift the entire burden of the Law from the gentiles' shoulders, he was not afraid, finally, to eat whatever food he liked, listening quietly to Paul's advice and acting upon it.[133]

In all his sermons, in all his letters, what is Paul, the foremost herald of Christ, proclaiming, if not that we should 'break their fetters and throw off their yoke from us'? And yet the leaders of the synagogue continued their storms of protest; see how often they stirred up riots against Paul, how

* * * * *

127 Cf Matt 9:10, Mark 2:15, and Luke 5:29.
128 Mark 7:1–4
129 Matt 11:25 and Luke 10:21; the Greek word means infants who cannot speak.
130 Cf Matt 9:15 and John 3:29.
131 Cf Matt 26:3.
132 Cf Acts 2:13, during the descent of the Spirit at Pentecost; on its importance for Erasmus, see Screech 72–4.
133 A résumé of Peter's vision and his reactions to it in Acts 10–11

often he was in danger of being torn apart by the Jews, had not the pagan judges, more equitable than the Jews, rescued him.[134] Moreover, no disease is more dangerous to true religion than over-enthusiasm for ritual, however convincing it may be in its show of religiosity. In short, the synagogue remained resolute in its plotting against the Lord's anointed, and had not Paul, in chains and in great peril of his life, cried out with still greater resolution: 'Let us break their fetters and throw off their yoke from us' – indeed, had he not continued to cry out the same thing even after his death – we would still be circumcised, we would still be burdened with the unforgiving yoke of Moses' law. Greece clung on fiercely to the teaching of Paul, her own son, and was thus always less susceptible to Judaism. For the rest, Augustine complains, many years after Paul's time, that among certain people the influence of the Jews was more powerful than that of the Christians, and that Jewish superstitions had been established so strongly in Africa that drunkenness, adultery, and many other sins were considered a joke by people who thought it an unforgivable crime to touch the earth with the naked foot on the sabbath; all because Africa had been connected with the Hebrews by links of both language and race.[135]

Someone may ask what moved the Pharisees to fight so hard against gospel freedom and to defend a set of petty, futile, and unpleasant regulations. The gospel story provides a complete answer: they were spurred on by ambition, greed, and spite. The common people, in their ignorance, are dazzled by things which they can actually see, and are never more easily led, or rather misled, than by a false show of religion. The Pharisees wielded a particular kind of power; they laid down rules for the people and piled one burden on another simply to make the people more beholden to them; they were highly esteemed, they were considered demigods – and meanwhile they worshipped their bellies and looked to their private interests. A tyrant must make every effort to keep his people in ignorance and to repress any sign of spirit among them, and similarly the Pharisees had to ensure that the people persisted in their childishness, without an interruption which might move them to throw off their yoke. It is splendid, it is Christlike, to rule over free men – but it is also difficult. It is tyrannical – and all too easy – to rule over asses and dolts. This is why the high priests and the Pharisees fought to preserve their power: they were pursuing their personal interests – at the people's expense.

* * * * *

134 See for example Acts 21–6.
135 On the general theme, cf Augustine Ep 55 PL 33 221; for detailed references, see ASD V-2 119–121:721–6nn.

How I wish we could foresee an end to all this agitation against Christ! There has been no period, there will be no period, without its Pharisees, its Caiaphas, its Herod, its Pilate, its people led along by the fury of the Pharisees and princes. To rage against the gospel's message is to incite violence against Christ; to conspire against the heralds of the gospel's teaching is to conspire against Christ's apostles. The selfsame things which stirred up the Pharisees against Christ continue to rouse the world against the gospel message. Those who belong to the world hold dear the things of the world. They like to have the seat of honour at the feast, they like to stroll around showing off their robes and their phylacteries, they like to be greeted as Rabbi in the marketplace;[136] they enjoy their ease and live at the expense of others. They love riches, the pleasures of the flesh, and tyranny. And so they cannot endure the gospel message, since it challenges their desires and their deeds. Hence these outbursts of frenzy, arising first among the hypocritical Pharisees, but spreading rapidly, as they are joined by the other sects and by the high priests and elders. In the end, many of the people were also drawn into their frenzy, and the civil power, the governor, was pressed into support of a madness which had nothing to do with him. Then, having mustered all their forces, as it were, they hastened single-mindedly towards certain victory and Christ's destruction; the world is not so blind that it does not see that great strength is required to crush the truth.

What, meanwhile, of the powerless Christ? He is deserted, taken, bound, beaten, condemned, crucified; he dies and is buried. The Pharisees mock him: 'Let him come down from the cross now! He wanted to pull the temple down, did he? He saved others, but he cannot save himself!'[137] This, of course, is the world's voice, celebrating its victory over the gospel message. What, meanwhile, of Christ's tiny flock? They take flight, they seek refuge, they keep silence. And yet inwardly they never cease to say, with a groan: 'Let us break their fetters and throw off their yoke from us.' As I had begun to say, the pagans' yoke is the sin which binds them, as it bound the paralysed man to whom Jesus said: 'Your sins are forgiven you.'[138] The Pharisees' yoke consists of the heavy bundles of purely human rules and regulations which, as the gospel says, they make up and pile on others' shoulders, an intolerable burden which they will not raise a finger to lift themselves.[139]

* * * * *

136 An echo of Christ's sarcasms in the Gospels, particularly in Matt 23:5–7
137 Adapted from Matt 27:39–43 or Mark 15:29–32
138 Matt 9:2, Mark 2:5, and Luke 5:20
139 Matt 23:4

How can the disciples of Christ hope to escape these snares, these chains, this yoke when, powerless and without guile, they face a world which rages against them with such unanimity? Will they not be downhearted? Will they not throw off Christ's gentle yoke and offer their necks to the irksome yoke of the world? Of course not! But where are they to find solace? Where are they to find protection? Let them listen to their Lord: 'Be not afraid,' he says, 'little flock';[140] and again: 'Be of good cheer, for I have conquered the world.'[141] So much for solace: what of protection? Listen: 'He who dwells in heaven will laugh at them, and the Lord will laugh them to scorn.' So far from the princes of the earth winning a victory against Christ, they will win only scorn and mockery, instead of the expected triumph, from their mad agitation. But what will the little flock do in the meantime? Surely they must fight the world's violence with violence, and counter deceit by deceit, trickery by trickery, force by force? I think not: but what then will they do? In earnest prayer they will implore the aid of their Prince, who is in heaven, and, lifting up their eyes, their hands and their hearts, they will say with the congregation of apostles: 'Now, O Lord, mark their threats, and grant that your servants may speak your word with every confidence.'[142] Paul, though bound by the magistrates' chains, did not cease to cry out with pride: 'But the word of the Lord is not bound.'[143] The leaders of the world must not be provoked, as far as is possible, but the word of God must not be silenced. There will be some against whom we must shake the dust from our feet in protest,[144] but there will be others who will receive with gladness the message of the gospel, and will bear fruit, some thirtyfold, some sixtyfold, some a hundredfold.[145]

Now, before I venture further across this ocean of exposition, it will be useful to discuss a couple of small points beforehand: first, the identity of the speaker, and second, the figures of speech and style used in this passage. If the preceding verse, 'Let us break their fetters etc,' is spoken by Christ's disciples, it may well be asked who is speaking here: 'He who dwells in heaven will laugh at them etc.' Hilary seems to attribute these words to the prophet himself, comforting Christ's disciples and bolstering their courage

* * * * *

140 Luke 12:32
141 John 16:33
142 Acts 4:29
143 2 Tim 2:9
144 Cf Matt 10:14, Mark 6:11, Luke 9:5, and Acts 13:51.
145 Cf Matt 13:8 and Mark 4:8.

against the world's futile machinations.[146] But then there is a second problem: does the entire verse, which falls into two parts, refer to one Person, or does one part refer to the Father, and the other to the Son? Hilary suggests that here the same distinction between the Persons is maintained as in the earlier verse 'against the Lord, and against his Christ.' Just as Father and Son alike feel the affront, so they both have a part in avenging it; another proof that Father and Son share the same nature. Power and the exercise of power are shared by them: for example, 'the Father raises the dead and gives them life, just as the Son gives life to those he chooses,' and in this way they share the honour. 'For the Father judges no man, but has passed on each judgment to the Son, so that all shall honour the Son as he honoured his Father.' They also share the affront: 'To refuse honour to the Son is to refuse honour to the Father who sent him.'[147] Similarly, those who conspire against the Lord also conspire against his anointed.

Here too, in the same way, the one laughs at them, and the other laughs them to scorn. But there is still some doubt as to which part of the verse should be applied to which Person. In fact, when Hilary discusses this passage, his language is rather obscure, but he seems to apply the first part to God the Father, the second to the Son.[148] The psalm appears to him to designate the Father by the metonymy 'he who dwells in heaven'; not because the Son was not in heaven, since he is considered to have also been in heaven at the time that he walked the earth clothed in human form; but because, at the time to which this prophecy refers, the Son of God had descended to earth, assuming human nature, whereas this putting on of an assumed body is not appropriate to the Person of the Father. Moreover, the Father is never described as 'being sent,' but as the sender, whereas we read that the Son and the Holy Spirit *were* sent. In addition, students of Hebrew culture tell us that the phrase 'he who dwells in heaven' is one of the sacred names of God. Therefore the Father laughs, the Son laughs to scorn – but it is the same laughter, the same scorn.

As I said earlier, St Augustine does not think that any distinction between the Persons is intended but rather that the same idea is repeated, with no more than a change of wording,[149] which, as we noted earlier, is a

* * * * *

146 *Tractatus in 2 psalmum* 10–12 PL 9 267–8, which also uses the Trinitarian text from John 5 that Erasmus cites below
147 John 5:21–3, slightly adapted
148 Cf n146 above.
149 *Enarratio in psalmum* 2 PL 36 70; cf 86 above.

recurrent characteristic of the mystical writings. Now, although both these views are defensible, my opinion, for what it is worth, is that in this instance we should accept Augustine's conclusion.

So much for the Persons. Now, as promised, I shall discuss the imagery of the verse. In the Holy Scriptures, human emotions are frequently attributed to God: fury, anger, regret, joy, grief, pity, although none of these is appropriate to the divine nature, which is utterly immutable; none the less, following the tradition of the mystical Scriptures, words expressing the emotions which result from changes in *our* fortunes are applied to God.[150] For example, he is said to be angry whenever our crimes are punished by the infliction of some misfortune, and when the affliction is still more grievous he is said to be furious. He is said to show compassion whenever we enjoy more good fortune than we deserve or whenever, by some lightening of our misfortunes, we are urged to return to our right senses. He is said to be regretful whenever we live in such a way that we seem quite undeserving of his kindness and he must deprive us of his gifts which we are wasting. Thus either the causes or the effects of these passions are within ourselves, while God remains serene and unmoved; and since he is free from all the abstract emotions, physical feelings are still less applicable to him. God is Mind, and utterly undivided;[151] in no way can he be called body, unless you call body anything that subsists in its own nature. Moreover, when someone laughs at us he stretches his mouth wide open; the physiologists think that laughter is produced by movement of the spirits around the pericardium, which separates the heart from the lower organs, and they say that its origin is the spleen.[152] It is usually the result of joy, but sometimes of bitterness, when it is called sardonic laughter.[153] However, when someone 'laughs to

* * * * *

150 This subject is discussed in this context by both Hilary (cf n146) and Augustine (cf n149).

151 *simplicissimus*, a technical theological term defining God as the most uniquely and totally One, a uniquely undivided essence; see the elucidation of the term and its background in Erasmus' work and elsewhere in Screech 93–6. Cf also the exposition of Ps 1 43 above and the related n202.

152 Pliny *Naturalis historia* 11.205 reports the theory that laughter originates in the spleen, but it was a matter of great controversy, and others attributed it to the head, the heart, or the diaphragm. See for example Laurent Joubert *Traité du ris* (Paris 1579) 41–5 and 282–8 on the controversy in both the ancient and modern worlds; also M.A. Screech and Ruth Calder 'Some Renaissance Attitudes to Laughter' in *Humanism in France* ed A.H.T. Levi (Manchester 1970) 216–28. On the action of the spirits and the pericardium, cf Aristotle *De partibus animalium* 3.10 (673a) and Joubert 90–3.

153 *Adagia* III v 1

scorn,' he wrinkles his nose in mockery; the ancients particularly associated the nose with scorn.[154] These expressions are all quite inappropriate to God, since they are even considered unbecoming in the better sort of men, but the Holy Scriptures have adopted the language of human emotions in order to increase our understanding.

God is described as 'laughing' at the impious when their plans go wrong and when, in plotting the downfall of others, they fall into their own trap; the divine wisdom has a particular talent, so to speak, for dealing with the plots of evil men in such a way that their impiety is converted into greater glory for itself; the mischief which was intended for others is turned into ruin for its authors and success for the virtuous. For example, God's wisdom allowed Pharaoh to torment his people for a time, in order to make the redeemer's glory all the greater, and to make it clear to all that an impious king and his impious followers had perished by a just act of divine vengeance.[155] Thus he is in a sense playing a game when, in full awareness of what is happening, he allows impiety to go its wanton way until it entangles itself in the doom it deserves. Hence, of course, the words of the Virgin Mother's prayer: 'He has scattered the proud in the imagination of their hearts.'[156] Similarly, in another psalm we read: 'Behold, he gives birth to sin; he has conceived sorrow and produced iniquity.'[157] This refers to the conspirators' schemes; next we hear how he who dwells in heaven mocks them: 'He has made a pit and dug it deep, and he falls into the trap he has made. His mischief shall recoil upon himself, and his iniquity shall fall on his own head.'[158] You can hear a similar tone of mockery in Psalm 56: 'The sons of men have teeth which are spears and arrows, and their tongues are like sharp swords.' This refers to the conspirators as they rage and threaten. But, to make it clear that he who dwells in heaven transcends all human powers and ingenuity, the psalm continues: 'Be exalted, O God, above the heavens, and let your glory shine over all the earth.' Next, see how God's wisdom mocks their unholy enterprises: 'They have prepared a snare for my feet and they have bowed down my soul; they have dug a pit in my path but have fallen in it themselves.'[159] Similarly, Psalm 36: 'The sinner will keep close watch on

* * * * *

154 Cf *Adagia* I vi 81: *Odorari* 'Scenting out,' and especially the many examples in I viii 22: *Naso suspendere* 'To turn up the nose.'
155 See Exodus 1–5 and 14.
156 Luke 1:51
157 Ps 7:14
158 Ps 7:15–16, slightly adapted
159 Ps 56/57:4–6

the righteous, and will grind his teeth at the sight of him. But the Lord will laugh at the sinner, because he foresees that his time is drawing near.'[160] The eternal wisdom speaks out in similar vein in the Hebrew proverbs; there too the wicked are hatching plots and saying: 'Let us lie in wait to shed blood, let us conceal a snare for the helpless innocent, let us swallow him alive like a demon, and whole like a man going down to the pit.' But what reply do they get from the wisdom they scorn? 'I in my turn will laugh at your doom and will mock you when your fears are all realized and sudden calamity overwhelms you, when death descends on you like a whirlwind, and anguish and distress fall upon you. Then they will call my name, and I shall not answer; they will rise early, but they will not find me.'[161]

It is possible to find similar ideas in secular poetry as well. In Homer, Jupiter sends a baleful dream to make Agamemnon confident of taking Troy, when in fact he was preparing disaster and death for all the Greeks;[162] that is why the poet calls him ἀγκυλομῆτιν or 'crooked of counsel.'[163] Similarly, the Lord put a lying spirit in the mouth of his prophet to deceive those who refused to listen to the truthful spirit.[164] In the Gospel, too, the rich man is mocked when he decides to enlarge his storehouses and to live at ease on their contents; it is as if God were mocking him when he hears the words 'You fool, this night your soul is required of you; who will own your hoard now?'[165] Again, in his letter to Timothy, Paul reminds him of the delusive spirits by whom those who obstinately conspire against the true gospel spirit are led to perdition.[166] This is what Paul teaches elsewhere: 'God makes the wisdom of this world look foolish' and 'entangles the wise in their own cleverness,' giving them up to their own depraved reason, which makes them perform all kinds of immorality because, being blinded by pride, they preferred to worship the creature and not to acknowledge the creator; they receive a fitting reward for their errors.[167]

If we look at the gospel story in the light of this prophecy, it is easy to see how often, and in how many different ways, the Lord laughed from heaven and mocked the scheming of evil men. The very first is Herod,[168]

* * * * *

160 Ps 36/37:12–13
161 Prov 1:11–12, 26–8
162 *Iliad* 2.1–15
163 In fact the epithet applied by Homer to Kronos; *Iliad* 2.205 and 4.59
164 1 Kings 22:22–3 and 2 Chron 18:21–2
165 Luke 12:18–21
166 1 Tim 4:1
167 1 Cor 1:20, 1 Cor 3:19, and an adaptation of Rom 1:25–8
168 There follows a résumé of Matthew 2.

who, plotting to destroy the child, consults the Scribes, elicits from the Magi the time of the star's appearance, and urges them to seek out the child, pretending that he too will worship him if he is discovered. What is the result of this foxlike cunning? By consulting the Scribes, he confirms the truth of the prediction; they knew from prophecy that he would be born in Bethlehem, and he was born there. The Magi, who arrived in Jerusalem guided by a star, also have their story confirmed, and the report is given wider currency as a result of the prince's unease. The Magi are fired with enthusiasm by the king's show of piety, and they devoutly worship the child they sought, while the impious king is frustrated when the Magi, warned by an angel, return to their country a different way. Helpless with rage, Herod quickly discards the fox's skin and puts on the lion's:[169] with unconcealed fury he unleashes his frenzy against those whose age should inspire pity even in an enemy. His ruthless edict orders the murder of every male child under two years of age born in the Bethlehem district; he enlarges the area to avoid any mistake over the prophet's words, which said Bethlehem, but perhaps meant not the village itself but the countryside surrounding the village. He raises the age, and no one is spared, to prevent any finding an escape. And by all his actions he is showing that he too believes the prophecy, that he believes the Magi's story that Christ is already born – and once again his godless cunning is frustrated. The first martyrs for Christ are sanctified; Christ alone was sought, and Christ alone escapes; Herod's death-deserving cruelty is displayed to all mankind, and Egypt, which was then in the grip of a superstitious cult of demons, is sanctified as the cradle of its saviour.

Later, the eternal enemy of mankind's salvation, who plotted to destroy Christ by means of Herod, was frustrated again. He attempted various traps and trials, and, had he been able to extract the secrets of the divine plan with any certainty, he might have endangered the world's salvation; but he was beaten by Christ, and indeed by his own sword: he kept trying to use the words of Holy Scripture to outwit Christ, but he was always beaten back by those selfsame words. Finally he gave up, realizing that his quarry was quite unconquerable, but still not entirely sure that he was God, since he saw him hunger like a man.[170]

How often too did his followers cry out, in the mouths of the tormented: 'We know that you are the Son of God; you have come before your time

* * * * *

169 Cf Luke 13:32; *Adagia* III v 81 describes the more usual reverse process in a metaphor made famous by Machiavelli, but found first in Plutarch *Lysander* 7.4.
170 Cf Matt 4:1–11; the temptation in the wilderness is the basis for the whole paragraph.

to destroy us'?[171] However, although he did not reject recognition from the blind and from women, he would not accept it from impure spirits. Here then was the serpent, the most cunning creature on earth, who had once deceived old Adam by beguiling his wife; but all his wiles were frustrated by the new Adam, though he did not realize he was beaten until the very moment when he thought himself most assured of victory. But then, who could have expected that the road to everlasting glory lay through the ignominy of a wooden cross? Who would believe that a kingdom could be won by an execution, that life could be redeemed by death? Here then was that past master in trickery, repeatedly setting traps for Jesus through his instruments, the Pharisees and Scribes, the hunters who hoped to bring him down by their captious quibblings; but in fact all they did was to demonstrate their folly and spite, even to the untutored mob, and to enhance Christ's glory and strengthen his power.

They denigrate his miracles, saying that they were performed in the name of Beelzebub,[172] but their calumny is transformed into praise of God when Christ gives irrefutable proof that they could only be performed by God's power. The more they strive to lower his reputation among the people, the more they excite admiration for him, since on every occasion divine wisdom triumphs over the spurious wisdom of mankind. Sometimes they make covert allegations against him, but here too they are thwarted, when Jesus replies to their unspoken thoughts, or else frames his reply so as to strike a covert blow at their guilty consciences. Again, as he slips from the hands of those who would stone him, and escapes through the midst of the crowd who would throw him from the cliff,[173] are not the people's plots frustrated twice over? On the one hand, they are denied the power to do him harm, as they want to, and on the other it is proved to us that he sought death voluntarily on our behalf, since he chose to die, but in his own time, not theirs.

I will not weary the reader with every single example, but finally there was the plot, which the Jews considered so very crafty, to have Jesus killed with an appearance of due legal process, so that everyone would think him a criminal and a malefactor: how well it turned out for us, and how badly for them! In this case the plot is hatched in a packed meeting between Pharisees, Scribes, elders, and high priests. The people are brought in too, so that all may be aware of the fate of the sacred victim, who was to be sacrificed for the

*****

171 Cf Matt 8:29 (the Gadarenes possessed by devils); see also Luke 4:34.
172 Matt 12:24–8, Mark 3:22, and Luke 11:15
173 Cf John 8:59 and 10:31–9, and Luke 4:29.

salvation of the whole world. Cleverly, they decided not to have him killed on a feast-day,[174] but in fact their helpless rage was made to serve the divine plan, which had decreed from all eternity that the true paschal lamb should be sacrificed on the day of the Passover.

Money obtains the services of the disciple who is to betray his Lord, but when he throws down the coins at their feet and inflicts his own punishment upon himself, does he not give conclusive proof, even to them, of Christ's innocence? Moreover, they themselves decide, in a perverse display of religious zeal (for which they even summon another council), that the money is not to be put into the temple treasury, but will pay for a field for the burial of paupers and foreigners, whose very name[175] testifies that an innocent life has been sold for the price; in all this, are they not themselves giving spontaneous testimony of their spite and of Christ's innocence?

False witnesses are bribed to accuse him before that impious high priest Caiaphas, and yet even in such a court their evidence is rejected; does not their malice add lustre to the Saviour's peerless innocence, since not a single credible charge could be fabricated against him? When Caiaphas prophesies by virtue of his office, when he extracts a confession from the accused, when he tears his garments in the sight of all,[176] does he not give evident proof of the plan for redemption?[177] Did he not reinforce our faith, since we are now more certain than ever that Jesus is the Son of God who shall come one day with his angels to judge the living and the dead?[178] Did we not learn, from the tearing of his garments, that the priesthood of Moses was to be abolished?

The only result of the meeting was that, to avoid the odium of executing a man whom they knew to be innocent, they took him off to the governor, Pilate.[179] Moreover, this pagan, who did not know the Law and had never seen Christ perform miracles or heard him preach, made every effort to rescue an innocent man from the effects of their demented fury. He said that he found no crime in him worthy of death, and by invoking the custom of the feast-day and asking them to choose between him and Barabbas, a murderer

* * * * *

174 Cf Matt 26:5; the passage as a whole is a résumé of Matthew 26–7.
175 'The Field of Blood' or 'Blood Acre'; Matt 27:8
176 John 11:49–52 (Caiaphas' prophecy), Matt 26:59–65 and Mark 14:55–63 (false witnesses against Jesus, Caiaphas' interrogation of him, and Caiaphas' tearing his robe)
177 *consilium redemptionis*; the phrase could also mean 'the plan of bribery,' and Erasmus is perhaps playing on the double sense of *redemptio*.
178 Cf Acts 10:42, 2 Tim 4:1, and 1 Pet 4:5.
179 Erasmus' account of this episode is largely based on Luke 23, with some additions from Matthew 27.

and a rebel, he tried to help this Christ who was famous for his many good deeds; he brought him out after a flogging, hoping that this punishment would satisfy them and soften their anger. He was warned privately by his wife not to stain his hands with an innocent man's blood, but finally, after making every effort, he washed his hands and declared himself guiltless of Christ's blood.

Does not all this evidence, resulting from the meeting of the Jews, provide astonishing proof that Christ was considered innocent even by the gentiles? And then the Jews, unmoved by so many appeals, and as if driven to distraction, no longer troubled to conceal their madness, but cried out: 'Crucify him! Crucify him! His blood be on us and on our children!' and 'We have no king but Caesar';[180] did they not make it obvious to all that they deserved the destruction which, we find, was later visited upon their race? In condemning Jesus, Pilate absolved him, declaring first that he was not responsible, and then pronouncing the death sentence, not because he was convinced, but because of their fury. Anyone who argues against the sentence of the law is obviously proclaiming the innocence of the man he is condemning; and anyone who declares that he is not responsible is attacking those whose malice is destroying an innocent man. The evangelists did not overlook this point when they wrote: 'For Pilate knew that they had handed Jesus over out of malice.'[181] The Jews damned themselves in court, and brought divine retribution upon their own heads.

To continue: Christ was then taken to Herod,[182] which merely produced further evidence of his innocence. Herod sent him back disdainfully, but without condemning him, and disdained him for his silence rather than for his guilt, despite the many charges against him. We read that Jesus was warned by the disciples to beware, because Herod might seize the opportunity to kill him; but the king, despite his impiety and his hostility, recognized Christ's innocence. While he knew him only by reputation, he sought to kill him; after meeting him, he sent him away, from which we may conclude that purity of spirit radiated from the Lord's very face.

What of the scarlet mantle, the crown of thorns, the reed given him as a sceptre, the beating, the blows to the head, the spittle, the flogging, the insults, the jeering, the mockery, and all the other things with which Pilate's soldiers amused themselves at Jesus' expense, before the sentence

* * * * *

180 John 19:15
181 Matt 27:18 and Mark 15:10
182 The account of this episode is based on Luke 23; for Herod's earlier attitude see Luke 13:31.

was carried out? There can be no doubt that the Jews encouraged it all, and of course this wickedness of theirs also fulfilled the forecasts of the prophets,[183] who predicted it all, and drew the world's attention to the extraordinary meekness of our Christ. Similarly, the fact that they deliberately chose the most ignominious kind of death, that he was crucified between two criminals on a hill outside the city, that his hands and feet were pierced, that he was given vinegar to drink, that, as he hung on the cross, the most cruel taunts were flung at him, the fact, besides, that all this was arranged by the Jews, as if they were anxious that no part of the prophecies concerning Jesus should be overlooked: the more that all these facts reveal the insane and irremediable hatred of the Jews towards Christ, the more they increase the gratitude and love we feel for him in our hearts.

Who could have done more to strengthen belief in the resurrection than the Jews? They took such care to obtain an official guard from the governor and, not content with that, they sealed up the tomb to prevent any possibility of the disciples removing him in secret; finally, seeing that all their precautions were useless, and that the results were quite different, they followed their previous bribery of the disciple by using money to persuade the guards to tell lies, and gave them a large bribe, as the evangelist says, to say that the disciples had come and stolen Jesus' body while they were asleep.[184] Could they have been more stupid? The guards had already told everyone how they had been filled with terror by the glory of the angel, and that they had heard him speaking with the women; that they had seen the stone removed, although it had been sealed earlier and was too big to be moved by just a few men; but now they claim to have seen the disciples creep in and steal Jesus' body – while they were asleep! Could anyone have convinced the world of the true facts, had not the Pharisees' impious persistence provided so much evidence to confirm our beliefs?

Through all these machinations, did not 'he who dwells in heaven laugh' at the impious and their earthbound ragings, and did not the Lord 'laugh them to scorn'? They heaped shame upon him, and yet he lives in the glory of God the Father;[185] they thought him entirely obliterated, and yet he brought salvation to all nations; they believed him dead, yet he rose again and will live for evermore; they brought him lower than any man, made

* * * * *

183 For example Isa 50:6 and 53:5; this account of Christ's passion is based largely on Matthew 27 and Luke 23.
184 Matt 28:12–13
185 Cf Matt 16:27 and Mark 8:38.

him a worm, and an object of derision among the people,[186] and yet he is worshipped and adored throughout the world as God and man. The cross, once a sign of infamy, is the glory of princes and of all the faithful. At the name of Jesus, which they were planning to wipe out completely, every knee bends, and all the highest powers in heaven and earth bow down.[187]

What do you say now, unhappy Jew? Do you see how God has made all your plans miscarry? Do you see how your wickedness has fallen on your own head? Do you see that you have fallen into the pit which you dug?[188] Do you see that the temple is utterly destroyed, and not a trace of it remains, that your religion is virtually extinct, that nothing survives of your priesthood, law, principate, cities, tribes, holy places, nothing, in fact, but a few scattered exiles, witnesses to the old madness and to your downfall, and that these few are only preserved on the advice of Paul,[189] whom they persecuted so cruelly, and by the clemency of Christians, whom they hate so insanely. You are left, unhappy Jew, to enjoy the fruits of the innocent blood which you took upon your head and on your children's heads. You are left to enjoy the rule of Caesar, whom you preferred to Christ.[190] And despite all this, will you still not come to your senses and admit that you have been blind? Do you still seethe with hatred for the King of the Jews, whom we adore?

What have you to say, Satan, author and prime mover in their misfortunes? Do you not see that all your plots have been baffled by heaven? You had swallowed your prey, but you were forced to disgorge him. You were planning to destroy the human race, but you hastened its salvation. You were trying to make your tyranny secure, but you lost your kingdom. Do you recognize the wood, which you sent your servants to mix with his bread?[191] Do you recognize the triumphal symbol which strikes fear into your troops? Do you acknowledge the name of Jesus, at which the demons, the agents of your wickedness, leap up and flee? Now that the tables have been turned, may not the victor justifiably boast of your defeat: 'Death, where is your sting? Death, where is your victory?'[192] And when, even though beaten and laid low, you kicked against the victor, as you did when you goaded the Pharisees and the gentile kings into a frenzy against the martyrs, what was the

* * * * *

186 Cf Ps 21/22:6.
187 An adaptation of Phil 2:10
188 Ps 7:15–16
189 For example, in Romans 3
190 Cf Matt 27:25 and John 19:15.
191 Jer 11:18–19; on the symbolism, see n85 above.
192 1 Cor 15:55

result of the chains, the cells, the stones, the whips, the racks, the claws,[193] and the fires? What good were all those terrible torments, all those deaths? You merely strengthened faith in Christ; you established and spread the kingdom of Christ, and multiplied the torments of hell for yourself and your limbs. The name of the Lord Jesus Christ is famous throughout the earth, and we owe this, in part, to your stubborn and senseless behaviour; moreover, he who is in heaven laughs, every day, at your jealous plots; every day the Lord mocks your machinations, since he knows how to turn all your traps and tumult to the advantage of his people, and thus to add to the sum of eternal bliss.

Now, let us pursue our interpretation of the prophecy. The next words are 'Then he will speak to them in his wrath, and in his fury he will confound them.' First, we must recall here what I said earlier, that the divine nature cannot be disturbed by passions, and that such expressions as these refer, by synecdoche,[194] not to an actual stirring of the emotions, but to the effects normally produced in us when our spirit is perturbed or otherwise moved.[195] For example, whenever our blood boils up around the heart, we are roused to seek revenge, and thus it is quite usual for the divine eloquence to describe as wrath the just vengeance of God, by which he punishes the incorrigible, and as fury his more severe or final vengeance. Similarly, if someone takes advantage of our good nature, we are touched by regret, being sorry that our kindness was misplaced; God may thus be said to be sorry, not because something turns out contrary to his expectation, or inadvertently (as it might for a man lacking in foresight), since God has foreknowledge of everything before it happens, but because something has happened which will bring us sorrow.

It is not only in the Old Testament that punishment inflicted on sinners is called the wrath of God; in the New, these are the words of John the Baptist in the Gospel: 'Generation of vipers, who warned you to flee from the wrath that is to come?'[196] And Paul, to the Romans: 'For the wrath of God is revealed from heaven.'[197] He also describes as 'the day of wrath' that final

* * * * *

193 An instrument of torture, like a large pair of pincers, used on Christian martyrs; see the illustration in PL 60 7 (tabula XIII).
194 Normally meaning the use of a part for the whole, or the whole for a part, but given a broad range of metaphorical applications by Erasmus in *De copia*; cf n57 above.
195 Cf 102 and n150 above.
196 Matt 3:7
197 Rom 1:18

season when every man shall be paid for what he has done,[198] whereas for the moment it is the season of mercy.

Now the word which the Latin translator renders as *furor* [fury] is not the Greek μανία, which describes people who are ill and not in their right mind (though according to the principles of the philosophers wrath is nothing other than a brief madness),[199] but θυμός, which in Greek sometimes means simply 'the spirit' and sometimes 'a disturbance of the spirit' when it has been violently upset. Latin tends to use the plural *animi*, rather than the singular *animus*, when describing this sort of disturbance: hence the satirist's words: *Animos a crimine sumunt* 'they take mad courage from their crime.'[200] Apparently there is little difference in Hebrew between the words translated 'wrath' and 'fury,' and it is thus clear that the same idea is repeated, as it was earlier with 'laugh' and 'laugh to scorn.'

While on the subject, we must not pass too quickly over the force of the word *tunc* [then]: it indicates the position in time of these events, relative to those which have gone before; it shows that they will be long in coming, but it also suggests a particular, well-defined time. Thus, after the nations have raged, and the peoples have carried through their futile plots, after the kings of the earth have gathered, and the leaders, conspiring together, have woven all their plots against the Lord, and against the Lord's anointed; after all their plots have miscarried, so that their wiles can be seen to have been duly frustrated by divine counsel; and when, in the blindness of their souls, they have for many years poured out their fury against the Redeemer, and God, foreseeing everything, has looked down from heaven and mocked their impious schemes: then, finally, he will speak to them. How will he speak? When will he speak? 'He will speak to them in his wrath, and in his fury.' He will speak on that awesome day when, as Christ prophesied, 'the powers of heaven shall be shaken.'[201] In his wrath on that day, he will speak in a fearsome voice: 'Depart you cursed ones: go into the eternal fire which is prepared for the devil and his angels.'[202] For the moment, he speaks to us in his mercy, he bears with us, he urges us to return to our senses, he does all he can to draw us to him.

* * * * *

198 Rom 2:5; cf Rom 11:30–2 on the 'season of mercy.'
199 Cf Horace *Epistles* 1.2.62; the 'philosophers' are presumably Seneca (*De ira*) and Plutarch, whose *De cohibenda iracundia* (*Moralia* 452E–464E) Erasmus translated in 1525.
200 Juvenal 6.285; as used here, *animi* means something like 'impetuosity, rashness.'
201 Matt 24:29
202 Matt 25:4

Augustine suggests that here the 'wrath of God' could mean that mental darkness which descends on those who, despite many and varied calls to repentance, have abused God's goodness, so that what was intended as a source of improvement has become a source of still greater wickedness.[203] We are saddened to see this kind of 'wrath' persisting in the remnant of the Jewish nation, even though they can see that all that their prophets foretold concerning the Messiah has been fulfilled in Christ, and even though they can learn from the gospel story that it is none other than Christ whom now the whole world worships. They know that not only God, but all the nations of the world, laugh at them, and yet they still curse Christ in their synagogues and await some other Messiah; they will not see him, except in the 'day of wrath,' they will not hear him, except when 'in his fury, he shall confound' every impious creature. Their present sufferings ought to teach them that the wrath of God is clearly upon them, and yet their spiritual blindness is such that not even such notable afflictions as these can give them 'understanding of what they hear.'[204] This is undoubtedly the wrath of which Paul speaks in his letter to the Romans: 'For this partial blindness has fallen upon Israel, until the gentiles have been admitted in full strength.'[205] This is the wrath which finally 'comes upon them at the last,'[206] as the same writer says; not only upon the Jews, but also upon those gentiles who have stubbornly resisted God's gospel, as Paul wrote to the Ephesians: 'They are estranged from the ways of God by the ignorance which is in them because of the blindness of their hearts and, being without hope, they have abandoned themselves to vice, falling prey to greed and all kinds of immorality.' And, a little further on: 'For these reasons the wrath of God falls on his rebellious children.'[207]

It is true that Augustine's reading contains nothing that clashes with the orthodox interpretation, but I prefer to take this 'wrath' and 'fury' of the Lord as both a punishment and a reproof, by which God seeks to bring us back to our senses. For in speaking to us, through the prophets long ago and now through his son Jesus, he frequently changes his tone. Sometimes he grants us prosperity and encourages us to love him, since he freely bestows upon us much that we do not deserve; at other times he sends disaster in an effort to make us repent. At times he gently coaxes us with promises, at others he threatens punishment and inspires terror to make us mend our ways, just

* * * * *

203 *Enarratio in psalmum* 2 PL 36 70
204 Cf Isa 6:9 and Matt 13:14.
205 Rom 11:25
206 1 Thess 2:16
207 Eph 4:18–19 and 5:6

as a father sometimes coaxes his son, encouraging good behaviour by a gift, but sometimes threatens to disinherit him, and occasionally even administers a thrashing to induce better results. Similarly, a doctor will sometimes cut and burn, but sometimes he will ease the pain of a wound with soothing ointments and poultices.

For example, here is the Lord coaxing his children, as it were, with the promise of a modest reward: 'Honour your father and mother,' he says, 'as the Lord your God has commanded, that you may live long, and that it may be well with you in the land which the Lord your God shall give you.'[208] An example of the stern tone in which the Lord rebukes and threatens? Here are his words in Isaiah: 'Woe to this sinful nation, a people weighed down with iniquity, a worthless race of wicked children. They have deserted the Lord, they have blasphemed the holy one of Israel and turned their backs on him. Where shall I strike you now, since you continue to betray me?' And so on, a great deal more in the same vein. What is the purpose of such a long and harsh rebuke? It is like bitter medicine given to a patient. But now, here is a passage in the same chapter where this tone of wrath and fury changes to a tone of mercy: 'Wash yourselves, be clean, remove the evil of your thoughts from my sight. Cease to do evil, learn to do right. Pursue justice, help the oppressed, do justice to the orphan, defend the widow, and come and argue it out with me, says the Lord. Though your sins may be like scarlet, they will become as white as snow; though they be as red as crimson, they will be as white as the lily. If you will listen and do my will, you shall eat the fruits of the earth.'[209]

But woe to those who remain persistently deaf to both these voices of the Lord! The next verse in this passage is reserved for them: 'If you refuse, and provoke me to anger, the sword shall devour you; the mouth of the Lord has spoken.'[210] But why does he say: 'If you provoke me to anger'? Surely most of the preceding passage sounds like someone who is thoroughly angry? However, we have shown that the wrath of God can be taken to mean retribution, and so we must distinguish between two kinds of retribution, the one merciful, by which he reforms us, and the other vengeful, by which he destroys us. Persistent rejection of the first kind leaves only the second. To save us from this, the Holy Spirit cries out in the psalm: 'If you hear his voice today, do not harden your hearts.'[211] 'Today' means all through our earthly

* * * * *

208 Deut 5:16
209 Isa 1:4–5 and 16–19
210 Isa 1:20
211 Ps 94/95:8

lives: let us therefore hear his voice 'today' and mend our ways; if we fail, we shall hear his voice, whether we like it or not, at a later date – and we shall perish for all eternity.

If you have time, you can find a thousand similar passages in the Old Testament, in which the Lord constantly changes the tone of his voice, but it is enough for us to have mentioned one or two. Even in the New Testament, which preaches the law of grace and heralds the season of mercy, you may still find God speaking, through his Son, in both tones of voice. This, for instance, is his awesome tone: 'Bind him hand and foot, and cast him into the outer darkness, where there shall be weeping and gnashing of teeth.' And again: 'He shall cut him off, and shall place him among the hypocrites.' And, yet again: 'Woe to you Pharisees, woe to you Scribes, woe to you rich men!'[212] Is not this the voice of wrath? But it is wrath exhorting the nearly-deaf to repent. Now listen to the other voice: 'Come to me, you who labour and are heavy-laden, and I will refresh you. Take my yoke upon you, and you will find rest for your souls. For my yoke is easy and my burden is light.'[213] Here, again, is the tone of admonition: 'You are children of the devil, and you do your father's work.'[214] But then the opposite: 'Father, forgive them, for they know not what they do.'[215]

The Lord also spoke in this way to Paul as he breathed his murderous threats against the Lord's disciples: 'Saul, Saul, why do you persecute me? It is hard for you to kick against the pricks.'[216] He was thrown to the ground, he lost his sight, he was confused by a sudden bright light. This was undoubtedly an illustration of the words 'And in his fury he will confound them.' In this case his anger brought healing, and Paul, cured at once by the treatment, replied: 'Lord, what do you want me to do?' In the same way a doctor may shock his patient's body with a convulsive drug, so that the illness is expelled and good health takes its place. God worked in this way through the prophets, through his Son, and through his disciples, and every day he continues to work in this way through good teachers and bishops.

How often does Paul change his tone in his Epistles? At times he coaxes, pleads, and consoles with the tenderness of a mother; at others he threatens the disobedient with all the authority of the Apostle. However, whether coaxing, or rebuking and threatening, the leaders of the church should have

* * * * *

212 Respectively Matt 22:13, 24:51, and 23:13 (cf Luke 6:24)
213 Matt 11:28–30
214 John 8:44
215 Luke 23:34
216 Acts 9:4–6

no other aim than to give guidance. The language may be changed, but the intention is the same; the nature of the medicine may be changed, but it is directed towards the same end. Paul always prefers to use pleasant and soothing words, but sometimes he is obliged to grieve the hearts of his audience. Nor does this mildest of apostles regret the fact, although he had once regretted it; it grieved him to bring sorrow to his most dear children, but he rejoiced to see the medicine doing them good. He writes in his second letter to the Corinthians: 'Perhaps I grieved you by the letter I sent, but I am not sorry for it. Even if I was sorry when I saw that my letter had grieved you for a time, I am happy now, not because you were grieved, but because that grief brought you to repentance. For your grief was inspired by God and thus you suffered no harm at my hands. Grief which is inspired by God brings that earnest repentance which leads to salvation, whereas worldly grief brings death.'[217]

In fact, God addresses us in two different ways: through his Scriptures and through events themselves. We must therefore spend much time in studying the sacred books, to hear what God says to us there – and let us be sure that his words do not fall on deaf ears. But in addition, he often speaks to the unlearned through events, and here the inward ear must be kept open so that we do not miss the Lord's voice. If some good fortune comes our way, we must not act like the man described by the psalmist elsewhere: 'The beloved grew fat and unruly; he grew sleek and bloated. He forsook God who made him, and abandoned the God of his salvation.'[218] If we know that we have sinned, we should give thanks for God's mercy, which, although we deserve punishment, still urges us by kindness to mend our ways; on the other hand, if we are sure that we have done no wrong, we must strive to increase still further our previous devotion to God. If illness or some other calamity befalls us, we should give thanks for God's goodness, which calls us to reform when we forget ourselves, scourging his children here and now to keep them from eternal death.

Paul writes of this to the Corinthians: 'When we are judged by the Lord, he is disciplining us, to save us from damnation with the rest of the world.'[219] If we suffer some affliction even when we are guiltless, we should none the less give thanks to God, whose goodness gives us an opportunity to increase and strengthen our faith. This is the teaching of the apostle

* * * * *

217 2 Cor 7:8–10
218 The quotation is in fact from Moses' song in Deut 32:15; the 'beloved' in question is Israel.
219 1 Cor 11:32

James: 'Count yourselves supremely happy, my brothers, whenever you have to face the various trials of life, knowing that this testing of your faith breeds steadfastness; allow steadfastness to perfect its work, so that you may become whole and perfect, lacking nothing.'[220] We should beg the Lord to go on scourging us in his fatherly wrath, confounding us in his fury, so that we tremble at the recognition of our sins, and are inspired with godly grief, for our salvation's sake. Let us shake with fear of the Last Judgment and of hell, or else the Lord may speak to us in his wrath as he spoke to Herod, when the angel of the Lord struck him down with a fearsome death,[221] or as he spoke to Jerusalem and to the whole nation of Israel, when the Roman conquerors unleashed their fury against them, showing mercy to none, whatever their sex or age, and left not one stone standing upon another; all this because of their stubborn refusal to recognize that the time of their visitation had come.[222] It was not enough for them to have crucified the Lord of glory, but they had to continue, with relentless hatred, to persecute him after the resurrection through his disciples. As a result, their homeland stands desolate: they have no city, no temple, no kingdom, no priesthood, no people; but worst of all, they have no eyes to see the Lord's will, no ears to hear the Lord's words, no heart to help them mend their ways, to understand and turn towards their king, to whom they once preferred Caesar.[223] The Lord also 'spoke in his wrath' to many gentile princes: Nero, Diocletian, Maximin, Julian,[224] who all, manifestly, died in the blindness of their hearts by acts of divine retribution; suddenly, as they reached for the sky and waged war on God, they were flung headlong into Tartarus.

Thus the prophet, inspired by the heavenly Spirit, has taught us that all the commotions made by kings and peoples were vain, frivolous, and laughable, and that there is no power in heaven, on earth, or under the earth[225] which can escape God's vengeance if he should speak in his wrath and confound his enemies in his fury. Next, the prophet reveals to us the contents of the decree, proclaimed by the eternal wisdom, which men have tried in vain to overthrow. The Jews doggedly clung to their Law, the

* * * * *

220 James 1:2–4
221 See Acts 12:23.
222 An echo of Christ's prophecy, in Luke 19:43–4, of the destruction of Jerusalem, which was accomplished by the Romans under Titus in AD 70
223 Cf John 19:15.
224 Roman emperors notorious for persecuting Christians; all except Diocletian died violently.
225 An echo of Phil 2:10

Pharisees defended their power, the high priests vied with one another for prestige, the philosophers would not drop their arrogance, the kings battled fiercely to maintain their power or the laws they had made, and the people could not be detached from the superstitions to which they had become accustomed or from the vices which had become second nature to them. They all had different aims, but they were united in their opposition to the Lord's anointed. The Jew disagreed with the pagan over religion, but concurred in hating the Christian. The kings were divided by their wars, but were united in their determination to stamp out Christ's disciples. The people hated their princes, calling them tyrants and oppressors of civic liberty, but applauded them when they turned their fury on the Christians. Philosophical sects could agree on nothing among themselves, but they all swore enmity to the gospel philosophy.

Amid all the uproar and confusion, however, the eternal king's decree remains, proclaiming steadfastly: 'I have enthroned (or 'anointed') my king on my holy mountain of Zion.' This is the meaning of the original Hebrew, if we accept Jerome's reading:[226] according to this reading, these words must be given to the Father who, after mocking and laughing at them, now begins to speak and to make known his power and his authority, to which all human power must necessarily yield. A handful of disorderly soldiers used to elect the Roman emperor, and the emperor appointed kings and governors. All too often the foolish people appoint foolish and impious kings; for example, long ago the people of Israel, in their dislike for Samuel, demanded Saul from God,[227] like the frogs in the fable who rejected King Log and demanded that Jupiter give them a heron to rule them.[228] But he who dwells in heaven has established one king alone, immortal, eternal, invincible, immutable, supremely wise, supremely powerful, and to him alone every creature in heaven and earth must bow. He is the Lord Jesus: it is vain for the world to oppose him, since the Father has given him all power in heaven and on earth.[229]

According to the Septuagint version,[230] this verse should be given to the Son: 'But I have been made king by him on his holy mountain of Zion.'

* * * * *

226 In Jerome's version of the Psalms based on the Hebrew text, the *Hebraica veritas* PL 28 1130B. For Jerome's different versions see Introduction xxi and also n230 below.
227 See 1 Samuel 8–10.
228 A story in the *Fables* of Aesop and Phaedrus (1.2); in some versions the new king was a water-snake or eel, but the result was the same.
229 Cf Matt 28:18.
230 In contrast to Jerome's version from the Hebrew (see n226 above), his earlier revision of the Latin text in the light of the Septuagint, the so-called Gallican

Now, since the Hebrew text is quite straightforward, I cannot see that the translators of the Septuagint have done more than avoid a rather harsh, abrupt change of speaker. The preceding verse: 'Then he will speak to them in his wrath, and in his fury he will confound them,' does not run smoothly into the next: 'But I have enthroned my king, etc,' since the former is the prophet's description of the Father, while the latter is spoken by the Father himself. Moreover, the next words, 'I will proclaim God's decree,' are spoken by the Son. Thus, to smooth the flow of the passage while preserving the sense of the prophecy, they have changed the speaker from Father to Son. It is not uncommon for the translators of the Septuagint to permit themselves this kind of thing, for example in a later verse [verse 12] of this psalm: 'Lest perchance the Lord be angry, and you are struck down from the righteous path.' Here they have added two words of their own, 'Lord' and 'righteous.'

On the literal level, this verse is appropriate enough to David, who defeated the Jebusites and built his palace on Zion (that is, the citadel of Jerusalem),[231] but let us dismiss such an insipid, watered-down interpretation, a product of the 'letter which kills';[232] we prefer to drink from the new wine of our king. What interest have we in David, who ruled a precarious kingdom, soon to be destroyed, in Palestine, a mere dot on the map? What importance, in the historical sense, has this hillock of Zion, which had been inhabited by idolaters, and even during David's reign; it brought the death of prophets, and in the end the death of the Lord of the prophets himself.[233] In killing him, however, the inhabitants enhanced his glory, and ensured the very result they had tried to avoid. In fact, our king rebukes them for this in the selfsame prophecy: 'Why, unruly peoples, do you hatch your futile plots in vain? Why, kings of the earth, do you conspire in vain? I alone have been made king, not by men, but by God, whose will no man can resist, that I may rule a kingdom without end on his holy mountain of Zion.'[234]

In Hebrew, Zion means 'a watch-tower'; it symbolizes, no doubt, the mountain so often invoked in the mystic writings, the mountain of the

* * * * *

Psalter, allots these verses to the messianic king; see PL 29 122B. The same reading is given in the *Breviarium in psalmos* PL 26 826B.

231 See 2 Sam 5:6–7.
232 Cf 2 Cor 3:6; the next clause is probably an allusion to the miracle at Cana, when Christ turned water into wine (John 2:1–11), allied with the symbolism of 'new wine in new bottles' (Matt 9:17, Mark 2:22, and Luke 5:38), indicating the break with the Judaic past.
233 Cf Matt 23:37.
234 The passage is loosely based on the opening of Ps 2.

gospel teaching, from which we look down on whatever the world considers exalted, and on which, with heaven at hand, we are made worthy to receive the heavenly Spirit. The temple of Moses is said to have been built on it, and David's palace, and the house, the prototype of the church, in which the disciples joined together in harmony and were made fire instead of clay.[235] On this mountain is built that gospel city which cannot be hidden,[236] and against whose foundation the gates of hell cannot prevail;[237] it is protected, not by human sentinels or an earthly garrison, but by a wall of good works, the rampart of faith; its king is Christ and its protector is God. As Isaiah wrote: 'The city of Zion is our stronghold; there the Saviour will take his place as our wall and our rampart.'[238]

Let us ask the prophet to describe the inhabitants of this city, a new people, who foster peace and the truths of the gospel: 'Open the gates,' he says, 'and a righteous nation shall enter, the guardians of truth. The old errors have vanished: you will keep the peace, because we have confidence in you.'[239] In another psalm, too, the prophet's spirit is moved to wonder by this: 'Glorious things are said of you, O city of God,' and 'The Lord loves the gates of Zion more than all the dwellings of Jacob,' and again 'Her foundations are on the holy mountains.'[240] Similarly, in a different psalm: 'Those who trust in the Lord shall be like Mount Zion; he who dwells in Jerusalem cannot ever be shaken.'[241] Honourable mention is made of this mountain, and of the city built on it, Jerusalem, in many other places in the sacred writings, and whenever it occurs we must interpret it either as the universal church, or as the heavenly city[242] of which the church is, as it were, a portion, a first beginning. Anyone who has been uplifted to the love of heaven looks down from a pinnacle, as it were, on anything that the world can display, however fine and lofty; such a one dwells on Mount Zion, and is truly a citizen of the church.

* * * * *

235 Cf Acts 2:1–4, the miracle of Pentecost.
236 Cf Matt 5:14.
237 Matt 16:18, meaning the church; in their commentaries, Augustine and Jerome both consider that Zion here prefigures the church, whereas Hilary makes it the heavenly Jerusalem. All point out that in Hebrew it means 'watch-tower.'
238 Isa 26:1
239 Isa 26:2–3
240 Ps 86/87:1–3; the verses are put in varying order by different versions of the Scriptures.
241 Ps 124/125:1
242 Cf Heb 12:22, Rev 3:12 and 21:10.

In Hebrew Jerusalem means 'a vision of peace.' Even if they cannot yet achieve perfect peace, at least the inhabitants of this city, raising their eyes to their heavenly fatherland, can glimpse everlasting peace from afar, and sigh for it with ardent prayers, awaiting the time when 'God shall wipe away every tear' from the eyes of the faithful, and 'there will then be no more grief or crying, or pain any more.'[243] On the summit of a mountain Moses once hailed the promised land from afar,[244] and similarly the faithful constantly hail their mother Jerusalem, saying: 'How lovely are your dwelling-places, O Lord of hosts! My soul longs and faints for the courts of the Lord.'[245] But in order to glimpse that land, one must be in the watch-tower; it cannot be seen by those who pursue baser interests, preoccupied by the squalid concerns of this world, their eyes bleary in the aftermath of worldly pleasures and of the fool's wisdom.

There are mountains in this world, but they are cursed by the Lord. There is the mountain of pride: the first man to take his seat there was he who said in his heart: 'I shall be like the most high.'[246] There are the mountains of Gilboa, which David curses, praying that neither the dew nor the rain from heaven may make them fertile.[247] There are mountains which pour forth smoke when the Lord touches them.[248] In Jeremiah, too, God threatens a deadly mountain which is infecting the whole world.[249] But the mountain of which I speak was blessed by the Lord, and described by Isaiah in the verses: 'In the last days, the mountain of the Lord shall be set above the mountains and be raised above all the hills; all nations shall stream towards it, and many peoples shall arrive there and say: "Come, let us climb to the mountain of the Lord, and to the house of the God of Jacob."'[250] Jerusalem was a small city, containing only the Jews, and not even all of them. But the house of the Lord is spacious enough to lodge all the nations of the world together. Many different mountains stand around us, but this mountain is unique. There are different dwellings, but the house of the Lord is unique.

* * * * *

243 Rev 21:4; cf Augustine *De civitate Dei* 19.11 PL 41 637.
244 Deut 32:49 and 34:1–4
245 Ps 83/84:1–2; the heavenly Jerusalem as 'mother of us all' occurs in Gal 4:26, echoed by Hilary in his commentary on this verse; *Tractatus in 2 psalmum* 26 PL 9 276B.
246 Isa 14:14
247 2 Sam 1:21
248 Ps 103/104:32
249 Jer 51:25; the 'mountain' in question is Babylon.
250 Isa 2:2–3

There are numerous churches but, just as there is but one King, so there is but one universal church, compassing all others in her embrace. The head of the whole church is Christ, 'supreme above all, God blessed for ever.'[251] The king is unseen, because the mountain is invisible; you cannot point a finger and say: 'There is Mount Zion,' just as you cannot point at Christ and say: 'There is Christ.'[252] Wherever the gospel faith is found, there is Mount Zion.

It is well worth hearing how exactly the Son will reign on the Father's holy mountain. The principal authority of a king resides in his edicts and laws. Our king's 'sword' is his teaching of the Father's message or, as the psalm says, 'announcing his decree' (the Hebrew text reads: 'I will proclaim God's decree'). The princes of the earth often make unjust and impious laws; the Pharisees inculcate worthless, man-made regulations, always with an eye to their own profit; the philosophers expound the useless speculations of mere mortals, and all disagree with one another about everything. The king of Zion teaches nothing that is base, or artful, or false, but preaches the Lord God's decree from on high. You can talk about philosophers' decrees, Moses' decrees, the Pharisees' decrees, kings' decrees (there are a lot of those!), but the Lord's decree stands alone, proclaimed in a unique way by our king on Zion.

What is his decree? The decree of mutual love. 'This is my decree, that you should love one another.'[253] But are we complying to the full with this decree if we love one another? Not entirely, for he adds: 'As I have loved you.' He loved us purely and selflessly, unto death. All the teaching of the Law and the prophets is comprised within this gospel of love. Anyone who loves God with all his heart will also trust in him, will find good hope in his promises, and will be wary of offending him. Paul was thus right to name love, or charity, as the greatest of the three outstanding virtues, since it includes both faith and hope.[254] 'Charity believes all things, hopes for all things.'[255] 'But,' someone will remark, 'you have said nothing about works!'[256] Charity is not idle; on the contrary, it 'does nothing in vain,'[257] but never ceases in its work. This, then, is the one unique decree of God the Father; the Son calls it his

* * * * *

251 Rom 9:5
252 This sentence was recommended for deletion in the *Index expurgatorius* LB X 1820B.
253 John 15:12
254 1 Cor 13:13
255 1 Cor 13:7
256 Erasmus' view of works is expounded most cogently in *Ecclesiastes* LB V 783–5; as so often, he rejects empty ceremonial and ritual, but approves of works inspired by evangelical charity; cf 143–4 below.
257 1 Cor 13:4 in the Vulgate

own, but only to give it the full weight of the Father's approval, with whom he is associated in all things. He also bears witness to this in the Gospel: 'My teaching is not mine, but his who sent me,'[258] that is, the Father's.

Christ could have conquered the world by force of arms; he could have obtained from the Father many legions of angels, had he not preferred to save rather than to punish; he chose to conquer all the powers of the world for the Father by means of heavenly teaching. Isaiah remarked on this too, in the text which I quoted a little earlier: 'Come, let us climb up to the mountain of the Lord, and to the house of the God of Jacob, and he shall teach us his ways, and we will walk in his paths. For from Zion comes the Law, and from Jerusalem the word of the Lord.'[259] One can hear in this 'the sword cleaving through to the place where life and spirit, joints and marrow, divide.'[260] The prophet's next words relate to the same theme: 'And he shall judge the nations, and shall rebuke many peoples.'[261] How will he judge them? By proclaiming the truth. How will he rebuke them? By refuting falsehood. The world's darkness is shown up in the light of the gospel.

Now, see what follows once the truth is known. The strife which always accompanies false beliefs and arrogance will be replaced by that devotion to peace which is the hallmark of the Christian. 'And they shall beat their swords into ploughshares,' he says, 'and their spears into pruning-hooks. Nation shall not lift up sword against nation, neither shall they make war any more.'[262] Why should this be? Because, recognizing the new king's authority, all the overweening pride of the world shall submit, and the prophet's subsequent words shall be fulfilled: 'Mankind's haughty eyes shall be cast down, and men's pride shall be abased; the Lord alone shall be exalted on that day.' Similarly, a little later: 'Mankind's arrogance shall be brought low, and men's pride shall be humbled; the Lord alone shall be exalted on that day, and the idols shall be utterly destroyed.'[263] It is fitting that idols, or images, the empty shadows of the real, should have faded away once the light of truth has shone upon them. It is fitting that the swelling clamour of human philosophy should have fallen silent once the teaching of heaven has begun to be revealed by Christ, about whom the Father alone gave his

*****

258 John 7:16
259 Isa 2:3
260 Heb 4:12; I have used the New English Bible version for this rather difficult (and gruesome) metaphor evoking the action of the word of God.
261 Isa 2:4
262 Isa 2:4
263 Isa 2:11 and 2:17

testimony: 'This is my beloved Son, in whom I am well pleased: hear him.'[264] It is appropriate that arrogant mankind should be crestfallen[265] when once they have begun to listen closely to Christ, who says in the Gospel: 'Learn from me, for I am gentle and humble in heart: and you shall find rest for your souls.'[266]

Some people[267] claim that 'the Father's decree' is in fact the Son's public declaration that he was truly the Son of God, that the Father might be glorified through the Son.[268] I do not disagree with this view entirely; but see, too, how well the prophecy accords with the gospel story. In the Gospel[269] we find: 'This is my beloved Son,' and in the psalm [verse 7]: 'The Lord said to me: "You are my son, this day I have begotten you."' If Moses, Elijah, Elisha, Isaiah, and the other ancient prophets, who were mere servants or heralds, enjoyed so much authority, how great must be the authority of the Son; especially since, unlike so many of the others, he did not become a son by adoption, in the usual way, but by a special, inexpressible process. He stands alone and unique in being called the Son of God by nature.

Now, the Lord said 'this day,' but this refers, not to a particular time, but to eternity, which knows neither beginning, nor end, nor the passage of time. For us, the past has already ceased to exist, and the future does not yet exist; even the present is always passing away. But for the divine nature, it is always 'this day,' it is always the present, and there is no passage of time. Thus the Son of God is always being born of the Father 'this day,' just as he is always 'coming from' the Father.[270] St Augustine also interprets the passage in this sense,[271] although not denying that it could also be applied to the nativity, by which the Son became man, born of the Virgin; on that day he began to exist in a new form, but did not cease to be what he had always been.

Hilary is attracted by a different hypothesis,[272] which states that Christ was born of the Father, by some mystical process, more than once, although nothing was added to his divine nature but only to the human; or else that

* * * * *

264 Matt 17:5
265 *cristam ponat*, literally 'lay down the crest'; cf *Adagia* I viii 69: *Tollere cristas* 'To raise one's crest,' ie be conceited.
266 Matt 11:29
267 Cf Hilary *Tractatus in 2 psalmum* 27 PL 9 276B–277B.
268 John 14:13
269 Matt 3:17 and 17:5
270 Cf John 16:27–8.
271 The preceding passage follows closely Augustine's *Enarratio in psalmum* 2 PL 36 71.
272 *Tractatus in 2 psalmum* 27–8 PL 9 277–8

he is said to be 'born' in the sense that his existence is revealed. For in a certain sense he is born for us when first we understand that he plays a role of which we were previously unaware; and in a certain sense the Father begets him when he acknowledges him publicly as his Son. In support of this, we find terms similar to those of the present prophecy used on two occasions in the Gospels, in words addressed by the Father to his Son. On the occasion of his baptism in the Jordan, the Lord first sent the sign of the dove, and then, in his own voice, he commended him to all, saying: 'This is my beloved Son.' Mark and Luke record it as: 'You are my beloved Son.' In addition, the psalm continues: 'This day I have begotten you,' while the Gospel reads: 'In you I am well pleased.'[273] This Gospel text seems to accord marvellously with the prophecy, for I take the view that in the psalm the statement 'You are my Son' is echoed and reinforced by the similar clause 'This day I have begotten you'; similarly, in the Gospel the Father says: 'You are my best beloved Son,' and emphasizes it by repeating: 'In you I am well pleased.'[274] Again, the words added in the Gospel, 'Hear him,'[275] correspond to the psalm's phrase 'announcing God's decree,' thus:[276] 'He is my best beloved and only Son; there is no reason to await any other. He is sent from me, and will speak on my behalf: therefore hear him, and you will hear me.' God used the same words to glorify the Son on the mountain, when Jesus had transfigured himself before the three disciples.[277]Peter also recalls it, in his second epistle:'We became witnesses of his majesty; for as he received honour and glory from God the Father, a voice came down on him from the sublime glory and said: "This is my beloved Son, in whom I am well pleased: hear him." We heard this voice, which came from heaven, when we were with him on the holy mountain.'[278] Again, when Jesus was praying to his Father that he should glorify his own name through his Son, the Father's voice came from heaven, saying: 'I have glorified it, and I will glorify it again.'[279] This too was a voice full of majestic power: some of the witnesses said that it had thundered, others that the angel of the Lord had spoken to him. As the Son brought honour to the Father by his death, so the Father in

* * * * *

273 Matt 3:17, Mark 1:11, and Luke 3:22
274 At the second of the two occasions mentioned, the transfiguration; Matt 17:5
275 Added only on the second occasion, the transfiguration; Matt 17:5, Mark 9:7, and Luke 9:35
276 The passage following is apparently a summary of Erasmus' interpretation of God's words.
277 Cf n274 above.
278 2 Pet 1:16–18
279 John 12:28–9

turn brought honour to the Son by the resurrection: not because it brought
some new honour to him, but because he began to enjoy among men the
honour which his Father always gave him.

Thus the prophet's words, 'This day I have begotten you,' could refer
to the day the Lord made,[280] on which he raised his Son from the dead. We
do not find that the words 'You are my beloved Son' were heard on this
occasion; here the Father spoke through the deed itself. For he glorified his
Son once more, as he had promised, when 'he placed the stone which the
builders rejected as the cornerstone,'[281] raising him, by his divine power, to
be the first-born from the dead; the apostle Paul suggests that he was in some
sense reborn when he calls him 'the first-born from the dead.'[282] He was the
first-born of all creation, since all things were made through him,[283] but also,
being proclaimed the founder and source of resurrection, he has become the
first-born from the dead, and again hears from his Father the words 'This
day I have begotten you'; for the mortal being, born of the Virgin, was given
immortality by his Father.

Someone may find this interpretation rather strained, and based more
on human ingenuity than on the rules of Scripture, but in the Acts of
the Apostles Paul, preaching Christ to the Jews, also applies this verse of
our psalm to the day of the resurrection, saying: 'When he had fulfilled
everything that was written of him, they took him down from the tree and
placed him in a tomb. But God raised him from the dead on the third day; he
was seen over many days by those who had come up with him from Galilee
to Jerusalem, and who up to now are his witnesses to the people. And we
now give you the news that God, who made the promise to our fathers, has
fulfilled it for your sons by resurrecting Jesus, as it is written in the First
Psalm: "You are my son, this day I have begotten you." And because he
raised him from the dead, never again to return to corruption, he also said:
"I will give you the holy mercies of David." '[284] What, then, is implied by
his statement 'You are my son'? I have proclaimed to the world that you are
my son. And what of 'This day I have begotten you'? On this day I have
consecrated you to immortality; on this day I have made you the first-born
of the dead; on this day I have given you all power in heaven and earth.[285]

* * * * *

280 Ps 118/119:24
281 1 Pet 2:7, quoting Ps 117/118:22; cf Matt 21:42 and Acts 4:11.
282 Col 1:18
283 Cf John 1:1–3.
284 Acts 13:29–34
285 Cf Matt 28:18.

On this day I have enabled the world to understand that you sit at my right hand, sharing dominion over the whole world. On this day I have glorified you before men, with the same glory which you have always enjoyed in my sight. Moreover, that all may understand that you are my true and only son, I have made you the heir and joint ruler of my kingdom, the prince of the gospel kingdom.

The psalm continues: 'Ask it of me and I will give you the nations as your inheritance, and the ends of the earth as your possession.' The Father has given the Son complete jurisdiction over the church's kingdom. It remains for the Son to proceed, with the aid of the gospel teaching, to bring the nations of the whole world under his Father's sway. But the aim of his conquest is to save rather than destroy them. They are to be subjected, not to tyrannical slavery, but to the 'liberty of the children of God.'[286] Christ does not aspire to a kingdom of this world, although by his human nature he was also made king of kings and lord of lords.[287] On the contrary, he asked his Father for a kingdom of the gospel, in order to free the whole world from the tyranny of sin and to make it listen to the heavenly Father, who does not wish the death of a sinner, but that he should turn from his wickedness and live.[288] Should you wish to know where the Son asked this of the Father, here are his words to him in John's Gospel: 'Father, the hour has come; glorify your Son, that your Son may glorify you. You have given him power over all flesh, to give eternal life to all that you have given him.'[289]

Moreover, should anyone think that he was asking the Father only for the Hebrew race, from which at that time he had chosen his disciples, he added: 'It is not only for these that I pray, but also for those who through their words shall believe in me, that they may be one; as you, Father, are in me, and I am in you, so may they be one in us, that the world may believe that you sent me.'[290] What bounds did he set to his disciples' preaching? 'Go,' he said, 'into the whole world and preach the gospel to every creature.'[291] What are they to demand, what laws of peace are they to prescribe? 'Whoever has believed, and been baptized, he shall be saved.'[292] This is how he lays claim to the gospel kingdom: 'So that all may be one in us, as you are in me, and I

* * * * *

286 Rom 8:21
287 Rev 17:14; cf 1 Tim 6:15.
288 Ezek 33:11
289 John 17:1–2
290 John 17:1–2
291 Mark 16:15
292 Mark 16:16

am in you.' I have proclaimed your decree, and nowhere have I strayed from your commandment. Those who believe in me will accept my teaching and, summoned by me and by my disciples, will submit themselves to your will. Thus I shall finally deliver to you a kingdom at peace, free from all sedition, just as in heaven no one opposes your will.

A different point: Augustine thinks that the sense of the words 'I will give you the nations as your inheritance' is repeated, and indeed expressed more clearly, in the next clause, 'and the ends of the earth as your possession.'[293] However, Hilary disagrees, arguing at some length that the one refers to the boundaries themselves, the other to what is enclosed by them; the furthest regions of the earth, he says, are enclosed by different elements: the earth is bounded by the air above, and by the deep waters, which he calls the abysses, below, and these also have their denizens who are alive, not dead. In pursuit of this idea, he bends Paul's words, 'That at the name of Jesus every knee shall bow, of things in heaven, on the earth, and below the earth, and every tongue shall confess that Jesus is Lord, to the glory of God the Father';[294] moreover, he says, the author of the Apocalypse used a similar formula, writing that no one, be he in heaven, on earth, or below the earth, would be found worthy to open the book of seals.[295] This is Hilary's reasoning, more or less.[296]

I favour Augustine's view that we should interpret the 'gospel kingdom' as stretching out in every direction to the most remote peoples of the world, in accordance with the text 'Their sound went out into all the earth, and their words to the ends of the world.'[297] I suspect that Hilary dug his ideas out from the commentaries of Origen, who says something somewhere about freeing those who have been condemned to hell, and about redeeming demons.[298] Moreover, besides the strained interpretation of 'boundaries' as anything which surrounds anything else (although we do sometimes say things like this, for instance that the earth is bounded by the ocean, or that the earth's atmosphere is bounded by the sphere of the moon), it is not true that the

* * * * *

293 *Enarratio in psalmum 2* PL 36 71
294 Phil 2:10–11
295 Rev 5:3
296 *Tractatus in 2 psalmum* 32–3 PL 9 280B–282B
297 Rom 10:18
298 These are recurrent themes of Origen's writing; see for example his *Commentary on John* PG 14 47 n63, 81 n35, and 512 n64. They were among Origen's more controversial tenets, often castigated by the later Fathers, which explains Erasmus' apparent desire to excuse Hilary here.

earth is covered only by the air above, and bounded by the abyss below, since the waters touch the earth on all sides, and air surrounds the earth on all sides. And if we must allot a particular position to the infernal regions, it is more likely that they are to be found in the depths of the earth, sometimes called its centre, than in the abysses of the waters. In any case, the psalm is using the title 'king' (which suggests in human terms the most extensive power) and the expression 'the ends of the earth' (which means possessions so widespread that they cannot be spread wider) in order to make a contrast with the weakness of Christ's human form, which was a stumbling block for the Jews,[299] and with the narrow-mindedness of the Jewish people, who did not want the gospel kingdom to be extended beyond their own race.[300] The titles of king and priest are both equally appropriate to Christ, since we translate Melchizedek, who was a prototype of Christ, as 'king of righteousness,' and he is also described as king of Salem, meaning king of peace.[301] Christ says that his kingdom is not of this world,[302] not because he was not lord of all, but because at that time he was trying for a moment to convey to his disciples an image of the gospel kingdom. He went about with a band of followers who were quite unarmed, and, so far from owning fortresses, he had not even a resting-place for his head; he conquered the people by kindness, he used only the gospel teaching as a sword to strike down impious passions, so that, once the sinful man was slain, the new man could be born, and be worthy of God.[303] He triumphed by suffering, he triumphed by dying; but after the resurrection he speaks like a king: 'All power is given to me, in heaven and on earth.'[304] In fact, he did not refuse the title of king in the Gospel,[305] but when speaking to Pilate he differentiated between types of kingdom; when asked if he was a king, he replied: 'The words are yours,'[306] avoiding any hint of arrogance in his reply, but without impairing the truth. Moreover, as he hung on the cross, he both heard and spoke words appropriate to a king. The

* * * * *

299 Cf for example 1 Cor 1:23, Rom 9:31–3, and 1 Pet 2:8.
300 This whole section rehearses the argument of the Epistle to the Hebrews, which is of great importance to Erasmus in his insistence on the church as a spiritual community beyond sectarian and political divisions, as in his later expositions of Pss 83 and 14.
301 Melchizedek was both king and priest; cf Gen 14:18 and Heb 6:6 and 7:2.
302 John 18:36
303 Cf Eph 4:22–4 and Col 3:9–10.
304 Matt 28:18
305 See John 18:33–6.
306 Matt 27:11, Mark 15:2, and Luke 23:3

thief said: 'Remember me, when you enter your kingdom,' and Jesus replied: 'Amen; I say to you, this day you shall be with me in paradise.'[307]

The prophets use similar terms in their inspired verses: 'Behold,' says Zechariah, 'your righteous king and saviour shall come.' But to dispel any impression of a proud and tyrannical ruler, he added: 'Righteous, and your saviour, yet poor, mounted on an ass and on a colt, the foal of the ass.' In the next verse Zechariah shows that the gospel kingdom is to be extended far and wide by mercy, not violence: 'He shall speak peace,' he says, 'to the nations, and his power shall extend from sea to sea, and from the rivers to the ends of the earth.'[308] Similarly, Isaiah said: 'Unto us a boy is born, unto us a son is given, and the government is set upon his shoulders; his name shall be called wonderful, counsellor, the mighty God, the everlasting father, the prince of peace.' A kingdom and a government very different from earthly kingdoms! Next we are told of the extent of his power: 'His dominion shall be multiplied, and of peace there shall be no end.' Earthly rulers increase their dominion by bloodshed and, as they thrust and parry by turns, there is no end to their wars. But here is something more truly regal: 'He shall take his seat on David's throne, and in his kingdom, that he may build and strengthen it in righteousness and justice.' Where justice and righteousness make themselves heard, there is no room for the tyrant. As for the duration of his reign: 'From now to eternity.'[309] He was that 'priest for ever, after the order of Melchizedek,'[310] a victim whose sacrifice removed the need for any other. Similarly, he is king for ever more, being immortal, and thus admitting no successor; he sits enthroned as God for all eternity, governing the universe with a nod of his head.

However, his kingdom on earth is not yet entirely secure: the church's net still catches and brings in both good fish and bad, the gospel's harvest still contains tares mixed with the wheat;[311] Paul too declares that there are many Antichrists.[312] The kingdom includes weak members; within each of us the lusts of the flesh still foment rebellion against the spirit. But when he has conquered all, and delivered the kingdom to God the Father,[313] then all things will exist in perfect peace.

* * * * *

307 Luke 23:42–3
308 Zech 9:9–10
309 Isa 9:6–7
310 Ps 109/110:4; cf n301 above.
311 Cf Matt 13:47–8 and 24–40.
312 Paul does not mention Antichrists; this is probably a reference to 1 John 2:18.
313 Cf 1 Cor 15:24–8.

Up to here, the prophet's words have been appropriate enough to our Christ who, although supreme and lord of all, yet descended from the heights to show his apostles, and the apostles' successors, the paths of mercy and gentleness; to show that the princes of the church's realm must stand aloof from any form of worldly tyranny. But the words which follow appear to strike a note of harshness and violence, and the exegetes have to twist and turn to apply them to our Christ, who is both the teacher and the exemplar of peace, mercy, and humility.[314] Having given him the nations as his inheritance and the ends of the earth as his possession, the psalm adds: 'You shall rule them with an iron rod; you shall break them like a pot of clay.'

At first sight, the word 'rule' itself seems to many rather hard and violent, since at one time the very title of 'ruler' offended the ears of free citizens.[315] The next words have a still more fearsome ring: 'With an iron rod.' 'Rod' conveys a threat, which is exacerbated by the adjective 'iron'; but the next sentence seems the harshest of all: 'You shall break them like a pot of clay.' What could be more cruel than to achieve the desired control over the nations, only to destroy them, utterly and irrevocably – for a clay pot, once broken, cannot be repaired. Such cruelty seems quite incompatible with the supremely merciful ways and gentle teaching of Christ and, in short, with the reign of him who says: 'Take my yoke upon you, and you will find rest for your souls, for my yoke is gentle, my burden light.'[316]

Earlier commentators have therefore tried in many different ways to extricate themselves from this difficulty. If one takes the text in the historical sense, these harsh terms are appropriate enough to the Jews' impiety, which has led them to struggle obstinately against Christ and has been punished by their miserable ruin. They refused to accept him when he came in peace, and so finally God's harsh retribution descended upon them; not only was this rebellious nation most severely chastised, but it was almost brought to the point of extinction. Some commentators relate the text to the Day of Judgment; by inspiring fear of it beforehand, God calls on the nations to abandon their persistent sinfulness; if they continue to rage and conspire against the Lord, who for the moment invites them – gently – to change their ways, then in the future they will feel the iron rod of everlasting punishment and will be consumed in everlasting ruin. They are threatened with this in Isaiah: 'Suddenly, when it is least expected, destruction shall come upon

* * * * *

314 In particular Hilary; *Tractatus in 2 psalmum* 34–41 PL 9 282B–286B
315 Latin *regere* 'to rule' and *rex* 'king.' The title 'king' was unpopular among the republican Romans; cf *Institutio principis christiani* CWE 27 226 and n85.
316 Matt 11:29–30

them; they shall be overthrown like a jar of clay that breaks with a great crash, and among the fragments there shall not be found a shard large enough to take a flame from the fire.'[317] It is even more clear in Jeremiah 19: 'I shall break that people and that city as a clay pot is broken and cannot be mended again.'[318] Jerome touches on both these interpretations, and sketches a third in a couple of words,[319] which is the only one of the three to be followed by Augustine.[320]

Hilary too does not shrink from an attempt to tone down the harshness of the passage in a number of ways.[321] First, he says that 'to rule' must be defined, not in terms of tyranny, but of government by reason and the rule of law, and that it is a term applied to Christ elsewhere: 'A leader shall arise, who shall rule my people Israel.'[322] Moreover, the Greek word used by the translators of the Septuagint is much less harsh: it is ποιμανεῖς, meaning 'you shall tend, or guide, like a shepherd'; according to experts in the language, the Hebrew word has similar overtones. And indeed, says Hilary, Christ is the good shepherd who feeds and tends his sheep with such devotion that he even laid down his life for us, the sheep of his pasture.[323] Moreover, the rod is not always an instrument of punishment, but may be a symbol of power, indicating the king's duty to direct his people towards the principles of law, and to prevent them straying from virtue; as we read elsewhere in the Psalms: 'The rod of justice shall be the rod with which you rule';[324] thus this psalm calls a 'rod' what the Greeks call a sceptre. Moreover, says Hilary, the addition of 'iron' does not imply harsh, tyrannical government, but an authority which is strong, permanent, incorruptible, and unyielding. Those whose lives are governed by the moral code of human law often stray from the path of rectitude, but those whose lives are controlled by the code taught by the gospel will never wander from true piety. This rod is light to the obedient, unyielding to the wilful; those who resist will feel the iron, but not those who comply. In the same way, Christ is a strong rock, a safe refuge for

* * * * *

317 Isa 30:14
318 These two sentences were added in the 1525 Basel edition; the second quotation, which is Jer 19:11, was there erroneously attributed to Isaiah.
319 *Breviarium in psalmos* PL 26 826C; in the 'couple of words' he suggests that Christ is the potter and mankind the clay, with a reference to Jer 18:6.
320 *Enarratio in psalmum 2* PL 36 71
321 Cf n314 above.
322 Matt 2:6
323 Ps 99/100:3 and John 10:11
324 Cf Ps 44/45:6; Erasmus in fact quotes the version of this in Heb 1:8, though Hilary quotes the original *virga directionis* 'rod of guidance' of the psalm.

those who stand on him; but those on whom he falls, or who dash themselves against him, are destroyed.

It is really no surprise that Christ, sole ruler of all mankind, should have a rod, since Paul, his servant and steward, has a rod, with which he threatens the Corinthians if they do not mend their ways: 'Which do you prefer? Am I to come to you with a rod, or in love and the spirit of mercy?'[325] What exactly is the Apostle threatening? That he will come into the church, flanked by guards, brandishing the praetor's rod?[326] Of course not: he is seeking to improve his children by gentleness, like a loving father. But he warns those who resist that he will go on to exert his apostolic authority, by giving them a sterner rebuke in public or, if need be, by excommunicating them. He made use of the rod in consigning to Satan the man who had taken his father's wife for himself, and he threatens the Corinthians with it when he says: 'Do you seek proof that Christ dwells in me?'[327] In the Acts of the Apostles Paul used this rod against Elymas, the sorcerer who opposed the gospel message, and said: 'You trickster, you deceiver, son of the devil and enemy of all righteousness, will you not cease to pervert the straight paths of the Lord? Now, behold, the hand of the Lord is upon you, and you shall be blind, and for a time you shall not see the sun.'[328]

Peter also brandished the rod, when he said to Ananias: 'Ananias, why has Satan tempted your heart to lie to the Holy Spirit and to hold back part of the price of the land?'[329] On hearing these words Ananias fell down and died; the same happened to his wife, who was a party to the theft, although Peter, who was otherwise so gentle, was not the direct cause of the punishment but merely laid information against them. The apostles' successors also have a rod, with which to correct and rebuke opponents who impede the progress of the gospel, but not to avenge private grievances. However, they rarely produce it, except on occasions when, all else having failed, necessity compels them to adopt extreme remedies. Paul consigned only four or five people to Satan: one who had had intercourse with his father's wife, bringing great shame on the whole congregation, because he kept her in his house, in full

* * * * *

325 Cf 1 Cor 4:1 and Titus 1:7; the quotation is 1 Cor 4:21, and Erasmus is here following closely St Hilary's commentary, *Tractatus in 2 psalmum* 36 PL 9 283A–B.
326 An emblem of secular justice; in ancient Rome the praetors, the chief magistrates, were preceded in solemn processions by lictors bearing the bundles of rods (with an axe projecting) called *fasces*.
327 1 Cor 5:1–5, followed by 2 Cor 13:3
328 Acts 13:8–11
329 Acts 5:3

view, as his wife; Paul consigned him to Satan for a time, which means that he
ordered him to be ostracized, in order to shame him into a change of heart.[330]
But soon he tempered the strictness of the rod with the spirit of mercy, asking
the Corinthians to look after the man and receive him with charity in their
hearts after his punishment, and to comfort him lest his shame should drive
him to deeper despair.[331] He consigned Hermogenes and Phygellus to Satan,
to teach them not to blaspheme, but only when they persisted in attacking
the gospel.[332]

Thus, Peter and Paul could truly ask: 'Do you seek proof that Christ
lives in me?'[333] They healed the sick, they raised the dead, they endured all
suffering for Christ's gospel; their gentleness brought many thousands to
accept the gospel, and they had no rod but reproaches and, when persistent
sinners drove them to extremes, excommunication, which only prescribed
that the incorrigible offender be ostracized; if he could not be shamed into
improvement, at least he could not infect others with his disease. But how
remote their example seems to be from certain people who have at their
disposal, not only the apostolic rod, but prisons and chains, the right to
confiscate property, a 'secular arm,' artillery, even, and armed guards – not
to mention poison and countless other horrors which equip them to avenge
private grievances rather than the gospel. At the same time, they instruct
no one, nor do they gently admonish; they bring not one soul to Christ, yet
destroy so many with their violence and their evil ways. We must therefore
pray to Christ, the prince of shepherds,[334] that he will rule them too with an
iron rod, and make them exercise their power like the apostles and not like
tyrants.

The next sentence is 'You shall break them like a pot of clay.' There
is nothing cheaper or more fragile than potter's clay, and yet those who
are truly religious 'keep the Lord's treasure in a vessel of clay,'[335] and this
dwelling, though made of clay, is a temple of the Holy Spirit, if our lives
are pure. On the other hand, nothing is more presumptuous than that a pot

* * * * *

330 The clauses 'which means . . . change of heart' were recommended for deletion
in the *Index expurgatorius* LB X 1820B.
331 1 Cor 5:1–13 and 2 Cor 2:5–8
332 2 Tim 1:15
333 2 Cor 13:3. The rest of this paragraph, with its implied contrast between apostolic
lenity and contemporary harshness, was recommended for deletion in the *Index
expurgatorius* LB X 1820B.
334 1 Pet 5:4
335 Cf 2 Cor 4:7.

of clay should set itself up against God, the potter;[336] for God's hand has more power over man even than the potter's hand as it shapes, reshapes, and squeezes the clay at will. Now, if a clay pot happens to be broken while the clay is still moist, it can be repaired, but if it is smashed once it has been baked in the sun or the kiln, then it is irretrievably destroyed. As long as we live this life, we are like moist clay; we are broken, but we can be remade, if the potter deigns to set his hand to it. It is difficult to restore those who have become hardened by long acquaintance with sin, and yet no man is to be despaired of; what is impossible among men is possible with God.[337] Once he has hurled you into hell, there is no hope of reparation; but if he breaks the useless vessel through repentance on this earth, or dashes it down by humbling the spirit during this life, then the words of another psalm will be fulfilled: 'O God, you will not despise a contrite and humbled heart.'[338] If moist tears are mixed with the fragments of a broken vessel, our clay will soften again, and God in his mercy will deign to reshape the penitent, and turn a worthless vessel into a vessel fit to honour and serve the Lord. Happy are those who are broken by this potter, happy those who are slain by this king, happy those who are struck with his sword, happy those who are scourged by his rod! He kills in us the being that we were, that a new being may live; he strikes us with the sword of the Spirit,[339] the word of God, in order to cut away all sinful desires from a heart dedicated to the heavenly Spirit. The rod strikes and lays us low in order to raise us up. Saul was struck by it: he fell to the ground as the persecutor of the church; he arose as the herald of eternal salvation.[340] It destroys in us all the slimy residue of the sin we inherited from our first parent. It shatters the murky preoccupations of the former creature, it shatters earthbound passions, so that from this moment, being baked in the fire of love, we may be guided and moved by the Spirit of God.

Up to this point in the psalm, God has threatened, with the might of his power and the severity of the punishment to come, all those who join in the impious conspiracy and revolt against the Lord and his anointed. But now the king in his mercy shows them a path by which they may escape the penalty and reach bliss: 'And now,' he says, 'you kings, understand; learn your lesson, you judges of the earth.' Until this point in history, there had been some sort

* * * * *

336 Cf Isa 45:9 and 64:8; for the development of the image see Rom 9:20–3.
337 Cf Matt 19:26 and Luke 18:27.
338 Ps 50:19/ 51:17
339 Cf Eph 4:22 and 6:17.
340 See Acts 9:1–9.

of excuse for revolt against the Lord and his anointed, although it was still a heinous crime. The law of Moses was obscure, and was not proclaimed to everyone; the philosophers were still lost in idle speculation;[341] the princes of the earth were wise only in the things of earth; God had wrapped everything in sin[342] and error, that he might show mercy to all. But now that the gospel truth has been revealed through Christ and his apostles, do not rebel against the Holy Spirit; henceforth there will be no excuse for error. 'Believe and understand,' for unless you believe, you cannot understand. Faith alone will win salvation, and will blot out, once and for all, all previous sin.[343]

The first problem here is the identity of the kings to whom the king of Zion – or God the Father – is speaking. If you are looking for a historical interpretation, then he is speaking to those kings and princes who, a little earlier, blinded by ignorance, had been raging and plotting against the Lord and his anointed, and had been using their various instruments of torture to butcher those who preached the gospel's peace. He recalls them to a sound mind, so that at last they may know and understand, through the gospel's teaching, that Christ alone has been given by God the Father, that in his name all nations may find salvation, and that to him every knee must bow.[344] Until now there has been a season of darkness, but now that the light of gospel truth has shone forth, you must understand, and turn from the worship of idols to the pursuit of true holiness. You must worship the victim of your persecutions; you tried to blot out his teaching, but he offers you salvation; you persecuted him as a man, but he is God.

The second problem arises on the tropological level. Does this verse apply to secular princes, or to the apostles' successors, the bishops? St Jerome suggests that it applies to both.[345] Augustine applies it more readily to churchmen, but in such a way that his words could be applied to both groups.[346] We shall therefore take it to mean both, after we have dealt with a small point: although previously 'the nations raged, the peoples carried through their futile plots, the kings of the earth stood ready, and the leaders

* * * * *

341 Rom 1:21

342 Cf Gal 3:22.

343 This sentence was recommended for deletion in the *Index expurgatorius* LB X 1820B; it can be read as having Lutheran overtones, in the context of the dispute over faith and works, although it is unlikely that Erasmus intended to enter that controversy here. Cf n256 above.

344 Cf Phil 2:10.

345 *Breviarium in psalmos* PL 26 826D, though he suggests the apostles themselves rather than their successors

346 *Enarratio in psalmum* 2 PL 36 71

conspired together,' there is no mention in this verse of the nations and the peoples. I imagine that only kings and judges are specified here because, once they have changed their ways, the people will be easily persuaded to follow their good example; in any case, all the rest are included in the general conclusion at the end of the psalm: 'Blessed are all those who put their trust in him.'

It is thus incumbent upon rulers to 'understand,' whereas all too often the concomitant of high office is foolishness. It is essential that those who have to think for many thousands of people should be particularly thoughtful, and that those who oversee so many cities should be more than usually clear-sighted. Foolish monarchs are highly dangerous to the world, just as wise ones are highly beneficial to it. It is certainly not enough to be born a prince to be a good one.[347] It takes long study to learn the art of governing a people, and at the same time help must be no less assiduously sought from the Lord. For this reason, when God is offended by mankind's sins, he threatens them with a foolish prince, like some deadly plague. For example, he says, through Isaiah: 'And I shall give them mere boys as princes, and weaklings shall rule over them. And the people shall run wild, man against man, each man against his neighbour.'[348] Later in the same book, having been mollified, he says, as if promising a great favour: 'Behold, a king shall reign in righteousness, and his princes shall govern with justice.' And then: 'The fool will no longer be called prince, nor the scoundrel be thought noble.'[349]

Solomon, wisest of youths, understood this, for when he had succeeded to his father David's kingdom, and was told by the Lord to ask for whatever he wanted, he asked, not for wealth, or glory, or the death of his enemies, but for an understanding heart to help him govern a great nation wisely.[350] And yet the kingdom of Judaea, which Solomon ruled, was tiny by comparison with those which some monarchs now possess. He prays for the same thing in the book called Wisdom: 'O Lord,' he says, 'grant me Wisdom, who sits beside your throne . . . Send her from your holy heaven, from your majestic throne, to work at my side that I may learn what pleases you.'[351]

* * * * *

347 An important theme in the first chapter of the *Institutio principis christiani* CWE 27 206–45; see also *Adagia* I iii 1: *Aut regem aut fatuum nasci oportere* 'One ought to be born a king or a fool.'

348 Isa 3:4–5

349 Isa 32:1 and 5; the latter verse reads rather differently in the Vulgate and the Authorized Version.

350 Cf 1 Kings 3:5–11.

351 Wisd 9:4 and 10

The first part of the verse refers to judgment, which is that part of our understanding which enables us to decide what it is best to do; the second part of the verse refers to control of the emotions. 'Understand, you kings,' that you may perceive what is best for the state; 'learn your lesson, you judges': the Greek is παιδεύθητε, which often refers to moral improvement rather than scholarship, since it comes from the Greek for 'children,' whom we bring to heel by the use of strict discipline. The fool who lacks judgment always chooses the worst instead of the best, and similarly, if a man is distracted by anger, hatred, love, ambition, lust, pride, or spite, his mental perceptions are disturbed and he cannot discern the best course. It is the mark of a philosopher to be free from such distractions. Plato recognized this when he declared that the well-being of the state depended upon its rulers being philosophers as well.[352] How can a man properly rule others, if he is himself subject to blind emotion? How can a man properly take care of his own people, if his council consists of foolish passions?

Once more, Augustine thinks that in this verse the same idea is being repeated in different words, that the same people are addressed first as kings and then as judges, and that the same group are first told to understand and then commanded to learn their lesson.[353] How I wish that the psalmist had put this idea in so often that it would stick, just once, in the minds of our own princes, who are constantly throwing the world into disarray by their endless disorders!

But if a monarch can threaten mankind with total ruin by following his foolish, untamed passions, like Phaethon endangering the earth by driving the sun's chariot,[354] it is all the more essential that those who are the custodians of God's mysteries[355] should overflow with understanding of the divine law, and that their minds should be purged of all dangerous passions. How can they be called the rulers of the earth, if they are subject to earthly passions? If we are to deserve the name of rulers, we must be superior to our subjects. Spiritual leaders who are wise in the ways of heaven, who aspire to the realm above,[356] whose every thought and action is directed towards heaven, who trample on

* * * * *

352 An allusion to Socrates' celebrated ideal, expounded particularly in Plato *Republic* 5.473C–D

353 *Enarratio in psalmum* 2 PL 36 71

354 A son of Phoebus Apollo, the sun-god, Phaethon was struck down by Zeus' thunderbolt when he lost control of his father's horses and threatened to cause universal conflagration; see Ovid *Metamorphoses* 2.1–332.

355 1 Cor 4:1

356 Col 3:1

all that is earthly in their love for the celestial: such people deserve to be called the judges of the earth. Paul writes to the Corinthians as follows: 'Do you not know,' he says, 'that the saints will judge this world? And if the world is to be judged by you, are you unworthy to judge the smallest matters?'[357]

We have learned how Christ chooses from among men those who are to judge the world, and by their very lives they teach scorn for all the superficial attractions and temptations of this world. But, to puncture any pride that they may take in being named rulers and judges of the earth, he added: 'Serve the Lord with fear, and rejoice with trembling.' Immense prestige attaches to rulers: they fear no one, but are feared by all, and consequently they often think that they can do as they please. The psalm therefore warns them that they too must know fear; they are rulers of the people, but there is a ruler above them all in heaven. They are not taken to court by mankind, but they will have to stand with everyone else before the eternal judgment-seat. They may lord it over the people, but there is a lord above them all, on high, whose might and judgment they can never escape. Therefore, you kings, do not trust to your own powers and scorn the Lord of heaven, but 'serve him with fear.' In the Scriptures, to serve often means to worship. You have worshipped idols, you have worshipped the world, now worship the Lord. Moreover, to worship him is to obey his commandments 'with fear,' which means that you must always be on your guard against giving the slightest offence to the Lord of all.

Some princes worship the Lord by attending services or by reciting the set prayers called hours; I am not saying that this does them no credit, but if, at the same time, they impose harsh taxation and plunder the poor, if they appoint wicked and unworthy candidates to high office for money, if they divert into their own coffers the money destined to relieve the needy and persecute the innocent while condoning violence, if, unmindful of their oath, they tyrannically suppress the liberties of the state and plunge the whole world into the turmoil of war to satisfy their ambition, their anger, or their other passions – then they are not serving the Lord 'with fear.' If they truly feared him, if they were really convinced that they would have to account for each one of these crimes before the eternal and ineluctable judgment-seat, that the greater the power they wielded on earth, the heavier the penalties they would suffer, and that they would hear, with the impious, the words 'Go, accursed men, into the eternal fire'[358] – then they would not do whatever they please with such unconcern.

* * * * *

357 1 Cor 6:2
358 Matt 25:41

But now, in case the words 'serve the Lord with fear' might suggest only wretchedness, the psalm adds: 'and rejoice.' It is no unhappy task to serve the Lord; it will not diminish your status, but rather enhance it. In days gone by you served wood and stone,[359] you feared Jupiter and Neptune, or people bereft of life, or deadly demons; now you serve God, the ruler of the ages, and fear to offend him, since his displeasure alone can 'send you body and soul into hell.'[360] Rejoice in the service of a master who, if you have exercised your power in accordance with his decree, will reward your faithful management of an earthly kingdom with immortality in the kingdom of heaven.

However, to prevent this rejoicing from turning into irresponsible excess, the psalm adds the timely words 'with trembling.' The rewards are immense, but the task of kings is difficult. Many things may tempt them to overstep the mark: the sheer magnitude of their power, for example, which frequently makes a man who gets whatever he wants want more than he can get. Again, the position of great men makes them especially vulnerable to the plague of flattery by their suite; similarly, the press of business makes them prone to ignorance or inattention. It is thus essential that those who fear no mortal man should fear the Lord, and always be on guard, for if they sleep great harm may befall the state.

Next, the psalm repeats and reinforces the advice it has already given more than once: 'Grasp this instruction.' Here, the Greek text reads not καταλαμβάνετε but δράξασθε, meaning, more or less, to run after a fugitive.[361] They must thus act quickly, putting aside all other business to learn this lesson, unless they would rather give up their power. Indeed, it should be a constant preoccupation of those destined to rule; they cannot afford to waste the best part of their lives in dicing, drinking, wenching, hunting, travelling, parading, and other trifles. Whatever time they may be allotted is still short for rulers and noblemen to grasp this instruction. But the wisdom which princes gain from experience comes too late and is unreliable. Humanity will suffer if the princes must wage war for years before they realize finally, as old men, that war is in every way the most pernicious of occupations, even to the victor; if they only discover that high office must not be entrusted to just anyone when they see the state tottering from their misdeeds; if they

* * * * *

359 A reminiscence of the Lord's threats in the Old Testament, for example in Deut 4:28 and 28:64
360 Matt 10:28
361 Erasmus' point is that, instead of the usual verb 'to understand,' the Greek uses a forceful metaphor.

eventually learn to issue proper decrees only when they realize that the ones they issued so hastily have brought ruin on the state; and if it is only after many disappointments that they learn not to put their trust in flatterers.[362]

The same may be said of all the other duties of kings and leaders. But how can they 'grasp the instruction' in time? The principles of kingship can be absorbed more quickly from books than from experience; they can be learned more rapidly from respected and upright counsellors than from dangerous adventures. When St Thomas, archbishop of Canterbury, was raised to this office at the king's behest, he had more previous experience of the court than of the Holy Scriptures; realizing what a burden he had taken on his shoulders, he made great haste to 'grasp the instruction.' In that country it was customary for the archbishop, as primate of the whole kingdom, to invite the leading courtiers to feast with him. To avoid seeming miserly or mean, he provided for the nobles tables laden with everything their hearts could desire, but himself admitted no one to his table except a few scholars. Throughout the feast a reader read aloud or, if occasion arose, the meaning of the scriptural text was discussed; this shows how anxious he was to lose no time which could be spent 'grasping the instruction.'[363] How I wish that all the bishops of our own time would sing these verses more often, and that they would sing them 'with their understanding as well as with their spirit.'[364]

All this might indeed apply to the people who are in their charge, but it applies to them particularly, as the next part of the verse shows: 'Lest the Lord be angry, and you are struck down from the righteous path.' An ordinary person is in danger if he incurs the king's wrath, but the king is in still greater danger if he incurs the wrath of the Lord. Here again the psalm describes righteous wrath in terms of vengeance, which falls here on all who wander from his 'instruction': 'The way of the Lord is straight, the ways of the iniquitous are crooked, and the Lord does not know them.'[365] In our world, straying from the right road does not always spell disaster; often it merely involves us in extra expense, and occasionally a mistake has actually led a traveller to safety. But all who have strayed from the straight path of

* * * * *

362 All these admonitions to the prince resume the advice of the *Institutio principis christiani*, and are characteristic of Erasmus' attitude towards contemporary monarchy; see J.D. Tracy *The Politics of Erasmus* (Toronto 1978) passim.

363 Thomas Becket; cf David Knowles *Thomas Becket* (London 1970) 56, citing Becket's biographer Herbert of Bosham.

364 Cf 1 Cor 14:15.

365 An adaptation of Prov 4:27

the Lord have perished, even if they are still alive. Those who remain with Christ will not wander, for he is the path which leads to life, and all who have modelled their lives upon his teaching and example remain with him.

St Jerome notes in his commentary that the Hebrew text has a double meaning, and that the words translated in the Septuagint as 'grasp the instruction' could have been rendered 'worship or kiss the son' or, as he himself translates the Hebrew text, 'worship in purity,' because the ancients used to worship with a kiss and in some places the translators of the Septuagint render the Hebrew word for worship as καταφιλήσατε 'to kiss tenderly or caress.'[366] But 'bar' usually means 'son' in Syriac, whereas in Hebrew it means 'in purity' and, according to some, 'wheat.' However, there is no need to cudgel our brains with the complexities of these barbaric languages![367]

Having awaited the promised son for centuries, the Jews preferred to kill rather than worship him, and by that very fact, though they tried to establish their own righteousness by the legality of their action, they were struck down from the righteous path, which is Christ Jesus. They did indeed worship God, but not with purity: they sacrificed animals, they washed their bodies and their cups, but their innermost hearts overflowed with filth, the evil passions of anger, spite, avarice, and pride. This is why, in Isaiah, the Lord rejects their festivals, sacrifices, and sabbaths with such anger,[368] for he wishes to be worshipped 'in purity,' that is, in purity of spirit. He is spirit, pure and absolute, and wishes to be worshipped with a pure spirit rather than with sacrificial victims. Those who attribute salvation to man's own works do not worship the Son in purity, since eternal salvation is offered to all through the gospel, faith, and grace. Finally, anyone who honours the Father, but insults his Son, does not worship in purity; anyone who does not receive the Son does not receive the Father either.[369]

Next, to prevent the wicked from finding solace in the slowness of divine vengeance, the psalm adds: 'For his wrath flares up in a moment.' As long as he is holding back his vengeance, the Lord conceals his wrath, as it were, calling us to repentance by his mildness, patiently waiting to see if the sinner will perhaps mend his ways, and live. But we cannot be

* * * * *

366 *Breviarium in psalmos* PL 26 827A
367 The pun on *bar* is Erasmus' own, but most of the other material here is derived from Jerome's *Psalterium iuxta Hebraeos*; see Introduction xxi.
368 Isa 1:11–14
369 An echo of 1 John 2:23 or John 5:23

certain that his wrath will not suddenly flare up. The Hebrew words for
'in a moment' are rendered by the translators of the Septuagint ἐν τάχει,
which refers to something sudden and unexpected; we can take this to mean
either the Last Day, which will come 'like a thief in the night'[370] and steal in
unexpectedly, or the day of individual death, which also frequently strikes
down the unsuspecting while they are still half asleep. No one is so young
or strong, no one so powerful, that he can guarantee himself another day.
Even the greatest rulers are carried off unexpectedly by death; thus perished,
some time ago, Philip, son of the emperor Maximilian, at the height of his
career.[371] Similarly, sudden death has removed from the world Leo x, at a
time when all Rome resounded with the noise of triumphs and thanksgiving
– and his destination is uncertain:[372] he could not, indeed, be taken to task
by any man on earth,[373] but only he knows how good a case he has to make
before Christ's judgment-seat.

We must therefore be constantly on our guard and not wander, at any
time, from the righteous path. Let us always have a good conscience before
God, so that whenever the day of death may come, we may put our trust in
his goodness. It will be an unhappy day for those who put their trust on earth
in wealth, power, fortune, riches, or good deeds; but 'blessed are all those
who put their trust in the Lord.'[374] Indeed, how can those who, throughout
life, have put their trust in the world put their trust in the Lord at the hour
of death? Although our confidence is bred above all by the knowledge of
God's mercy, it cannot coexist with corrupt thoughts and a guilty conscience.
Anyone who trusts in man is accursed; anyone who trusts in riches is a
fool.[375] This is what the rich man in the Gospel was told: 'You fool, this night
they come for your soul; who will now possess the money you have made?'[376]

* * * * *

370 Cf 1 Thess 5:2 and 2 Pet 3:10.
371 Philip the Handsome, archduke of Burgundy and a patron of Erasmus, who
     died suddenly in Spain in 1506; see Ep 205.
372 Leo died on 1 December 1521; in Ep 1248 Erasmus, hearing rumours of his
     death, wrote a eulogy of his character, patronage of letters, and favours to
     himself, and had no doubt that he would reach 'a more lasting bliss.' However,
     the note of caution here is echoed in Ep 1342, where Erasmus refuses to judge
     Leo's career, on the grounds that that would be to usurp God's privilege.
373 Cf *Julius exclusus* CWE 27 179–80 for an ironic passage on papal invulnerability
     – on earth!
374 Ps 2:12
375 Cf Jer 17:5.
376 Luke 12:20

To put your trust in works is to follow the Jews. There are two kinds of works, however, those of Judaism and those of charity: it is dangerous to trust in the former unless the latter are also present. But confidence even in these is vain unless, mistrustful of our own merits, we have cast our sheet-anchor, as the saying goes,[377] into the boundless goodness of God.

St Augustine has pointed out the forcefulness of this line. Having struck terror into evil men by saying: 'For his wrath flares up in a moment,' it did not go on to say that the good would be merely safe, but 'blessed.'[378] Not only will they be freed from danger, but they will also win eternal bliss, if they have ceased their rebellion against the Lord's anointed: if, apprehensive of eternal punishment, they have acknowledged that he is ruler of heaven, earth, and hell, head and shepherd of the whole church, outside which there is no hope of salvation; that life must be lived according to his decree; and that he is the Son of God, God and man, whose power none can resist, whose vengeance no one, however strong, can escape if they have scorned his commandments. If they have worshipped him with reverence and diligence, if they rejoice in him, but 'with trembling,' if they have devoted all their energies to understanding his teaching, and if they have persevered in it – then, when the great and terrible day of the Lord suddenly arrives, the misfortune of those judged most fortunate by the world will be revealed, and at the same time all those who have put their trust, not in the weapons of this world, not in their works, but in the goodness of our Lord Jesus Christ, will be called 'blessed.'

It is now time to go on to the next psalm, and I intend to do so, with the inspiration of Jesus Christ; but first, let me demonstrate that the mystical sense of this psalm can be extended more widely, to different persons and different times, so that even today it applies to every one of us. First, although the historical meaning is often rather dull when set beside the allegorical, yet it sometimes sheds much light on the mystical meaning, and adds not a little to it. Anyone wanting to make trial of this should read Arnobius' commentary on the psalm in which David grieves over his sins, beginning: 'Have mercy on me, O God, according to your great loving kindness.'[379] Nor is it essential that every part of a prophecy should fit perfectly into either a historical or an allegorical reading, because often

* * * * *

377 *Adagia* I i 24; appropriately, the sheet-anchor was called the 'sacred anchor' in Latin. On the image applied to theology see Boyle 59–61.
378 *Enarratio in psalmum 2* PL 36 72
379 *Commentarii in psalmos* PL 53 396–8; the psalm in question is Ps 50/51.

certain elements are included to ensure chronological coherence while others, which are out of place in the historical context, compel us to have recourse to allegory.

The next step is to show that the prophecies are particularly appropriate to Christ, and that already, long ago, these prophetic oracles foretold the story which the Gospels narrate openly and without concealment. This level of meaning in particular is almost inexhaustible in the Psalms, and has indeed been shown to be irrefutable, on the authority of Scripture, as I have made clear. This, in my opinion, is the most challenging aspect to deal with, because once it has been properly established, it is not very hard to transfer the same reading from the head to the limbs, and from the time when Christ walked the earth to earlier or later periods. The sufferings inflicted on Christ by the Pharisees, the rulers, and by his own people had earlier been inflicted on the pious by the impious, and were again inflicted on the apostles after Christ. Indeed, from the beginning of time the world has persecuted the true worshippers of God, and so it shall be until the end of time. This psalm mentions other things which, so to speak, have always been done and have always existed, such as God's mocking of men, his wrath and fury, his appeal for a return to the worship of his Son, and the terror of the Last Judgment.

Christ is the truth of the gospel, the world is the cause of its own impermanence; in the final analysis, Christ suffers or is revived in his limbs. There thus remains the final step, when the meaning of Scripture is applied personally to each one of us, and the deeds ascribed to various groups in the other readings are applied to a single individual: for example, whenever anger, lust, ambition, or avarice distract our thoughts to those things that are contrary to the teachings of the gospel, then, so to speak, 'the nations rage and the peoples carry through their futile plots.' Again, if reason gives way to unbridled passions, then 'the kings of the earth stand ready, and the leaders conspire together against the Lord and against his anointed.' But whenever our minds are restored and, sickened by the harsh bondage which our sins have imposed, we remember our former freedom, then we cry out: 'Let us break their fetters, let us throw off their yoke from us.' Moreover, the Lord assists our efforts from heaven, by mocking and laughing us to scorn; he allows us to be swayed by our passions for a while, until we are taught by our misfortunes that the very things in which we placed our hopes of wondrous bliss have brought us total ruin. Next, he speaks to us in his wrath, exposing to our eyes the terrors of eternal torment, and filling us with horror of the life we have led. Then, in our terror and confusion, he shows us the source of our hopes of salvation, he sets his Son before us, who says to us all: 'Come to me

all you who labour.'[380] He warns us that our instincts must be made to obey
his laws, that human reason must conform to his decree, and that we must
so serve this single ruler of us all that we must both rejoice in his boundless
goodness towards us, and yet be always fearful; that is, we must mistrust our
own deeds and our own strength, since we are not our own judges, but must
place all hope and trust in his inestimable kindliness, through which eternal
salvation is won by those who turn to him for help with all their heart; to
him be praise and thanksgiving, with the Father and the Holy Spirit, for all
eternity.

* * * * *

380 Matt 11:28

A PARAPHRASE ON THE THIRD PSALM, 'O LORD, HOW HAVE MY TORMENTORS MULTIPLIED!'

Paraphrasis in tertium psalmum,
'Domine quid multiplicati'

Near the end of his commentary on the Second Psalm (144 above) Erasmus says: 'It is now time to go on to the next psalm, and I intend to do so, with the inspiration of Jesus Christ.' The implication is that Erasmus chose to discuss the Third Psalm simply because it was 'next,' and perhaps that he was about to take up the challenge of writing a commentary on the whole Psalter. In the letter to Melchior of Vianden which prefaces the present work, he claims that his correspondent 'leaves no stone unturned to persuade me to do over again for the mystical psalms what I had done for the New Testament.' There is thus some evidence that this *Paraphrase on the Third Psalm* gives us a glimpse of what might have been, that Erasmus is here assessing the practicability of continuing his programme of scriptural exegesis by undertaking a paraphrase of what he considered the most important and rewarding of the books of the Old Testament. The project got no further than this; the *Sermon on the Fourth Psalm*, when it appeared a year later, returned to the type of lengthy and painstaking exegesis which Erasmus had given to the first two psalms, and thereafter in his commentaries on the Psalms Erasmus made no attempt to follow the chronological order or to achieve completeness.

Thus the *Paraphrasis in tertium psalmum*, by far the shortest of Erasmus' writings on the Psalms, appeared from Froben's presses in 1524 not as a separate work but as an annex to the first edition of the *Exomologesis sive modus confitendi*. It reappeared, naturally enough, in the two subsequent Froben editions of Erasmus' writings on the first four psalms, as well as in a subsequent edition of the *Exomologesis*.[1] It shares a number of characteristics with other Erasmian paraphrases:[2] in particular it eschews textual criticism and seeks rather to elucidate the text by means of a sustained meditation in the first person. In the letter to Melchior of Vianden, Erasmus mentions the peculiar problems posed by the Psalms, such as their linguistic and structural complexity, but he makes no attempt to resolve them here, as he had in his other writings on the Psalms. Neither does he make any obvious use of the patristic commentaries which sustained him elsewhere; for example, he merely mentions in the prefatory letter a disagreement between Jerome and Augustine over the status of David in this psalm: in his work on other psalms he always has at least a few words to contribute to such controversies.

It is interesting that Erasmus' predecessors all considered the Third Psalm to be an allegory of the crucifixion, and that the words were spoken by

* * * * *

1 Cf ASD V-2 93.
2 See the excellent discussion of the genre in CWE 42 xi–xix and also Chantraine 692.

Christ upon the cross; Augustine also saw it, on another level, as a prophecy of the events surrounding the crucifixion.[3] Erasmus was to make just such an interpretation of the Fourth Psalm, but here he concentrates upon a different branch of the allegorical meaning, the application of the psalm to the limbs of Christ. He begins with a relatively brief typological examination, in which he demonstrates that the story of David and Absalom (which provides the historical background to the psalm) foreshadows the passion and resurrection of Christ. The main body of his meditation, however, dwells on the role of the psalm as a comfort in tribulation and an exhortation to piety. He uses the first person plural to involve the reader in his evocation of a faithful congregation beset by enemies, specifically the Jews and the heretics; it is noticeable, however, that Erasmus neglects the opportunity thus offered to satirize or denounce these opponents, no doubt because the detachment of the satirist would disrupt the unity of tone he had achieved by assuming the complicity and compliance of his audience. Thus almost every allusion is to the Bible, rather than to earlier commentators or to contemporary events; the true 'source' of this paraphrase is Erasmus' immersion in the Scriptures and his desire to promote the *philosophia Christi*.

The text translated here is that established by S. Dresden in ASD V-2 163–79 and based on the first edition. Most of the variants noted there come from a manuscript, now in Gouda, which appears to be a copy of Erasmus' own autograph draft of the treatise.[4] These variants consist almost entirely of unimportant variations in word order or marginal summaries omitted from the printed editions; I have not thought it necessary to note them, as they make no difference to the sense. In translating Scripture, in referring to the Psalms, and in establishing a 'working text' of Psalm 3, I have followed the principles described in my introductory note to the exposition of the First Psalm (4).

MJH

*****

3 Augustine *Enarratio in psalmum 3* PL 36 72–8
4 See ASD V-2 92.

PSALM 3

1 Domine quid multiplicati sunt, qui tribulant me! Multi insurgunt adversum me.

2 Multi dicunt animae meae: 'Non est salus tibi in Deo.'

3 Tu autem, Domine, clypeus [susceptor] meus es; gloria mea, et exaltans caput meum.

4 Voce mea ad dominum clamavi, et exaudit me de monte sancto suo.

5 Ego dormivi, et soporatus sum, et exsurrexi, quia Dominus suscepit me.

6 Non timebo millia populi circumdantis me.

7 Exsurge, Domine; salvum me fac, Deus meus; quoniam tu percussisti maxillam omnium adversantium me, et dentes peccatorum contrivisti.

8 Domini est salus; et super populum tuum benedictio tua.

1 O Lord, how have my tormentors multiplied! Many are they that rise up against me.

2 There are many who say to my soul: 'There is no salvation for you in God.'

3 But you, O Lord, are a shield to cover me; you are my pride and have raised my head high.

4 I cry aloud to the Lord and he answers me from his holy mountain.

5 I lie down and sleep, and I wake again, for the Lord upholds me.

6 I shall not fear the peoples that surround me in their thousands.

7 Rise up, Lord; save me, O my God; you strike the cheek-bone of all my enemies, and break the teeth of the wicked.

8 Salvation belongs to the Lord; may your blessing be upon your people.

ERASMUS OF ROTTERDAM TO DOCTOR MELCHIOR OF VIANDEN THE
THEOLOGIAN, GREETING[1]

I had lately finished a paraphrase on the Acts of the Apostles,[2] dearest Vianden, and thereafter it never crossed my mind that anyone would challenge
me with a request for a paraphrase. Lo and behold, out of ambush, as it were,
appears your letter,[3] to rob me of this peace of mind; for it leaves no stone
unturned[4] to persuade me to do over again for the mystical psalms what I
had done for the New Testament. What a well-disciplined phalanx of arguments you advance, sufficient, if you cannot persuade me, to compel me to
comply with your suggestion! First you move forward your right wing, and
what praises you pile on me! But praise, however ingratiating, is more than
anything a means of applying force; while your method of praising is to try
to persuade me that all you say is true, so that to contradict you is out of the
question. But with your left wing you launch a much more formidable attack.
You overwhelm me under arguments like a cloud of arrows, and if I shoot
any against you they are either caught on your shield and turned aside or
(what makes it still more one-sided) actually turned round and used against
me. You block every avenue, that I may have no way of escape. And then, to
leave nothing undone, you urge me and adjure me and, as the poet puts it,
'add threats to prayers, as monarchs used to do.'[5] You point out the danger
that, if I refuse your request, I may lose all the benefit of my previous efforts,
and may in fact reap discredit instead of the reputation I was aiming at. This
was presumably the object of that marvellous exaggeration of the worldwide
fame achieved by my Paraphrases – to make me all the more frightened at
the risk of losing so notable an asset, just as a tyrant might say to a father:
'Think of your children: what a good-looking lot they are, so virtuous, so
well educated, so clearly born for a glorious future! I will kill them all unless you do as I tell you.' And to leave me no scope to refuse to do what I am
urged to do, unless I wish to appear both ungodly and unhelpful, you de-
pict the whole of Christendom prostrate at my feet, making the same request
in unison. So you threaten me that, unless I comply, I shall be commonly regarded, and rightly so, as a creature of silly disclaimers, selfish excuses, and
artful dodges back and forth. The famous exaggerations of Demosthenes, the

* * * * *

1 The dedicatory letter is Ep 1427; its concluding lines come at the end of the
  Paraphrase (168 below).
2 See CWE 50. The dedicatory letter is Ep 1414.
3 Not extant
4 Adagia I iv 30: Omnem movere lapidem CWE 31 340
5 Ovid Metamorphoses 2.397

lightning and thunder of Pericles – these are nowhere, and all would seem cold and flat when compared with your torrents of rhetoric.

But the way you go on, my dear Melchior, is compulsion, not persuasion. Who would have thought that our Melchior, a man almost worn out by the niceties of logic and philosophy, would have had so much eloquence in him? For my part, my dear Vianden, at my age and in my state of health and in the embittered times in which we live, in which it is not safe to put pen to paper, if I were to demand my discharge, my freedom, I do not say from paraphrases but altogether from the whole business of writing, no fair-minded person would think my demand selfish or my assumptions unreasonable. Yet, though I see that this subject simply does not lend itself to paraphrase, I cannot risk having this powerful and menacing letter followed by another even more ferocious; and so I have provided a sample in the Third Psalm to show how vain will be the efforts of anyone who attempts anything of the kind. For in this psalm, short as it is, one is at once confronted by so many problems, the inversion of historical order (for many psalms have a subject which from a chronological point of view is earlier than the story of Absalom making war on his father David), the insertion of *Selah*, the question whether this psalm as a whole can be adapted to the person of David, which Jerome does not deny, maintaining that it is suitable to David and Christ and through him to all the saints,[6] while Augustine raises objections[7] – in view of all this, what will the maker of a paraphrase say about the title, about the complexity of the meaning, which is often threefold, since it is impossible, once a character has been assumed, to drop it again? None the less, I will try to give you in one psalm a taste of what I have tried to do, to make it clear that I did not lack the will to oblige you.

When I asked you to put a little work into demonstrating the corruptions of the logic and philosophy which are now so tediously and wastefully ground into the young at our universities, and into pointing out some system of teaching more suitable than this, my reason was that I can see many gifted minds put off from learning subjects that would be really useful by the dreary and pointless way in which they are taught. In fact, in many institutions such subjects, together with theology itself, are no longer taught; and at the same time the ancient tongues too and humane studies in general are neglected. The age is wasted solely in quarrelsome disputations and in bitter polemical pamphlets. This is a great scandal, and no one was better

* * * * *

6 In the commentary on the Psalms printed in volume VIII of Erasmus' edition of Jerome (fol 3 in Froben's edition of 1516) but now regarded as spurious
7 *Enarrationes in Psalmos* PL 36 72–3

fitted to deal with it than you, who have spent so many years working in that field and have achieved no mean reputation. You will earn the gratitude of both sides; for those who have learned nothing except those subjects, however they may have been taught, will prefer to see them lectured on differently in the universities rather than die out altogether, and the young who thirst for a more literary education will express their gratitude to you for pointing out a more suitable method. Farewell.

Pray give my greetings to your excellent Maecenas[8] and your most friendly and humane circle, in which I think you highly fortunate. Since you mention my *Colloquia familiaria* in your letter, it occurs to me to wonder at the part played by fortune in human affairs. What subject could be more lightweight? And yet you would hardly believe how many thousand copies have been published[9] and the appetite of purchasers is not yet satisfied. It appears again this year,[10] enlarged by added matter at the end. Such is the nonsense I write to please my friends; though there are some grave divines who maintain that these trifles have a serious purpose.[11] You may praise my *Spongia*,[12] but you will never persuade me not to hate it; I cannot forgive those who drove the poor fellow[13] to this. Some people are so misguided. He died, I think, before he had read my *Spongia*. Farewell once more. Now for the psalm!

* * * * *

8 Perhaps Pierre Cotrel; see Ep 1237 n8.
9 See Ep 1341A:285–301.
10 See Ep 1476.
11 See Ep 1296 n10.
12 See Epp 1378 and 1389.
13 Ulrich von Hutten

A PARAPHRASE ON THE THIRD PSALM

'O Lord, how have my tormentors multiplied!' O Lord God, who can accomplish with a nod[1] whatever you desire, whose will none can resist, whose counsel is unfathomable, even to the angels: though Lord of all and creator of all things, you have set us apart from all the nations as your chosen people and, through the blood of your only begotten Son, have claimed this people for yourself, although we were mean and powerless in the eyes of the world; you require us to abandon the world and depend on your aid alone. Therefore hear, I pray, the complaint of your people. We speak with a single voice, a single cry, since the misfortune is common to us all; when one limb is struck, all feel the blow in equal measure.[2]

You are the one true God; our defence and our salvation lie in your hands alone; no other bosom will receive our tears, no other ears will hear our cries, no other power will offer us refuge. Why then have you allowed your beloved people to stand alone, attacked in concert by so many foes, the weak by the strong, the unarmed by the armed? In the same way, it is true, Cain, standing in his day for the godless legions of the gentiles, rose up long ago against his brother Abel, standing then for the whole congregation of those who depend on you; at once the sinner prevailed and crushed the unresisting innocent.[3] In similar ways, impious rulers struck down your servants the prophets, and a whole rout of priests, Pharisees, Scribes, elders, Herod, Pilate, and finally the whole mass of the people, conspired, as it were, against your only Son Jesus, and crushed him.

Moreover, what was fulfilled in him had previously been foreshadowed in your beloved servant David, against whom Absalom stirred up a most

* * * * *

1 A common image in antiquity: see Homer *Iliad* 1.528 and Virgil *Aeneid* 9.106; cf also 2 Macc 8:18.
2 Cf 1 Cor 12:26.
3 Cf Gen 4:8.

terrible revolt.[4] David was king of the Israelites, Christ the king of the Jews, that is, of all who confess your name. Absalom, whose renowned beauty and luxuriant hair[5] filled him with unbridled arrogance, made wicked plans to destroy David and to claim his kingdom. Absalom was the prototype of the Jewish people, who took similar pride in the renown of their God-given law, in their father Abraham, their prophets, God's splendid promises to them, their temple of the Lord, their sacrifices, the prestige of their priests, Scribes, and Pharisees, and all the rituals in which they paraded a dazzling display of piety; and so they turned all their strength against the king of the Jews. They even had their Ahithophel: he had formerly been one of David's closest advisers, but quickly defected to Absalom, and showed him how, once David himself was dead, he could bring over the whole people to his side.[6] Similarly, Judas the disciple became a traitor to his Lord.[7] David did not possess the physical beauty, the luxuriant hair, the smooth, insidious eloquence of Absalom. But these are the ornaments and the weapons of a woman. Our David has a vigorous disposition which delights those manly spirits who pursue moral health instead of aesthetic pleasures and strength instead of beauty. David, considering his people's security before his own, took to his heels and left the city;[8] Absalom, marshalling his chariots and horsemen, advanced menacingly with his army. Christ escaped more than once from the Jews' fury, as on the occasions when they tried to stone him or to fling him down from a cliff.[9] Absalom's followers grew riotous and arrogant; the fugitive David's companions wept and wailed. Today, similarly, the world takes arms against Christ and his adherents and unleashes its fury on those who preach the gospel. Absalom reigned in Jerusalem and practised tyranny in a palace not his own; David and his followers had to flee and hide.

In all this, heavenly Father, we recognize the image of everything that, in accordance with your will, befell your Son Jesus and his disciples. Your Son 'was in the world, and the world was made by him' (just as David had built Jerusalem), 'and the world knew him not';[10] he was driven out and thus withdrew into the wilderness, to dwell among the gentiles. The image

* * * * *

4   See 2 Samuel 15–18. The heading of Ps 3 in most versions relates it to David's flight from Absalom, thus making the 'literal sense' simple to elucidate.
5   Cf 2 Sam 14:25–6.
6   2 Sam 17:2–3
7   As described in all the Gospels: Matthew 26–7, Mark 14, Luke 22, John 13 and 18
8   2 Sam 15:14
9   Cf John 8:59 and 10:31, and Luke 4:29.
10   Cf John 1:10.

corresponds to the gospel story in yet another detail: as David fled, he crossed the brook of Kidron,[11] which our David, Jesus, also crossed before his death. Moreover, at the moment of greatest peril, David tried to ensure that his endangered followers should not share his peril; similarly, your Son said: 'If it is me you seek, let them go.'[12] David ordered that the ark be carried back to the city of Jerusalem, wishing to rely for everything on the Lord's prophecy, not on the resources of mere mortals: 'If the Lord should say: "You do not please me," I am here, let him do what he wishes with me,'[13] he said, 'I shall go where I am to go.'[14] Your Son, our true king, said: 'Your will be done, not mine,' and 'The Son of Man goes as it is written of him.'[15] David, his feet bare and his head covered,[16] climbed the Mount of Olives in order to pray; Christ, with bare feet, went up to the place called Golgotha,[17] climbed to the summit of the cross, and there prayed to the Father for the salvation of the whole people.

Shimei, a kinsman of Saul, seething with inveterate hatred of David, hurled bitter taunts at him,[18] which, in the midst of other woes, can indeed be the most bitter pill to swallow. David, the outcast, the fugitive, destitute and in hiding, had to listen to him: 'Get out! get out! you man of blood, you man of Belial! The Lord has repaid you for all the blood of the house of Saul, whose kingdom you stole; see! your sins have caught up with you!' Not content with curses, he even hurled stones at David and his servants. Our David, the true and eternal ruler of your people, also had to listen to them: 'You are a Samaritan, and you are possessed by a devil,'[19] and 'You cast out devils in the name of Beelzebub.'[20] His friends also had to listen to them: 'You were steeped in sin from birth, and yet you give us lessons?'[21] And again: 'You are one of them; you too are a Galilean.'[22] Such words, more hurtful than any stone, were hurled at Jesus' disciples in those days. Moreover, when

* * * * *

11 2 Sam 15:23 and John 18:1
12 John 18:8
13 2 Sam 15:25–6
14 2 Sam 15:20
15 Matt 26:39 and 24
16 2 Sam 15:30; this is apparently the sense of the Latin and is the rendering in the Authorized Version; later English versions read 'with bare head.'
17 Matt 27:33, Mark 15:22, Luke 23:33, and John 19:17
18 This story is told in 2 Sam 16:5–8.
19 John 8:48
20 Matt 12:24, Mark 3:22, and Luke 11:15
21 John 9:34
22 Mark 14:70

Jesus was hanging on the cross he could hear the taunts of the soldiers, the Scribes, and the Pharisees, which were more painful even than the cross: 'You would pull the temple down, would you? If he is the Son of God, let him now come down.'[23] David bore Shimei's taunts with patience, and would not permit Abishai the son of Zeruiah to avenge him.[24] Our king restrained Peter when he tried to exact vengeance, and, as if deaf and unable to hear them, he remained silent beneath the taunts of the scoffers; he prayed meanwhile to the Father to forgive them,[25] just as David wept at the death of Absalom, saying: 'O Absalom, my son, why am I not allowed to die in your place?'[26] David wished that he could save one individual; Christ offered salvation to the whole Jewish people, and Paul, the imitator of Christ, desired to become an outcast for the sake of the Jews who were pursuing him with implacable hatred.[27]

Finally, the outcome was similar in each case. David, restored by God's aid to his kingdom, sings a hymn to his deliverer, in these words: 'Therefore will I praise you among the nations, O Lord, and sing psalms to your name. He is a tower of salvation to his king, and shows mercy to his anointed David and to his seed for evermore.'[28] Similarly our David, having conquered all his enemies by his death, and having established dominion over the whole world, says: 'All power in heaven and on earth is given to me.'[29] Ahithophel went home and hanged himself; Judas Iscariot returned to his house with an unquiet mind and met his doom in the same manner.[30] What is more, when we see the Jewish people clinging obdurately to the rituals of the Mosaic law, to the extent that, as strangers to Christ, they cannot obtain a place in heaven, or even on earth, since they are shunned and oppressed in every land: do we not see Absalom, caught by his hair, hanging from a tree?[31] His pride was his downfall.

We confess, Lord, that nothing happens on this earth by accident or by chance, but that all things are governed by your eternal design; what was foreshadowed in King David, we see fulfilled in the king of our Jerusalem, which is the church; and what happened to the head, we confess, happens

* * * * *

23 Matt 27:40–2
24 2 Sam 16:9–10
25 Cf Matt 26 and Luke 22–3.
26 2 Sam 18:33
27 Rom 9:3
28 2 Sam 22:50–1
29 Matt 28:18
30 2 Sam 17:23 and Matt 27:5
31 2 Sam 18:9

also to the body. There are, and there always will be, people like Absalom, self-satisfied and arrogant, with their titles, their prestige, their honours, and their show of religion. There are plenty of people like Ahithophel, and like Shimei, Saul's kinsman; plenty like Annas and Caiaphas, like the Scribes and Pharisees, like the leaders of the people, like the ungrateful mob, the fickle multitude swayed by the breath of princes; like Herod and Pilate, and the impious throng who persecute and afflict your anointed in his members. It has pleased you in your wisdom to make trial of your people's trust in you in this way, and to teach us to rely on your aid alone. But still, so long as we dwell in this weak body, hemmed in on all sides by evil, we cannot but groan, and sigh, and bewail our immediate fate; but only to you, in whom alone we fix all our hopes. When others are in distress, they find help or consolation in various things: riches, beauty, physical strength, noble birth, fame, position, power, cunning, armies, horses, chariots, fleets, cannon, kings' alliances, princes' plots, worldly wisdom, the hope of revenge, sensual pleasures and delights; all of these help, it seems, to soften the blow. Some even have recourse to enchanters and soothsayers. But we have learned from our Lord, your Son, to place our hopes in none of these, lest we be deprived of your aid, since you wish all the glory of victory to be attributed to you. We have learned to give thanks to you alone if good befalls us, and to address our complaints to you if misfortune overtakes us.

It is difficult enough to resist a determined attack by one enemy. But see how many now surround your flock, alone and weak as it is; how many men and weapons are deployed against us by this warlike world; evil spirits with fiery darts never cease to assail our souls from the heights, and besides all this we carry with us an enemy within the walls, our flesh, which endlessly rebels against the spirit. It is no wonder that these many foes, ever ready for the fray, do not allow your people peace of mind; many fearsome wolves, many roaring lions, seeking their prey, prowl about your sheepfold.[32] They are at their most dangerous when they join forces to attack us with all their might; they are lofty and exalted, we are humble; they are armed, we are unarmed; they are the conquerors, we are the underdogs. We are sent into exile, thrown into prison, stripped of our possessions, struck, beaten, reviled, condemned, killed. Even if no human foes are assailing your people, for once, there is no lack of enemies yet more dangerous, because invisible: from one side we are assailed by the spirit of lust, from another by the spirit of anger, or ambition, excess, avarice, and often, to outwit us more speedily,

* * * * *

32 A reminiscence of 1 Pet 5:8, describing the devil; for the prowling wolf, see for example Matt 10:16 and Luke 10:3.

this cunning foe disguises himself as an angel of light.[33] But who could count their numbers, their weapons to batter us, their tricks to entrap us; who could describe the fierceness of the charge when the mighty join forces to overwhelm your people, O Lord?

However, amid all these woes, distressing though they may be, we find singular consolation in our hope of an end to adversity, of suffering turned to joy, like storm-tossed travellers cheered by the prospect of returning calm. But our enemies seek to snatch even this last hope from us, for there are many who delight in tormenting our souls by saying that there is no hope for them in God.[34] If you will not or cannot save your people, where can they hope to find salvation? An insult that is flung in our faces can be borne, but this most bitter of taunts is aimed at our souls. The death of the body can be endured, but who could bear the loss of his soul? However, your only-begotten Son heard a similar taunt long before us when these hostile words were directed at him: 'Now that he is sleeping, surely he will never rise again.'[35] Then, while hanging on the cross, he heard: 'He put his hopes in God; let God rescue him now, if he wants him.'[36] Then there was the unfounded reproach: 'You are a Samaritan, and possessed of a devil.'[37] Is there anything more cruel than to taunt a man already suffering in extremity and to make him despair of salvation? O Lord, stop up the ears of our souls, to keep out such cries as 'There is no salvation for you in God.'

There are indeed many who assail us with this most bitter of taunts: the votaries of this world tell us that 'whoever falls asleep in Christ is dead';[38] the mockers of the church's sacraments cry out: 'A sprinkling of water does not wash away the stain from your spirit, nor do words atone for the deeds you have done.' The heretics cry that there is no hope for those who have relapsed since baptism.[39] One sect of philosophers cries that there is no God, while another maintains that God is not concerned with human affairs,[40] and that

* * * * *

33 Cf 2 Cor 11:14.
34 An adaptation of Ps 3:2
35 Ps 40/41:8
36 Cf Matt 27:43.
37 John 8:48
38 1 Cor 15:18
39 A marginal note in the manuscript attributes this view, rightly, to the Novatian heretics (third century AD).
40 Atheistic philosophers were something of a rarity in the ancient world; Cicero (De natura deorum 1.1.2 and 1.23.63) cites only Diagoras of Melos and Theodorus of Cyrene. The second 'sect' mentioned resembles the Epicureans, frequently reproved by Cicero (ibidem 1.2.3, 1.99.51, 3.32.79).

we should eat and drink now, for tomorrow we die.[41] From another quarter, the Sadducees cry that souls do not survive the death of the body, and that the whole being perishes at death.[42] But what are all these yapping voices trying to tell us? Simply that we are wrong to have placed our hopes of salvation in you, our God. And since on this earth we are done to death all the day long for your sake, and treated like sheep destined for the slaughter,[43] are we not truly more wretched than any others, if our expectations cannot extend beyond this life?[44] Are we not irredeemably dead when slain by our foes? That godly man Tobit heard similar words from his wife and neighbours;[45] the saintly Job also heard them from his wife: 'Bless God, and die.'[46] There are also parts of our own being which aim such thoughts at our souls, from close range, removing hope and instilling despair. For our sakes, your Son Jesus had to listen to remarks of this kind, the most wounding of all, as he hung on the cross: 'My God, my God, why have you forsaken me? The words of my confession are far from saving me.'[47]

Sins, too, have speeches to make, but of a different kind; their voices are soft and persuasive as they tempt our souls. How persuasive, for example, was ambition's voice when it said: 'You shall not die, but shall be like gods, with the knowledge of good and evil.'[48] Unchastity speaks in this way: what could be sweeter? So does intemperance: what could be more attractive? And the mania for power: what could be more dazzling? And avarice: what could be more satisfying? But when the soul has drunk the sweet poison, there is a change of tone, and it hears these bitter words: 'Your sin is too great to deserve pardon.'[49] God is just; you can expect nothing except punishment. The sentence is harsh enough when passed on us for a single crime; who could bear it if all our many crimes, adultery, robbery, murder, theft, were to cry out together to our souls: 'There is no salvation for you in your God'?[50] Hard words, bitter words indeed!

Now, if we could not see, here on earth, beyond the enormity of the crimes we have committed, beyond our own resources and our own deserts,

* * * * *

41 1 Cor 15:32, quoting Wisd 2:6
42 Cf for example Matt 22:23, Mark 12:18, and Luke 20:27.
43 Cf Ps 43/44:22.
44 Cf 1 Cor 15:19.
45 Cf Tob 2:8 and 14.
46 Job 2:9; the English versions read 'Curse God, and die.'
47 Ps 21/22:1; cf Matt 27:46.
48 Gen 3:4–5
49 Gen 4:13, adapted
50 Ps 3:2, echoed throughout the preceding passage

and God's sentence upon us, what indeed would be left to us but to despair? But your mercy, which surpasses and masters even your just judgments, says something different to our souls. Your judgment lets us descend to the depths of despair, but, at the time of trial, your boundless mercy[51] makes provision for us to survive. 'We are troubled on every side, but we are not distressed; we are bewildered, but our wits do not desert us; we suffer persecution, but we are not abandoned; we are humiliated, but we are not perturbed; we are struck down, but we do not perish. We appear to be dying, but, see, we are alive, chastened but not done to death.'[52]

However much we may be tempted to despair by the sheer numbers of those who strike at our little band, by the arrogance of their attacks upon our humility, and by the bitterness of those who taunt us, like a defeated army, with the absence of hope, yet you alone, O Lord, stretch out a helping hand against the throng of our assailants; those whom you have taken under your protection cannot perish. In the face of these boasters who would trample us underfoot, we take pride in you alone; you lift up our heads in expectation of a victory against those who, as proud as any conqueror, used to taunt us as if we were a beaten army. If you, O God, are on our side, who can be against us?[53] Who can cut us off from the love of your Son Jesus? Shall it be misfortune, poverty, hunger, nakedness, danger, persecution, or the sword?[54] We are assured that nothing, not death or life, not angels, principalities, or powers, not the present or the future, not strength, height, or depth, nor anything else in creation, can cut us off from your love, O God, which is in Christ Jesus our Lord.[55] Anyone who confesses your Son with a whole heart will be delivered by him from all the storms of temptation. You offer to all his limbs the same aid that you gave him. When 'the nations raged and the peoples carried through their futile plots against him, when the kings of the earth stood ready, and the leaders conspired together,'[56] when they all unleashed their fury against a single man, abandoned by all, then you protected him with the shield of your power. In their pride, they all made mock of him, beating him with a cane, boxing his ears, cuffing him, spitting in his face,

* * * * *

51 The phrase echoes the title of the *De immensa Dei misericordia* (LB V 557–88), completed by Erasmus by July 1524; see Ep 1474.
52 2 Cor 4:8–9 and 6:9. Erasmus now turns to the consolation offered by Ps 3:3–4, of which verbal echoes are scattered over the next few paragraphs.
53 Cf Rom 8:31.
54 Cf Rom 8:35.
55 Cf Rom 8:38–9.
56 Ps 2:1–2

mockingly crowning him with thorns and giving him the cane as a sceptre, dressing him in a scarlet mantle,[57] making bitter gibes about him and then hurling insults at him as he hung between two criminals. But although in every way he had been made less than human, a mere worm, a reproach to humanity, and an object of scorn to the people,[58] he none the less took pride in you alone because, in the face of all the world's contempt, you found so many ways to glorify your Son, even in death itself. Finally, after his burial, when they set out to obliterate his very name, you raised his head high and 'gave him the name which excels all others, so that at the name of Jesus every knee should bow, in heaven, on earth, and under the earth.'[59]

The sufferings of our head are a lesson to us; his exaltation brings hope and pride to his limbs. Though weak in ourselves, we are made invincible by you; although there is nothing in us to make us proud, we take pride in you and in our Lord Jesus Christ; though mean and despicable in ourselves, we are raised high by him, and can look down on all the wiles of Satan. We know that this is your way: you wound in order to heal, you strike down in order to raise up, you kill in order to give life, you humble in order to glorify. Therefore, we too shall take a willing pride in our affliction, our humiliation, and our disgrace, so that in you we may find consolation, exaltation, and glory. From this day your people will not listen to the mocking voices which say: 'There is no salvation for you in your God'; but whenever a storm of troubles breaks upon us, in all confidence we shall cry out to you with our own voices, and you will answer us from your holy mountain.[60]

There are cries from the synagogue which ring in your ears: 'I fast twice on the sabbath, I give a tenth of all my property to the poor, and I am not as other men are.'[61] The church has a different cry, in which it confesses that the Lord is good and that his mercy endures for ever.[62] The voice of faith is powerful, and obtains all that it asks of your mercy, O Lord. Your Son promised: 'Not a hair of your head shall perish.' He also promised: 'Whatever you ask of the Father in my name, he shall give you.'[63] You too made a promise, O God: 'He shall cry out to me and I shall answer

* * * * *

57 Based on Matt 27:28–31
58 Cf Ps 21/22:6.
59 Phil 2:9–10
60 Cf Ps 3:4.
61 Cf Luke 18:11–12.
62 Cf the opening verse of a number of psalms: 105/106, 106/107, 117/118, 135/136.
63 Luke 21:18, followed by John 15:16 (cf 16:23)

him.'[64] We trust in your promises, and cry out with the voice of faith: 'You who cannot fail, answer us from your holy mountain.' The synagogue cries out in a temple made by men's hands,[65] and demands an answer from the mercy-seat.[66] But we know that your majestic presence cannot be limited in space, and cry out to you from every region of the world; we are sure that, from your lofty throne which you never leave, you will answer us according to your own good pleasure, even if you seem not to answer us: for you know what is good for us. We do not prescribe a time or a place or a particular way for you to help us, so firm is our confidence that your aid will not fail a people who put their trust in you.

While hanging on the cross, your Son called out to you in his own voice, and 'he was answered because of his devotion.'[67] Crying out in a loud voice, he commended his spirit into your hands,[68] and you brought him back to life on the third day since, confident and sure of your protection, he willingly fell asleep in death, taking his rest in the tomb; soon he was roused and brought back to life, while the Jews guarded the tomb in vain. All this, because you never deserted him, and did not abandon his soul in hell, that death might have no power over him.[69] The impious held a celebration because, as they thought, they had brought an innocent man to certain death, and they said: 'Surely he will never rise again.'[70] But to you he was sleeping, to you he was resting, and would be awakened whenever you wished. We worship and reverence this experience of our head as a mystical symbol, in the hope that your goodness will offer the same gift to the limbs as it gave to the head. We who die in the faith of Jesus Christ, since we die in the certain hope of a better life, fall asleep rather than die, and meanwhile the body, which is to live again at the trumpet-blast of the angel, is not dead in the tomb, but is at rest, free now from all the pain of sorrow and hardship with which it was afflicted, and will live again in the fullness of time; our souls too enjoy a peaceful sleep until each one shall renew its companionship with its body.[71]

* * * * *

64 Ps 90/91:15
65 Cf Acts 17:24; a derogatory expression.
66 The place of expiation in the Holy of Holies in the synagogue; cf Exod 25:17 and Heb 9:5.
67 Heb 5:7
68 Luke 23:46
69 Cf Rom 6:9.
70 Cf Ps 40/41:8.
71 On this passage, with its echoes of 1 Thessalonians 4 and other Pauline descriptions of the resurrection, see Screech 174–5.

Secure in this belief, we are both alive and dead, knowing that, whether we live or die,[72] we live and die for you, since both living and dying we belong to you; whatever belongs to you does not perish. Those who belong to you are all those who have been grafted into the body of your only-begotten Son by the gospel faith; there is no damnation for those who are in Christ Jesus,[73] and indeed their earthly lives are a reflection of his: by repentance they are dead to sin,[74] by baptism and by the avoidance of evil works they are buried with him who spent the sabbath at ease in the tomb, and they rise again with him into newness of life, so that now they do not live for worldly desires but for righteousness. Just as Jesus Christ died once for our sins, and lives the life everlasting, so they too shall one day live again in blessed immortality since you have bestowed righteousness upon them.

In all these ways your compassion welcomes and protects us. In this world we are struck down and killed, as it were, but when you set us free we breathe again; through repentance we are mortified in the flesh, but we are made to live again by your Spirit; this feeble body falls asleep in death, but is revived by you in the resurrection. Our leader's example shows us the way to total victory. He conquered the world, he conquered the prince of this world, he conquered death, he conquered sin,[75] he conquered his persecutors' fury; but as he conquered them all for us, our faith in your Son Jesus gives us too the courage and boldness to oppose them all, and, rejoicing with him, we sing a triumphal song: 'I shall not fear the peoples that surround me in their thousands.'[76]

We have seen your only-begotten Son, deserted, given up for lost by everyone, even his closest friends, triumph over all his enemies with your protection. We have seen all your saints subjected to extreme peril in this world, but all were granted your aid. For ourselves, we have been hemmed in by so many misfortunes as to make us despair of salvation, yet we have learned by experience that your help is closest at hand when our own resistance is at its lowest ebb; so, from now on, confident in your goodness, emboldened by your power, we shall not fear the peoples that surround us in their tens of thousands. Your power to protect us is too strong for all the multitudes of enemies that beset us; your wisdom, working for our salvation,

* * * * *

72 Rom 14:8
73 Cf Rom 8:1.
74 Rom 6:1; the following passage contains many echoes of Rom 6:1–5. See also Screech 123.
75 There are echoes here of John 16:33 and 12:31, 1 Cor 15:54, and 1 John 1:7.
76 Ps 3:6

is too subtle for the wily enemies who plot our destruction. Your goodness, which we have seen and felt so often, has more power to implant confidence in us than has the fury of all our enemies to terrorize us. For all these reasons we give you constant thanks, most merciful God, both when we are visited by adversity, by which you make our confidence in you all the more notable, and when we are rescued, and win through, for the consolation of others and the glorification of your name.

We must, however, expect constant attacks by the enemy for as long as we remain in this mortal frame, until we have come to terms with death, and can say in safety: 'Death, where is your victory; death, where is your sting?'[77] Therefore, do not leave us to our own devices but, whenever we are beset by an army of troubles, threatening us with imminent ruin, do you, O Lord our God, rise up to defend and preserve[78] your little flock, and to let our enemies know that God is for us, that we are in his care, and that none can stand against his power.[79] We know the numbers, the power, and the fury of our foes, but you have guaranteed our safety against them, for you are our God, in whom we have placed our hopes of salvation. Already, through your only Son Jesus, you have shown us that none of our foes is invincible; by patient suffering he defeated the spiteful Jews, he overcame all Satan's temptations, and he conquered a world which had always looked on him with hatred. He was engulfed by death, but he returned and broke death's power. Descending to hell he crushed the tyranny of the prince of this world. But his conquests were made for us, and so he bade us all, however weak, to take heart from his victory: 'Be of good cheer,' he said, 'for I have conquered the world.'[80]

In this way, O God, through the Son, you have 'struck the cheek-bone' of your people's foes, and 'broken the teeth of the wicked';[81] they may attack us, but they cannot devour and swallow us. How often have the Jews' intransigence, the princes' cruelty, the philosophers' arrogance, the rhetoricians' eloquence, or the heretics' obduracy opened their mouths wide to swallow your little flock, saying: 'Let us be like devils and swallow them alive and whole, like men going down to the pit.'[82] But your wisdom has struck them across the cheek-bone for us, and in such a way that, the more they unleash their frenzy against us, the stronger the gospel message

* * * * *

77 1 Cor 15:55
78 Cf Ps 3:7.
79 Cf Rom 8:31.
80 John 16:33
81 Ps 3:7
82 Prov 1:12

becomes. Today, too, our great enemy prowls about like a roaring lion seeking its prey,[83] but you, O Lord, have broken his teeth. Even today, the Jews sharpen their teeth against us, but they are broken, so that, although they may bark, they cannot bite. The heretics too sharpen their teeth, but in vain, since you turn all their efforts to the advantage of your church. Hell opens its mouth to engulf those who invoke the name of Jesus, but in vain, since he said that not even the gates of hell should prevail against the gospel faith.[84] Christ is a strong rock,[85] and anyone who is in Christ is a rock: broken teeth cannot grind it down.

Some wild beasts, such as lions and bears, do their killing with their teeth, but there are others which carry a deadly poison in their fangs. Similarly, there are people 'whose teeth are their spears and arrows, whose tongue is a sharp sword, and whose lips conceal the viper's lethal poison.'[86] This is undoubtedly that generation, sprung from the devil, not from God, which, in Solomon's description, 'has swords instead of teeth, and grinds with its teeth until it has eaten the helpless off the earth and the poor from among men.'[87] But you, O Lord, have fulfilled through Christ the promise which the prophet made in your name, long ago: 'God will break their teeth in their mouths; the Lord will smash the lions' fangs.'[88] And again, elsewhere: 'You shall tread on the viper and the basilisk and shall trample the lion and the dragon.'[89] Once, an impious assembly gnashed its teeth against your servant Stephen, but they were broken, for they could not resist his wisdom and the Spirit which spoke in him.[90] The same people whipped the apostles and ordered them not to preach in the name of Jesus; they were, in a manner of speaking, baring their fangs at the apostles, but what they heard in reply was this: 'It is for you to judge whether more obedience is due to man than to God.'[91] People who press false charges against the innocent, who heap insults upon the pious, who lure the unwary into acts of impiety: all these are 'sharpening their teeth' against their victims. Similarly, when Satan said to Christ at one point: 'I will give you all this, if you will fall down and worship me,' he was sharpening his poisoned teeth against him; but Christ shattered his teeth by saying: 'It is written: you shall worship the Lord your God, and

* * * * *

83 1 Pet 5:8
84 Cf Matt 16:18.
85 Cf 1 Cor 10:4.
86 A conflation of Ps 56/57:4 and Rom 3:13
87 Prov 30:14
88 Ps 57/58:6
89 Ps 90/91:13
90 Acts 7:54
91 Acts 4:19; for the occasion, see Acts 5:29 and 40.

serve him alone.'[92] Those who accused him of various crimes before Annas and Caiaphas, and again before Pilate, 'bared their fangs' at him. The people who shouted: 'Away with him, away; crucify him, crucify him!'[93] had teeth like spears, with which they could kill him – but not conquer him. When they shouted at him, as he hung on the cross: 'He said he was the Son of God; let him now come down from the cross!'[94] they were sinking their poisoned fangs into him, but their teeth were broken by the Lord's patient suffering.

Why, therefore, should we fear people who, in a similar way, bare their broken fangs at your church, saying: 'There is no salvation for them in their God.'[95] On the contrary, 'salvation belongs to the Lord';[96] without him, even those who seem to be saved will perish, but with him even those who seem to be dead will be saved. If they were to say: 'You cannot hope for salvation from your own efforts, from earthly powers, from Moses' law, from moral philosophy, or from the merits of mankind,' we might agree and we might lose heart. But because they say: 'There is no salvation in God,' we can reply with perfect confidence: 'Salvation belongs to the Lord.' Why do you threaten us with extinction, when you have no power to destroy or to save anyone at all? When the body is slain, only God can cast the soul into hell,[97] and only he can recall a soul from the regions below. Why do people who cannot save themselves threaten others with extinction? Pilate claimed this power for himself: 'Do you not know,' he said, 'that I have the power to kill you, and also the power to save you?'[98] But Pilate could do no more than kill the body, and not even that without your permission, for without your consent not even a little sparrow falls to earth.[99] There is no hope of salvation by mankind; anyone who puts his trust in mankind is accursed.[100] There is no hope of salvation in pagan gods, in earthly princes, in angels, in saints. Only you, O Lord, can perform what you proclaim through the lips of your prophet: 'See, I am, alone, and there is no god beside me. I kill, and I give life; I wound, and I heal; there is no one to rescue you from my hand.'[101] Those who seek to be the agents of their own salvation perish for all eternity; those who place their hopes of salvation anywhere but in you are making another

* * * * *

92 Matt 4:9–10; cf Luke 4:6–8.
93 John 19:15
94 Cf Matt 27:42–3.
95 Cf Ps 3:3.
96 Ps 3:8
97 Cf Luke 12:5.
98 See John 19:10.
99 Cf Matt 10:29.
100 Jer 17:5
101 Deut 32:39

god for themselves; but there is only one God, and he is the source of true salvation. For there is a false salvation, which in the end drags men down to extinction: to have preserved the existence of the body, which is none the less destined soon to die, by denying the truth which your Son taught us, is true perdition; but those whom you have undertaken to save cannot be destroyed by anything in creation. This, then, is your own special gift, O Lord God, that we place our trust in you, that we depend only on your will, that we say, with all our hearts: 'Salvation belongs to the Lord.'

Bless your people,[102] as in the beginning. Let our enemies curse us, if only you will bless us. We care nothing for human blessings, which lead simple hearts astray, when 'the sinner is praised for his soul's desires, and the unjust is given blessing.'[103] Such blessings are cursed by you. There will always be people who will hire Balaam to curse your people,[104] but your Son declared that those whom men cursed for his sake would be blessed.[105] David patiently endured Shimei's curses,[106] and we too bless those who curse us, we speak well of those who revile us, we pray for those who execrate us, following both the example and the teaching of your Son, so that your blessing shall always rest upon your people.[107] Grant that we may always remain your people; we trust that we shall never lose your blessing. Meanwhile we in turn shall bless your holy name, which is blessed for evermore, until we hear your final blessing from the lips of your blessed Son Jesus: 'Come, you that are blessed of my Father, and possess the kingdom prepared for you since the beginning of the world.'[108]

So here is your sample, my dear Vianden, taken on the spur of the moment. If you do not like it, I shall not be disappointed; that is what I expected. But whether or no, you must for the moment approve my desire to oblige. Farewell; and farewell too to all those who love the Lord Jesus Christ with all their hearts.

Basel, 25 February 1524

* * * * *

102 Deut 26:15, intended by Erasmus to echo the final words of Ps 3
103 Ps 10:3
104 Cf Num 22:6 and Deut 23:4.
105 Cf Matt 5:11, the Sermon on the Mount, which, with its echoes in St Paul (eg Rom 12:14 and 1 Cor 4:12) provides the development here.
106 2 Sam 16:5–12
107 Another echo of Ps 3:8
108 Cf Matt 25:34.

A SERMON ON THE FOURTH PSALM

In psalmum quartum concio

In psalmum quartum concio was first published by Froben at Basel in February 1525 at the end of a re-edition of Erasmus' writings on the first three psalms. We may conclude from the appearance of this edition that the public had shown considerable interest in Erasmus' efforts, and this is confirmed by the rapid appearance of another edition at Antwerp and a possible third at Cologne.[1] In the dedicatory letter to John Longland, Erasmus describes this treatise as another attempt to find a genre which he may use to expound the whole of the Psalter, in response to many pressing requests. In fact, this *concio* marks the end of the quest. Erasmus' later writing on the Psalms embodies no systematic treatment of this most awe-inspiring of Old Testament books, but is prompted either by a request from an individual or by Erasmus' observation of the increasingly disturbed political and religious scene, as he seeks a remedy for current troubles in the eternal wisdom of the Holy Spirit. It is in any case inconceivable that Erasmus should have been able to devote to all 150 psalms the time and effort that he expended on this *Sermon on the Fourth Psalm*, very nearly the longest of his writings on the subject.[2]

After a few words on the literal sense,[3] Erasmus divides this homily into two parts: the first deals with the allegorical meaning, where Erasmus follows St Jerome in associating the words of the psalm with the scene at the crucifixion, and applies its wisdom to the church in general; in the second, longer, section, Erasmus expounds the tropological sense as 'it relates to each of us individually, and deals with the conduct of our everyday lives' (212). It is in this section that the choice of form is particularly appropriate: Erasmus appeals from the pulpit for the undivided attention of his 'dear brothers,' especially of those who may be nodding off, and exhorts them earnestly to practise the *philosophia Christi*: to put their trust in God, to exercise charity towards their less fortunate fellows, and to make the appropriate sacrifice by avoiding vanity and falsehood. The language of the psalm clearly authorizes this exposition of many of Erasmus' favourite moral themes, and indeed provides the opportunity for passages of satire which recall

* * * * *

1 See ASD V-2 187.
2 It is slightly shorter than the commentary on Ps 38/39, and about equal in length to that on Ps 85/86, the *Expositio concionalis*, which was also dedicated to John Longland. On the project for the whole Psalter, see also my introductory notes to the previous two works.
3 See 176–7; Erasmus is at his most cursory here, and gave the historical context considerably more weight in discussing the first three psalms. On this *concio* as a model of Erasmus' exegesis, see Chantraine 699–700.

contemporary additions to the *Colloquia*.[4] Even the attacks in the first part on the Jews and pagans of Christ's own time are related to the contemporary ethical and spiritual themes of the homily; it is there that Erasmus brings in from the modern world the examples of the wine merchant and the money-lender, and of course Judaism and Pharisaism had become metaphorically identified with excessive devotion to ritual and formalism in the Christian community.[5]

Erasmus also turns his attention once more, after an intermission in the *Paraphrase on the Third Psalm*, to the thorny textual questions whose complexity he attributes, piously, to God's desire to 'rouse us from our torpor' (239). As usual, his unfamiliarity with Hebrew led him to rely heavily on Jerome, while Cassiodorus, Arnobius, and Augustine supplied varying interpretations to stimulate Erasmus' critical faculties. Augustine's discussion of the musical form and the heading of the psalm provided the stimulus for two brief passages, but even there Erasmus' preoccupation with Christian ethics surfaces, when he defines the instrument upon which the psalm of praise must be played as the deeds of our hands rather than the words of our mouths. Similarly, while he looks to the commentators for advice on broad interpretation and textual detail, when it comes to doctrine and the provision of persuasive examples, he turns, as always, to the Scriptures.

On textual questions, Erasmus generously allows that 'salvation is not imperilled by a slight departure from the original sense' (239), and it has to be said that his own treatment of the language of the psalm creates problems for the translator into English. Erasmus delighted in the Psalms' unusual metaphors, whose intriguing presence he considered to be another divinely inspired stratagem to 'rouse us from our lethargy' (226); at one point he acknowledges cheerfully that his pursuit of a particularly stimulating image has led him far from his original path (235). But the subtle wordplay which the psalm's imagery inspired in him is sometimes beyond the resources of English. In particular, a phrase in the first verse, *in angustiis dilatasti mihi*, has a number of resonances, exploited thoroughly by Erasmus, which cannot be conveyed by a single English expression: *dilatare* means literally 'to expand' or 'to dilate,' but in this context can also mean 'to relieve' or 'to make

* * * * *

4 See for example 219–20 and 259; I have pointed out in the notes how such passages clearly struck home and were recommended for deletion in the *Index expurgatorius*.
5 See Introduction xlix–lvi. For a bibliography of Erasmus' views on the Jews, and his use of them as symbols of Christian degeneracy, see ASD v-2 88:16n.

room for'; *angustiae* may be translated literally as 'narrows' or 'straits,' or metaphorically as 'anguish.' Again, *iusticia* in verse 1 may be either 'justice' in the ordinary sense, or 'righteousness'; a similar problem arises over *sanctus* (verse 3), which means both 'holy one' and 'saint.'

The text translated here is that established by Ch. Béné in ASD V-2 191–276 and based on the first edition. The work does not appear to have been revised by Erasmus and there are no significant variants in the 1540 Basel edition or in LB, though some errors crept in there. However, the ASD text omits several phrases which are present in all the original editions; I have restored and translated these and pointed out these occurrences in the notes. In translating Scripture, in referring to the Psalms, and in establishing a working text of Psalm 4, I have followed the principles described in my introductory note to the exposition of the First Psalm (4).

MJH

PSALM 4

1 Cum invocarem, exaudivit me Deus iustitiae meae. In tribulatione [angustiis] dilatasti mihi. Miserere mei, Deus, et exaudi orationem meam.

2 Filii hominum, usque quo gravi corde, ut quid diligitis vanitatem, et quaeritis mendacium? [Selah]

3 Et scitote quoniam mirificavit Dominus sanctum suum. Dominus exaudiet me cum clamavero ad eum.

4 Irascimini; nolite peccare; quae dicitis in cordibus vestris, in cubilibus compungimini. [Selah]

5 Sacrificate sacrificium iustitiae et sperate in Domino.

6 Multi dicunt: 'Quis ostendit nobis bona?' Signatum est super nos lumen vultus tui, Domine.

7 Dedisti laetitiam in corde meo. A fructu frumenti, vini et olei sui multiplicati sunt.

8 In pace in id ipsum dormiam et requiescam, quoniam tu, Domine, singulariter in spe constituisti [habitare fecisti] me.

1 When I called, the God of my righteousness heard me. In tribulation, you relieved me. God have pity on me, and hear my prayer.

2 Children of mankind, how long will your hearts be burdened [with pride]? Why do you love vanity and seek out falsehood? [Pause]

3 And know that the Lord has performed wonders for his holy one [or 'has made his holy one an object of wonder']. The Lord will hear me when I cry to him.

4 Be angry; do not sin; say these words in your hearts and examine your conscience in your private chambers. [Pause]

5 Offer the sacrifice of righteousness, and place your hopes in the Lord.

6 There are many who say: 'Who will show us these good things?' O Lord, the light of your countenance has appeared on high as a sign to guide us [like a banner].

7 You have brought joy to my heart. They have been multiplied by the ripening of their [or 'his'] corn, their wine, and their oil.

8 I shall sleep in peace and take my rest in it, for you, O Lord, have set me apart in hope [or 'made me dwell in hope'].

TO THE MOST REVEREND FATHER JOHN, BISHOP OF LINCOLN IN
ENGLAND, FROM ERASMUS OF ROTTERDAM, GREETING[1]

Several years ago at Calais, most honourable bishop, you were the first
to encourage me to produce a commentary on the Book of Psalms and in
frequent letters since then you have returned again and again to the same
theme. Later others made the same request, not only men of learning but
even princes. When I saw that my excuses, though I thought them perfectly
justified, were not well received, I tried repeatedly to look into this holy of
holies of the divine Spirit. But whenever I tried, other obligations turned my
attention elsewhere or a feeling of awe and reverence for the grandeur of the
work frightened me off from the attempt. Some time ago, as a sort of prelude,
I wrote something on the First Psalm; then I added a regular commentary
to the Second; for the Third I tried a paraphrase. Now I am sending you a
homily on the Fourth, leaving nothing untried in the hope of discovering
the right road to success. But I am not yet satisfied. The work by its nature
scarcely admits of paraphrase, and yet I realize that, where there is such a
host of commentaries, if I am to hold the reader's attention, there must be
some novelty in the treatment. I shall press on if you approve this sample of
my work and if you remember my efforts in your prayers to God. Farewell.

Basel, 5 January 1525

* * * * *

1 The dedicatory letter is Ep 1535, to John Longland (1473–1547), one of Erasmus'
most consistent English supporters. A graduate of Oxford, Longland became
confessor to Henry VIII in 1520 and bishop of Lincoln a year later. Thomas
More refers to him as 'another Colet': he was a noted preacher and, in spite
of administrative and court obligations, he was an active diocesan bishop,
committed to Catholic reform and, initially, to the royal supremacy. According
to his own account he had urged Erasmus to undertake a commentary on the
Psalms when they had met at Calais in 1520; his response to *In psalmum quartum
concio* can be found in Ep 1570, and in 1528 he received the dedication of
the *Interpretatio in psalmum 85*. For details of his career see CEBR; J.W. Blench
Preaching in England in the Late Fifteenth and Sixteenth Centuries (Oxford 1964)
20–8 and passim; M. Bowker *The Henrician Reformation: The Diocese of Lincoln
under John Longland* (Cambridge 1981) 4–16.

A SERMON ON THE FOURTH PSALM

Dear brothers in the Lord: interpretation of this psalm is fraught with difficulties, and we must therefore give it all our attention; if not, you will be deprived of much pleasure and profit, and I shall have laboured in vain to instruct you. In order to enjoy the kernel of a nut, you do not begrudge the small effort involved in removing the hard shell and bitter rind; you should not therefore be reluctant to concentrate your thoughts for a while, in order to feed them with the wholesome and delicious nourishment which this psalm offers you. The Holy Spirit inspired the composer of this psalm and will honour both you and me with its presence if we can show that our minds are ready and eager to learn.

I shall not tax your patience with the heading, as there are a number of different versions. The translators of the Septuagint probably put in the heading 'Towards an end, a psalm of David among the hymns.'[1] St Jerome appeals to the authority of the Hebrew text in beginning 'To the victor, or towards victory, a psalm of David among the canticles.'[2] Some manuscripts of doubtful provenance have the heading 'Towards an end, the psalm of a canticle of David.' The words 'Towards an end' signal the presence of some more hallowed hidden sense which will reveal to us a sacred truth concerning Christ, since he is the End of all Law, that is, its fulfilment.[3] The words 'victor' or 'victory' signal a reference to the holy mystery of Christ's death, by which he defeated and overthrew Satan's tyranny, helping us also to emerge victorious from all our battles with Satan. The words 'the psalm of a canticle' suggest a

* * * * *

1 For another discussion of the headings of psalms, see *In psalmum* 2 75–6. The phrase 'towards an end' (*in finem*) probably translates a Hebrew term meaning 'dedication.'
2 *Divina bibliotheca* PL 28 1130A
3 Erasmus is following Augustine's interpretation (*Enarratio in psalmum* 4 PL 36 78), based on Rom 10:4. Augustine also goes on briefly to discuss the musical forms.

spiritual kind of music which will give special pleasure to our King David, that is, the Lord Jesus, when our deeds and our lives fulfil the promises that our lips have made; we are told that a psalm is accompanied by a musical instrument, while a canticle is a setting for the voice alone.[4] Christians do God more honour by leading godly lives than by singing hymns and praises; an ideal melody would combine the two, but if goodness of life precedes the song of praise, then that is the correct order, reflecting the example given us by the Lord, who began his task by teaching and by performing good works. On the other hand, the words 'the canticle of a psalm' give priority to the song of praise; but if the canticle alone is heard, and not the instrument, God will be displeased with the music and stop his ears, saying: 'What need to recite my righteousness?'[5]

The Hebrews associated music with religion and used it in their ceremonies; it was clearly a particular interest of King David, who not only appointed musicians to make music for the Lord on their different instruments, but also did not consider it beneath his own dignity as a king to dance and sing before the Ark of the Lord.[6] But all that they did was mere symbolism; we must strive to make that special kind of music which delights the ears of God. Socrates concluded that philosophy was the supreme music.[7] We should realize that our music is sweetest to God when every part of our lives is in harmony with his commandments, when our words are in tune with our lives, when the mellifluous chorus of brotherly concord is not marred by the discords of conflict and disagreement, when a plangent lyre bewails our misdeeds, when we give thanks with a clash of cymbals, and the trumpet boldly sounds the gospel message.[8] This is the music which drives away the evil spirit that possessed Saul, and which, as Elisha demonstrated in the Book of Kings, calls down the good Spirit from God.[9]

So much for the heading: now for the psalm itself. I shall not deal with its literal meaning; not only do the authorities disagree about it, but also it

*   *   *   *   *

4 For further discussions of music in the context of the psalms, see Erasmus *Enarratio in psalmum 38* LB V 417C–E, and Ep 1304; cf J.-C. Margolin *Erasme et la musique* (Paris 1965) 24–9. For Erasmus the 'instrument' here represents men's deeds.

5 Ps 49/50:16

6 See, for example, 1 Chron 15 and 2 Sam 6.

7 In Plato the harmony (συμφονία) of faculties in the moral life is frequently compared to music, making philosophy the greatest of the arts; see eg *Phaedo* 61A and *Laws* 3.689D.

8 There are echoes here of 1 Chron 16 (cf n6 above) and of Ps 150.

9 See 1 Sam 16:14–23 and 2 Kings 3:15.

will not contribute much to the advancement of piety, which is our present aim. Jerome judges that the psalm cannot be applied in the literal sense to David;[10] others think differently. But even those who agree that in the literal sense it does concern David do not agree on the historical details. I shall leave on one side these contentious and unprofitable speculations, and divide my exposition of the psalm into just two parts: first, the ways in which this psalm is a prophecy concerning Christ and, second, how it may apply to all the members of Christ, that is, Christ's body, the church.

St Augustine thinks that these are words spoken by Christ after the resurrection, but Arnobius[11] prefers to see them as words spoken on the cross, which I find a more convincing theory; for it was there, as a priest of the order of Melchizedek,[12] that he offered himself as a sacrifice to God the Father, that he interceded for us, and was heard, out of respect for his person. This interpretation implies the presence of four different characters: Christ, his followers, the Father, and the ungodly who do not yet acknowledge Christ. Clearly, we who have been redeemed by Christ's death must listen all the more attentively to our high priest's prayer for us, and strive to ensure that his prayers are not in vain. Our high priest had taken upon himself the most onerous of burdens, the sins of all humankind, in order to deliver us from all sin. Thus, turning to his friends, who were indeed believers, but were discouraged by his death, he rejoiced in the fact that his Father had heard him and had deigned to accept the death of his own Son, for the salvation of all humankind. This had always been his desire, and often had he begged it of his Father. 'God heard me when I called,' he says, 'God, the author and judge of my righteousness,[13] who knows that I alone am free from all sin; therefore he was pleased, in his goodness, to grant righteousness to all who believe in me, through the death of one who is guiltless. I was condemned by the Jews and Pilate, I hang between criminals, and from all sides abuse is heaped on me – but men judge only by appearances. God sees into our hearts, and he alone knows that I am righteous; that is why I did not resist my persecutors, but entrusted my soul's destiny to God.'

This much to his friends; then, turning to his Father, he says: 'In tribulation, you relieved me.' He gives thanks to the heavenly Father, since

* * * * *

10 *Breviarium in psalmos* PL 26 828B

11 Respectively, *Enarratio in psalmum 4* PL 36 78 and *Commentarii in psalmos* PL 53 330D

12 Cf Heb 7:17 and 21, quoting Ps 109/110:4; the author of Hebrews is demonstrating that Christ's priesthood surpassed that of the Jews.

13 An adaptation of Ps 4:1

he alone brought comfort to both his body and soul as afflictions crowded in from every side. No part of the Lord's body was spared the torment:[14] nails had pierced his hands and feet, a lance had been thrust into his side, the thorns and the reed had injured his head, bruises and spittle disfigured his face, the whip had scourged every inch of his flesh, and every joint and sinew was strained and racked by the utmost pain; his eyes could see the Pharisees, mocking and wagging their heads, his ears could hear them: 'Woe unto you, who destroy the temple of God; he saved others, but cannot save himself.'[15] This indeed was harder to bear than the cross itself. His heart was drained of blood and his body racked by a thirst more painful than death; a mixture of sour wine and myrrh was offered to him, so that even his palate and tongue should not escape the torment. The many sins of the world, for which he alone was atoning, racked this most holy of souls, and what torture is more painful than that of a guilty conscience? Yet all this he had taken upon himself. The unbelief of the many for whom he suffered in vain made it all the more cruel; he had borne our weakness and carried our sorrows, fulfilling the prophecy of Isaiah.[16] He became the scapegoat,[17] and on his head the Father heaped the sins, not just of Israel, but of all nations and of all times.

Here, truly, was a man beset by all the miseries of death,[18] overwhelmed by the deepest anguish; and yet, in the midst of unparalleled suffering, the heavenly Father did not desert his Son, but answered his pleas by granting him the comfort of good hope. He was hemmed in on all sides by misfortunes, which pierced and wounded him from every quarter; despair, the ultimate evil, weighed him down. 'But,' he says, 'in such a state of anguish you, O Lord, relieved me. You gave me strength to suffer and renewed my greatest hopes, granting my mind the capacity to withstand my afflictions, however numerous and painful they might be.' He was given ample hope: not only would he himself be restored to eternal life, and Israelites who believed in him be saved, but all those, in every corner of the globe, who confessed the name of the crucified, would find eternal salvation. The Father gives him this assurance in the words of the Second Psalm: 'Ask it of me and I will give you the nations as your inheritance, and the ends of the earth as your possession.'[19] He called out, he begged that the promise be fulfilled, and this

* * * * *

14 The details are taken from Matt 27 and John 19.
15 Matt 27:40–2
16 Isa 53:4
17 See Lev 16:20–2.
18 An echo of Ps 17/18:5 and 115/116:3
19 Ps 2:8

renewal of his fondest hopes brought comfort to this spotless lamb beset by all calamity.

At that moment he was an outcast among men, bereft of all grace and beauty, 'not human, but a worm, a reproach to humankind, scorned by the people';[20] no one could have answered his cry but the Father; indeed, he cried out only to the Father, and his cry was answered by the one being who can sustain those who are deprived of all human aid, first by offering them good hope in their sufferings, and then by changing transient suffering into perpetual joy. This is, of course, the meaning of Psalm 21: 'All the seed of Israel shall fear him, for he has not scorned or spurned the prayers of the poor. He has not turned his face from me, and he heard me when I cried out to him.'[21] He it was who became a wretched beggar for our sake, and poured out to the Lord his prayer for us all in Psalm 101: 'O Lord, hear my prayer, and let my cry come unto you.'[22] Picture, if you will, the Lord imprisoned by anguish on our behalf: 'I am not human, but a worm,' he says, 'a reproach to humankind, scorned by the people.' Now, picture him set free: 'When I am lifted up from the earth, I shall draw all things to me.'[23] He was imprisoned in the guise of a slave, beaten with rods, nailed to a cross; he was set free by the glorious resurrection. Like him, we must be shackled by the flesh and all its ills, that we too may be set free, through him, by the lifegiving Spirit.

The next line is 'God have pity on me, and hear my prayer.' It might be asked here how the plea 'Have pity on me' could apply to Christ, who had no need of pity; moreover, can it be right that someone who has just given thanks, who has rejoiced at being heard, and who has been uplifted by the renewal of his hopes, should now be lamenting, once again: 'Have pity on me, and hear my prayer'? However, we should not be surprised that he cried: 'Have pity on me,' as in fact he was praying on behalf of so many pitiable wretches, having taken all our wretchedness upon himself. He gives thanks for God's answer, then quickly cries out again to remind us that we must never cease to pray. We must continue to thank God for all his gifts; we must continue to beg that, in his mercy, he will watch over the gifts he has already given us, increase his bounty, fulfil his promises in this life, and bring them to perfection in the life to come.

Having made this prayer, Christ does not wait for an answer, but directs his thoughts towards unbelievers on whom the light of faith has not

* * * * *

20 Is 53:2 and Ps 21/22:6
21 Ps 21/22:23–4
22 Ps 101/102:1
23 John 12:32

yet shone, such as the Jews, who, in their ignorance of God's justice and in their preoccupation with their own forms of justice, condemned Jesus, and the pagans, who worshipped silent stones as gods and sacrificed to things which could not help them. Our merciful Lord wants them all to recover their wits and accept the forgiveness proffered by God, and he was praying on their behalf when he cried out: 'Have pity on me.' Believers, who are implanted in Christ through faith and baptism, have become already the children of God;[24] therefore he calls those who do not yet believe 'the children of mankind'; bearing the impress of the earthly Adam, they know nothing but earthly wisdom; they are obsessed by base and trivial concerns and cannot lift their thoughts to heaven, where true bliss is found; they place their trust, not in God, but in illusions and in the shadow of reality. In his boundless love, the Lord desired that all should be saved, and should come to know the truth; hence his impassioned cry to them: 'O children of Adam, why do you not hasten to be made the children of God? How long will your hearts be burdened and dragged down by love for all that is inferior, when heavenly treasure is freely offered to you? Why do you persist in loving vanity when the truth has been revealed to you? You Jews have glimpsed the heavenly light, yet still you cling so obstinately to the shadowy illusions of the Law. You pagans have been offered knowledge of the true God, and of true religion, yet still you hanker for your empty images of gods. For centuries God allowed you to persist in your ignorance, but now, when the light has come into the world, why do you still delight in the night of ignorance? Why do you not greet the rising sun, which will dispel all these empty shadows of the truth?' When day has dawned and flooded the world with its welcome light, is there anyone so senseless that he will take refuge in a gloomy cave,[25] as if eager to turn day into night? What man, given eyes to see, will yearn to be blind and in the dark once more? It was utter blindness to worship man instead of God, but it is an act of even greater blindness to deify oxen, apes, crocodiles, serpents, or dragons, or, similarly, to worship as deities the moon, sun, and stars, entities created by God for the service of humankind. But it takes the most disordered mind of all to bow down before onions,[26] wood, stones, bronze, and images made by men's hands, in

* * * * *

24 An echo of John 1:12
25 Probably a reference to the famous illustration of the difference between substance and shadow in Plato's *Republic* 7.514–17. The preceding passage contains echoes, in particular, of John 3:16–21.
26 Onions were venerated by the Egyptians, according to Pliny *Naturalis historia* 19.32.101. Juvenal too mentions this superstition in a passage (15.1–9) which also alludes to their worship of crocodiles, serpents, and apes.

which there is neither life nor feeling. And yet this darkness reigned over all the earth for thousands of years. It can only be described as 'seeking out falsehood.'[27] How vain it was to believe that some divinity inhabited the sun or the moon, rather than to perceive in them the hand of the true God, their creator. People were misguided to worship such things, even before the gospel trumpet had sounded throughout the earth and proclaimed that they must worship only God, the Father, Son, and Holy Spirit. But now that the gospel trumpet has been heard, it takes an incurably wretched mind, and one vowed to death, to continue to burn incense to a block of wood, or to say to a stone: 'Save me!' To believe that dead men could become gods was a pitiable fallacy, but to seek falsehood where there is none, that is, to lie to oneself and to concoct an illusion with which to deceive oneself: this is the mark of an even more pitiable blindness. No one, says the Preacher, can escape vanity in this life;[28] every creature, says Paul, is the unwilling prey of vanity, but so little does he delight in it that he groans, as if in the throes of childbirth, as he waits for God's children to be revealed; the vanity which gives delight is deadly dangerous.[29] Again, falsehood is something ingrained in human nature: 'Every man is a liar,' we are told.[30] But the deadly dangerous falsehood is the one which is sought out, pursued, and taken to one's heart.

My own opinion is that the whole of this second verse, which falls into three parts – the first dealing with the proud-hearted, the second with lovers of vanity, the third with seekers after falsehood – applies equally to both groups, namely to the Jews and to the pagans. Despite the coming of Christ, the embodiment of truth, there were still lovers of vanity and seekers after falsehood in both camps, as there are even today.

To possess a body is a burden shared by all mortals. 'A corruptible body weighs down the soul, and our thoughts and our understanding are often inhibited by their earthly habitation.'[31] Even Paul is oppressed by this burden, and cries out: 'Unhappy man that I am, who will free me from this body doomed to death?'[32] Again, writing to the Corinthians, he groans under the weight of his earthly frame, yearning for a heavenly habitation to be put on over it. However, this burden will be lifted from us at the resurrection

*****

27 Cf Ps 4:2.
28 Ecclesiastes: the remark is not a quotation but a summary of the book's conclusions.
29 The sentence is based on Rom 8:19–22.
30 Rom 3:4, quoting Ps 61/62:9 or 115/116:11
31 Wisd 9:15, also cited by Augustine *Enarratio in psalmum* 4 PL 36 82
32 Rom 7:24 and 2 Cor 5:2

when, like a seed entrusted to the earth, a spiritual body will arise to replace this earthly, animal body.[33] But before that day, how wretched it must be to be burdened also by one's heart, like the Jews, who were so intent on the letter of the Law that they could not lift up their hearts to understand its spiritual meaning; they could see no more in Christ than what they perceived with the eyes of the flesh. To an extent, the Lord's disciples too were like this before the heavenly Spirit took away the earthbound part and gave them hearts soaring aloft towards heaven.

The Greek philosophers' hearts were burdened by their concentration on the created world; they had only the haziest notion of beings distinct from matter, and still less of the utterly undivided nature of God.[34] Perhaps a few did conceive some idea of it, deducing, from the miracles of the creation, the existence of a creator, but even those enlightened by this imperfect perception of God did not worship him as the true God, who, since he is eternal mind, is worshipped by a pure mind; on the contrary, they lived sinful lives and reduced the glory of God to the likeness of mankind. It is not surprising that Paul wrote to the Romans: 'They became vain in their imaginings, and their foolish minds grew dark.'[35] He says elsewhere that drunkards are drunk at night:[36] when the light of the gospel had shone out through Christ, night had flown, day was drawing near, and it was time to 'cast off the deeds of darkness and put on the armour of light.'[37] Some people, their eyelids drooping after the night's debauchery, remain blind to the daylight long after the sun has risen. This kind of physical sickness can be dissipated by sleep and is relatively harmless, but sickness of the heart is grim, and cannot so easily be dispelled. The Lord warns his disciples against it in Luke's Gospel: 'Take care, do not let your hearts be so burdened with dissipation, drunkenness, and the cares of this life that the great Day take you unawares.'[38] For thousands of years this spiritual sickness dragged down the hearts of mortal men, not only among the pagans, but also among the Jews, who often relapsed into the worship of idols.

The word here rendered 'vanity' is in the Greek ματαιότης, which is closer in meaning to 'something superfluous, done to no purpose'; in general Latin uses *vanum* for something which is empty and lacking in truthfulness.

* * * * *

33 Cf 1 Cor 15:44.
34 See *In psalmum 1* 43 and n202.
35 Rom 1:21
36 1 Thess 5:7
37 Rom 13:12
38 Luke 21:34

Moreover, anyone making false boasts is called *vanus*. It can be shown that in many scriptural texts idols are called 'vanities'; for example, in the First Book of Kings, the phrase 'provoking the Lord God of Israel with their vanities' is in Greek ἐν ματαίοις αὐτῶν.[39] There is a similar passage in Jeremiah: 'They provoked my wrath with their images and their foreign vanities,'[40] where the Greek reads ἐν ματαίοις. Similarly, in the Acts of the Apostles, chapter 14, Barnabas and Paul use the term 'vanity' to describe the worship of false gods, saying: 'We declare to you that you must turn from these vanities,' which in Greek is ἀπὸ τούτων τῶν ματαίων.[41] These pagan practices were not only ungodly, but superfluous: what could be more pointless than to appeal to a statue, which cannot hear, to burn incense before a stone, which cannot smell, to lay votive offerings before an idol, which cannot see, to offer food to an image of brass, which cannot taste, to entrust your own life and your family's to an idol, which has no life of its own,[42] to demand protection from a stone, which cannot protect itself, which cannot right itself when knocked over, or mend itself when broken in pieces? Imagine, indeed, the depths of sickness and confusion to which their minds must have sunk, when you read about them cutting down timber and getting a craftsman to carve one block of the wood into some fanciful shape, while they cook their food on the wood left over; the surviving piece, set up by men's hands in the temple, is considered a god![43] Clearly, this is the kind of sickness which Isaiah describes in chapter 29: 'Be senseless and dumbfounded, waver and reel; be drunk, but not on wine; stagger, but not with drunkenness.' There is another fine description of this intoxication with vanity in chapter 44 of the same book.[44] The pagans took such delight in their darkness that, for the love of it, they inflicted all kinds of cruel persecution on Christ's heralds for many years, and, far from abandoning their former errors, they happily deceived themselves with new superstitions: could there be a better example of 'seeking out falsehood'? It was not enough to worship their national gods: they had to import every fake deity from foreign lands as well! The true God was come, but they spurned him and sought out false gods.

* * * * *

39 1 Kings 16:13 and 26
40 Jer 8:19
41 Acts 14:15
42 The clause 'to entrust . . . life of its own' is omitted in ASD V-2 200:232, although it appears in all the earlier editions of Erasmus' text. The whole sentence is an echo of Ps 114/115:5–7.
43 The preceding sentence is clearly inspired by Isa 44:14–20.
44 Isa 29:9, 44:9–20

In much the same way, the Jews also loved vanity and sought out falsehood. Without the spirit, the letter of the Law is empty of substance; without its real body, a shadow means nothing; in the absence of truth, a symbol has no purpose. Yet the Jews still cling stubbornly to their sabbaths, circumcision, dietary restrictions, sacrifices, and other such mere symbols of the Law which Christ, whom they foreshadowed, rendered superfluous by his coming. The Jews still await fulfilment of the prophets' promises, even though the promised one has been revealed to them; they reject the true Messiah and await some fictitious saviour, even though there will be no other. Could there be a better example of 'seeking out falsehood'? Now it is true that, thanks to the gospel, we have been freed from the senseless cults of our forefathers, and that we acknowledge and confess the true God; but I could still wish that our hearts and minds were entirely clear of idols and false gods, since anything which a person prefers to God becomes a god to him. Those who are enslaved by their belly, their lust, or their greed are still sacrificing to idols; Paul calls this the worship of idols.[45]

Christ must still cry out to the Jewish people, as he cried on the cross: 'Children of mankind, how long will your hearts be burdened? Why do you love vanity, the empty shadows of the Law, when the truth has been revealed through the gospel? Why do you seek a false Messiah, when the true Messiah, fulfilling all the prophecies, has been so clearly revealed to you?' The Jews were deterred[46] because he came in humility, because he was condemned to death, nailed to a cross, died, and was buried; they were expecting some mighty king. But that lowly creature, reduced to nothing in the eyes of the world, was exalted by the Lord and given the name which is above all names.[47] Since this seemed unbelievable, he added: 'And know ...' If you believe in him, you will understand, but even if you do not believe, you cannot fail to see the evidence that 'God performed wonders for his holy one.' You saw the sun's light fail, you saw the earth tremble, you saw tombs open, you saw the rocks split, you saw the veil of the temple torn in two;[48] such was the power of his weakness and the glory of his humiliation. You cast this stone aside, but God recovered it and made it the cornerstone.[49] This is the psalm's message: 'And know that the Lord has

* * * * *

45 Cf Col 3:5 in particular, but this passage echoes much of Paul's teaching, for example Rom 16:18 and Phil 3:19.
46 The Latin phrase *offendiculum Judaeis* contains an echo of Rom 9:33.
47 Phil 2:9
48 Cf Matt 27:45–52.
49 Cf 1 Pet 2:6–7.

performed wonders for his holy one.' Similar words are found elsewhere: 'This is the Lord's doing, a wonder to our eyes.'[50] Who would believe that one man's death could obtain life for all? Who would believe that humiliation on the cross could destroy Satan's tyranny? Who would believe that the schemes of all of them, Pharisees, Scribes, high priests, people, and princes, could be overthrown? God offered salvation to all humankind through the one whom these conspirators did their best to destroy. They thought that they had wiped out all memory of him from among mankind, but God magnified his glory above the glory of mankind and of angels. At his name the earth's mightiest monarchs bare their heads, bow their necks, and bend their knees.[51] Legions of angels worship his name. At the sound of his name the dead are restored, demons tremble,[52] evil spirits squirm and flee.

The Latin translator's 'he performed wonders' is in Greek $\dot{\epsilon}\theta\alpha\nu\mu\acute{\alpha}\sigma\tau\omega\sigma\epsilon\nu$, meaning 'he made him remarkable and worthy of respect.' In this world, if someone is to be respected by others, he must wear cloth of gold, be decked in jewels and chains of office, mounted on a charger – not to mention the titles, statues, retainers, trumpeters, and solemn assemblies! If someone should wish to be numbered among the gods, he must deceive the uneducated masses with conjuring tricks and tall stories. But God, the king of heaven and earth, made men respect his holy one by quite different means. The world too has its holy ones, and even the sect of the Pharisees has its saints; but God has a single, unique 'holy one,' his only-begotten Son, untainted by sin, whom he sanctified and sent into the world, that through him should be sanctified all those who confessed his glorious name.

The expression 'Know that . . .' is used in Scripture both as an encouragement and as a rebuke. The apostles used it as they shook off the dust from their feet in places where the gospel was not welcomed: 'None the less,' they said, 'know that the kingdom of God has come to you.'[53] Similarly, the Lord said to the unbelieving Jews:[54] 'You have heaped all ignominy upon me, but know that, despite all your scheming to prevent it, the Father has glorified his Son. If you will only allow yourselves to see my radiance and my glory, there is hope of your salvation; if not, there is every chance that you will burn. God

* * * * *

50 Ps 117/118:23, quoted in Matt 21:42 and Mark 12:11; both the New Testament passages also allude to the symbol of the cornerstone.
51 An echo of Phil 2:10
52 James 2:19
53 See Luke 10:10–11.
54 Not a quotation, but a summary of Christ's charges against the Jews in various parts of the Gospels

changes your evil deeds into glory for his Son and you will learn, willingly or not, that no human design can prevail against God's design; no human power can match the power of God. He performs whatever he chooses, and is now using a new design, unintelligible to you, to carry out his decrees. The prophets are yours, but you refused to believe them; now the truth itself offends your eyes, and the rock on which you might have been saved has become for you a stumbling-block, an obstacle in your road.[55] You have continued to reject the holy one of the Lord, but now it is not merely five Egyptian towns,[56] but every nation on earth, which worships the name of the crucified. The cross, which the pagans found laughable and foolish, and the Jews a stumbling-block,[57] is now a mightier emblem than any king's.'

The next sentence reads: 'The Lord will hear me when I cry to him.' If Christ made a point of attributing all the glory to his Father, the creator, how much more should we, if our deeds ever deserve praise, assign all the praise to God, rather than claim the glory for ourselves. 'You will seal up the tomb,' he says, 'and sit beside it to prevent me from arising; but just as Jonah cried out from the belly of the whale and, against all expectation, returned alive, so too the Lord shall hear me cry from the depths below, and on the third day he shall restore me to life. For the Father always hears the Son, and whatever the Son desires, that too the Father desires. I shall not appeal to Moses, or to any other human agency; God alone restores the dead. Though my soul be in the depths of Tartarus, its cry shall reach up from there and enter my Father's ears.'[58] God will not hear the prophets of Baal[59] who cry out: 'Do not allow that impostor to be restored, or things will become worse than before; save our temple for us, save our sacrifices, save our priesthood and our dignities.' It is enough that Pilate heard your cries: 'Take him away, take him away, crucify him, crucify him, and let his blood be upon us, and upon our children! We have no king but Caesar!'[60] Those cries were answered in such a way as to convince you that God has glorified his holy one, whom you sought to humiliate. The only true glory is the glory given by God. Now even the pagans, whom the promises of the Law and the prophets did not

* * * * *

55 1 Cor 10:4, Rom 9:33, and 1 Pet 2:8
56 See Isa 19:18–22, a prophecy of conversion.
57 Cf 1 Cor 1:23.
58 This 'speech' is based particularly on Matt 27:63–6; the illustration is Jonah 2.
59 See for example 1 Kings 18 and 2 Kings 23; here the prophets are considered a prototype of the Pharisees. The phrase 'things ... become worse than before' is based on Matt 12:45.
60 Matt 27:22–5 and John 19:15

reach, believe the gospel and embrace the Lord, whom God has sanctified and glorified; unburdened by the Law, they glory in his cross and pursue righteousness and holiness. The Jews alone, to whom Christ was promised, find it vexatious and intolerable that this salvation should be communicated to all the gentiles; they would rather forfeit salvation than share it with the uncircumcised, unaware that God takes delight in circumcision, not of the body, but of the heart,[61] and that he considers all who emulate Abraham's faith to be children of Abraham.

The Lord rebukes the Jews for envy of this kind when he says: 'Be angry; do not sin; say these words in your hearts and examine your conscience in your private chambers.' 'What?' he says, 'Are you angry, envious Jew? Has some promise made to you not been kept, simply because God has extended his mercy to the whole world? This anger of yours is a sin almost more grievous than that of nailing me to the cross; you destroy yourself inasmuch as you envy your neighbour; you deny the Father inasmuch as you do not believe his Son. If you must be angry, let your anger be without sin. Be angry with your sins, and you will receive mercy. Why do you vainly flatter yourself that you are righteous, and shun the uncircumcised as unclean? I have found no one completely free from sin. Why do you boast of your works?[62] Why do you reproach the gentiles with impious and impure living? Salvation comes from faith, not from works.[63] If you would be angry to some purpose, emulate the gentiles' anger; God became more gracious towards them after they became angry with themselves and showed remorse for their former lives. You are steeped in vice, O Jew, and indeed your very acts of righteousness are stained with sin. Your fasts are impure, your sacrifices profane, your sabbaths unholy. Today the Lord demands none of this; he seeks purity of spirit, born of unblemished faith and unfeigned love.[64] Repent, be angered by your sins, and stop adding to them the most grievous sin of all, stubborn unbelief. Let the words on your lips be the words in your hearts, that God need not forever be complaining of you: "This people pays me lip-service, but their hearts are far from me."[65] The same complaint is made of you in the Psalms: "They loved him only with their lips, and lied to him with

* * * * *

61 Cf Jer 4:4 and Rom 2:29.
62 LB reads: 'Why do you boast of your works to me?' (248F).
63 Cf for example Acts 13:19, Rom 3:20–2, and especially Gal 2:16. In applying these texts strictly to the Jews, Erasmus was perhaps avoiding controversy; this passage escaped censure in the *Index expurgatorius*.
64 2 Cor 6:6
65 Matt 15:8 and Mark 7:6

their tongues; they were disloyal to him in their hearts, and were unfaithful to his covenant."[66] Your lips praise the prophets, but you turn your backs on the one whom the prophets foretold. You cling stubbornly to the law of Moses, but you spurn me, the one whom the whole Law proclaims. You worship God the Father, but utter blasphemy against his Son; with your lips you boast of the circumcision of the flesh, but your minds are uncircumcised.[67] You claim to keep the Lord's sabbath, because on that day your bodies are at rest; but that is a human sabbath, whereas to keep the Lord's sabbath you must maintain your spirit calm and free from all disturbance by sin. This sabbath you are constantly breaking. You boast of your cleanliness, the result of your frequent ablutions, but your hearts within you are full of uncleanness.[68] Your lips obey the letter of the Law, but you deny its spirit. You cry: "It is the Lord's temple, the Lord's temple,"[69] but you curse the church, the true temple of the Lord. How long will you lie to me like this? You are called Jews, which means "confessors,"[70] but you clamour more persistently than anyone against the gospel truth. How long will your lips tell a different tale from your hearts? Let us hope that some day, at last, your declaration of faith will become clear and unambiguous. Grasp the spiritual sense of the Law, and at once you will begin to say in your hearts what you say with your lips; you will begin to be angered with yourselves, acknowledging your blindness. Do not despair of salvation because you crucified God's Son; your crime was, in part, simply an error. God does not desire the death of sinners, but that they should change their ways and live.'[71]

All this could also be applied, quite aptly, to the pagans. Their philosophers had much to say about Deus Optimus Maximus, the Supreme and Perfect God,[72] whom they described as holy, boundless, all-powerful, all-ruling, all-knowing, infused into everything, yet understood by none. However, they did not glorify him as God; they chose to honour the creation rather than the creator of all. They often talked learnedly about the supreme good, the nature and practice of virtue, the pursuit of honour for its own sake –

* * * * *

66 Ps 77/78:36–7
67 Cf Rom 2:28–9
68 Cf Matt 23:27 on the Pharisees as whited sepulchres.
69 Jer 7:4
70 Cf Jerome *De nominibus Hebraicis* PL 23 853, who also gives the more conventional sense, 'praisers.'
71 Cf Ezek 33:11.
72 Optimus Maximus was one of the many surnames of Jupiter; cf Cicero *De natura deorum* 2.25.64. What follows is an eclectic survey of the religious and ethical teaching of a variety of ancient sects.

but their lives did not match their speeches! The poets, too, often wrote of
the rewards awaiting those whose earthly lives were innocent and godly, of
the endless torments awaiting the ungodly, of the immortality to which the
godly would be brought – yet they lived their lives as if they believed nothing of what they wrote. Thus the following[73] is very properly addressed to
them: 'Speak these words in your hearts, say them with all your heart; confess the truth and blush for your impiety; confess true justice and be ashamed
of your injustice. God makes no distinction between Greek and Scythian;[74]
the magnitude of your sins – however great they may be – does not disqualify
you from salvation. Admit your wrongdoing, trust in the gospel's promises,
and receive the salvation freely given. You have grievously offended God in
preferring demons and stones to him; you have shown great impiety in forc-
ing the Saviour to mount the cross. But he promises to forget all your evil
ways, if only you will mend them. He does not demand that you expiate your
guilt by endless burnt offerings. A victim has been sacrificed for the sins of
all; you have only to admit your sinfulness, cease to boast of your righteousness, and receive the grace of God. All this will happen if you "examine your
conscience in your private chambers." Pharisee,[75] why do you still parade
through the streets and squares, with your pale face, your wordy prayers,
your elegant robes, your broad phylacteries, hawking your sanctimony to
the people? Leave the public arena, where popular favour is canvassed, enter your private chambers, consider the inward meaning of the Law, and you
will see that I have fulfilled all that the prophets foretold concerning the
Lord's anointed. Then examine your conscience, confess your malice, and be
moved to repentance. A few moments of mental perturbation will win you
endless peace of mind. At present you take comfort, wrongly, in a law you
do not understand; you believe, falsely, that you are righteous because you
carefully observe rites which cannot guarantee true righteousness. The blood
of goats or calves cannot purge your conscience of sin;[76]these sacrifices were
but a symbol of true purification.'

The next words, appropriately, are 'Offer the sacrifice of righteousness,
and place your hopes in the Lord.' When reality appears, it is time for
symbols to disappear; now God must be appeased by very different sacrifices.
God demands from you the same offerings as from the gentiles; I think

* * * * *

73 An adaptation of Ps 4:4
74 Cf Col 3:11.
75 Cf Matt 23:5–7. Erasmus has provided no transition here, having apparently
   forgotten that the preceding remarks were addressed by Christ to the pagans.
76 Cf Heb 10:4.

these words apply to both gentiles and Jews, since neither offered him the sacrifice of righteousness. Now, the 'sacrifice of righteousness' could mean two things: either that it is performed righteously and lawfully, or that it confers righteousness upon the sacrificer. The gentiles' sacrifices, far from making them righteous, made them impious and impure, since they were imbued not merely with false beliefs but with impiety as well. What could be more impious than to slaughter your own children, as we read that Agamemnon did,[77] and as was common practice among the Africans and Scythians? What could be less righteous than to give to demons, humans, animals, onions,[78] and dumb statues the honour due to God alone?

At least the Jews did sacrifice their victims to God, but they could not truly be called sacrifices of righteousness either. In the first place, they did not confer righteousness on anyone, since they were mere symbols of the true sacrificial victim, through whom true righteousness was to be granted freely to all who believed and lived according to their faith, as Paul clearly points out in his letter to the Hebrews.[79] Similarly, in Romans 8: 'For what the Law could not do, being weakened by the flesh, God, sending his Son ... etc.'[80] And yet the Jewish people claimed credit for their righteousness, and by implication made God unrighteous, since God wished his Son to be sacrificed for all, which he would hardly have done had not Paul's words been true: 'All have sinned; all are in need of God's glory.'[81] In the second place, the Jews' sacrifices were in many ways impure and illegitimate. The Law prohibited a victim which had any spot or stain, which was lame or crippled, tainted by disease or infection, or acquired by theft or stealth.[82] Moreover, it condemned any offering which contained leaven, or had no salt in it. But the Jews' sacrifices were indeed leavened – with hatred and envy of their fellow men; they were crippled and unsalted because they involved the flesh but not the spirit. Food without salt has no savour,[83] and similarly the Law's flesh is tasteless without the spirit; anything lacking its better part must be far from perfect. The Jews were covetous, cheating and robbing

* * * * *

77 King of Mycenae and Argos, he sacrificed his daughter Iphigenia at Aulis in order to ensure safe passage to Troy for the Greek fleet. In some versions of the story Iphigenia offered herself as a sacrifice: cf *Ciceronianus* CWE 28 385.
78 Cf n26 above.
79 Heb 10:1
80 Rom 8:3
81 Rom 3:23
82 Cf for example Lev 2:11–13 and 22:20–2.
83 Cf Matt 5:13, Luke 14:34, and especially Mark 9:49–50, with additional references to sacrifice.

their neighbours, 'devouring the property of widows,'[84] and so the sacrifice they offered from among their booty was an abomination, as Solomon cries in [Proverbs] chapter 21: 'Wicked men's sacrifices, taken from the proceeds of crime, are an abomination.'[85] Similarly, in Ecclesiasticus 34: 'To offer a sacrifice stolen from the poor is like killing a son in front of his own father.'[86] God curses this kind of sacrifice in Malachi, saying: 'The food you place on my altar is defiled. Is it not wrong to offer a blind victim? Is it not wrong to offer one that is lame or sickly? I have no pleasure in you, says the Lord of Hosts, and I shall not accept an offering from your hand, says the Lord of Hosts.'[87] Again, in Isaiah the Lord turns in anger from a defiled offering, saying: 'What do I care for these countless sacrifices? I am sated. Offer no more sacrifices in vain, for your hands are full of blood.'[88]

Thus, from the cross, the Lord urges both Jew and gentile to change the nature of their offerings, to offer pure victims instead of impure, the spirit instead of the flesh. Isaiah describes this new type of sacrifice: 'Wash yourselves and be clean; remove the evil of your thoughts from my sight, cease to do wrong, learn to do right, pursue justice, help the oppressed, be just to the orphan, protect the widow.'[89] What does 'wash yourselves' mean? Recognize the unique sacrifice of the spotless lamb, whose precious blood truly cleanses men's consciences through faith. This, of course, is Peter's message: 'Putting aside all malice, all deceit, pretence, and jealousy, and all recrimination, like newborn infants, rational but without guile, you must crave for the pure milk which will enable you to grow towards salvation.'[90] Again, Paul says, in 1 Corinthians 5: 'Purge out the old leaven, that you may be new paste, as the unleavened bread you are; for indeed Christ our Passover has been sacrificed for us. Let us therefore keep the feast, not with the old leaven, or with the leaven of malice and evil, but with the unleavened bread of sincerity and truth.'[91] Abel's offering was like this, and the Lord received it with favour, whereas Cain's offering was unacceptable to God,[92] soured no doubt with the bitter leaven of envy and hatred. The Jews' sacrifice was like this too: they were afraid that if

* * * * *

84 Matt 23:14, Mark 12:40, and Luke 20:47; again, an attack on the Pharisees
85 Prov 21:27
86 Sir 34:20 English versions, 34:24 Vulgate
87 Mal 1:7–10
88 Isa 1:11–15
89 Isa 1:16–17
90 1 Pet 2:1–2
91 1 Cor 5:7–8
92 See Gen 4:3–5.

they entered the governor's hall, their Passover celebration might be de-filed,[93] but they were not afraid to shed an innocent's blood! They did not scruple to fix to a cross a fellow creature, and one who had done them so many kindnesses, even by the standards of this world – otherwise we might forgive them, since they did not yet understand God's hidden purpose.

Thus the Lord in person, as once through the prophets, now demands a new kind of sacrifice which will commend us to God. This kind is not per-formed in the temple at Jerusalem, in the profane shrines[94] of the pagans, or in sites of abomination, but in minds purified by faith, throughout the whole world. As he proudly cries in Malachi: 'From east to west my name is great among the nations, and in every place unblemished gifts are sacri-ficed and offered to my name.'[95] No doubt these are the 'calves of our lips' which delight the Lord in Hosea.[96] We offer such gifts whenever we confess our own unrighteousness and give thanks for the mercy of God, who has forgiven us all our sins through the death of his Son. Human righteousness consists in confessing our unrighteousness, and in glorifying God's right-eousness in fulfilling his promises.[97] On the other hand, the Pharisee who boasts of his own righteousness does not offer the sacrifice of righteous-ness; he lays claim to what is not his and robs God of the glory due to him. The prophet David recognized this when he said: 'O God, free me from bloodshed, O God of my salvation, and my tongue shall celebrate your right-eousness. O Lord, open my lips, and my mouth shall declare your praise.' Praise in the mouth of a sinner is unseemly, and no one can truly sing praises to the Lord unless the Lord himself has first opened a man's mouth so that he can curse his human sinfulness and beg for God's mercy. How-ever, his mouth is opened by the gospel faith, not by burnt offerings, in which the Jews put their trust. Indeed, the next verse reads: 'If you had de-sired a sacrifice, I should have offered one; but you take no pleasure in burnt

* * * * *

93 See John 18:28.
94 Erasmus plays here on *phanum* 'shrine or temple' and its compound *prophanus* 'lying before or outside the shrine.' For the general sense, see John 4:21–3 and Erasmus' paraphrase of the Gospel text, LB VII 528E / CWE 46 57–8.
95 Mal 1:11
96 Hos 14:2, quoted in Heb 13:15; the usual reading is 'the fruit of our lips.' Cf Erasmus' paraphrase (LB VII 1197C), which establishes the link between 'fruit' and 'sacrificial animals' ('calves').
97 This sentence was recommended for deletion in the *Index expurgatorius* LB X 1820B, presumably because it proposes a very narrow definition of righteous-ness (*iusticia* in the Latin).

offerings.' David then describes the sacrifice which God requires: 'My sacrifice to God is a broken spirit; you will not spurn a contrite and a humbled heart.'[98]

However, just as there is no forgiveness of sins outside the church,[99] so no sacrifice is acceptable to God unless it is offered within that temple which the Lord, its foundation and cornerstone, fashioned from living rocks.[100] David therefore added: 'Let it be your pleasure, Lord, to favour Zion, that the walls of your Jerusalem may be built anew.' Without your good will this building cannot rise, nor can this temple be preserved without your mercy, for among men nothing can be found except decay, collapse, and ruin. 'Only then will you accept the sacrifice of righteousness, gifts and burnt offerings; only then will men lay their calves upon your altar.'[101] Such sacrifices are made every day on our Zion, which spreads throughout the world, in the form of the confession of sins, thanksgiving, and the kind of incense which is most pleasing to God, heartfelt prayer. God takes no delight in the slaughter of cattle, the reek of burning flesh, or the heavy fumes of incense.

No animal is more brutal or dangerous than a godless man: let this be the beast that is slaughtered, to be reborn as a worthy offering to God. No wonder the apostle Paul exhorts the Colossians to become offerings of this sort: 'Mortify those parts of you which belong to the earth.'[102] If your ears are deaf to God's words, but open to scurrilous gossip, cut them off; if your eyes are without shame, pluck them out;[103] if your brow is arrogant, cast it off; if your tongue is untruthful and wanton, but silent when it comes to confessing your unrighteousness and God's righteousness, cut it out; if your neck is stiff and will not bend to God's will, strike it through; if your throat is always itching with greed, cut it; if your belly is always ravening, throw it out; if your heart is full of lust, cut it out; if your liver is full of envy, pluck it out; if your genitals are unchaste, destroy the rebellious part; if your hands wander or your feet waver, chop them off; in sum, slaughter the old creature that was defiled in every way, that a new creature may be born, renewed by submission to God who made him in his image. Not that the body, which

* * * * *

98 Ps 50/51:14–17
99 On Erasmus' views on penance and forgiveness see J.B. Payne *Erasmus: His Theology of the Sacraments* (Richmond 1970) 181–213.
100 Cf 1 Pet 2:5–6.
101 Ps 50/51:18–19, slightly adapted
102 Col 3:5
103 Cf Matt 5:29; this enumeration is clearly a development of Christ's counsel in this verse and the next, though it also draws upon the list of vices traditionally associated with the various parts of the body.

God bade us honour,[104] is to be harmed; but the passions of the flesh, which make war on God, are to be cut off. Paul enumerated those parts which typify the worldly heart: fornication, indecency, lust, foul desires, and greed, which is the slave of idolatry; anger, malice, blasphemy, filthy talk, and lying.[105] The apostle also listed the parts which belong to the new creature: deep compassion, kindness, humility, modesty, patience, gentleness, forgiveness, mercy. But who will slay this brute beast and enable a rational offering to arise in its place? None other than the one who, as the prophet says, kills and gives life, wounds and heals.[106] He kills the wicked that the good may be born; he strikes down the rebel that an obedient servant may arise. But his weapon is the sword of the Spirit, which is the word of God.[107]

Come, dear brothers, let us offer ourselves to be slain by that sword, for there is always a part of us which needs to be slain, and to be given new life. We shall make this offering if we believe the gospel with all our hearts, if we truly trust in its promises, and in this way offer a pure and spotless lamb to the Lord. He takes delight in such lambs, since he chose to work reconciliation through that spotless lamb, his Son. Let the dangerous beast in us be killed, so that we become as lambs ourselves, to be sacrificed to the lamb. What does it mean to be a lamb? To harm no one, to help all. No one can make us such lambs except the one true lamb sacrificed for us. When it is done, it only remains for us to dedicate to him all that we have received from him, and, as Paul teaches, to show that we are all 'a holy, living sacrifice, acceptable to God, which is our reasonable service.'[108] Let us, as Peter advises, offer spiritual sacrifices, acceptable to God through Jesus Christ.[109]

What must be done next? 'And place your hopes,' says the psalm, 'in the Lord,' or, as the Hebrew version has it: 'Put your trust in the Lord.' There is little difference between hope and trust. Those who distrust works and merits, and their own powers, and rely entirely on God's grace, 'place their hopes in the Lord.' Philosophers put their hopes in human wisdom, rich men in wealth, princes in chariots and horses; but the little lamb of Christ relies entirely on his shepherd's care.

These words too apply to both Jews and gentiles, who are being exhorted to abandon the things in which, until now, they have placed vain

* * * * *

104 Cf for example 1 Cor 6:18–19.
105 The development here is based on both Gal 5:19–22 and Col 3:5–13.
106 Moses, in Deut 32:39, echoed by Hannah in 1 Sam 2:6
107 Eph 6:17
108 Rom 12:1
109 1 Pet 2:5

hope, and instead to put all their trust in the Lord, who does not desert those whose hopes are in him. The Lord does not fail in his promises, and no one can snatch from his hands anything entrusted to his care. He will assuredly complete the task begun with his chosen followers. Therefore any true lamb devoted to God will not claim the credit for any good qualities he may have, but will ascribe them all to his creator and Lord, giving thanks even in times of trouble. He will not cling to life or shrink from death, confident that, under the protection of God to whom he has dedicated himself, he cannot perish; whether he lives or dies, he will remember at all times Paul's words: 'Whether we live or die, we are the Lord's.'[110] Moreover, as we learned earlier from Isaiah,[111] to live soberly, piously, and righteously in Christ Jesus is to offer the sacrifice of righteousness. No one can do so unless he puts his hopes in the Lord.

Let us take an example of the most trivial kind. To make money, a wine merchant knows a hundred ways of adulterating his wine, and sells expensive poison to his neighbour instead of wine. When his conscience pricks him, he replies: 'I am forced to do it, otherwise I could not look after my family or satisfy my creditors.' What should be our answer to him? 'Good man, you have only to make the sacrifice of righteousness, and place your hopes in the Lord; make up your income by being thrifty: parsimony can be very profitable.[112] Stop cheating your neighbour, help him rather, in time of need, and leave the rest to God. He will not abandon you, unless you have abandoned your trust in him.'

The wine merchant's example could be applied to all kinds of craftsmen and businessmen; if they truly placed their hopes in the Lord, amazing though it may seem, all their cheating and dishonesty would be eliminated entirely. Let us say that a prince's counsellor observes with sadness that many innocent people are being oppressed, and that many of the decisions made are unjust and unholy; he would like to put a stop to it, but other considerations deter him: 'If you are too bold in your opposition to the prince, you will be removed from office.' Such thoughts show his lack of trust in God. You must make the sacrifice of righteousness and place your hopes in the Lord. Sacrifice some hoped-for reward; if it is not paid to you in this life, you will be fully repaid in the life to come. There are many similar circumstances, in every walk of life, which lead us to deviate from righteousness, but anyone 'who trusts in the Lord shall not be moved, like

* * * * *

110 Rom 14:8
111 Isa 1:16–17; cf 191 above.
112 Cicero *Paradoxa Stoicorum* 6.3.49

Mount Zion,'[113] and anyone who stands on the firm rock which is Christ Jesus cannot be dislodged by any storm.[114] When Isaiah had condemned polluted offerings which were unacceptable to the Lord, and had defined the sacrifice of righteousness, he added: 'Come, let us argue it out, says the Lord.'[115] Had he failed to fulfil his promises, he would not reject accusations of betrayal. But what, in fact, did he promise? Anyone who for his sake has given up something, useful or not, in this world, was promised a hundred times more in this age, and eternal life in the age to come.[116] Anyone who firmly believes these promises will in no circumstances be deterred from making the sacrifice of righteousness.

However, since there are very few true believers, our psalm continues: 'There are many who say: "Who will show us these good things?"' Those who trust in the Lord are but a tiny flock compared to the multitude who do not, and yet this little flock whose hope is in the Lord was told: 'Have no fear, for yours is the kingdom of heaven.'[117] Fear shows a lack of trust. Peter was afraid and began to sink.[118] The Jews would not believe God's promises without some clearly visible evidence. The Greeks, carried away by their enthusiasm for human wisdom, refused to believe anything which could not be proved by human reasoning; thus Aristotle did not believe that the world was created, and he doubted whether the soul survived the body – indeed, he doubted the very existence of the soul.[119] Gideon refused to believe the angel's promises until flames had spurted from the rock and consumed the meat and the unleavened cakes, and the maker of the fire had disappeared from his sight; nor did he dare to attack the Midianites until reassured by the two signs involving the fleece.[120] The Jews demanded that the Lord show them some sign from on high.[121] Thomas did not believe what the apostles

* * * * *

113 Ps 124/125:1
114 Cf 1 Cor 10:4–5.
115 Isa 1:18, following the accusations against Sodom and Gomorrah in verses 10–17
116 Mark 10:30
117 Cf Luke 12:32.
118 See Matt 14:30.
119 Allusions to Aristotle's theory that soul is not a substance separate from body, but an added condition of body (see for example *De anima* 1.1 402–3), and to his discussion of 'becoming,' for example in *De generatione* 1.3 317, which Aquinas for one took to be a denial of the divine act of creation (*Summa theologiae* I q 45 a 1). For a more sustained attack on Aristotle's teaching on the soul, see the colloquy *Puerpera* (CWE 39 590–618).
120 See Judg 6:17–21 and 37–40.
121 See for example Matt 12:38, 16:1.

told him until he had seen it with his own eyes and touched it with his own fingers.[122] But true faith cares nothing for human reason, which tends rather to weaken faith. True faith is confident that whatever the Holy Scriptures promise will come to pass; it does not argue or debate whether that which is promised may involve a contradiction, as the rhetoricians call it; it asserts only that he who made the promises is all-powerful, that he is truthful, and cannot be forsworn.

There are many, even among those who boast the name of Christian, who say: 'Who will show us these good things?' They want to see and touch the things they hear about; they will not believe anything they cannot see with their eyes or hold in their hands. This is the sort of thing we hear from Christians: 'I know what I can have here and now, but I don't know what I may have hereafter.' But a farmer sows his seed in the earth, and hopefully awaits the crop, trusting in the earth; should we then distrust God's promises if he does not immediately place what he has promised before our eyes? In Isaiah, the Lord cries: 'A believer has no need to be impatient.'[123] Similarly, Paul says: 'Hope that is seen is not hope,' for 'faith is the substance of things hoped for, the evidence of things not seen.'[124] In the Gospel, the Lord describes as blessed those 'who have not seen, and have believed.'[125] Psalm 2 says: 'Blessed are all those who put their trust in the Lord.'[126] The apostle agrees, saying: 'For we are saved by hope, and since we hope for what we do not see, we can wait with patience.'[127] Similarly, the apostle John says, in his first epistle: 'My dear friends, we are here and now the children of God; what we shall be has not yet been revealed, but we know that when it is revealed, we shall be like him, since we shall see him as he is. Everyone who has this hope in him sanctifies himself, sanctifies himself as Christ is sanctified.'[128] What does 'sanctifying oneself' mean? What else but offering the sacrifice of righteousness, so that by this act we are made like him who sacrificed himself for us? Those who have become the children of God through faith[129] recall the ways of their Father in the blamelessness of their lives, and do not demand the premature fulfilment of his promises,

* * * * *

122 See John 20:24–9.
123 Isa 28:16
124 Rom 8:24, followed by Heb 11:1
125 John 20:29
126 Ps 2:12
127 Rom 8:24–5
128 1 John 3:2–3
129 Gal 3:26

being content with his pledge. For the moment they see with the eyes of faith, though 'through a glass darkly,'[130] until it is time for the consummation. The eyes of the flesh see only things that are near at hand, but faith sees things that are far distant, hidden away, and not yet apparent. Therefore the apostle John says: 'No sinner sees God, nor does he know God.'[131] Why does he not see him? Because, living in the twilight world of his sins, he is deprived of the light of faith. Without faith, there is no salvation, since eternal life implies the knowledge that the Father is the one true God and that his emissary is Jesus Christ. How indeed can we know him, unless we have seen with the eyes of faith? It should be enough for us, here and now, to see his promises in this limited way, and to touch them: for faith has hands as well as eyes. We can perceive these things by contemplation, and by some secret power of the mind we can also touch them.

His pledge is a spirit poured into the hearts of his children. Other signs do not make hope assured. Pharaoh saw frightful portents, but he did not believe.[132] The Jews saw Christ perform miracles, day after day, but none the less they did not trust him. But when a man is robbed, thrown in prison, beaten, tortured, and executed for righteousness' sake, and yet even in the midst of his woes he feels his heart rejoice with the hope of bliss to come, this is, for him, an unmistakable sign which faith itself provides. Faith is a gift of God which dispels the night of sin and floods our minds with light. Thanking the Father for this gift, in his own name and that of his church, Christ says: 'O Lord, the light of your countenance has appeared on high to guide us.'

Those who have no trust in the gospel's promises – the greatest number – say: 'Who will show us these good things, in place of the woes we endure? The righteous have plenty of troubles; we can see, feel and touch them. But where are the good things which are promised? We see the body perish and be reduced to ashes. We hear of a promised resurrection, but we do not see it.' Their attitude, if not their exact words, reminds me of the comic poet's pander who said: 'We don't pay cash for mere hopes!'[133] It is not surprising that men should distrust one another; all men are liars,[134] since, even if they make a promise in the best of faith, all too often they cannot produce the goods. Yet people do trust one another, so long as they can include in their agreement a

* * * * *

130 1 Cor 13:12
131 1 John 3:6
132 Exodus 7–12
133 Terence *Adelphi* 219 (adapted); cf *Adagia* II iv 5 CWE 33 191–2.
134 Ps 115/116:11; cf 181 above.

covenant, sureties, a deposit, witnesses, a written contract, a pledge, a treaty. But although God has given us all of these and much more, and has offered us much better security, we still distrust so reliable a guarantor. We will trust a person who has managed to fulfil his promises in good faith once or twice; shall we not then trust God, who has fulfilled all the promises he made through the prophets so many thousands of years ago? Yet we refuse to believe in the only two promises remaining to be fulfilled, the judgment and the resurrection. We have a written contract in the form of the Holy Scriptures, where his good faith has been proved to the hilt[135] in chapter after chapter; why do we still have doubts about the rest? We have thousands of witnesses, in the Old Testament and the New; in other transactions we make do with four or, at most, seven witnesses, but in this we refuse to trust thousands. Christ says to you: 'If you give anything to this poor man, you may put it on my account; I shall repay you a hundred times here, and later give you life everlasting.'[136] You may reply: 'But if I give, who will repay me? How will my wife and children live?' The moneylender is approached and asked for money, to be paid back over three years; contracts are exchanged, and we do not hear him say: 'But will you pay me back enough to keep my family?' The most cautious demand a pledge before they count out the money; but how many do we know who have been cheated by pledges? None the less, it is only God whom we refuse to trust; even though he gave us his only Son as a pledge, added the Spirit as a surety, and has fulfilled all the promises, however apparently incredible, that he made through the prophets; he guaranteed his promises in person, by performing countless miracles, and produced thousands of witnesses who testified to Christ by their pain and suffering and their eagerness to suffer death: and yet we continue to cry: 'Who will show us these good things?'

My brothers, we must have nothing to do with these cries of distrust; let us instead give thanks to the Lord by saying, with our psalm: 'O Lord, the light of your countenance has appeared on high to guide us.' Many are called, but few are chosen.[137] He has poured the light of his countenance upon those he has deigned to choose: happy are those on whom this light has shone! The sun is a wondrous creation, but God commands it to rise on the good and the evil alike;[138] however, he shows the light of his countenance only to those

* * * * *

135 *ad unguem*, literally 'to the nail,' an expression borrowed from craftsmen who tested finish or accuracy with their nails, as Erasmus explains in *Adagia* I v 91
136 A development of Matt 19:21 and 29
137 Matt 20:16 and 22:14
138 An adaptation of Matt 5:45

he has specially chosen. The sun's face belongs to this world; anyone at all may look on it when it rises. But God's countenance has not the same effect on all: when those who have rebelled against him see it, they shall be struck down,[139] whereas when the righteous see it they shall stand up with great steadfastness. The judge of the living and the dead shall some day act like this; at present he illumines the hearts of the elect through faith and turns his countenance away from those who are in love with this world. But observe the many ways in which he has shone into our hearts and allowed our sins no hiding place. God gave his human creature the light of intelligence, enabling mankind to perceive what to pursue and what to avoid. Even though this light was darkened by disobedience, yet it left behind a spark, like a seed in the earth, from which the light could be rekindled. God enlightened us by his wondrous construction of the created world; he enlightened us through the Law and the prophets; he enlightened us by sending to earth his Son, who was the light of the world;[140] he enlightened us through the holy books, through miracles, through the apostles and martyrs; even today he continues to enlighten us through the gift of faith and the breath of his Spirit.

The 'countenance of God' is God's favour towards us, which Paul calls grace.[141] This light has not merely appeared to us, but has appeared 'as a sign to guide us': the Latin word here, *signavit*, is not a translation of ἐσφραγίσθη, as St Augustine seems to suppose, since he comments here that it is 'like a coin stamped with the king's portrait,'[142] but rather a translation of ἐσημειώθη, a word describing, for example, how the Little Bear gives guidance to sailors on the deep, or how a lighthouse, shining from afar, guides the sailor towards harbour in the dark of night. It is thus an answer to unbelievers who mutter: 'Who will show us these good things?' Faith guides us towards the haven of immortal life, and the resurrection brings us into port. Sailors are often misled by their seamarks, but the guiding light which God has set before us, through faith and in Holy Writ, can mislead no one.

Jerome,[143] and some other scholars of Hebrew, have commented that in Hebrew this word means something like 'raise the ensign, or banner.' In

* * * * *

139 The Latin *exanimare* can mean both to deprive of breath or stun, and to deprive of life. It is likely that the latter is intended here, since the next sentence suggests an allusion to the Day of Judgment; cf Rev 1:7.

140 Cf John 8:12 and 9:5.

141 The Greek is χάρις, which does indeed have both these senses; cf Erasmus' commentary on 1 Cor 15:10 (*et gratia eius in me*) LB VI 735D.

142 *Enarratio in psalmum* 4 PL 36 81. Most texts and commentators agree with Erasmus here.

143 *Divina bibliotheca* PL 28 1130B

battle a banner is raised for the soldiers to follow through the press. But they are often misled by such devices, and both soldiers and sailors can be lured to their doom. But the banner which God raises for his people infallibly guides them all to safety. A prototype of this banner was the pillar of fire which guided the Israelites by night, as they journeyed through the wilderness towards the promised land; by day, a pillar of cloud preceded them.[144] We also have a light to guide us through the night of doubt and sorrow, and a cloud to cool our ardour for worldly success. The Israelites were given a bronze serpent as an emblem, and it was set up on a long pole for all to see; anyone who lifted his eyes to the emblem was cured of snake bite, but those who did not perished.[145] God's gift is set on high to make it easier for us to see and, as Jesus our teacher said: 'No one comes to me unless my Father has drawn him to himself.'[146] The three Magi were given a sign which led them to Jesus' cradle,[147] but the sign did not appear to the Scribes or to Herod. Why not? Because their eyes were not illumined by the light of faith. Why did they not see it? Because the sign was set on high, and their eyes were fixed upon the ground. Herod feared expulsion from his earthly kingdom; the high priests and Pharisees feared the loss of their wealth and power. It is no wonder that their eyes, cast downward like this, could not see a sign from heaven! Old Simeon's bodily eyes were now dim, but his faith was penetrating and sharp, and so he prophesied concerning this sign: 'This child is destined to be a sign which men shall reject; many in Israel shall fall and rise again because of him.'[148] Who were the 'many'? The majority of the Jews, who kept on asking: 'Who will show us these good things?' and who were outraged by Christ's miracles. 'The light came into the world, but the people loved the darkness more than the light.'[149] But since the Jews refused to see the sign set on high, it became 'a light to lighten the gentiles'[150] and, as Zechariah prophesied: 'The morning sun from heaven has visited us, though we were far away.'[151] God is light and his Son our Lord Jesus Christ is light proceeding from light; truth is an eternal light which never fails.[152]

* * * * *

144 See Exod 13:21.
145 See Num 21:9.
146 John 6:44
147 The account which follows is based on Matt 2:1–12.
148 Luke 2:34
149 John 3:19
150 Luke 2:32
151 Luke 1:78
152 Cf John 1:4–9.

However, to see this light, we need another light to lighten the darkness of minds blinded by sin, and to save us from the fate of the Jews, who saw but did not see,[153] because they did not believe what they saw; as Psalm 35 puts it: 'For the fountain of life is with you, and by your light we shall see the light.'[154] Unless God has first looked upon us it is impossible that we should see him. When, in his mercy, he turns his countenance upon us, then our mind's eyes are illumined and inspired to gaze upon him in their turn. This is why, in the mystic writings, holy men so often beseech God to turn his face towards them; for example, in Psalm 83: 'O God, our shield, look down, and gaze upon the face of your anointed,'[155] in Psalm 88: 'O Lord, they shall walk in the light of your countenance, and shall rejoice in your name,'[156] and in Psalm 31: 'I shall give you understanding, and teach you the way you must go; I shall fix my eyes upon you.'[157] In Psalm 43, again: 'For they did not win the land with the sword, and their arm did not save them; it was your right hand and your arm, and the light of your countenance.'[158] Anxiety comes with the night, but the light of day dispels nocturnal fears and restores confidence, as Psalm 26 says: 'The Lord is my light and my salvation: whom shall I fear?'[159] Psalm 117 also rejoices: 'God is the Lord, and he has given us light.'[160] Psalm 66 prays: 'God be merciful to us and bless us; may he make his countenance to shine upon us and be merciful to us.'[161]

When the sun is hidden by the clouds, it spreads gloom everywhere, but when it is bright and clear, it brings joy to the world; similarly, God has two faces, one clouded and one bright; holy men beseech him to turn away the one, and beg him not to turn away the other; as the prophet cries out in Psalm 12: 'How long will you forget me, O Lord? For ever? How long will you turn your face from me?'[162] Again, in Psalm 29: 'You turned your face from me, and I was troubled,' and in Psalm 43: 'Why have you turned away your face and forgotten our helplessness and our tribulation?'[163] Similarly, in Psalm 118 the prophet prays: 'Make your face shine upon your servant and teach me

* * * * *

153 Cf Matt 13:13 and Mark 4:12.
154 Ps 35/36:9
155 Ps 83/84:9
156 Ps 88/89:15
157 Ps 31/32:8
158 Ps 43/44:3
159 Ps 26/27:1
160 Ps 117/118:27
161 Ps 66/67:1
162 Ps 12/13:1
163 Ps 29/30:7; Ps 43/44:24

your statutes.'[164] In Psalm 79 he cries: 'Show me your face and we shall be saved.'[165] The same prayer is made in other texts too numerous to mention here. Moreover, the Lord himself makes this promise in the Second Book of Chronicles, chapter 30: 'For the Lord your God is gracious and merciful, and will not turn his face from you if you have turned back towards him.'[166]

However, as I have said, God has another face, which weak humanity cannot bear to look on: the face of judgment and vengeance, mentioned in Psalm 67: 'So let the sinners perish before the face of God, and the righteous make merry and rejoice in God's sight.'[167] Of course, the latter is his merciful aspect, which allows us hope of forgiveness. A later passage concerns the wicked: 'And they shall be scattered before his face.'[168] Jeremiah calls this face the face of wrath and fury: 'Peaceful lands lie in ruins before the Lord's face of wrath and fury.'[169] The psalmist also trembles at this face of God: 'Who can stand up in the face of his disfavour?' and again: 'Turn your face from my sins.'[170] The Israelites could not look upon this face, or bear the words it spoke.

But when the age of the gospel's grace arrived, God put on his other face, which is not only bearable, but lovable. He took on human form, that all might be saved and none perish. He freely forgave us all our sins through trust in his Son Jesus. But to return to the point: of course, God is by nature incorporeal and does not have a face which he turns this way and that, sometimes calm and smiling, sometimes grim and stormy; rather he views everything, both good and evil, past and future as well as present, in the same way; but the Holy Scriptures say metaphorically that he 'gazes down' when he bestows his favour, and that he 'turns away his face' when he withdraws his mercy – and when this occurs, a deep and numbing terror takes possession of us. Sometimes he does so when offended by our sins; sometimes he even turns his face from good men for a while, to remind them that they can do nothing for themselves unless they are constantly upheld by God's favour. He had turned his face from Peter, when he denied his Lord, but Jesus turned his own face towards him again, at which he began to weep bitterly.[171]

* * * * *

164 Ps 118/119:135
165 Ps 79/80:3
166 2 Chron 30:9
167 Ps 67/68:2–3
168 Ps 67:5 in the Vulgate, omitted from the English versions
169 Jer 25:37
170 Respectively Pss 147:17 and 50/51:11
171 See in particular Luke 22:54–62.

Thus, when all humankind despaired most deeply of salvation, when the gentiles were sunk in such complete ignorance of God that they worshipped silent stones as gods, when corruption was equally rife among the Jews as they clung to the letter of the Law, and when the night of error and vice had descended upon all mankind: then God in his pity sent a sign of his mercy, raised the gospel banner for all to see, hung his Son, the image of God invisible,[172] on a high cross, so that all who fixed their heart's gaze upon him, through faith, would be freed from all taint of sin. Through this sign he dispelled the gentiles' ignorance, he dispersed the shadows of Moses' law, and poured out over all the world the grace of the gospel's light. The Lord was crucified on a hill, hung on a high cross, so that the sign should be clearly visible to all. He says this himself in the Gospel: 'When I have been lifted from the earth, I shall draw all eyes to myself.'[173] This was his most ardent desire when he cried: 'Come to me, all you who toil and are burdened, and I shall give you relief.'[174] The Jews strove to conceal the light of grace, to thrust it into a corner, forever boasting that salvation was reserved to the circumcised. But God meant his sign to be bright and visible to the whole world, as Paul writes to Titus: 'The grace of God and of our Saviour appeared to all men, and enlightened us.'[175]

Where the Latin translator has 'appeared,' the Apostle wrote in Greek ἐπεφάνη, which means 'grew light' or 'became bright.' A little later, recalling the darkness which had descended on the whole world, Paul describes the coming of light: 'At one time,' he says, 'in our folly and unbelief we had gone astray, enslaved by desires and passions of every kind, living in malice and envy, hateful and full of hatred for one another.' A description of darkness with no hope of salvation: but now hear how the banner of good hope was raised: 'But when our Saviour and our God appeared, imbued with generosity and kindliness, he saved us, not because of any righteous works we had performed, but according to his mercy, through the water of rebirth and the reviving power of the Holy Spirit, which he poured out upon us abundantly through Jesus Christ our Saviour, so that, justified by his grace, we might become heirs in hope to eternal life.'[176] Here again, 'appeared' is in Greek ἐπεφάνη, which I explained earlier; moreover, the translator's 'generosity' [benignitas] is in Paul's Greek χρηστότης [mildness], the opposite of severity,

* * * * *

172 Col 1:15
173 John 12:32
174 Matt 11:28
175 Titus 2:11
176 Titus 3:3–7

while the Latin word *humanitas* [kindliness], is in Greek φιλανθρωπία, a word which conveys good will and benevolence towards the human race. What sign could be more worthy of our love? What could be more welcome than this face of God? But in case anyone might doubt the sign, the Apostle adds: 'You can trust my words.'[177]

As I have said, the Lord Jesus, in his love for us, burned with an unquenchable desire to save humanity, as he himself declared in the Gospel: 'I have come to bring fire to the earth, and my only wish is that it be set aflame.'[178] Therefore he thanks his Father that by his death he will win eternal life for so many: 'You have brought joy to my heart,' he says. The Lord could see what was to come and, convinced that his request had already been granted, he said: 'You have brought joy to my heart.' The Father consigned his Son to death, but it was for the sake of all. As the source and fountain-head of all salvation, he brought joy to his Son's heart. How could this best of shepherds not rejoice in his heart at the salvation of humankind, seeing that a human shepherd will joyfully lift to his shoulders a single sheep he has found and carry it back to the sheepfold, that a woman will rejoice to find a coin she has lost, and that God's angels feel such joy over one sinner who repents?[179] The greater the love, the greater the joy; the more we have paid for what is lost, the greater our delight when it is found. If the apostle Paul felt such joy in his heart, when just a few people were converted to the gospel, that he became, as it were, drunk with delight, why should he not constantly exult and boast, as he did to the Philippians: 'My dear brothers,' he says, 'whom I long to see, my joy and my crown, stand thus firm in the Lord, my beloved brothers.'[180] Similarly, to the Thessalonians: 'For what is our hope, our joy, our crown of glory? Is it not you, standing before our Lord Jesus Christ at his coming? For you are our glory and our joy.'[181] Elsewhere, he swears by this glory,[182] as by something holy. All his letters are infused with this glory, this joy, despite the many hardships he suffered for the gospel at the same time: chains, prison, the lash, wild beasts, stoning, shipwreck, hunger, thirst, nakedness,

* * * * *

177 Titus 3:8
178 Luke 12:49, cited here in a form which Erasmus discussed but rejected in his New Testament (LB VI 287D–E)
179 A passage based on Luke 15:3–10
180 Phil 4:1
181 1 Thess 2:19–20
182 In 1 Cor 15:31, according to Erasmus' reading of the Greek; see his note (*propter vestram gloriam*) LB VI 737F–738D.

dangers besetting him on all sides, his brothers' treachery, curses, labour, sorrow.[183]

If Paul's heart could feel such joy at the salvation of so few, how much greater the joy we must imagine the Lord feeling in his heart, which was all aflame with the fire of love! So we read in Luke that, before the time had come to perform the sacrifice, he exulted in the Spirit, giving thanks for the salvation of believers. 'In that hour,' we read, 'he exulted in the Holy Spirit and said: "I thank you, O Lord, Father of heaven and earth, that you have hidden these things from the learned and wise, and have revealed them to the simple. Even so, Father, for such was your choice. All things are entrusted to me by my Father."'[184] What the evangelist calls the Spirit, the psalmist calls the heart; in my opinion the statement 'you have brought joy to my heart' has considerable impact, for his whole body had been subjected to torture, and yet death itself could not take the joy from his heart. In John, he promised that this joy would be passed on: 'But I shall see you again, and your hearts will rejoice, and no one shall take this joy from you.'[185] This then is true, entire, and everlasting joy, which the heavenly Father grants, even in the midst of this world's turmoil.

The prophet indicates the cause of all this joy: 'They have been multiplied by the ripening of their corn, their wine, and their oil.' As our Lord says in the Gospels, his Father was a farmer;[186] he himself was a grain of corn, which was dead and buried in the earth, but none the less produced an abundant crop.[187] He was the mustard-seed, the least of herbs, which grew into a tree with spreading branches where birds built their nests. He was the true vine, which spread the shoots of its branches throughout the world. The farmer waits impatiently for his crops and vines to come to fruition, and hopes for the richest possible return from his planting and seeding, as he counts the days to the harvest. Ever in harmony with his Father's wishes, the Lord is most eager for the harvest, and says in Luke: 'The harvest is great, the reapers are few; ask the lord of the harvest to send reapers for his harvest.'[188]

* * * * *

183 The list is based on 2 Cor 11:23–7, a summary of the narrative in Acts.
184 Luke 10:21–2
185 John 16:22
186 Parables drawn from agriculture are very common in the Gospels, as the examples which follow demonstrate; this first remark could apply to a number of passages.
187 Cf John 12:24, followed by Matt 13:31–2 (the mustard-seed) and John 15:1 (the true vine).
188 Luke 10:2

And in John he tells the disciples to look around at the fields where the crops are already ripening and, as it were, begging to be scythed.[189] Before the Lord Jesus' death, the yield from the gospel was meagre and sickly: even his brothers did not believe in him.[190] But from the moment that the seed, planted in the good soil, bore fruit, and the vine began to spread its branches into every corner of the world, believers began to multiply. At Peter's first sermon, about three thousand people came into the church's barns.[191] It is a constant theme in the Acts of the Apostles that the number of believers grew rapidly; within a few years, by the efforts of humble, simple men, and not many of them at that, the religion of Christ was spread through every region of the world, although later, for reasons I cannot guess, it began to contract once more.

Where I read 'by the ripening of their corn,' others[192] read 'in the season of their corn,' but it does not make much difference to the meaning whether you speak of the ripening which occurs in due season, or of the season which brings the ripening crops. This mystical process had seasons of its own: it was foretold for centuries, it was promised for centuries by the prophets' oracles, but when it reached the season of its maturity, and God implanted his seed through his Son and the apostles, there began to spring up, among all the nations, an abundant crop of gospel corn, a bountiful harvest of wine, which the gospel vine poured out for us.

There is no mention in the Hebrew of oil, which was added by the translators of the Septuagint,[193] and is retained by our church. I do not know where the idea came from, but I certainly do not think that it should be rejected, since the Septuagint has a traditional authority, and church usage has approved it for so many years. I would accept, too, the interpretation of the old commentators, including Arnobius,[194] who relate the corn and wine to the communion of the Lord's body and blood, and the oil to the holy chrism with which we are anointed at baptism, so that we too are called 'Christs': 'Do not touch my Christs.'[195] For as long as their religion involved circumcision,

* * * * *

189 John 4:35
190 Cf John 7:5.
191 See Acts 2:41.
192 Most notably Augustine (PL 36 82 and n1) and Cassiodorus (PL 70 51); Erasmus follows the Vulgate reading current in his own time, which is accompanied by a note on the variant.
193 Jerome *Breviarium in psalmos* PL 26 828D denies this, but is equally puzzled about its origin.
194 *Commentarii in psalmos* PL 53 330
195 Ps 104/105:15; 'Christ' means 'anointed' in Greek.

pointless ablutions,[196] dietary restrictions, and the ritual slaughter of cattle, few converts joined the Jews, and most of those became worse than they were before. But then Jesus came and baptized us with the flame of the Holy Spirit and, as John says, our anointing began to reveal all things to us;[197] the seeds of the gospel teaching spread far and wide, the new wine[198] of gospel love fermented in the minds of men, and it was then that the worshippers of Christ were multiplied. As the Jews and the princes resisted it with ever-increasing ferocity, so the gospel harvest spread itself more widely. Thus were they multiplied, not by arms, or wars, or riches; but in the midst of persecution they were filled with joy, and with the Holy Spirit.[199] The gloomy hypocrites, who disfigured their faces,[200] knew nothing of this oil; the apostles had drunk of this new wine, when they seemed drunk to the people, speaking to the people in strange tongues.[201] On this corn were fed those who believed the apostles, who broke bread in private houses in memory of the Lord; this is mentioned in chapter 2 of the Acts: 'Some continued steadfastly in the apostles' doctrine, in fellowship, the breaking of bread, and prayer.' And, a little later: 'With one accord they attended the temple daily, and broke bread in private houses, and ate this food with gladness and singleness of heart.'[202] This was the badge of Christ's soldiers, these their provisions, these the church's fortresses as it grew. They formed alliances by the breaking of bread, they provisioned themselves with gospel teaching, they waged war with prayers. Thus, amid the world's tumults, was that heavenly band increased.

Augustine has drawn our attention to the possessive 'their' [sui], suggesting that a distinction is being made between God's corn and man's, God's wine and man's, God's oil and man's;[203] this is not meant to rule out the traditional interpretation concerning the consecrated bread and cup, but to make room for his own theory, which is more ingenious than convincing, and which he was alone in propounding: I shall have more to say about this shortly.[204] But why should we be afraid to call 'ours' what God has given us,

* * * * *

196 Erasmus plays on the adjective *frigidus*, meaning both 'useless' and 'cold.'
197 1 John 2:27
198 Cf Matt 9:17.
199 Cf Acts 13:52.
200 Cf Matt 6:16.
201 Acts 2:4 and 13
202 Acts 2:2 and 46
203 *Enarratio in psalmum* 4 PL 36 82
204 265 and 269 below; Augustine's theory is that the subject of this sentence is the unbelievers, rather than the faithful.

since he bestowed his Son wholly and entirely upon us, and together with him will give us everything, if we are members of the Son? He is bread for his children, and none of it is given to the dogs.[205] Every day we ask the Father for this bread, saying: 'Give us this day our daily bread.'[206] It should not be thought in any way irreverent or illogical to describe the gospel message as the bread and wine by which the disciples are multiplied, since in the sixth chapter of John the Lord himself teaches that he is the bread of life and, after the argument about his flesh, he added: 'In truth, I tell you, unless you have eaten the flesh of the Son of Man, you will have no life in you. Whoever eats my flesh and drinks my blood possesses eternal life; I shall raise him up on the last day. For my flesh is truly food, and my blood is truly drink; whoever eats my flesh and drinks my blood dwells in me, and I in him.'[207] The earliest commentators interpret this passage as a reference to the word of truth,[208] and indeed Christ is truth itself, and the Word of the Father; later in the same discussion there is this passage: 'It is the spirit which gives life; the flesh is of no avail. The words I have spoken to you are both spirit and life. But there are some among you who do not believe.'[209]

The implication here is that this bread and drink do not give life except to those who consume them spiritually, that is, those who believe the Holy Scriptures. Now there has been a decrease in the number of carnal Jews, and an increase in the number of spiritual Jews,[210] who eat the true bread which comes down from heaven, who drink Christ's blood, which gives life to the soul, and who are anointed with the oil of the Spirit, which, in the midst of this life's tribulations, brings a joy which cannot be expressed or ever taken away. The Jews had their manna[211] and boasted of it; they had their sacred bread,[212] which none but the priests were allowed to eat; they had

* * * * *

205 Cf Mark 7:27.
206 Luke 11:3
207 John 6:35 and 48, 53–6
208 For example Origen Περὶ ἀρχῶν or *De principiis* PG 11 244–7, Chrysostom *In Ioannem homilia* 46 PG 59 259A, and Tertullian *De oratione* 6 PL 1 1262–4. Erasmus repeats this in 1527 in his annotation on John 6:52 (*si quis manducaverit ex hoc pane*) LB VI 366F, taking issue with St Hilary's interpretation of the 'bread' as Christ's assumption of a human body; *Erasmus' Annotations on the New Testament: The Gospels* ed A. Reeve (London 1986) 242.
209 John 6:63–4
210 In the sense of 'confessors'; cf 188 and n70 above.
211 Erasmus is repeating Christ's argument in John 6:31–2 and 49.
212 Cf Matt 12:4, where Christ reminds the Pharisees of David's infraction of this law in 1 Sam 21.

oil,[213] made for particular ceremonies, which could not be used for ordinary purposes – it was a capital offence to copy the recipe. Christians have oil, still more sacred – but it is shared by all; they have bread and wine which bring eternal life and are available to all, so long as they have the faith, or the expectation of faith, which enables them to consume them. Anyone who is unworthy to eat the Lord's body condemns himself in the eating of it;[214] anyone who hears the word of the Lord and does not believe brings worse damnation upon himself. Judas ate the bread, and after one mouthful Satan entered into him.[215] The Pharisees heard the word and were so outraged by it that they plotted his crucifixion; but the apostles, who were at first a small group among the Jews, were multiplied among the gentiles, especially after the Holy Spirit descended on them because they readily accepted the gospel message: in other words, they ate the heavenly bread and drank the Lord's blood, and then, full of the Holy Spirit, they began to live in a state of constant joy, accepting with great alacrity of spirit whatever suffering was inflicted on them for the sake of the Lord Jesus Christ.

The Lord could see that by his death his Father would provide for him just such a church, thronged with people, rich and joyful, and so, having completed everything necessary for the sacrifice, freely and willingly he laid down his life, certain of resurrection, not only for himself, but for all those who should believe the gospel teaching. 'I shall sleep in peace and in it take my rest,' he says, 'for you, O Lord, have set me apart in hope.' 'In peace' and 'in it' is much the same as saying 'in peace and harmony,' signifying a conscience which is entirely calm and confident. There is no peace for the wicked;[216] but by his death[217] Christ brought peace to all things in heaven and on earth; not only did he reconcile individuals with God, but he united in Christian concord all the nations of the earth, Jews, Greeks, Latins, Scythians, and Indians, when they were divided by vast differences in laws, rituals, customs, and attitudes. He made them all one in himself. 'I shall sleep,' he says, since he is soon to live again, and 'I shall take my rest,' meaning 'I shall keep the sabbath in the tomb and shall make the Lord's day holy by my resurrection.' It is written that God kept the sabbath on the seventh day, after he had made the world;[218] but it was through the Son that he made

* * * * *

213 Described in Exod 30:22–33
214 Cf 1 Cor 11:29.
215 See John 13:26–7.
216 Cf Isa 48:22.
217 The phrase 'but by his death' is omitted in ASD V-2 222:951.
218 Gen 2:2

the world,[219] and so it was through him that he restored his creation. After performing everything necessary for the redemption of humanity, the Son too kept the sabbath, resting in the tomb.

Many people sleep restlessly, haunted by bad dreams. But the Lord not only slept, but rested, since his soul was free from all guilt and had complete confidence in God's promises. Anyone tormented by doubt or fear either cannot get to sleep or else finds little rest in sleep. Therefore he added: 'For you, O Lord, have set me apart in hope.' The Father had placed his Son in the hands of the wicked, and they could do whatever they liked with him, including the final humiliation of the cross; they left nothing undone in their efforts to erase all memory of him. But God, wishing to restore humanity through this sacrificial victim, took him away from their hands and from their sight; this is why the psalm uses the adverb καταμόνας, meaning 'apart,' 'separately.' For the Lord was buried in a new tomb, where no one had been laid before;[220] moreover, he alone among the dead was free, for although death claimed him, it had no power over him and was obliged to disgorge its prey; death itself was caught, as it snapped at the bait which concealed, beneath a morsel of human flesh, the steel hook of a divine nature. The Lord had earlier exposed himself publicly to all the indignities a man can suffer, but we are told that after the resurrection he appeared and made himself known only to those whom he had chosen out of the world of men.[221] In this way he is detached and separate from the world, and is now again taking his rest, free from persecution by the wicked; but he is taking his rest in the certain hope, confirmed by his father, that, as he himself has been raised above this world's woes to enjoy immortal glory, so his members will also be rescued one day from the world's mire and will share immortality with him.

It is worth pausing over the choice of language here.[222] The Latin version is *constituisti* 'you established me,' but the Septuagint version is closer to the Hebrew idiom, using κατῴκησας 'you have made me dwell,' or 'you have given me a home.' Someone may object that 'home' does not tie in very well with 'hope.' But when danger threatens, home is always the safest refuge; if you enjoy living in comfort and peace, you will always prefer to be at

* * * * *

219 An allusion to John 1:1–5
220 See Matt 27:60 and Luke 23:53.
221 All the Gospels agree on this aspect of Christ's resurrection, though the details vary.
222 Erasmus is following Augustine's discussion here; *Enarratio in psalmum 4* PL 36 83.

home, sheltered from wind and rain and other dangers from the skies, and safe from attack by beasts and men. The hope of resurrection is the one secure refuge from all the suffering inflicted by the world on the Lord's congregation. We pillow our heads on this hope, which the Father alone can give, while we await the hour when he will lead all his people to that same rest.

There, my worthy brothers, you have one interpretation of this psalm, showing how it can be applied to Christ the head and to the church, his body; but there are some incidental allusions to the moral sense which I shall now elucidate as briefly as possible. Everything I have said up to this point has, I think, great relevance to our salvation generally, but what I am about to say should be studied especially closely because it relates to each of us individually, and deals with the conduct of our everyday lives. Therefore I would ask that those of you who have nodded off should now rouse yourselves, and that those who have been wide awake should now pay even closer attention.

Returning to the beginning, therefore, we must run our eyes over the various participants again. First, on high, we must imagine God, the observer and governor of all that happens on earth, and, since he also gave his Son all power in heaven and earth,[223] it can make no difference if we imagine the Son alongside him. Next, in a high tower, we must imagine the prophet David or – it does not really matter – some other intelligence, raised by faith above the trivial concerns of the earth; his mind, filled with hope and longing, already dwells on heaven, but for the moment he is suspended between the two; sometimes his longing for the heavenly life draws his eyes upward, but at others brotherly love draws his eyes down again to earth. Finally, on earth we must imagine deep, impenetrable darkness, and disorder of all kinds. At the top, around God's throne, there shines ineffable light without a trace of shadow; in the middle, a tolerable half-light which, if compared with the lowest stratum, would seem like cloudless day but, if compared with the highest, would seem like night – but perhaps the time of night, just before dawn, when the shadows begin to thin out and the sky to lighten. Each of us has a cross to bear, the mortification of the flesh (by which I mean all human passions). When uplifted by this practice, we are troubled less by the earth's darkness but, as we draw closer to heaven, we long to fly higher. Let us add to the picture the companions of the crucified, listening intently and adding their voices to his song of thanksgiving.

* * * * *

223 Cf Matt 28:18.

With this picture fixed in our minds, let us proceed to examine the moral sense. As we have said, the heading mentions David, and he is a prototype of Christ. Now, David means 'physically strong,'[224] and you need strength if you wish to sing a psalm acceptable to God, to win victory in these canticles, and to be the victor 'towards an end,'[225] that is, to win the laurels, the prize of immortality. Victory implies a contest. The pagans held musical competitions, in which the winner received useless applause from the audience and some trashy prize. But Christians are not taking part in some frivolous musical competition, nor are they competing for trifling or silly prizes: if we produce a winning song, the prize is immortality. The body with its passions is like a musical instrument; if our sufferings strike the right note on it, and if the spirit, mortifying the flesh, puts it in proper tune, it will produce a melody most pleasing to Christ's ears. Anyone who perseveres in this contest to the end will be saved, and will be able to say, with Paul: 'I have fought the good fight, I have run the full course, I have kept the faith. For the future, a crown of righteousness is reserved for me, which the Lord, the just judge, will award to me on that great Day – not only to me, but to all who have set their hearts on his coming.'[226] This passage alludes to the adjudicator[227] in this particular musical competition. He is a judge, but a just judge who will not cheat anyone who deserves a prize. He is not biased towards any particular contestant, as often happens in singing contests between humans, when the judge is either wrong or corrupt.

The pagans were singing to their fellow men, and their prizes were the prizes of men. The Jews, however, were singing to God. The mystic psalms frequently urge us to sing, to play, to make a joyful noise[228] – but to God. Let us therefore also be Jews and sing a psalm to the Lord. Jew means 'confessor.'[229] Unless you confess that you are a sinner, and that you owe any good qualities you possess to God's mercy, you are not a true Jew and cannot sing a psalm to the Lord. Many of the philosophers treated their bodies very rigorously, and some even submitted to death voluntarily, but

* * * * *

224 Usually interpreted to mean 'beloved' or 'prince,' but Jerome also gives *fortis manu* 'physically strong'; *De nominibus Hebraicis* PL 23 813.

225 *in finem*; see 175 and n1 above.

226 2 Tim 4:7–8

227 Erasmus uses the rare technical term *agonotheta*, meaning the supervisor of the games; for patristic precedents see CWE 44 37 n12 (page 278).

228 For example at the opening of Pss 66, 81 and 95 (English versions)

229 Cf nn70, 210 above.

since in all this they were seeking human glory, and did not aim at the one true target,[230] the Lord Jesus, they were not 'singing to the Lord.' Similarly, the Pharisees were always torturing their bodies by fasts, or allotting a tenth of their income to succour the poor, or praying at inordinate length, but since in all this they were seeking praise for themselves, they were not 'singing to the Lord,' but to men; such seekers of reward should listen to the adjudicator: 'In truth, I tell you, you have your reward.'[231] But we have learned from the Gospels and from the apostles' letters that the branches can do nothing without the vine,[232] that we are unfit even to make plans by ourselves, and that we achieve salvation not by our own works but by faith and grace; let us therefore confess that the Lord is good, and let us sing of his mercy for ever; let us echo the psalmist's praise of his goodness: 'May my glory sing songs to you and never cease.'[233] In our acts of worship, we must not sing to ourselves, like the Aspendian lute-player in the classical proverb,[234] nor must we sing to our fellow men; let us rather sing our psalm to God, that we may win from him the prize of eternal life. Both the Jews and the gentiles had music performed during their religious ceremonies; but our music ought to be like our sacrifice: since our sacrifice is a rational one,[235] the appropriate music will be the confession of our sins, prayer, and thanksgiving, in the bad times as well as the good.

So much for the heading. Let us now turn to the psalm, although I am not unaware that there has been a dispute among modern students of Hebrew over the complexities of the heading and overall subject of this psalm. If anyone feels inclined to investigate, there is plenty of material here, but I prefer to pursue matters more relevant to the conduct of a life of piety. I have noted elsewhere that the First Psalm is like a preface to the whole book.[236] The words 'the victor' or 'for victory' are added to the heading of a large number of psalms, songs of thanksgiving to the Lord for shielding

* * * * *

230 *scopus.* The theological implications of the term are explored in Boyle 72–81; an alternative view is given in Manfred Hoffmann *Rhetoric and Theology: The Hermeneutic of Erasmus* (Toronto 1994) 252 n104.
231 This passage is inspired by Matt 6:1–7 and Luke 18:2; the ironical quotation which closes it ('you have your reward') is an adaptation of Matt 6:2.
232 Cf John 15:1–6.
233 Ps 29/30:12
234 Cf *Adagia* II i 30. This proverbial figure sang very softly and played his instrument only by fingering chords with his left hand. Cicero *In Verrem* 1.20 used him as a symbol of corruption and self-seeking.
235 Cf Rom 12:1 and 176 above.
236 See 8 and 74–5 above.

his people from the attacks of their persecutors. Other psalms have different headings but deal with a similar subject, since they all teach us that the most assured safeguard against all evil is to implore God's aid with confidence. For example, the Second Psalm begins with a complaint: 'Why did the nations rage . . .?' but it concludes: 'Blessed are all those who put their trust in the Lord.' The opening of the Third Psalm is plaintive: 'O Lord, how have my tormentors multiplied!' but the ending shows that help comes from the Lord: 'Salvation belongs to the Lord, and your blessing is upon your people.' The Fifth begins with a plea: 'O Lord, hear my words,' but the conclusion identifies the source of aid: 'Like a shield, O Lord, you have surrounded us with your favour.' The heading of this Fifth Psalm also mentions 'the victor,' as does the Sixth, which begins with a cry for help, but ends by proclaiming that God has brought about victory against the foe: 'Let them turn away in sudden confusion.' If you have the time to look into it, you will find the same thing in many other psalms.

All this makes the point that we need to be firmly convinced that in all our troubles we must seek no other refuge than God's protection; anyone putting his trust in him will be assured of victory against his foes. 'The victory which conquers the whole world is our faith.'[237] Similarly, this Fourth Psalm begins with a cry for help, but its ending shows that victory depends on faith: 'For you, O Lord, have set me apart in hope.' Many indeed are the sufferings of the righteous; none who choose to live in holiness with Christ Jesus can escape persecution in this world. However, we need not be downcast, for God, our one defender, is mightier than all our enemies together. We must simply make him the repository of our trust and constantly beg for his help. Why look for human support when once you have devoted yourself to God? Why rush hopelessly into the trap? Why seek help in perplexity from the forbidden arts or from demons, as Saul did when he called up Samuel through the witch?[238] Why weigh up your own merits? Why measure your own strength? You need only consider the goodness and power of the one who has undertaken to defend you. Moreover, to convince us that help is close at hand, the psalmist did not say: 'He heard me after I had called,' but rather: 'He heard me as I called.' This is St Jerome's translation of the original Hebrew text, and the Septuagint translated it ἐν τῷ ἐπικαλέσαι, which suggests that God's help was ready before the petitioner had finished speaking. What God expects from the suppliant is not the verbosity of the gentiles or Pharisees, but trust in him. When you beg him for

* * * * *

237 1 John 5:4
238 See 1 Sam 28, the story of the witch of Endor.

help, you are acknowledging both your own helplessness and God's loving kindness. The Pharisee in the Gospel, whom the Lord judged inferior to the publican, begged for nothing at all: he simply recited his good deeds. The publican, standing further away, cried: 'Have mercy on me, a sinner,' and was answered.[239]

It does not make much difference to the meaning whether Christ addressed these words to God (as Jerome's translation of the true Hebrew text suggests: 'You have heard me, O God of my righteousness'), to his devoted followers, or to the good and the wicked together. It is not clear why the translators of the Septuagint decided that there should be a change to the third person here.[240] If you use the second person, the words are a thanksgiving for assistance quickly granted; if you use the third, they become a cry of exultation, expressing his heartfelt joy to his friends. It is right that the devout should share their joys and sorrows, confirming Paul's words: 'When one of the members is sorrowful, all the members feel sorrow together; when one of the members rejoices, the other members too feel joy.'[241] If the verse is also addressed to the wicked, it becomes an exhortation to them to call upon God themselves: 'I cried out and was heard, and so you should be encouraged by my example: cry out and you too will be heard.'

As a thanksgiving, the verse has a threefold purpose. First, by acknowledging the source of the gift, the speaker ensures that he will be allowed to keep it; if someone claims the credit for his good fortune when it is entirely due to God who provided it, that person is unworthy to make long use of God's gift. Second, giving thanks to God is even now a means to repay his kindness; indeed, there is no other way for a human being to repay God than by proclaiming aloud his many kindnesses to us, and God demands no other payment from us than the sacrifice of praise[242] by which he delights to be honoured. Finally, thanksgiving is also a kind of petition. When a pauper thanks a rich man for an earlier favour, he is asking for another. People are sometimes offended by thanks of this kind, but God, the richest of the rich, whose generosity can never be exhausted, is glad to be encouraged to further

* * * * *

239 Luke 18:10–13
240 Jerome's third version, based on the Hebrew, uses the second person; the Septuagint uses the third person. Modern versions replace both by an imperative, which is more in keeping with the conventional opening line of psalms of invocation.
241 1 Cor 12:26
242 A phrase often used in the Psalms (for example in 49/50:14 and 23) and also in Heb 13:15

acts of generosity by having his liberality openly proclaimed. It is a matter, as the Greek proverb rightly puts it, of 'horses for courses.'[243]

Christian charity demands that we proclaim publicly God's goodness towards us, so that, from this sharing of comfort, spiritual joy will be increased among the faithful; Paul burned with desire to see the Romans, precisely because sharing the experience of the faith which God had given them, and exchanging good cheer with them, would gladden the hearts of both parties.[244] Moreover, there is always a chance that, when large numbers give thanks to God, the wicked and the slothful, wasting away, deprived of hope, amid all their woes, may come to realize where they must look for a remedy for their ills. As Paul wrote to Titus: 'For we too were once fools and unbelievers who had lost our way, and slaves to our passions'; in the next verse he points to the source of their good fortune: 'But when the kindness and generosity etc.'[245] Similarly, he wrote to Timothy: 'Before, I was a blasphemer, a persecutor, a slanderer, but I obtained the mercy of God.'[246]

Philosophers have looked for a way in which a man may praise himself without boasting.[247] The most certain way is to attribute all our misfortunes to ourselves and all our good fortune to the generosity of the deity, always conscious of Paul's dictum: 'By the grace of God I am what I am.'[248] It cannot be called self-praise to recall God's gifts and to give him the credit, so long as you let no hint of hypocrisy spoil your account. For example, it will be very profitable for a drunkard who has reformed with God's aid to make this sort of statement to a group of heavy drinkers: 'In the past, life meant nothing to me unless I was at a party, gorging myself with food and drink, but now, having cried out to God, I have reached a state where I find nothing more pleasant than sobriety, and nothing so repugnant as drunkenness. Previously I found it very difficult not to swear, but now, aided by God's grace, I find nothing easier than to refrain from it. In days gone by I found nothing so tedious as reading holy books, and I was infatuated with the tales of the poets; now I have made such progress, with God's help, that nothing delights me more than to meditate on Holy Writ. Once I used to enjoy slandering

* * * * *

243 *Adagia* I viii 82, quoted here in Greek. It means literally 'the horse to the plain,' and is glossed by Erasmus (CWE 32 169) as encouraging someone to do what they are best at, or most want to do.

244 Cf Rom 1:11.

245 Titus 3:3–4

246 1 Tim 1:13

247 For example Cicero in *De senectute* (on Nestor in Homer) and Plutarch *Moralia* 539–47, a whole essay on the subject

248 1 Cor 15:10

people, and listening to slander, but now, by constant prayer, I have been given the power to hate slander more than any other vice. I used to think once that I could never give up my infidelities and promiscuity, but I cried out to the Lord, and he made the apparently impossible quite simple, and the apparently bitter quite sweet: so much so that now I shudder to think of all the things that I used to find so enjoyable, and rejoice in my newfound liberty, having escaped from such maddening masters. My struggle against greed and ambition was long and dangerous; I placed all my hopes in the Lord, and my troubles were at an end.'

Anyone who has been enabled to share Christ's cross, and to mortify his earthly limbs through the spirit, has a duty to inspire others with the hope of the same freedom, by proclaiming the goodness of God the Liberator in terms such as these. Of course, physical problems and extraneous concerns[249] are of less importance, but even here God's generous response to our cries must not be passed over in silence. Those cured of illness speak in praise of the magic arts,[250] and those who have done well in battle make much of their lucky swords and undergarments;[251] why then do you say nothing of your Saviour's glory when you have been saved by imploring Christ's help? You should shout to everyone, everywhere: 'The Lord heard me when I called,' so that people who previously resorted to soothsayers,[252] magicians, and enchanters can be taught to resort instead to God's aid, since whether he rescues them from a particular danger or not, he always saves them when they call, whereas the others will not only cheat them, as usual, but will also ensure their perdition, precisely when appearing to offer salvation. I do not think that simple people are entirely to be blamed when, in time of danger, they invoke Christopher, George, Antony, or Nicholas,[253] provided that they fervently sing this psalm: 'The Lord heard me when I called.' No

* * * * *

249 The phrase 'extraneous concerns' recalls the *res extraneae* of the Stoics; see for example Cicero *De inventione* 2.56.168 and 2.59.177.

250 The reading in the original editions is 'magic arts,' which LB changes to 'medical arts'; in the light of the next clause, the original version seems acceptable.

251 Erasmus often condemned such superstitions, for example in his commentary on Ps 28/29, *De bello Turcico* (LB V 358E); on lucky swords, see the *Moria* CWE 27 129 and *Adagia* I x 97; on the excessive veneration given to items of saints' clothing, cf Ep 396:71–9.

252 *sortilegos*; LB reads *sacrilegos* 'the sacrilegious,' which makes less sense.

253 Erasmus is less severe here on the superstitious cult of saints than, for example, in the colloquy *Naufragium*, where vows to St Christopher, the patron saint of travellers, are mocked (CWE 39 355–6); the other saints mentioned here were also among those whose protection was most frequently invoked.

saint is a provider of such favours, only he who stands alone; but the others, themselves saved by God's aid, rejoice that we too may be saved by his aid, and are only too willing to join us in singing this psalm, which Christ sang before us. They called to him and were given relief; they desire salvation for all, and take their rest in hope, as God's children, awaiting the promised reward of immortality at the resurrection.

We have learned that there is no strength in us, we have learned that we must seek it from elsewhere, and we have learned that it is ready and waiting for us, according to God's promise, since he made this covenant in another psalm: 'He shall cry to me and I shall hear him. In the time of trial I am with him, and I shall praise and honour him.'[254] However, the contract he made in the Gospel is more binding: 'Whatever you ask of the Father in my name,' he says, 'he shall grant you.'[255] Of course, what we ask must be righteous, so he adds, in the psalm: 'The God of my righteousness heard me.' As a pagan poet wrote, quite cleverly and with some justification: 'It is a mistake to expect injustice from the just; but it is mere foolishness to demand justice from the unjust.'[256] Moreover, since God is justice itself, we must be careful not only to ask nothing unjust of him, but also to ask nothing unjustly. People who ask for long and prosperous lives to enable them to enjoy their pleasures for longer are making unjust demands; the same is true of demands for riches and prosperity which will enable people to take revenge on those they hate. People[257] who ask for eternal life as if they had earned it for themselves are making demands unjustifiably; that is, they do not say: 'O God, have pity on me,' but cry out: 'Give me the reward for my fasting, for my psalm-chanting, for my fish-eating, for wearing a cowl all these years.' I am not saying that such practices are wrong, if properly carried out; but it is unjustifiable to ask for a reward on these grounds as though you expect God to grant it as a right. I would venture to add that the same applies to pleas made on the strength of almsgiving or suffering imprisonment for the love of God. Those who were renowned for such things in the Gospel were unaware of their renown. How then can we hope to obtain reward

*****

254 Ps 90/91:15
255 John 16:23; Erasmus uses the word *chirographum*, an autograph document, to emphasize that this is Christ's personal guarantee.
256 Plautus *Amphitryo* 35–6
257 The rest of this paragraph and most of the next (down to 'is in itself a gift from God') were recommended for deletion in the *Index expurgatorius* LB X 1820B; as Erasmus was obviously aware, to judge by his disclaimer here, his attack on ritual and external works is a strong one, although of course it reproduced many of the themes he worked out elsewhere, especially in the *Colloquia*.

from 'the God of our righteousness'? Our righteousness lies in confessing our sinfulness, and in acknowledging God's spontaneous kindness towards us; God's righteousness lies in his fulfilment of his promises. He made the same promise in many parts of Holy Writ, including Joel 2: 'I shall pour out my spirit upon all flesh. And it shall come to pass that all who call the name of the Lord shall be saved.'[258]

Someone may ask why he is called 'the God of righteousness' in the psalm. It is because no one is righteous unless God makes him righteous, or justified, by faith.[259] But why then does the psalm say 'of *my* righteousness'? Because nothing is more truly our own than God's gifts to us, since he puts no conditions on them, and never asks for them back, unless we are ungrateful; 'his gifts are irrevocable.'[260] As I have said, human righteousness consists in trusting in God's promises, while acknowledging that we ourselves have earned nothing but damnation. God's righteousness lies in fulfilling his promises, not because humanity deserves it, but because it was he who made them. Nevertheless, the ability to confess our wrongdoing and, distrusting ourselves, to trust in God's promises is in itself a gift from God. Therefore David refers to it as 'his own' righteousness, but points out that God is the source of this righteousness. Those who suffer persecution by the wicked for righteousness' sake are called 'blessed' by the Lord in the Gospel,[261] and the chief of the apostles repeats the lesson: 'Who can harm you, if you are followers of good? But if you do suffer for righteousness' sake, you are blessed. Do not be afraid of their fear and you shall not be troubled.'[262]

In the same letter, a little earlier, Peter advised his followers not to provoke anyone without cause, but rather to see it as their duty to encourage everyone, good or bad, to love one another; he then added: 'For it is a mark of grace to be able to endure the pain of undeserved suffering for God's sake.'[263] Therefore anyone suffering for the gospel has a just cause in God's eyes, though his cause may appear unjust to men. Though condemned by mankind, he will not plot his revenge, but call on God as his judge, who said:

* * * * *

258 Joel 2:28 and 32
259 Another reason for the censure of this passage is this deliberate movement from the language of the psalm, *Deus iusticiae*, to that of Reformation controversy, *iustificat per fidem*. Though clearly based on Paul's teaching (for example Gal 2:16), the doctrine of justification by faith was open to wide interpretation; cf CWE 42 xxxvi and Introduction lxi–lxv above.
260 Rom 11:29; Erasmus quotes the adjective in Greek.
261 Matt 5:10
262 1 Pet 3:13–4
263 1 Pet 2:19

'Vengeance is mine; I will repay!'[264] If we achieve anything worthwhile, we must not demand a reward from God as if the credit belonged to us. If we suffer hardship for God's righteous cause, we must imitate our head, the Lord Jesus, who, as Peter tells us, 'committed no sin, nor was guile found in his mouth; when cursed, he did not return the curses; while he suffered, he did not utter threats, but commended himself to the one who judges justly.'[265] God alone judges justly, since he alone sees into the secret places of the human heart. Finally, you call on the 'God of your righteousness' when, though innocent, you are punished for some crime by the unrighteous, as Peter again teaches: 'If you suffer, it must not be for murder, theft, slander, or covetousness; but if anyone suffers as a Christian, he need not be ashamed, but should give glory to God for that name.'[266] When an innocent person is punished, but would rather put up with injustice than fight against it, he is suffering for righteousness' sake. Paul expounded this idea in his first letter to the Corinthians: 'There is now a grave fault among you, in that you go to law with one another. Why not rather accept injustice? Why not rather allow yourselves to be robbed?'[267] I shall not discuss here the ticklish question raised by the schoolmen,[268] as to how far and from whom injustice is to be accepted, and as to when and by what means it may be legitimate to hurl evil men's incurable malice back in their teeth. I could wish that Paul's next words were not so relevant to our own times: 'But you do commit injustice, and you do perpetrate crimes, and all this you do to your brothers.'[269] What indeed would Paul say were he to see Christendom today, torn apart by trials, lawsuits, brawling, banditry, and war, and where the winner is often the greatest loser? But when those true disciples of Christ suffered appalling torment for the name of Jesus, did they plan to revenge themselves with armies, swords, treachery, or poison? Of course not. What did they do? They cried out to the Lord, maintaining their innocence, and set out their whole case before 'the God of their righteousness.'

Some commentators suggest that instead of 'God of my righteousness' the Hebrew text could mean 'God my righteousness.' If this is true, it does

* * * * *

264 Rom 12:19 and Heb 10:30, both quoting Deut 32:35
265 1 Pet 2:22–3
266 1 Pet 4:15–16
267 1 Cor 6:7
268 Erasmus frequently expressed his distaste for the subtleties of scholastic theology; cf *In psalmum 1* 26 and n109. The involved language here is a mild parody of their style.
269 1 Cor 6:8

not affect the meaning much, except perhaps that the nominative case carries greater emphasis. For example, to call Christ 'the truth'[270] is more striking than to call him 'the teacher of truth,' and so it is to call him 'our life' rather than 'the source of life,' 'the way' rather than 'our guide on the way,' 'the light' rather than 'the bringer of light' and 'our righteousness' rather than 'the restorer of righteousness.' This is a common enough rhetorical device in the Scriptures, for example in Psalm 26: 'The Lord is my light and my salvation,' and in Psalm 34: 'Say to my soul: "I am your salvation."' Again, Isaiah says: 'That you may be my salvation unto the ends of the earth,' and similarly Paul, writing to the Corinthians about Christ, says: 'For he is our peace, who has made the two things one.'[271] Thus anyone whose righteousness is God must be sure not to lose God, or he will lose his case; but as long as God is with him, he may be confident of victory.

In Holy Writ, some importance is given to merits, but only if God is not thereby robbed of his glory. Thus, the next line of the psalm reads: 'In tribulation, you relieved me.' Why did he say: 'You relieved me,' rather than: 'You rescued me'? It was because God does not always rescue us from the troubles that beset us, for the simple reason that it is not always the best solution; none the less, to ensure that we do not succumb, in our natural human weakness, to the ills which beset us, he makes provision for us to withstand the trial that he sends. Let us listen to Paul's description of the straits in which all who wish to live a life of holiness in Christ Jesus will find themselves:[272] 'In much suffering, in tribulation, hardship, distress, wounds, imprisonment, betrayal, toils, vigils, and fasting.' That was how anguish pressed in on him from every side, but now hear how he made his case righteous: 'In chastity, knowledge, patience, kindliness; in the Holy Spirit, in sincere love, in the word of truth, in the power of God.' And now hear how he was given relief in such dire straits: 'By the weapons of righteousness in the right hand and the left, by honour and dishonour, praise and blame, as an impostor who yet spoke the truth, as unknown yet well known; dying, we still live on, chastened yet not killed, sad yet always full of joy, poor men who make many rich, paupers who yet possess all things.' All this conveys the fullness of the Apostle's courage in the straits of woe and affliction. But why does this most modest of apostles speak so boastfully of the relief he found

* * * * *

270 In this development, Erasmus has in mind John 14:6: 'I am the way, and the truth, and the life'; it is also in John that Christ is most frequently described as 'the light'; see John 1:4–5, for example.

271 Ps 26/27:1, Ps 34/35:3, Isa 49:6, Eph 2:14 (not Corinthians)

272 2 Cor 6:4–5, 6–7, 7–10, and an adaptation of 11–13

in his heart? In order to encourage the Corinthians, still weak and beset also by troubles from outside, to find a comparable courage in themselves. 'My mouth is opened for you, Corinthians,' he says, 'and, though beset by many ills, I may speak proudly to you; do not be surprised by my tone, for my heart has been relieved by joy. The source of your anguish is not in me, but in your own innermost selves; since you receive the same reward, I say to you as a father, you too shall find relief.' Later, in the second letter to the Corinthians, having described again the throng of cares, dangers, and troubles which constantly surround him, he adds that in these too the Lord brought great relief to his heart: 'Thus shall I gladly boast of my infirmities, that the power of Christ may reside in me. Therefore I take pleasure in my infirmities, in contempt, in hardship, in persecution, in distress – all for Christ.'[273]

Here is Paul, once more in dire straits, writing in the first letter to the Corinthians: 'We are treated, one might say, as the scum of the earth; even today we are the offscouring' (the outcasts, that is) 'of society.'[274] What could sound more depressing than this? But at once his voice is uplifted: 'Which do you choose? Shall I come to you with a rod, or in love and a spirit of gentleness?'[275] These are the accents of a king, not a tanner! Again, elsewhere, he says: 'For I am the least of the apostles, and am not worthy to be called an apostle, because I persecuted God's church.'[276] Could anyone seem more despondent? Yet again his voice is uplifted, as he writes to the Philippians: 'I can do all things, with him who comforts me.'[277] Could anything be more noble, more princely, than to be able to say: 'I can do all things'? However, he modifies this boast, in writing to the Corinthians: 'By the grace of God I am what I am.'[278] He also writes to them: 'We want you to know, brothers, of the harm which befell us in Asia, where we were injured beyond all reason, beyond bearing; we even became weary of life. Indeed, we felt in our hearts that we had received a death sentence.' That was the measure of his distress, but now hear how he found relief, and note that the distress comes from within us, the relief from God: 'This taught us that we must not rely on ourselves, but on God who raises the dead, who has rescued us from such dangers, and who continues to preserve us; our hope is in him, that he may

* * * * *

273 2 Cor 12:9–10
274 1 Cor 4:13
275 1 Cor 4:21
276 1 Cor 15:9
277 Phil 4:13
278 1 Cor 15:10

rescue us once more.'[279] Paul was once in chains, racked by anguish, when his heart found relief as he said: 'The word of the Lord is not bound.'[280] Peter was kept in a dungeon; he knew anguish there. But, having cried out to the Lord, he was set free by the angel. The apostles were beaten with rods, causing them much anguish, but they went rejoicing from the sight of the council. Stephen was battered by a hail of stones, but he saw the heavens open.[281] The greater the anguish, the greater the relief.

If we now seek examples in the Old Testament, we shall find that the pious were all afflicted by a multitude of troubles, but that none went without comfort, since they sought aid from no one but God. Joseph was attacked and thrown down into a pit, but God raised him to the pinnacle of glory. Jonah knew the depths of distress when swallowed by the whale, but from the belly of the beast he cried out to the Lord, and the Lord relieved his distress. What a predicament faced the three young men thrown into the fiery furnace! But from the midst of the furnace they cried out to the Lord, and the flames abated, allowing the innocents to walk through. When Daniel was thrown into the lion's den, he knew that his life was in great jeopardy, but even from there he cried out to the Lord and his distress was changed into courage.[282]

I am sure that I should not weary you if I were to go on to cite further examples of God-fearing men who had good grounds for singing this psalm: 'You heard me when I called, O God of my righteousness, and in tribulation you relieved me.' However, I imagine that we need not spend time recalling them all, since either you know about them already, or else you can easily find out about them by reading the holy books. I shall therefore presume on your good will only to remind you of one thing, which is that such people do not always obtain relief from their distress by the standards of this world. Peter was freed from prison, but John the Baptist was beheaded in prison.[283] At Philippi, Paul was beaten with rods, thrown into a tiny cell, and the officious jailer even came and put his feet in the stocks. Could distress be more distressing? But God was at hand to hear their cries and relieve their distress. This is the text in Acts 16: 'But around midnight Paul and Silas were singing praises to God; suddenly all the doors burst open and all the

* * * * *

279 2 Cor 1:8–10
280 2 Tim 2:9
281 These three incidents are related in Acts 12:1–11, 5:40–1, and 7:54–60.
282 The four examples are taken respectively from Genesis 37–41, Jonah 2, and Daniel 3 and 6.
283 See Acts 12 and Matt 14:10.

prisoners' chains were broken.'[284] How many kings have less freedom in their whole kingdom than those apostles had in prison? Now in this case the chains were broken, but not so the chains with which the tribune shackled Paul at Jerusalem;[285] the sword which struck off Paul's head was not blunted, and the cross on which Peter hung did not break.[286] This kind of physical comfort is not provided constantly, but only for a time, whenever it may contribute to humanity's salvation. But it is certain that spiritual relief is always at hand, if a man will cry out to the God of his righteousness with trust in his heart. That is why we often see the rich of this world, amid all their wealth and pleasure, worried and fearful, whereas those who have truly placed their hopes in God blithely endure both torture and death itself. In fact, the Spirit's consolation is never more plentiful than when someone who is bereft of all human resources delivers himself totally into God's hands.

I will not tax your patience by discussing all the difficulties which plague anyone who tries to elucidate every last detail[287] of the Hebrew text. No language is more confusing or more open to misinterpretation and disagreement among its translators. I shall simply mention the fact that Jerome translates the original Hebrew text here as *dilatasti mihi*, and that this is the version always cited by the Latin commentators and sung in church, whereas in the Greek text we find $\epsilon\pi\lambda\acute{\alpha}\tau\nu\nu\acute{\alpha}\varsigma$ $\mu\epsilon$.[288] This difference in the reading arises no doubt from the negligence of the copyists, who did not recognize the Hebrew metaphor, which should be rendered *dilatavit mihi*, meaning 'he made room for me' or 'enlarged me.'[289] However, it makes little difference to the meaning whether we read 'you relieved me' or 'you enlarged me.' God 'relieves' us when, being rescued from our distress, our minds are restored by the comfort he gives; he 'enlarges' us when, with misfortunes pressing in upon us, he bestows upon us the fullness of the Spirit, so that we welcome all our afflictions, knowing that true and everlasting joy is being made ready for us at the end of these unimportant and transient afflictions. When you

* * * * *

284 Acts 16:25–6
285 Acts 21:33
286 Both Paul and Peter were martyred in Rome c 67 AD; tradition has it that Peter was hung on an inverted cross.
287 *apices sectari: apex* can mean, appropriately, a Hebrew accent, but is used figuratively for 'the least particle, a jot' (Matt 5:18); *sectari* means 'to pursue (eagerly).'
288 The point at issue is the case of the pronoun 'me'; the Septuagint version uses the accusative $\mu\epsilon$ 'me,' Jerome's Vulgate and Hebrew versions the dative *mihi* 'to me, for me.' Revised Greek versions now also use the dative here.
289 On the various meanings of *dilatare* see introductory note 171–2 above.

force even fairly small objects into a narrow jar, it gets broken, but a wide jar will hold a great many objects, even quite large ones. In the same way, a narrow mind, which God's grace has not enlarged, will be shattered by the slightest misfortune, whereas, were it to be enlarged by faith, hope, and charity, it would be able to cry out, as Paul did in the midst of his afflictions: 'What can cut us off from Christ's love? Tribulation, or anguish, or hunger, or nakedness, or danger, or persecution, or the sword?'[290]

Now it is clear that the word 'enlarged' here means 'warmed' or 'gladdened' a heart that was sad; it may be of interest to inquire – with all due reverence – why the Holy Spirit preferred to use this metaphor rather than some more common form of words such as 'you gladdened my heart' or 'you warmed my heart.' The answer may be that very often an unexpected turn of phrase will rouse us from our lethargy, or make us more attentive when we are in danger of nodding off. Sometimes the apparent incongruity of an expression will have the same effect. If the psalm had said: 'In tribulation you made me joyful,' no one would have given the phrase a second thought, but as it is we have to seek out the hidden meaning of a pair of metaphors, since $\theta\lambda\hat{\iota}\psi\iota s$, which is translated sometimes as 'tribulation,' sometimes as 'pressure,' can equally well be rendered 'affliction'[291] or 'anxiety'; it normally relates to the body, but it is quite common practice to apply it to the mind. More importantly, hardly anyone would describe a mind that has been restored to health as 'enlarged,' although in common parlance the human body is often said to be enlarged. So in this text an unusual expression is employed to convey to us, by means of a familiar idea, how dejection can be turned into cheerfulness. Cold and grief shrink our bodies; heat and good cheer enlarge them. For instance, when people scowl they crease their foreheads and knit their brows, and when they are racked by grief they grow thin and waste away; on the other hand, when they are joyful they are said to uncrease their foreheads,[292] and their bodies grow stronger and fitter. For the same reason the inborn heat in young people causes them to grow and fill out, whereas in old age the heat begins to fail, and all the limbs begin to shrink; even the voice becomes thinner. Similarly, winter's cold makes

* * * * *

290 Rom 8:35
291 'Affliction' is indeed Erasmus' translation when the word appears in 2 Cor 1:4: see LB VI 752A; the Vulgate there renders it *pressura*. All the versions suggested by Erasmus are possible, though the literal meaning of the word is 'pressure' or 'squeezing.'
292 *exporrigere frontem*, literally 'to expand the forehead'; cf *Adagia* I viii 48, where the expression is discussed together with its opposite, *contrahere frontem*.

everything shrink, but the gentle warmth of spring brings universal joy and growth. For this very reason youth is usually cheerful, and old age is gloomy. The mind is bound by nature to the body, and is thus affected, willingly or not, by the condition of the body, just as the condition of the mind in turn permeates the body. Solomon also remarked on this: 'A joyful mind makes for a healthy life, but a gloomy spirit dries up the bones.'[293]

What is more, if we believe the doctors, the spirits are of great importance in the health or decay of the body; if they are constricted and confined, they weaken the body; if they are sufficiently lively and well dispersed they keep it healthy, but if they boil up too quickly they bring sudden death. There are a number of historical examples of people expiring as a result of sudden and unexpected joy,[294] while it is not unusual for people to fade away gradually as the result of grief. The doctors explain that joy opens up the channels through which the spirits pass, and grief shuts them down. Thus it happens that when excessive joy expands the channels more than usual, the spirits fly out all at once and bring sudden death; on the other hand, when the spirits are constricted they slowly squeeze out life from the body. The conditions which cause lethargy in the human body are like those which cause greed in the human heart, when love has grown cold.[295] On the other hand, it is excessive heat which brings on raving madness,[296] for example in a mind which, burning with the fire of hell, plans the death of a brother, or in a tongue which, as James said, is inflamed by the same fire to speak evil of a fellow man without cause.[297] But we burn with the fire of love which, as Paul says, is without sin.[298] Its warmth enlarges hearts which have been narrowed and shrunk by envy, hatred, or fear of poverty, persecution, and death; as Paul writes to the Romans: 'Let us take pride in our sufferings, knowing that suffering breeds endurance, that endurance gives proof of our qualities, and that such proof breeds hope; nor are our hopes deceived, since the love of God has flooded our hearts through the Holy Spirit which has been given to

* * * * *

293 Prov 17:22
294 Erasmus gives some examples in *Adagia* III v 1: *Risus Sardonius* LB II 826c, in particular those of the painter Zeuxis and the philosopher Chrysippus. On the theory of the spirits, see *In psalmum* 2 102 and n152; the subject here appears to be the vital spirits which, according to Galenic medicine, run through the arteries.
295 Cf Matt 24:12.
296 *phrenesis*, frequently regarded as the opposite of lethargy in ancient medicine; see Celsus *De medicina* 3.20.1.
297 James 3:6
298 Cf 1 Cor 13:4.

us.'[299] Whenever we suffer, we are diminished by our anguish; but the word 'flooded' here implies expansion and growth.

The earthly and the corporeal are indeed confined and limited, but the spiritual and the heavenly extend far and wide. Among the elements of the cosmos, earth occupies the smallest space; water, which surrounds it, extends more widely, and air more widely still, but even this is surpassed by the volume of fire; as for the heavenly bodies, the further each one is removed from the earth, the greater the space it occupies. Similarly, if we compare the confines of the body and of the mind, how much wider are the latter! How immense the space that our mind's eye can perceive compared with our body's eyes! How narrow the compass of this life when set beside the soul's immortality! Again, how limited are mankind's mightiest physical attributes when contrasted with the fullness of the Holy Spirit, by which it relieves our anguish. Thus anyone who desires its fullness must distance himself as much as possible from earthly concerns, release himself from his body, and ascend the lofty cross, thereby bringing himself closer to heaven.

In fact, there is a torment worse than the physical distress which this world can inflict upon good men – a guilty conscience. This text not only offers consolation to those who suffer physically for righteousness' sake; it also lifts up with hope hearts which are burdened with guilt and constrained by fear of God's vengeance; if they have no righteousness of their own, at least they have 'the God of their righteousness.' We are constrained by fear of punishment, but this is the beginning of wisdom,[300] and we are given release through love. It can thus be useful to be constrained by guilt, so that later, when love has driven out fear,[301] we may be happy to be released by the freedom of the Spirit. The world's manner of regret brings only death, but regret according to God's law brings certain salvation. Paul caused the Corinthians great sorrow when he told them to consign the incestuous man to Satan. But Paul was not sorry that he had inflicted this anguish, since love was soon to bring relief. 'On the contrary,' he says, 'because of this you must now give him more, and console him, lest perhaps a man of his sort be overwhelmed by excessive sorrow.' Where can relief be found, if not in love? 'Let your love for him be reaffirmed,' says Paul.[302] In sinfulness are found suffering and anguish, as Paul confirms in his letter to the Romans: 'But for those who are quarrelsome and will not accept the truth, believing rather in iniquity, there will be wrath and retribution;

* * * * *

299 Rom 5:3–5
300 Cf Ps 110/111:10 and Prov 1:7.
301 Cf 1 John 4:18.
302 See 1 Cor 5:1–5 and 2 Corinthians 2; the quotations are 2 Cor 2:7 and 8.

tribulation and anguish for every human mind following the paths of evil.'
But if anyone breaks the bonds of sin and turns to works of love, this is the relief he will receive: 'Glory, honour, and peace to all who do good.'[303] Similarly
in Psalm 118 the guilty sinner says: 'Tribulation and anguish have descended
on me!' But relief quickly follows: 'Your commandments are my continual
delight.'[304] No one can keep God's commandments unless he loves God.

Perhaps you would like to know just how far the mind can be relieved
when it is filled with love. Listen to our Lord Jesus' words in John: 'Anyone
who loves me will heed what I say; my Father will love him and we shall
come to him and make our dwelling with him.'[305] Paul states several times,
not least in Romans 8, that the spirit of God dwells in the minds of the
pious.[306] Imagine how spacious a dwelling that breast must be which can
accommodate the Father and the Son and the Holy Spirit. Again, John points
out in another passage the narrow-mindedness of the Jews: 'My message
has no effect on you.'[307] The pursuit of wealth, the love of pleasure, the
desire for office, hatred and envy of one's neighbour, all these so narrow
the mind that there is no room for the seed of the gospel message. Any
creature of the flesh is confined and constrained by anguish, but when the
Spirit is present, freedom is unconfined. A body empty of spirit shrinks and
withers with the cold, and similarly a mind from which God's Spirit is absent
becomes constrained and narrow. The alternatives are these: when the flesh
is mortified, the spirit lives; when the flesh lives, the spirit dies. As Paul says:
'For if you have lived according to the flesh, you shall die; but if by the spirit
you have killed the deeds of the flesh, you shall live.'[308] A branch which is
not nourished by the sap of the vine is cut off and dries up, but one which
remains on the vine grows ever broader and bears abundant fruit. Anyone
who will not offer a helping hand to a friend fainting from hunger is a dry
and withered branch; but those who have been nourished by the sap of divine
grace and broadened by brotherly love 'will do good to all, but especially to
the household of faith.'[309]

None the less, it is worth noting that, as I mentioned earlier, expansion
and contraction are both praised and condemned, by turns, in Holy Writ.

* * * * *

303 Rom 2:8–10
304 Ps 118/119:143
305 John 14:23
306 Rom 8:11
307 John 8:37
308 Rom 8:13
309 Gal 6:10

Many bodies are swollen with harmful humours, but on the other hand some grow strong and muscular on the richness of their sap. Here in Moses' song is a description of a kind of corpulence which is harmful: 'My beloved grew fat, he grew fat, bloated and sleek.'[310] Anyone swollen with pride in his worldly success has 'expanded' in a bad sense. On the other hand, anyone who has repented of his sins and dried up through fear of the Lord has 'shrunk' in a good sense, like the poor sufferer who speaks in Psalm 101: 'My bones have been burned like dry twigs; I have been cut down like the hay, and my heart has grown dry because I have forgotten to eat my bread.'[311] In Ezekiel too, the bones of the melancholy dried up, but to good effect, for they were later revived by the Spirit of God.[312] Similarly, a good doctor will drain and empty a body, almost to the point of death, to draw off the harmful humours, and will ensure that afterwards it is refilled with more healthy fluids. Some giants are hateful to the Lord, as Psalm 32 testifies: 'The giant shall not be saved by his mighty strength.'[313] The enormous Goliath, revelling in his powers, was struck down by David.[314] On the other hand, in Psalm 18 praise is bestowed on that wondrous giant, in his mildness the least of the kingdom of heaven, but in his divine strength the greatest, who rejoiced to run his race after descending from the heights of heaven.[315] The Lord loves these giants whose feet touch the ground, though their eyes and hearts are in heaven, as in the Gospel's words: 'Where your treasure is, there is your heart also.'[316] Such giants are immensely tall, but at the same time supremely humble. A proud heart is accursed before God, as the psalm says: 'O Lord, my heart is not proud, nor are my eyes haughty.'[317] On the other hand, a heart may be proud when God permits it to be exalted. The psalmist's heart swelled up, in a good sense, when he said, in Psalm 118: 'I have run in the paths of your commandments, since you have enlarged my heart.'[318]

Jesus loved and embraced the little children,[319] and warned that the giants of this world must be cut down to their size if they wished to enter the kingdom of heaven and be born a second time. The gate to the kingdom is

* * * * *

310 Deut 32:15
311 Ps 101/102:3–4
312 Ezek 37:1–14
313 Ps 32/33:16
314 1 Samuel 17
315 Ps 18/19:5–6
316 Matt 6:21
317 Ps 130/131:1
318 Ps 118/119:32
319 Cf Matt 19:14.

narrow; camels laden with wealth and honours cannot get through. The path which leads to life is narrow;[320] it requires great restraint to proceed along it. On the other hand, there are those little children whom Peter wishes to grow up in Christ: 'As newborn babes, reasonable and without guile, desire new milk, that you may grow into salvation.'[321] Similarly, Paul will not allow us to remain children for ever, as he writes to the Ephesians: 'Until we all join together in the unity of faith and the knowledge of the Son of God, reaching full manhood, measured by nothing less than the full stature of Christ; thus we shall no longer be little children, tossed and turned by every wind of doctrine.'[322] The Corinthians were such children, and so he wrote to them: 'As children in Christ, I gave you milk to drink, not solid food, because you were not ready for it, and indeed you are still not ready.'[323] The Galatians were such children, to whom he says gently: 'My sons, I must give you birth again and again, until Christ is fully formed in you.'[324] The letter to the Hebrews rebukes such children, who never move on from the very first lessons of God's word, and never progress to the solid food of more complete righteousness.[325] None the less, the same apostle tells those who wish to be strong and mature in mind to be children in malice; he made himself a little child, reducing himself to a child's weakness in his moderation and brotherly love, as he wrote to the Thessalonians: 'We have become a child in your midst, like a woman cherishing her children.'[326]

But let us return to the origins of the anguish and constraint experienced by so many of these 'little children,' of whom, I fear, there is a large number among you, my dear friends. The Apostle explained this when he expressed his regret that the Corinthians should remain like infants so long: 'For you are still bound to the flesh.'[327] It is the flesh, then, that constrains us, and the spirit that sets us free. Where the spirit is, there is love; where there is love, fear is driven out;[328] where there is no fear, there is liberty; where there is liberty, there is no constraint. People who are unimpressed by anything they cannot see in this world remain bound to the flesh and suffer great mental constraint; people whose religion depends on physical observances remain bound to the

* * * * *

320 Cf Matt 7:13–14, but with a possible allusion also to Matt 19:24.
321 1 Pet 2:2
322 Eph 4:13–14
323 1 Cor 3:1–2
324 Gal 4:19
325 Heb 5:12–14
326 1 Thess 2:7
327 1 Cor 3:2
328 1 John 4:18

flesh and will be driven to distraction by a joyless fastidiousness: do not taste this, do not touch that, do not handle the other. Any of you who used to be like wretched schoolboys, terrified by the imaginary dangers associated with these restrictions, but who have since progressed into the freedom of the Spirit, will understand what I am saying. Those who enjoy the fruits of the Spirit's bounty should meanwhile tolerate the weakness of the little children, until they too progress to liberty, to the measure of Christ, and we should pray for them, as Paul prayed for the Ephesians, that the heavenly Father may give them strength from the treasure-house of his glory, that the inner man may be strengthened through the Holy Spirit, that through faith Christ may dwell in them, that they may be rooted and made firm in love, that with all the saints they may learn the length and breadth, the height and depth of his love, and know the love of Christ, surpassing all knowledge, that they may be filled with the fullness of God.[329]

Human regulations are necessary, but only for the weak; ceremonies are useful, but only to the 'little children.' We must all grow to maturity in Christ; there is a curse on the child of a hundred summers who asks for nothing but milk and pap, who must always be wrapped in cotton wool and carried like a babe in arms, and who is constantly paralysed by his fear of imaginary bogeymen. On the other hand, 'there is a blessing on Gad in his wide domain,' as Moses' prophecy says; 'Abraham held a splendid feast on the day that Isaac was weaned.'[330] But the unhappy Jews, who to this day still suck the milk of the letter, have never put aside their childishness. However we, who are the descendants of Isaac, father of the spiritual family, never stop digging wells until, having spurned and dismissed the Philistines, we uncover the source of the spirit which springs up to eternal life.[331] When Isaac found it he gave the place a name meaning 'plenty of room,' saying: 'For now the Lord has made room for us, and has made us multiply upon the earth.'[332]

Divine wisdom, which is not natural but spiritual, is limitless, and thus requires a spacious and ample heart to dwell in. It cannot enter a spiteful

* * * * *

329 Eph 3:16–19
330 Quotations from Deut 33:20 and Gen 21:8; Gad was the grandson of Isaac. Erasmus uses this typology to reinforce his contrast with traditional Judaism; Gad's '*wide* domain' and Isaac's name for the well (*latitudo*, a few lines later) echo verbally the antithesis (derived from verse 1 of the psalm) which Erasmus is exploiting here.
331 Cf John 4:14 and Gen 26:18.
332 Gen 26:22

soul or dwell in a body sunk in sin. Where ill will exists, there can be no love, and the absence of love brings anguish and constraint. Therefore when God gave Solomon his wisdom, he also gave him ample room in his heart for it. As we read in 1 Kings 4: 'And God gave Solomon wisdom, and great understanding, and ample room in his heart.'[333] We all know what dreadful strife can arise from quite trivial causes among those who are puffed up with the world's wisdom, which James calls 'devilish.'[334] Why? Because of the narrowness of their minds, which God's Spirit has not broadened. Human wisdom is so narrow that it can allow a man to hate even his friends, whereas the wisdom which descends from on high so broadens the understanding that a man will love his enemies, bless those who curse him and return good for evil,[335] and of course, as James says, it is 'full of mercy and good fruits,'[336] for these are the things by which Christian love extends itself to all. Love is a fire, wisdom a light. Nothing spreads more rapidly or more widely than fire; nothing is more gently diffused to everyone than light. 'God is love' and 'the father of light.'[337] Moreover, 'the spirit of the Lord has filled the world.'[338] This elemental spirit which surrounds the earth is also infused into the very waters and into all the veins of the earth. I mention this in passing, to show that this scriptural imagery eulogizes spiritual breadth and condemns spiritual narrowness.

A particular feature of the spiritual world is that opposites are produced by their opposites and that one and the same thing produces opposites, although some examples of this can also be found in the material world: foul-tasting medicine can lead to good health, the sun can both melt wax and harden mud, fire can both melt lead and harden a pot, a bolt of lightning can melt copper but leave wax untouched,[339] water poured onto most things will put out a fire, but when poured onto quicklime will start one, and one end of a magnet attracts metal, while the other repels it. Similarly, Christ's Spirit and divine love can affect the same man in different ways, freeing and constraining, softening and hardening, raising and lowering. It sets him

* * * * *

333 1 Kings 4:29
334 James 3:15
335 Echoes of the Sermon on the Mount; Matt 5:44 and Luke 6:27–8
336 James 3:17
337 1 John 4:8 and James 1:17
338 Wisd 1:7
339 Reading *cera* 'wax' rather than *sera* 'bolt' as in the early editions or *fera* 'wild animal' as in ASD. The allusion, repeated in the *Parabolae* CWE 23 243, is to Pliny's claim (*Naturalis historia* 2.137) that lightning will melt gold, silver, or copper in bags while leaving untouched the bags themselves and their wax seals.

free to do good to all, but constrains him to be wary of injuring anyone; it softens his desire for vengeance, but hardens his endurance; it elevates him so that he may look down on opponents of the gospel, but humbles him so that he may serve everyone for the love of Christ. Listen to Paul, a man both freed and constrained by this love: 'And to the Jews I became like a Jew, in order to win the Jews; to those subject to Moses' law, I became like a subject to the Law; to those outside the Law, I became like an outlaw (although I was not outside God's law, being subject to Christ's law), in order to win those outside the Law. To the weak, I became weak, in order to win the weak; I became all things to all men, in order to save all men; but all this I have done for the gospel's sake, to play my part in proclaiming it.'[340] What freedom, to be able to say: 'I became all things to all men'! But what constraint in 'I made myself a servant to all.'[341] Again, could anything be more generous than this declaration: 'Everything belongs to you, but you belong to Christ, and Christ to God,' or this: 'The kingdom of God is not food and drink'?[342] On the other hand, could anything be more restrictive than this: 'It is a good thing not to eat meat or drink wine or do anything to make your brother stumble, or be weakened or upset'?[343] Paul could be uncompromising, as here: 'For I am sure that nothing, neither death, nor life, nor angels, nor principalities, nor powers, nor the present, nor the future, nor strength, nor height, nor depth, nor any creature, can separate us from the love of God, which is in Christ Jesus our Lord.'[344] But he could also be flexible, as his words to the rebellious Galatians show: 'My brothers, I beg it of you; you have not offended me at all.'[345] Similarly, he wrote to the Romans concerning the Jews, whom they considered their worst enemies: 'I could wish to be cast out myself by Christ for the sake of my brothers, who are my kinsmen according to the flesh, and are Israelites.'[346] But he could also be ruthless, as he was for example in the Acts, when he spoke to Elymas the sorcerer, fixing his eyes on him, and full of the Holy Spirit: 'You are full of all guile and all deceit, a child of the devil, enemy of all righteousness; you constantly pervert the straight ways of the Lord. Now the hand of the Lord is upon you, and you shall be blind, and shall not see the sunlight

* * * * *

340 1 Cor 9:20–3
341 1 Cor 9:19
342 1 Cor 3:23 and Rom 14:17
343 Rom 14:21
344 Rom 8:38–9
345 Gal 4:12
346 Rom 9:3–4

for a time.'[347] Similarly, he wrote to the Corinthians: 'Do you dare to ask for proof that Christ dwells in me?'[348] On another occasion, he admitted humbly to Timothy that he was the first among sinners, but a few lines later he steeled himself to add, concerning Alexander and Hymenaeus: 'I have consigned them to Satan, that they may learn not to blaspheme.'[349] Yet again, he wrote to the Romans in all humility: 'I beg you, brothers, by the mercy of God, that you should make your bodies a living sacrifice' etc,[350] and in a similar tone to the Corinthians: 'We beseech you, through Christ, be reconciled with God.'[351]

Do I seem, dear readers, to have strayed too far in my discussion of these wide open spaces? I might fear so, were I not confident that your minds are so broadened by the love of God that you will take this digression in good part. To return to the rest of the psalm: we have learned that sure and swift assistance from God is available to all who call on him; if any of us feels himself caught up in the toils of sinners, if he is beset by misfortunes, such as poverty, illness, or persecution by the wicked, or if he is still bound to the flesh and shackled by the cares of the visible world, let him call on the Lord with confidence, so that, set free by the spirit of love, he may give thanks for God's goodness, singing the words of Psalm 17: 'He brought me into a spacious place; he rescued me because he delighted in me.'[352]

The next words are: 'Have pity on me, and hear my prayer.' St Augustine wants to know how these words, and the preceding ones, 'you relieved me,' can apply to Jesus Christ, since they suggest that he had at some time been abandoned by God, and could thus only have been raised up, in the nick of time, by God's aid, and also that there was something piteous about him, which compelled him to cry out: 'Have pity on me.'[353] I am not unsympathetic to Augustine's solution, which is to attribute these words to the members of Christ, through whom he is hungry and is filled, is struck down and raised up.[354] But it is not far-fetched to suggest that Christ, racked by physical pain, prayed for deliverance from death and for the joy of resurrection, not

* * * * *

347 Acts 13:9–11
348 2 Cor 13:3
349 1 Tim 1:20; the preceding allusion is to 1 Tim 1:15.
350 Rom 12:1
351 2 Cor 5:20
352 Ps 17/18:19
353 *Enarratio in psalmum* 4 PL 36 79
354 Augustine quotes Matt 25:35, paraphrased here, in support of his interpretation. Erasmus' reading recalls the subject of his treatise *De taedio Iesu*, published in 1503; see Ep 108.

because he despaired of it unless he prayed, but to teach us that in time of trouble we must cry to God for mercy. I certainly do not think it impious to suggest that, for a time, Christ experienced an anguish of the spirit from which he was later freed, just as he experienced weariness and grief, such as he had not known before, as the moment of death drew near; he was soon relieved from them, too, for in Luke we read that the angel of the Lord came to comfort him.[355] There can be no objection to describing as piteous someone who is suffering cruel treatment, though undeserving of it; indeed, every affliction is called piteous, whatever the deserts of the person it strikes.

Our lives are subject to constant alternation between joy and sorrow; they are never free from dangers and cannot be lived entirely without sin; therefore, just as we must always give thanks to God for whatever he may send us, so we must constantly cry out: 'Have pity on me.' All God's gifts to us may be called God's pity or mercy,[356] since he freely bestows them on us when we need his aid. Sometimes he shows his mercy in greatest measure when he sends us troubles; in that case, we must beg him, in his mercy, to grant us patience. In times of prosperity we must again beg him, in his mercy, to save us from corruption. Without God's mercy, adversity and prosperity are equally dangerous to us. But ordinary people only cry: 'Have mercy on me!' when they are beset by troubles; the Pharisee, who thinks himself righteous, never cries: 'Have mercy on me!' but merely gives thanks.[357] But just as the true Christian always gives thanks for everything, so he always adds a fresh plea for mercy, since we know, first, that God's gifts need protection against theft by the unworthy, and, second, that we must prepare to receive still greater gifts; neither can be achieved without God's mercy to help us. There are other psalms in which we can find the same thing that we see here, that is, thanksgiving followed closely by a cry for help; for example, in the song of degrees: 'I cried to the Lord in my distress, and he answered me.' Set free, his prayers answered, he none the less cries out again: 'Lord, deliver my soul from lying lips and hurtful tongues.'[358]

By far the most pitiful of all is the person who believes he has no need of God's pity. Since we have constant need of it, our plea must be constantly

* * * * *

355 Luke 22:43
356 It is difficult in English to convey the play here between *miser* 'pitiable' or 'piteous,' and *misericordia*, which can mean 'pity,' but is more often rendered in this context as 'mercy' or 'compassion.' The subject here recalls Erasmus' 1524 treatise *De immensa Dei misericordia*.
357 Cf Luke 18:11.
358 Ps 119/120:1–2

reaching God's ears: 'Have pity on me, hear my prayer'; we are like a man afflicted by many ills at once, old age, disease, infection, poverty; his life is full of sighing, for if one of his woes is alleviated, another at once takes its place. Mere mortals are often wearied by the importunate pleas of such people, but God rejoices to hear his people sing the sad refrain 'Have pity on me!' as they await the great day foretold by John in the Apocalypse: 'And God shall wipe all tears from their eyes, and there shall be no more death, or weeping, or crying; there shall be no more pain, because the old order will pass away.'[359]

It is also worth stressing, I think, that when the psalmist cries out: 'Have pity on me!' he does not explain exactly what he wants. It is a mark of the most perfect confidence in God's mercy to ask nothing in detail but to entrust ourselves completely to his will, since he knows better than we what is necessary for salvation. But it is the duty of a pious Christian, who has been granted a measure of bliss by God in his mercy, not to turn on his heel and spurn the pitiful creatures who, wallowing in fleshly desires, do not know enough to want heavenly riches; rather, with brotherly affection, you must urge them on to better things. It is only right that someone who has experienced God's mercy at first hand should also show mercy towards his fellow slaves. Beg them, warn them, teach them, exhort them, argue with them, rebuke them, in season and out of season.[360] If one of them changes his ways, you have won your brother for Christ; if not, you have salved your conscience, you have done your best.

The next verse reads: 'Children of mankind, how long will your hearts be burdened with pride? Why do you love vanity and seek out falsehood?' Where the Septuagint translates 'children of mankind,' Jerome translates, from the original Hebrew, 'children of the man'; where it has: 'How long will your hearts be burdened with pride?' he translates: 'How long, my illustrious friends, will you shamefully love vanity?' Others translate this: 'How long will you turn my glory (or honour) into shame, and love vanity and seek out falsehood?' There are other disagreements on this verse, too. Some take 'the man' to mean Abraham, that outstanding hero in whose name the Israelites glory: 'We are the seed of Abraham, we have never been any man's slaves.'[361] Others take 'the man' to mean Adam; but in the sense in which the Hebrews use it, it is more likely that this word should be understood to refer to Abraham, whose name was the most renowned of

* * * * *

359 Rev 21:4
360 Cf 2 Tim 4:2.
361 John 8:33

all among the Hebrews, like Cecrops among the Greeks and Scipio among the Romans;[362] anyone descended from them was considered a hero. Thus those who swelled with pride because they were descended from Abraham are called by the translators of the Septuagint βαρυκαρδίους, that is, 'proud-hearted,' in the same way that we say 'tenderhearted'; in Greek βάρος often indicates pride,[363] and in Latin we call men of distinction and authority 'men of weight.' I suppose that this also accounts for the vernacular word 'barons,' men outstanding by virtue of both their parentage and their character.[364] In the Gospels the Lord thus upbraids the Jews because, although they took pride in the name of their father Abraham, they fell far short of his achievements; they behaved rather as if their father were the devil, and a liar, and a murderer, since they opposed the truth and plotted the death of an innocent.[365] Such a reading thus produces the following: 'How long will you Israelites persist in your unbelief? How long will you take pride in the names of your patriarchs, yet fall short of their faith and piety, tarnishing your ancestor's glory, loving vanity instead of the things necessary for salvation, and seeking out falsehood instead of truth?' The alternative reading ('Children of the man, how long will you turn my glory into shame?' etc) produces: 'Children of Abraham, how long will you dishonour my name among the gentiles, turning my glory into shame? You are called the chosen people, you are called the children of God, but because of your unholy way of life I am reviled among the gentiles, who think that the deity must resemble his people. Your showy titles are vain unless accompanied by piety in your lives; to call yourselves the children of God is to lie, since by your deeds you proclaim yourselves the children of the devil.'

However, the charges which our Lord once made against the unbelieving Jews can now quite justifiably be made against Christians, who proudly invoke the gospel, the apostles, and Christ, but whose entire lives belie their pretensions. It is a splendid thing to be called 'the children of God, brothers

* * * * *

362 Cecrops was a legendary early king of Athens, whose descendants formed an aristocracy; according to Juvenal 8.46 the name became synonymous with boasting about one's ancestry, and Erasmus demonstrates this in the *Panegyricus* CWE 27 19. The Scipios were perhaps the most distinguished Republican Roman family.

363 The Greek word literally means 'weight,' but its associated adjective, in particular, had many metaphorical uses.

364 In fact the word is of Frankish origin, though there may be a very indirect connection with the Greek.

365 Matt 3:9 and especially John 8:39–44

and heirs to Jesus Christ,'[366] but we bring these glorious titles into disrepute
if our entire lives conflict with the claims we make. What is more, to some
extent we also bring into disrepute the glorious names of God the Father and
the Son; what will unbelievers say when they observe that the most eminent
bearers of our name are more wicked, almost, than worshippers of pagan
idols? 'Does God have children like this? Is this what Jesus Christ's disciples
and brothers are like?' The gospel, too, is exposed to hatred and contempt by
the vicious lives of those who glory in its name. Today, all sorts of people can
be heard holding forth about Christ, the Spirit, the gospel, faith, the word of
the Lord; but if you look at the lives and morals of most of them, alas! everything they do conflicts with these splendid ideals. Among those who most
loudly proclaim their allegiance to them we will find misers,[367] swindlers,
debauchees, perjurers, slanderers, liars, self-lovers, people full of poison and
empty of any good instinct, intolerant of any slight, vengeful, haughty; will
we not then hear many unbelievers say: 'Goodbye to this gospel of theirs,
which has brought such people into the world to plague us!'? If the gospel
is on our lips, should we not try instead to enhance its reputation by our
lives and deeds, just as Paul won honour for his gospel? Of course, it is blasphemy to judge the gospel by observing the behaviour of mere mortals, but
such blasphemy is encouraged by those whose words proclaim the gospel but
whose deeds proclaim the opposite. The holy man, the true follower of the
gospel, will justifiably rebuke them: 'You haughty children, how long will
you dishonour your principles by your evil way of life? It is vanity to be
called what you are not; it is falsehood to seek glory in a name with which
your entire lives conflict; it is hypocrisy to solicit praise for bearing a name
which your deeds belie, and to have constantly on your lips what is not in
your hearts.'

The large number of different readings here should surprise no one.
There can be no doubt that what the psalmist wrote, at the behest of the Holy
Spirit, was simple and unambiguous; but God allowed these variations, the
work of copyists and translators, to appear in the holy books, so that these
extra difficulties would rouse us from our torpor. Salvation is not imperilled
by a slight departure from the original sense of the Scripture, so long as
the new reading conforms to piety and truth; even if our interpretation
does not entirely fit into its original context, our labours will have been
worthwhile if our reading contributes to moral improvement, and fits in

* * * * *

366 Cf Rom 8:16–17.
367 Erasmus uses the phrase *attentus ad rem*, meaning someone who thinks too
    much of money, used by Terence of old men in *Adelphi* 834 and 954.

with other scriptural texts. However, I shall not take up here the onerous burden of discussing which reading is the most acceptable. Jerome carries great weight with me, and the authority of the Septuagint version is not to be ignored, especially since that authority has been strengthened by its general use for centuries in both the Greek and Latin churches. Whether we read 'children of man,' meaning 'children of Adam,' or 'children of mankind,' both expressions serve to diminish man's self-esteem. It was out of humility that, in the Gospels, the Lord called himself 'the Son of Man,'[368] whereas the Jews boasted of Abraham, Jacob, David, and other patriarchs whose memory they held sacred. Paul also says: 'Do I say these things according to men?' and: 'If I still sought men's favour, I should be no servant of Christ.' Elsewhere, he says: 'Are you not bound to the flesh, and walking in the ways of men?' followed by: 'Are you not merely men?'[369] In each case he is implying something lowly, far removed from perfection.

Since so many of us are like this, each one should consider that this verse is addressed particularly to him. You have been baptized, you have professed the gospel creed, through which men become the children of God, 'who are reborn, not by blood, or by the will of the flesh, or the will of man,'[370] but in a heavenly way, through the Spirit regenerating and renewing the mortal man; you have put on the Lord Jesus Christ,[371] you have been grafted on to his body – and yet, despite all this, you remain no more than 'the children of mankind.' When will you move on to higher things? How long will you think of nothing but the flesh and the world?

A certain kind of light-heartedness is also condemned in Holy Writ, as Ecclesiasticus teaches: 'To trust a man hastily shows a fickle heart.'[372] This is true of those who are swayed and tossed by every wind of doctrine,[373] of whom another psalm says: 'Their heart is empty.'[374] For this reason a certain gravity of heart is required, which steadies the mind with the ballast of gospel truth and prevents it from being tossed around by the fickle winds of

* * * * *

368 The expression appears dozens of times in the Gospels; a relevant occurrence for this context is John 8:28, which is followed by an attack on the Jews' pride in their ancestors.
369 Respectively 1 Cor 9:8, Gal 1:10, and 1 Cor 3:3 and 4
370 John 1:13
371 Cf Rom 13:14.
372 Sir 19:4
373 Cf Eph 4:14; the English versions render the subsequent passage from Ps 5 rather differently.
374 Ps 5:9

human fancy. Paul showed this quality when he said that we must not trust even an angel if it brings a contradictory gospel.[375]

However, in other circumstances a certain lightness of heart is recommended. This was the case with those described in Isaiah: 'Who are these that float like clouds and fly like doves to their dovecotes?'[376] Eagles show this quality: 'they gather wherever the corpse is,'[377] but from there every day they fly up, by instinct, to where Christ sits at God's right hand. The priest demands this quality of the people as he commences the sacred mysteries, saying: 'Lift up your hearts,' and the response is made: 'We raise them up to the Lord.'[378] How I wish, my dear friends, that everyone could make this response truthfully. Hearts of lead, burdened by the weight of a guilty conscience, cannot fly up to the Lord. Earthbound hearts, weighed down by the cares of this life, have no wings and cannot be borne aloft. Only hearts of fire, hearts of air (by which I mean hearts full of the Spirit) can fly aloft. They are the opposite of those 'heavy hearts' whom the prophet exhorts in this verse to cast off base and trivial concerns, to take wing and fly up to the source of peace of mind. Those who are burdened with sin make no effort to end their sinfulness, putting off their reformation until their last day dawns. Those who take pride in the spurious rewards of this world, honours, wealth, pleasure, are not only wasting their time, but wasting themselves,[379] constantly beset by worry and gloom; whereas those who have rejected all this, and have lifted their thoughts to the eternal, are quickened by hope, ever rejoicing in the Lord, endlessly singing hymns and spiritual songs of praise to the Lord in their hearts.[380] If your heart has been enlarged by God's favour, you must never cease to cry out to those whose hearts are still burdened with pride: 'You proud of heart, how long will you spurn heaven and cling to the earth? How long will you love vanity instead of reality, and seek out falsehood instead of goodness and truth?'

I said something earlier on the difference between vanity and falsehood; we are disappointed by vanity, but deceived by falsehood. Similarly, we might discuss the difference between 'loving' and 'seeking.' We love things

* * * * *

375 Gal 1:8
376 Isa 60:8
377 Cf Matt 24:28 and Luke 17:37 ('vultures' in the New English Bible); Erasmus is making paradoxical use of the proverbial high flying of eagles, evoked symbolically for example in Exod 19:4 and Isa 40:31.
378 Part of the introduction to the Eucharistic prayer in the mass
379 A play on *immorantur* 'delaying' and *immoriuntur* 'dying'
380 Cf Eph 5:19.

which are within reach, but we seek things which we desire but which are not here. We love things which delight our minds here and now; we seek things which we must strive to obtain from elsewhere. It is true that the world knows many ways to tempt and entice us; it lays before our eyes, as if they were real treasures, beauty, strength, youth, wealth, nobility, power, good health, pleasure, long life, learning, wisdom, glory; on the other hand, it also sets before us many apparent terrors: old age, weakness, poverty, ill health, low birth, contempt, ignorance, torture, death, infamy. They are all vain delusions, but if his poor judgment leads a man to think that he should really pursue the former as good things, or shrink from the latter as evils, he is 'loving vanity' in pursuing the tempting ones, and is confounded by vanity in dreading the others. Anyone who loves the wrong things will also hate the wrong things. From this source spring all life's disasters: either our judgment is faulty, and we mistake good things for bad, and bad things for good, or else our judgment is perverse, and we make far too much of them altogether.

Impaired judgment gives rise to insane desires, just as an impaired palate leads us to demand poison rather than good healthy food; in this way we move on from loving vanity to seeking out falsehood. I am not speaking merely of things which everybody admits are frivolous, such as singing and dancing, play-acting, fun and games generally. Every human action is vanity, indeed every human being, however mighty, is vanity,[381] when compared to God and the divine world, which truly exist. Martha, too, was fussing and fretting about many vain things, when one thing alone was essential; Mary had chosen the one part that was best, sitting at Jesus' feet and listening to him.[382] Mary, seated there, represents the mind at rest from all carnal passions, Others sit at the feet of Aristotle, Averroes, Bartholus, and Baldus,[383] but blessed is the pupil who sits at the feet of Jesus listening to the voice of eternal truth. A man will never again love human vanities when once he is possessed by the love of true perfection. That is what we must love, that is what we must desire and seek. All the rest, which does not

* * * * *

381 The clause 'indeed ... vanity' is omitted in ASD V-2 248:796.

382 Luke 10:41–2; cf *Moria* CWE 27 152 and n644 (CWE 28 489). For a commentary on this text and its use elsewhere by Erasmus to illustrate Christian folly, see Screech 180–2.

383 A glancing attack on two of the favourite targets of the humanists, the schoolmen (cf n268 above), disciples of Aristotle and his commentator Averroes, and the medieval legists, represented by the fourteenth-century commentators Bartolo de Sassoferrato and Baldo degli Ubaldi; cf *Ciceronianus* CWE 28 421 and Ep 134:30–1.

lead to that end, is vanity; a promise of bliss from any source other than this alone is falsehood. The wise Ecclesiastes saw this when he said that every act of mortal life is pure vanity, except the fear of God and the keeping of his commandments.[384]

Now, why do Christians, who profess the gospel truth, live lives of such vanity? Why is there turmoil and strife on every side? We sail, we trade, we wage war, we make treaties (and break them again), we contract marriages, we have children, we write wills, we buy and sell land, we make friends, we build and knock down; we are tonsured, anointed, and take the cowl; we are schooled in the various arts or, with much outpouring of money and sweat, we seek degrees in the two kinds of law[385] or in theology; others choose to seek the mitre and the crook. We torture our minds over these things, we grow old with them – and in the long years we spend on them we lose the single most precious thing of all, which cannot be regained. And now the day of death has dawned and we must go before that judgment-seat where truth alone, not vanity, will find a place – and then, at last, as if waking from a dream, we realize that it has all been an empty simulacrum of reality, beguiling us as we slept.

Someone will object: 'So Christians should not concern themselves with what you call vanities?' No, you can concern yourself with some of them, but only from necessity, and sparingly, aware that they must be abandoned whenever they endanger your pursuit of the one true good. The nature of this good is well defined by Paul himself: 'The time is short,' he says, 'so it remains that those who have wives should be as if they had no wives, and those who mourn should be as if they did not mourn; those who are joyful should be as if they did not rejoice; those who buy, as if they owned nothing, and those who use the world, as if they used it not; for the outward form of this world is passing away.'[386] He is describing how to endure the vanity of this life, but not love it; how to use the world, but not to abuse its pleasures. Paul means 'vanity' when he speaks of its outward form. The Jews clung to outward forms, which they still doggedly maintain to be true reality.

* * * * *

384 Eccles 12:13
385 That is, canon and civil law; many contemporary lawyers bore the title *doctor utriusque iuris*, doctor of both kinds of law. It will be noticed that, at the beginning of the next paragraph, Erasmus hastens to qualify this pious but misanthropic rhetorical tirade, which resembles those of the Cynic philosophers and includes a number of Erasmus' usual targets – but also some surprising ones, such as friendship, marriage, and the study of the humanities.
386 1 Cor 7:29–31

Just as there are two laws, of the flesh and of the spirit, so there are two worlds. The world in which we live teems with vanities; another world will follow, in which the phantoms will be scattered, and all will be revealed. There, wasted words will have to be justified; what will be the answer of those who doted on Aristotle's philosophy, on erudite quibbling, on sophistical nonsense, or on mitres and crowns, to the extent that they hardly spared a thought for the one thing which should have occupied their lives? Before that court, it will not matter that you were king or peasant, monk or carter, philosopher or ignoramus. One question only will be asked: did you place all your hopes of bliss in the Lord, and cling to his commandments with all your might?

Love is born in the eyes, according to the Greek proverb.[387] It is therefore dangerous even to look upon the vanities of this world, which is why the psalmist prays: 'Turn my eyes from seeing vanity, and make me live in your paths.'[388] The vanities press in upon us from every side, and men have no power to avert their eyes unless God turns them away and directs them into his paths. 'Eve saw that the tree was good to eat, pleasing to the eye, and delightful to behold; she plucked its fruit, ate of it, and gave it to her husband; he ate of it and their eyes were opened.' Eve saw and loved vanity, and at the same time she sought out falsehood, since the serpent had promised: 'You shall not die, but shall be like gods.'[389] The beginning of all evil is to have seen and loved vanity. But in what way were their eyes said to be opened, since the text says that they already had their sight? They had seen before, but as if in a dream; once awakened and aware of reality, they understood that they had been beguiled by the empty shadows of reality. Therefore, instead of a treasure they discovered coals,[390] instead of true good they discovered only tokens of reality. David saw Bathsheba, he saw vanity, and he loved it. Soon he sought out falsehood as, having tricked and slain her husband, he hoped that his plot would remain secret and go unpunished. Later he realized that the pleasure he had loved had played him false.[391] If Eve had turned her eyes from vanity, and turned her steps into the Lord's paths, she would not have been the agent of our death. The apple was pleasing to the eye, but the Lord's command should have stopped her: 'Do not eat from the tree of the knowledge of good and evil, for on the day on which you shall eat

* * * * *

387 *Adagia* I ii 79
388 Ps 118/119:37
389 Gen 3:6–7, followed by an abridgment of 3:4–5
390 *Adagia* I ix 30
391 See 2 Samuel 11–12.

from it, you shall surely die.'[392] Again, if David, having seen the woman, had turned his eyes towards God's path, and heeded the commandment not to covet his neighbour's wife,[393] he would not have heard the sentence of death, and would not have bought a moment's pleasure at the cost of endless tears, troubles, and shame.

The alluring charms of the world do not only play us false when it comes to the life hereafter, but even in this transitory life. In the life to come, all who scorned the truth and sought out falsehood on this earth will say: 'What use was our pride, what did our bragging of our wealth bring us? All that has passed away like a shadow, like a messenger galloping by; it is like a ship crossing a wave-tossed sea, for when it has passed, not a trace can be found, no track of the keel among the waves' etc.[394] Similarly, ambition, greed, and lust play us false on this earth, as the bait deceives the fish. 'You lucky fellow!' people say, if you own a lot of land, or have received some splendid gift from the prince, or have found yourself a pretty girl. But whenever one of our cherished hopes is fulfilled, do we not always find ourselves enmeshed in a great web of fresh troubles and anxieties? In the end, we learn to distrust someone who has cheated us time and again, however much he tries to wheedle, and yet, although we have so often been deceived by the world's wiles, we still look on them, love them, and seek them out, allowing ourselves to be deluded yet again. Childhood passes by, and can be forgiven its foolishness; youth rushes past, and we pursue vanity still more eagerly. We reach maturity, but still we continue to seek out falsehood; old age creeps up, but we do not change our ways; death is knocking at the door, yet still we cling to our delusive dreams. How appropriate is this verse to all these states: 'Children of mankind, how long will your hearts be burdened with pride? Why do you love vanity and seek out falsehood?'

At this point the word διάψαλμα is inserted in the psalm.[395] Surprisingly, Augustine is not sure whether it is Greek or Hebrew; it is well known that the Hebrew *Selah* is translated by the Septuagint, by Symmachus, and by Theodotion as διάψαλμα; only Aquila translates it ἀεί, meaning 'for ever.'

* * * * *

392 Gen 2:17
393 Cf Exod 20:17.
394 Wisd 5:8–10
395 What follows is a conflation of the discussions by Augustine *Enarratio in psalmum 4* PL 36 80 and Jerome *Breviarium in psalmos* PL 26 828c. In fact Augustine casts doubt on the theory that *diapsalma* is a Hebrew word. Jerome provides the references to Symmachus, Theodotion, and Aquila, second-century AD translators of the Old Testament into Greek (included in Origen's *Hexapla*), as well as the last two theories mentioned by Erasmus here.

However, the commentators have markedly different views on the meaning of *Selah*; some think that it means 'silence,' a pause in the singing of the psalm, whose opposite is σύμψαλμα, while others, on the contrary, consider it a sign that the psalm is to be continued; some think that *Selah* is some sort of musical notation, others that it is a sign put in to underline the everlasting and unchanging truth of the text. Numerous other hypotheses are advanced, but I shall not for the present discuss how each may be refuted or confirmed, as I have no wish to impose on your good will a discussion which would be rather uninspiring in itself, and also far too long.

The best guess seems to me to be that there was in the Hebrews' performance of the psalms a convention similar to that found in ancient comedy, where during the performance of the dialogue a particular type of music was played on the flute to help the audience to recognize, from the tune, the mood of the scene, serious or light-hearted, to fix what was being said in the spectators' minds, and at the same time to encourage applause and cries of approval. Thus, whenever *Selah* is inserted in a psalm, we must fix in our minds what is being said, and sing it over time and again until it has taken root in our minds. Let everyone who still clings to vanity and falsehood say to himself: 'How long will your heart be burdened with pride? Why do you love vanity and seek out falsehood? When will you extricate yourself from the petty concerns which obsess you?' Cry out to the Lord, and he will relieve your heart; say to him: 'Have pity on me,' until he hears your cry. However, while the mind, under the influence of this mystic song, is considering abandoning vanity and rejecting falsehood, the flesh is singing it a very different song. 'If you throw away your wealth, your position, your pleasures, will anyone be more wretched, more abject, than you? Do you want to be like X or Y – is there anyone more contemptible and hopeless than they? Look what happens to people who want to live a life of holiness in Christ Jesus: humiliation, poverty, exile, prison, and in the end, death.'

This is how the flesh speaks to a bishop or abbot, who counts his annual revenue in thousands, who maintains a huge retinue, who outdoes kings in his luxury and pleasures, if he should happen to consider turning from vanity towards true goodness: 'What are you doing? Do you fancy living like the apostles? Do you want to be Bernard or Hilarion or Antony?'[396] A mind which is weak and humble in itself, but lofty and exalted in Christ, will

* * * * *

396 St Bernard of Clairvaux, twelfth-century co-founder of the Cistercian order, wrote a number of ascetic and mystical treatises; St Hilarion of Gaza was the disciple and successor of the celebrated fourth-century anchorite St Antony of Egypt, acknowledged as the founder of monasticism.

reply to this damnable tune: 'And know that the Lord has made his holy one an object of wonder.'[397] The Lord does not need rings, family trees, palaces, camels, horses, or hordes of courtiers to make his holy one an object of wonder and admiration. Instead of derisory pleasures tinged with much bitterness, he imparts the endless joy of an untroubled conscience, and arms his soldier with faith to defy the assaults of the world and Satan;[398] he gladdens him with hope and endows him with the gifts of the Spirit; instead of a glory that is illusory, he crowns him with everlasting glory and inviolable honour. It is this which is a source of astonishment to the 'children of mankind' as they observe those who have been truly reborn in Christ: 'How can they be so generous to the poor when they have so little? How can they be so contemptuous of wealth? How can they be so eager to endure all those vigils and fasts, all that wearisome toil? How can they be so unafraid when they are so utterly vulnerable?' It is in these ways that, even in this life, 'the Lord makes his holy ones (whom he has made holy) an object of wonder.'

The great men of this world possess much, but they lack even more. The true 'holy one' has everything within his grasp. The world says: 'How can this be, since you have been forsaken by all?' The holy one will reply, with great confidence: 'The Lord will hear me when I cry to him. I have an all-powerful master, who is always listening, and provides whatever is needed by the suppliant. I owe nothing to myself, and I am all the more confident that my welfare is guaranteed and in safe hands.' The princes of this world spend years trying to guarantee their own safety; the lords who depend on them, and have not taken thought for themselves, will often beg the prince's aid in vain. But if someone relies on God to guarantee his safety, he has a ready defence for all emergencies; he has only to cry out with true feeling and he will be answered. No one can intercept a cry from the heart; before you can get the emperor's help, you need the services of endless intermediaries and letters of introduction; all too often, the petitioner dies waiting; even if help does arrive, it does not always assist the suppliant. Our holy one receives swift and certain succour from the Lord who made heaven and earth. Those who have the Lord to give them all they need are a dozen times richer than Croesus.[399] Doctors have innumerable drugs, an infinity of potions, but surely everyone would prefer a doctor who used no more than a single panacea, such as the famous

* * * * *

397 This Greek reading of the verse (cf 185 above) is preferred by Erasmus in this context to the Latin version, 'has performed wonders for his holy one.'
398 Cf Eph 6:11.
399 The Lydian king proverbial for his wealth; cf *Adagia* I vi 74.

fifth essence.[400] Ancient myth tells of the cornucopia,[401] which provided everything you could ask. But our holy one has a true cornucopia which will deny him nothing, since his request is made in holiness, and is addressed to him who can do all things.

Roman law defines as 'holy' anything considered inviolable by divine command, such as the walls of a city or the laws of the state.[402] None the less, however 'holy' they may be, they are all too often violated. But the 'holy one' whom the Lord has taken under his protection cannot be harmed by men or demons, by creatures below or above, by death or by life.[403] No one can steal from the Son what his Father has given him. But God does not listen to sinners; if you wish your prayers to be heard, you must be holy. If you are ashamed of yourself, you have already ceased to be a sinner. The princes of this world have their own 'holy ones,' whom they hold exceptionally dear, permitting no one to do them harm[404] – but how can they offer their holy ones something they cannot guarantee for themselves? They have their castles, their cannon, their armies, their tasters to detect poison; they have magic rings, saints' undergarments, lucky swords,[405] but none of these can guarantee their safety. Immunity from all ills is granted only to those whom God has accepted and taken into his safe keeping,[406] by taking them from the world. What can the world do to someone who is not in the world? The true holy one is moved by nothing in this world, and so the world cannot harm him. His feet touch the earth, but his heart is in heaven. 'If you dwell in me,' Christ said, 'and my words dwell in you, you may ask for anything and it shall be granted to you.'[407] What monarch has the power to promise this – convincingly – to his friends? But this is the promise given to his holy ones by God, who can

* * * * *

400 Supposedly the substance of which the heavenly bodies were composed, and a term especially associated with alchemists and quack doctors; cf Epp 225:12–16 and 404:6–8.

401 The horn of plenty. Ovid provides two versions of its origin: in *Fasti* 5.121–8 it is the broken horn of Zeus' nurse, the goat Amalthea; in *Metamorphoses* 9.88–9 it is a horn of the bull into which Achelous changed himself to escape Hercules.

402 Cf the *Digest* of Justinian 1.8.8–9 (*De divisione rerum*), which gives both the examples mentioned here in its definition of *sanctus*.

403 An echo of Rom 8:38–9

404 Erasmus frequently attacks princely favouritism, for example in chapter 7 of the *Institutio principis christiani* CWE 27 273–5. It is possible, however, that this is a reference to the court fools who were considered inviolable in their divinely-inspired madness.

405 Cf 218 and n251 above.

406 The clause 'and taken into his safe keeping' is omitted from ASD V-2 254:957.

407 John 15:7

do whatever he wills and will not fail anyone. These are the words of the holy one, who fears nothing, under his God's protection: 'If God is for us,' he says, 'who can be against us?'[408] From his impregnable tower he boldly casts these words upon the world; here is a similar expression of his confidence: 'The Lord is my shepherd,' he says, 'I shall want for nothing.'[409]

Students of Hebrew have noted that the Latin translator's 'performed wonders' [*mirificavit*] represents a Hebrew word meaning 'separated.' God, who sees into every heart, separates the wheat from the chaff and stores it in his barn; he separates the good fish from the bad, and puts them in his basket.[410] One day he shall cut off his own people from all contact with the wicked, but in the meantime it is in their hearts that he cuts his chosen people off from the world, and through his spirit eradicates in them the love of the ephemeral, enrapturing them with the love of heaven; by this separation he makes them holy. This is what John tells us: 'They are not of this world, as I am not of this world. Make them holy in truth; your word is truth.'[411] Thus no one can be truly holy, unless the Father has made him so; no one is truly cut off from the world unless the Father has drawn him to himself. Anyone who puts his trust in God's words is already made holy, even if he is not entirely free from guilt; he is already cut off from the world and changed into another person entirely. Thus he is made an object of wonder by this sudden metamorphosis which those not yet separated from the world see in him, as Peter explains in his first letter: 'They are full of wonder when you do not plunge with them into their reckless dissipations.'[412] They say: 'What has happened to him? Why this astonishing change? How has he become so gentle, so generous, so temperate, so chaste, when he used to be so violent, greedy, drunken, and promiscuous?' To these expressions of wonder, the holy one replies: 'Why are you astonished that I have become another? The Lord, who makes all things new, has changed me; this transformation is the work of his heavenly hand. I am no longer the man who was your companion in debauch; the Lord has slain the old Adam in me, and now I do not live, but Christ lives in me. Beg the Lord to change you as well, and straightaway your astonishment will be turned into thanksgiving.'[413]

* * * * *

408 Rom 8:31
409 Ps 22/23:1
410 Matt 3:12 and Luke 3:17; Matt 13:48
411 John 17:16–17
412 1 Pet 4:4
413 There are numerous Pauline echoes in this speech; see for example Rom 6:6–8, 2 Cor 5:17, Gal 6:14–15, and Eph 4:22–4.

Long ago the disciples too were astonished by Paul, as he changed suddenly from a wolf to a sheep, or rather became the shepherd of the flock.[414] Long ago God made his holy one, the prince of holiness, an object of wonder, when the Jews said: 'Who has given him this strength and this wisdom?'[415] Similarly, they wondered at Peter and John, when those simple, uneducated men were able to instruct the people with such dedication.[416] He made Stephen an object of wonder: as he prepared to address the court, he did not turn pale, his expression did not change, nor did his voice stick in his throat; his face appeared to them like the face of an angel standing among them.[417] I shall not mention here the miracles with which God often honours his holy ones, not only in this life but especially after their body's death; it is certain that in that day, when all that is now hidden shall be revealed,[418] the Lord will make his holy ones an object of wonder, and the ungodly shall say: 'These are the people we once held up to ridicule and considered a reproach to humankind. Like fools, we held their way of life to be madness and their end to be dishonour. But see, they are numbered amongst God's children; their destiny is to be among the saints.'[419]

Let us therefore beseech the Lord, my brothers, that he will deign to make us holy in truth, not in our clothing, our food, our ritual, which on their own result in hypocrisy, not holiness; we should not seek ways to make ourselves worthy of notice, soliciting the praise and admiration of mankind, but rather let him who has made us holy also make us objects of wonder. Only those whom he has made holy are truly holy; only those whom he has made remarkable are truly remarkable; all the rest is vanity and falsehood. It is mankind that provides the mitre, the crook, the cowl, the cloak, the chain, the crown, the skull-cap; these gain the respect of fools, and that only for a season.[420] The Lord provides qualities of the mind, which no one can steal, he provides outward signs in works of a kind that no mortal could perform unless God were at work in him. He chooses to work through the weak, the despised, and the uneducated, to ensure that men's wonder at

* * * * *

414 Acts 9:21
415 Cf Matt 13:54.
416 Acts 4:13
417 Cf Acts 6:15.
418 Cf Matt 10:26 and Luke 12:2.
419 Wisd 5:3–5, slightly adapted
420 The passage 'not in our clothing . . . for a season' was recommended for deletion in the *Index expurgatorius* LB X 1820B, although it is by no means Erasmus' most outspoken attack on priestly vestments and ritual.

his divine power will be all the greater. A 'holy one' whom this world has made holy can be stung by a word, can plot to destroy the offender, can be hit by financial ruin, and can even plan murder. The Lord's holy one will repay the most outrageous insult with brotherly admonition; he will give thanks to the Lord when stripped of his property and, when brought to a humiliating death, will pray for those who have procured his death. These are the outward signs which truly make the Lord's holy one a source of wonder.

Now, be attentive while I quickly deal with the rest of the psalm. Among mortals, similarities breed love[421] and differences breed hatred. This is why the holy one, whom the Lord has made an object of wonder by the sudden change in his ways, becomes hateful to those who used to love him dearly because he shared their faults. Until they understand the operation of the Spirit within him, they grow angry and indignant at this deserter, this renegade who has left their band, and use threats to try to steer him back into their former relationship; often they are parents, who say: 'If you do not give up this futile way of life, I shall disinherit you.' The Lord's disciple tries, gently and fraternally, to turn their anger into repentance, saying: 'Be angry; do not sin. Say these words in your heart and examine your conscience in your private chamber.' Christian anger is full of good will towards its object; such anger is no sin, for Christian charity does no wrong, even when it starts a quarrel. When the world is angry it kills, and when it loves, it corrupts. When charity loves, it rejoices in doing good; when it grows angry, it heals. The Lord made his Son an object of wonder; the synagogue was angered and killed him. He made the apostles a source of wonder, and the Jews hounded them mercilessly. The gentiles too were disturbed by the unexpected ways in which God made his followers a source of wonder, and were incensed to be deprived of their gods, laws, luxury, lust, and general licence to sin, and so they practised every kind of cruelty against them.

Even today, worldly people become incensed when someone is transformed by God's Spirit into a new creature, and they chide him, laugh at him, persecute him as though he were an enemy, for no better reason than that he is different. 'He is casting aspersions on us,' they say, 'by pretending to be better than we are.' It is like a blind man rebuking someone who can see: 'You are showing up my blindness by having your sight,' or a cripple upbraiding someone healthy: 'You shame me by walking upright,' or a

* * * * *

421 Cf *Adagia* I ii 21.

stammerer getting angry with someone who speaks clearly: 'You are a living reproach to my stumbling tongue because you speak differently from me.' But this is in fact how the world is judged and rebuked by the lives of the devout, as Paul writes: 'Then their uprightness, like a light shining in, shows up the others' darkness.'[422] This happens not only in royal courts and secular assemblies, but also in ecclesiastical communities and even in monasteries: people become incensed against those whom they ought to imitate. But, amid all this, what does the Lord's holy one do? He does not return their insults, he does not reproach them for their madness and blindness, he does not make them jealous by boasting of his bliss; rather, he invites them lovingly to share his bliss. 'Why are you angry with me,' he says, 'when I hurt no one? The change you observe in me is not hypocrisy, but a gift of God; I seek no credit for it, but neither do I deserve your anger. This anger of yours is sinful, for "anyone who grows angry with his brother is a murderer."[423] If you wish to be angry without sin, be angry with your own faults, be angry with your darkness and accept God's gift, which is offered to all.'

This verse could have two meanings. The first is: 'If anything angers you, be angry in such a way that your anger does not erupt into wrongdoing'; in this reading, we are not ordered to be angry, but to moderate our anger once it has started. The alternative is: 'Grow angry, indeed, but with yourselves, not with me.' Such anger involves no sin. Ordinary people habitually make excuses for their own faults and denounce even the good deeds of others. But one might call 'blessedly angry' people who, observing someone else's virtues, are annoyed with themselves, are angry with themselves, quarrel and fight with themselves; they might reproach themselves thus: 'You wretch, that young man is blooming with good qualities, and you, an old man, are withering away in squalor. You poor creature: while the ignorant rise up and, breathed on by Christ's Spirit, conquer heaven, you, with all your learning, wallow in flesh and blood. You coward: while adolescent girls can scorn the pleasures of the flesh and embrace those of the spirit, you, with your manly beard, are a slave to every vice.' This is surely the struggle between the spirit and the flesh, in which every Christian should be constantly engaged. I am aware that at this point some commentators have written at length about control of the emotions, saying that our initial reactions are not under our control, and thus cannot be considered sinful so long as our reason and judgment are not engaged. Augustine and some of his

* * * * *

422 Not an exact quotation; cf Rom 2:19, 2 Cor 4:6, and 6:14.
423 1 John 3:15; cf Matt 5:22.

followers have advanced this view;[424] I am not rejecting their view, but I have preferred to discuss ideas which seemed to me more appropriate in this context.

It does not make much difference to the meaning whether we read 'be angry' or 'tremble,' which some commentators suggest for the Hebrew word, perhaps because violent anger results in trembling. Impotent rage produces two effects in man, pallor and trembling; pallor because the blood becomes concentrated round the heart, and trembling because of the violent movement of the spirits; the same effects are produced in us by extreme fear.[425] But no anger is more violent than a sinner's when he acknowledges his worthlessness and boils with rage against himself, to the point that he may rush off to find a noose or the edge of a cliff. Again, no fear is greater than a sinner's when he considers the magnitude of his crimes and shudders at the thought of God's justice and the punishment he deserves. Thus the righteous man says: 'Why are you raging at me? Tremble for yourselves, acknowledge your miserable condition, change your ways and cease to sin. Say these words in your heart and examine your conscience in your private chamber.'

Augustine suggests that an unspoken word should be added to this passage: 'What you are saying, say it in your hearts.'[426] This figure of speech is indeed found in Holy Writ, for example in Paul's letter to the Romans: 'For a man is not a Jew in external appearance, neither is true circumcision the external mark in the flesh.'[427] We must understand: 'For a man is not necessarily a Jew, who is a Jew in external appearance ...' However, the meaning of the psalm can be grasped without any addition: 'What you say in your hearts, when angered, examine this in your private chambers.' Do not follow the impulses of the first flush of anger, but the course suggested by reason, after you have carefully weighed the matter in your own mind, something usually done in one's private chamber. In fact, St Augustine

* * * * *

424 *Enarratio in psalmum* 4 PL 36 80, followed very closely in the preceding sentence. It must be pointed out that Augustine also proposes the interpretation, which Erasmus accepts here, that the verse is a call to repentance. Cassiodorus *Expositio in psalmum* 4 PL 70 49B–D writes at greater length on the nature of anger, but also provides the same alternative interpretation as Augustine.

425 Erasmus' discussion here owes something to Plutarch's *De cohibenda iracundia*, of which his translation was also published in 1525. Cf *De copia* CWE 24 332:19–20.

426 *Enarratio in psalmum* 4 PL 36 80; he suggests adding the imperative *dicite* 'say.' To avoid awkwardness, I have already included this in my version, as the English versions have generally done.

427 Rom 2:28

suggests that, instead of 'examine your conscience,' we could read 'open';[428] the Greek text has κατανύγητε [be pricked], but either he had a defective copy, or he was deceived by the similarity with κατανοίγητε [observe well, understand]; the latter comes from ἀνοίγω [I open], the former from νύττω [I prick]. Jerome translates this verse, from the original Hebrew: 'Be angered and do not sin; speak in your hearts, in your private chambers, and be silent.' There is no doubt that 'speak' here stands for 'think,' for to 'speak in one's heart' is to weigh the truth of a matter with oneself. To do this, people hide away in the privacy of their bedchambers, where strong emotions, which may prevent the perception of the truth, are silenced; what is more, the Hebrews often call rest 'silence.'

I shall not tax your brains with these and other knotty problems which do not make all that much difference to the meaning; I prefer to get on with my task. We often hear people say, when holy men are praised for their virtue: 'I wish that God would make me like them'; Balaam said something of the sort.[429] At the beginning of the mass how many beat their breasts and intone repeatedly: 'Have mercy on me, a miserable sinner'? How many say to the priest: 'I confess, I have sinned'?[430] But they say it only with their lips, observing formal custom. They ought to say it in their hearts and examine their conscience in private; they ought to say it to themselves, and say it to God who hears and sees in secret.[431] People rarely speak the truth in public. If you wish to pray truthfully to the heavenly Father, hide yourself in your chamber; if you wish truly to repent of your former life, examine your conscience in your chamber.

I imagine that you understand the prophet's figure of speech here; he is not referring to a room in a house, but to the innermost chamber of the heart. The heart is in fact the most inaccessible organ of the human body, a sort of inner room where secrets are stored, but there is a still more secret place within the heart, which is here called the private chamber. It is well known that the heart has various recesses and chambers, and the image of the heart is used in two different ways, in that people are said to speak both 'in their hearts' and 'from the heart.' But we can only search our consciences properly *in* the inner chamber of the heart, where we speak to God and

* * * * *

428 *Enarratio in psalmum 4* PL 36 81; the confusion does seem to originate with Augustine, who associates the 'opening up' here with the 'dilation' of verse 1. The Latin reads *compungimini* 'prick [your conscience].'
429 See Num 23:10.
430 References to the *Confiteor* and to the opening formula of confession
431 Cf Matt 6:6.

not to other people. David said: 'I have sinned against the Lord,'[432] and he obtained mercy. Saul said: 'I have sinned, for I have transgressed the Lord's command,'[433] but he was not answered because he did not say it in his heart, and did not examine his conscience in the innermost chamber, as David did. Thus people 'grow angry and sin' if, seeing their neighbour turn from a life of evil to piety, not only do they not change their lives as, swayed by his example, they should; they even despise the man they should congratulate, and, rather than emulate him, they try to lead him back into the sinfulness he has abandoned; thus the opportunity to mend their ways leads them deeper into sin. A few people 'examine their conscience,' to a limited extent, when they are moved to find fault with themselves by comparison with their neighbour, but they soon relapse into their former self-indulgence, and thus they do not speak these words from the heart,[434] or examine their conscience in their private chamber.

Again, *Selah* concludes this verse, an indication, as I said earlier, that we must take this particular passage very seriously. How I wish that the heavenly Spirit would pluck our heartstrings and produce a melody which would stay in our minds and never be dislodged once there. Our hope of bliss depends on our being stirred to wholesome anger by our faults and welcoming brotherly admonition; on confessing our lack of righteousness and begging for God's mercy: but we must confess in our hearts and examine our conscience – in our private chambers. The Lord pays no heed to a change of clothes or to sunken cheeks, but he will look kindly upon a contrite and a humble heart.[435] Do not think that all this applies only to those who are notorious for the great and manifest wickedness of their lives; every one of us has some reason to be angry with himself, to quarrel with himself in his heart, to examine his conscience in his private chamber. Every day we make so many mistakes, and carelessly let slip so many chances to do good – even our good deeds are so often imperfect.

Perhaps some of your hearts are heavy, burdened with the weight of your offences, because up to the present you have loved vanity and sought out falsehood; if you have been moved by the sweet sounds of this psalm and have begun to be angry with yourselves, to speak in your hearts, and to

* * * * *

432 2 Sam 12:13. Erasmus adopts the same contrast between David and Saul made by Augustine in *Contra Faustum* 22.67 PL 42 442.
433 1 Sam 15:24
434 *ex corde*; one would expect *in corde*, as this appears to be a quotation from the psalm, but all the texts including ASD have this reading.
435 Cf Ps 50/51:17.

examine your conscience in your private chamber, then listen carefully to the next part and discover how to complete the task you have begun: 'Offer the sacrifice of righteousness.' In days gone by, God was appeased with burnt offerings; this phrase could refer to them, were it not that the term 'sacrifice *of righteousness*' is used. St Augustine interprets 'the sacrifice of righteousness' in two ways.[436] On the one hand, it could mean repentance, through which someone who is thoroughly dissatisfied with himself sacrifices himself as a burnt offering to the Lord; this sacrifice is mentioned in Psalm 50: 'A troubled spirit is a sacrifice to God.'[437] Augustine explains that this may be called a 'sacrifice of righteousness,' since nothing could be more righteous than to be angered by your own sins rather than other people's, and consequently to wreak vengeance on yourself rather than on others. I think that Augustine is right here, except that it is still more righteous, when you see your brother converted to a new way of life, to praise God's gift to him and thereby to acknowledge your own sinfulness; in this way you give God his due, and take upon yourself the burden of the sinner, which is tribulation and anguish. Conversely, could anything be less righteous than to pride yourself on your righteousness, though you are thoroughly steeped in sin, and to feel no need of God's mercy, belittling your neighbour who has mended his ways? Alternatively, Augustine suggests that the 'sacrifice of righteousness' may mean righteous works performed after repentance; remember John the Baptist in the Gospel, exhorting the Jews, who were flocking to be baptized, to produce worthy fruits of repentance.[438] When a diseased tree is cut down and a healthy tree planted, it must be expected to produce good fruit instead of bad. The works of the flesh are bad fruit, the fruits of the spirit are good works.

Anger is the first step towards murder, wounding words are the second, and, when anger is well established, the final step towards murder is to plan how to kill the object of your hatred. The Jews sacrificed by slaughtering cattle; Christians sacrifice by slaughtering the 'former self'[439] and all his ways. Thus a sinner, inspired by the change in his brother, first becomes angry with himself. Anger is followed by self-reproach as he scolds himself in his heart;

* * * * *

436 *Enarratio in psalmum 4* PL 36 81, followed very closely by Erasmus on this verse as a whole
437 Ps 50/51:17–19
438 Matt 3:8 and Luke 3:8
439 Literally 'the old man'; a favourite phrase of Paul: see for example Rom 6:6, Eph 4:22, and Col 3:9–10. The expansion here, however, is taken almost word for word from Augustine's commentary on the psalm.

then he conceives an infallible plan for killing the former self: he strikes him down by repentance, buries him in baptism, and then lays the new self, born to replace the old, on the altar of faith, there to be consumed by the divine fire, the Holy Spirit. As Paul eloquently demonstrates in chapter 12 of the first letter to the Corinthians, sins were washed away by baptism and the confession of faith, and then the Holy Spirit distributed its gifts, the ability to perform good works, according to the measure of each man's faith.[440]

There are two stages involved in changing your life: abandoning what you once were, and starting to be something new. For this reason St Augustine suspects that *diapsalma* here means the same thing as *privatio*, a word used by natural philosophers to mean the moment of passage from one state, which has ceased to exist, to another which is now beginning.[441] However, that most unassuming of men presents this as a hypothesis, rather than a certainty, in the following terms: 'It is perhaps not unreasonable to suggest that the insertion of *diapsalma* implies the transition from an old life to a new.' I could wish that all commentators on Holy Writ would imitate his diffidence! And here is further proof of his modesty: 'The former self,' he says, 'has been snuffed out – or at least weakened – through repentance.' He did not venture to echo exactly Paul's words: 'Mortify your limbs which are on earth,'[442] because in this life no one can claim to be completely dead to sin.

Augustine derived some of these ideas from his knowledge of secular philosophy, which he tried to relate to the meaning of Holy Scripture, although he always did stern battle with those Stoics who recommended that the wise man practise apathy.[443] The same influence is detectable in his next remarks, as he builds a link with the next verse: 'There are many who say: "Who will show us these good things?"' Augustine says that this refers to 'internal' good things, which alone are worthy of our love; the others may be used in cases of necessity but are not to become a source of joy and delight to us. Now, while I admit that it is not unreasonable to discuss here the various degrees and differences between good things which are debated by

* * * * *

440 1 Cor 12:11
441 Cf Aulus Gellius 2.6.12 and Cicero *De finibus* 1.11.37–8; the word means 'deprivation' and thus 'absence,' a void between two contrasting states; Cicero discusses Epicurus' rejection of its existence. This allusion to the pagan philosophers is Erasmus' rather than Augustine's, but the two quotations which follow are indeed from the *Enarratio in psalmum 4* PL 36 81.
442 Col 3:5; Erasmus means that Augustine's qualification, 'or at least weakened,' makes due allowance for human frailty, including his own.
443 For example in *De civitate Dei* 9.4 PL 41 258–60; Augustine argues that the Stoics' claims to dominate their passions are mere verbiage.

the Peripatetics and the Stoics,[444] I think it more fitting to expound Holy Writ in terms of Holy Writ, lest we substitute mere human cleverness for the divine Spirit.

The apostle Paul is always proclaiming that man is justified, not by works, but by faith; none the less, true faith is not idle, but works through love.[445] If our works are evil, they prove that our faith is not pure. Therefore the 'sacrifice of righteousness' is offered by those who distrust their own powers, their own learning, their own acts, and who trust with all their hearts in the divine promises, never doubting, or quibbling over their reward. For example, Abraham received a promise from God that he would be the father of many nations and that through his descendants all peoples would receive a blessing; later, when ordered to sacrifice Isaac, his only son and his only hope of progeny, he did not give way to doubt and mutter to himself: 'What becomes of the promise if I slay him?'[446] He knew that the promise came from the source of all truth and power. Thus those who have drunk deeply of the gospel faith believe, first of all, that their innocence has been restored through Jesus Christ's death, and this is one part of righteousness. But it is not enough to be free of guilt, unless this is followed by the fruits of the good works which faith works through love, and so, once our innocence has been freely restored by the wiping out of sin, we are again told to 'offer the sacrifice of righteousness,' proffering to our neighbour the fruits of our good works by faith; at the same time, these represent a sacrifice to God, if we claim no credit for them ourselves, recognizing that all things proceed from God's bounty.

To clarify this idea, let us consider a fruit tree.[447] The root is faith, which rises up towards God through a healthy, straight stem; soon love spreads out branches for the benefit of neighbours, inviting all and sundry, as it were, to pick its produce; the tree so devotes itself to men's service that sometimes its branches, laden with fruit, bow down to the ground. Thus the root is responsible for the tree's produce, and if the fruit is sweet, it proves that

* * * * *

444 Aristotle divided good things into three classes (*Politics* 7.1 1323a), as Erasmus often recalled (see CWE 27 32 and 196, for example), but the wording here suggests that he had in mind the essential Stoic distinction between internal and external reality; cf 218 and n249 above. The principle that Scripture should be expounded in terms of Scripture was of course accepted by St Augustine; see for example his *De doctrina christiana* 3.2.2 PL 34 65.

445 See, for example, Rom 3:28 and Gal 2:16; the second proposition echoes Gal 5:6.

446 Gen 18:18, followed by an account of Genesis 22

447 Cf the exposition of the First Psalm 34-7 above.

the root is filled with healthy sap. Moreover, since our root is a gift of God, freely given, we must attribute all that it produces to God's goodness, and so, once more, it is a 'sacrifice of righteousness' not to claim for ourselves what is not ours, or to rob God of the praise and glory due to him. Thus philosophers who claim to derive the supreme good from the forces of nature do not 'offer the sacrifice of righteousness,' and neither do the Pharisees who claim that they have themselves earned the credit for their righteousness.[448] 'For anything which does not arise from faith is sin,' says Paul.[449]

Now let us consider[450] people who, overwhelmed by penitence for their earlier lives, set out for Jerusalem, or sail to Compostella, thinking that they are 'offering the sacrifice of righteousness.' I do not intend here to condemn such expeditions entirely, but I am afraid that those who hope to achieve righteousness by them are mistaken. If God has promised anyone righteousness as a result of them, then his promise must be believed; if not, then what is done is not done out of faith. I feel that the same must be said of those who, disgusted by their earlier life, enrol themselves in communities of Benedictines, Franciscans, or Carthusians. I do not condemn their way of life, but I do condemn people who put their trust in special clothing or diet, in the chanting of psalms and other rituals; they are not 'offering the sacrifice of righteousness' but rather revelling in the sacrifices of the Pharisees. It is impertinent of those who live lives of infamy to 'place their hopes in the Lord,' promising themselves what God has promised to others, and similarly, even if your life is blameless, it is wrong to place your hopes in your own merits. Do the best you can, but at the same time place your hopes in the Lord, not in any human agent, still less in yourself. No one 'hopes in the Lord' unless he mistrusts everything else and has placed all his expectations of salvation in the Lord's promises and mercy.

However, not everyone has faith; indeed, true faith is found in very few, and thus there are many who say: 'Who will show us these good things?'

* * * * *

448 The nature of the 'supreme good' (*summum bonum*) was a constant topic of discussion among ancient philosophers; see for example Seneca *Epistulae morales* 117 and Cicero *De finibus* 1.9–13 for discussions of the Stoic and Epicurean theories. On the Pharisees, cf especially Luke 18:9–14.

449 Rom 14:23

450 The paragraph 'Now let us consider . . . promises and mercy' was recommended for deletion in the *Index expurgatorius* LB X 1820B; it echoes Erasmus' frequent criticism of superstition and reliance on externals, voiced particularly in such colloquies as *Peregrinatio religionis ergo, Concio sive Merdardus,* and *Exequiae seraphicae.*

Peter was still bound to the flesh when he said: 'Lord, we have left all and followed you, what then will you give us?'[451] If we haggle with God over merits and rewards as if we were his equals, we are not 'offering the sacrifice of righteousness.' There is a reward for worshipping God, but we must not worship him simply in order to carry off the prize; it must be because by his very nature he is worthy to be worshipped by all. If you worship God in the right way, you possess God; and what can you lack if you possess God? Is that a small reward? In Genesis he speaks these words to Abraham, the father of all who trust in God: 'Have no fear, Abraham, I am your shield, and your reward shall be very great.'[452] But people who say: 'Who will show us these good things?' are not satisfied with spoken promises; they want to see the evidence as well. When people only believe what is immediately visible, it is called 'ocular' faith.[453]

In this sense, then, the psalm's words 'place your hopes in the Lord' are addressed to those who have no confidence in God's promises. It can also be applied to those who despair of ever being able to mend their ways, either because of the number and gravity of their sins, or because the habit of sinning is ingrained in them. They say, with Cain: 'Our sin is too great to be forgiven us,'[454] or they use the words in Jeremiah: 'We have broken away, we shall not return to you again.'[455] Those who disbelieve his promises say: 'The Lord will not come, and there will be no judgment of the just and the unjust at the death of the body. These worshippers of the Lord, how are they better off than we? They are not spared all the usual misfortunes, lightning, shipwreck, earthquake, plague, famine, war, disease, old age; they suffer just as we do. In fact, no one lives more miserably than these devotees of God.' To counter such impious arguments, the righteous man replies, with great confidence, that there is certain hope for all, if only they will lift their heart's eyes to see the banner which displays God's mercy, and which is raised for all.

I said a good deal about this earlier,[456] so I will not overburden your ears by repeating myself; but I would advise you to fix my words in your minds and, once you have conceived hope of forgiveness through God's mercy, to hasten to take up the Lord's cross; it may seem bitter at first because you must

* * * * *

451 Matt 19:27
452 Gen 15:1
453 *fides oculata*, an expression Erasmus found in the *Institutes* of Justinian (3.6.9, *De gradibus cognationum*) and explained in *Adagia* II vi 54 LB II 602B–D
454 Cf Gen 4:13, the Vulgate and the alternative reading in the Authorized Version.
455 Jer 2:31
456 See 197–205 above.

repent of the evil you have done, but it will also bring sweetness in the joy which follows pain, just as bitter medicine brings a special joy when health is restored. Put on with confidence the yoke of the Lord,[457] which is more pleasant by far than the yoke of this world. Taste the sweetness of the Lord and you will agree that 'blessed are those who place their hopes in him.'[458] In the midst of his sufferings, Paul cries out: 'I am filled with consolation, I overflow with joy in all our tribulation.'[459] This joy is poured into pious hearts by the spirit of Jesus Christ, which is given to us as a pledge of the bliss promised at the resurrection of the righteous.

You may be surprised by the sudden change of person in the next lines: 'The light of your countenance has appeared like a banner to guide *us*,' but: 'You have brought joy to *my* heart.' The banner is raised for all to see, but joy is not granted to all; thus only someone who has gazed on the banner with the eyes of faith can say: 'You have brought joy to my heart.' This world too can bring joy, but it is fleeting; it brings joy to the ears, to the palate, to the gullet, to the belly, and to what lies beneath the belly; it brings joy in clothes and in buildings, but the Lord alone can bring joy to the heart, a joy so well concealed that none may steal it away. If at present you enjoy the world and its wickedness, you should welcome the salutary pain of repentance, so that when you have felt this joy in your heart, you may dare to hope for joy in heaven, the priceless joy which knows no end. When once you have sampled this joy, you will not envy the world its pleasures, but will cry out with Peter: 'Lord, to whom shall we go? Your words are the words of life,' and, again: 'It is good for us to be here, let us make three tabernacles here.'[460] For it is in Christ that pious minds find rest, whereas those who follow the world's way find solace in very different things: 'They have been multiplied by the ripening of their corn, their wine, and their oil,' as the psalm says, if we accept for the moment Augustine's view that this verse applies, not to the pious, but to the impious, who love vanity and seek out falsehood.[461] Every other creature, having satisfied its natural desires, takes its rest and asks for nothing more. Only man's mind can never find rest in this life, because it has not yet obtained that supreme good which alone can fulfil the longings of mankind. As for those who seek satisfaction in the good things of this world,

* * * * *

457 Cf Matt 11:29–30.
458 An adaptation of Ps 33/34:8
459 2 Cor 7:4
460 John 6:68, followed by Matt 17:4 (Mark 9:2, Luke 9:33)
461 *Enarratio in psalmum* 4 PL 36 82; Erasmus again follows Augustine's thought very closely in his exegesis of this verse.

the greater the efforts they make, the further they are from true satisfaction and the greater the cares that beset them; whereas the upright man has but a single aim, those who aim elsewhere miss the target in many different ways. The result is that, having tried everything which holds out some illusory promise of profit, they realize that all this merely makes them more restless, and are compelled to go on crying: 'Who will show us these good things?' While they pursue a hundred good things, which in truth are no good to anyone, they miss the one thing which is truly good, and which alone can put the human mind at rest. The things perceived as good by the physical senses do not satisfy the mind, even of the most avid pleasure-seeker; in fact, indulgence in them merely causes a thirst for more; they are tinged with much bitterness, and, if you take the trouble to think about them, you will find in them far more gall than honey. Thus, when the mind has strayed along all these paths but has found that all that the human world has to offer is vanity and affliction of the spirit, then at last, wearied, it turns towards the single true path, and, mistrustful of all the good things of the world, and also contemptuous of all its bad things, it delivers itself entire to God, through the gospel faith, and now finds in the One the rest which it could not find in the many others. Therefore, when the psalm says: 'They have been multiplied,' it does not imply an abundance of good things, but a multiplicity of cares; the Greek word ἐπληθύνθησαν is used of an increase in population, rather than of extra production of things.

Now, just as it is excruciating for a body to be cut to pieces, so it is very painful for the mind to be so torn between various different concerns that it seems to become not a single coherent mind, but several minds at once. For this reason Paul calls a woman who has married a husband 'divided,' because she cannot give all her time to the Lord, but is distracted by her duty to her husband and her care for her children, whereas an unmarried woman can always devote herself entirely to the Lord and not be separated from him by other concerns.[462] The same conclusion may be drawn from the story of Martha, who was distracted by her many tasks, when one thing alone was essential. Mary had chosen that one thing instead of the many, and therefore sat, instead of rushing about, and found rest at the Lord's feet.[463]

Augustine brings in at this point a text from the Book of Wisdom: 'The body, which is corrupt, burdens the soul, and an earthly habitation inhibits our understanding as it teems with different thoughts.'[464] He suggests that

* * * * *

462 Based on 1 Cor 7:34
463 Cf Luke 10:41–2 and n382 above.
464 Wisd 9:15

'corn, wine, and oil' stand not only for the things named, but also for the great mass of temporal possessions which have a characteristic effect on all who own and love them, driving them to distraction with fear and anxiety, and thus preventing them from finding true satisfaction in the manner prescribed by the same book: 'Think of the Lord in goodness, and seek him in simplicity of heart.'[465] The Gospel parable of the seedlings choked by thorns makes a similar point, and the Lord himself interprets the thorns as riches, the source of much unhealthy anxiety.[466] But faith cuts a swath through these innumerable distractions and, by directing us back towards singleness of mind, brings us to God. However, most of humanity is distracted by things which bring lustre or comfort to their lives, and among these riches play a leading role, since they are supposed to be able to procure anything you want; thus this line could very well be intended to designate all the vain concerns which deflect our minds from the one thing we ought to love. As Psalm 143 says: 'Their barns are full, their ewes are fruitful' etc. The psalm ends: 'Men have said that the people who possess such things are blessed; blessed is the people whose Lord is God.'[467] People are distracted, not blessed, by a multitude of possessions; God alone, who is one, can bless mankind. Similarly, Psalm 72 says: 'These are the sinners, who prosper in the world; they have obtained riches.'[468] Again, in a letter to Timothy, Paul gives a full description of the ruinous prosperity which people achieve when, unsure of God's protection, they take refuge in worldliness and mistake profit for piety: 'But piety does bring great profit to the man who is self-sufficient. For we brought nothing into this world, and it is certain that we can take nothing out; but if we have food and shelter, we should be content. Those who want to be rich fall into temptation and into the devil's snares, into many harmful desires which plunge a man into ruin and perdition. For the love of money is the root of all evil, and many who have sought it have strayed from the faith and exposed themselves to much torment. But you, man of God, must shun these things.'[469]

If you ask for worldly goods, you ask for countless different things; you will be confused by countless distractions and plunged into countless sorrows, since you will be straying from faith, which turns us from diversity towards unity; but the man of God will escape all this by placing his trust

* * * * *

465 Wisd 1:1
466 Matt 13:7 and 22, Mark 4:7 and 18, Luke 8:7 and 14
467 Ps 143/144:13, 15
468 Ps 72/73:12
469 1 Tim 6:6–11

in the one and ignoring the many. Truth is indivisible, and anyone who strays from the truth will be confounded by a thousand distractions. Paul was afraid that this would happen to the Corinthians: 'I betrothed you to a single husband, presenting you to Christ as a chaste virgin; but I fear that, as the serpent in his cunning deceived Eve, so your thoughts may be corrupted and you may lose your single-minded devotion to Christ Jesus.'[470] Christ is the truth, and anyone who departs from him becomes at once less than single-minded. A bride depends entirely on her husband's resources; what need has the Christian soul, betrothed to the Almighty, to depart from its single purpose and be distracted by a multitude of nagging cares? Thus the spiritual creature, who feels that he has been given a taste of the good thing which he sought, will say: 'You have brought joy to my heart.'

However, the majority, confused and distracted, are never satisfied, and continue to cry: 'Who will show us these good things?' When they have acquired enough of all the things they desire in this world, they say to themselves, like the rich man in the Gospel who was thinking of extending his barns: 'My soul, you have many good things stored up for the years to come; take your rest, eat, drink, and be merry.'[471] This fool preferred to trust in his transient wealth rather than in the gospel's promises, but he did not find the peace he promised himself. This parable is clearly describing a surplus brought about by the ripening of his corn, wine, and oil, which meant that his barns were too small to hold all the produce. He had many good things, but he lacked the one essential thing, which alone brings peace of mind – incomplete in this world, it is true, but to be completed in the world to come. Anyone who has tasted this one good thing trusts in the Lord and 'lies down in peace and takes his rest.'[472] I mean that he is detached from all thoughts of his temporal existence and forgetful of everything which belongs to this world, taking his rest in the certain hope of eternal life.[473] In a way, sleep is an image of death.[474] For this peace of mind, which the world cannot give,[475] the prophet gives thanks to God, whose grace has rescued him from the numberless throng of things which come to birth and die; God has set him apart, self-sufficient (that is, restored to singleness of mind), and has

* * * * *

470 2 Cor 11:2–3
471 Luke 12:19
472 Ps 4:8
473 A variant in the 1540 Basel edition and in LB gives the reading 'taking his rest on earth in the hope of eternal life'; this makes equally good sense.
474 Cf Cicero *Tusculan Disputations* 1.38.92 and Ovid *Amores* 2.9.41.
475 Cf John 14:27.

allotted to him a safe and peaceful place, none other than the hope of eternal rest.

St Augustine interprets the whole psalm in this way, in book 9 of his *Confessions*.[476] He read the Psalms as a catechumen, with his fellow catechumen Alypius, and writes that he was particularly moved by this psalm. Later he discourses fluently upon the man who is driven to distraction by love of the temporal, but is restored to wholeness through faith. All this is expounded most devoutly by that excellent man, but it is not certain that this is the true meaning of the psalm. It would be best of all, of course, if our understanding were able to grasp every particle of the meaning which the Holy Spirit secreted in its mystical writings, but since that is not possible in this life, at least let our mistakes be happy ones. I am not sure whether or not Augustine erred here, but if he did, he erred as a beginner, and erred happily, too, since this misconception led him on to better things. I wish that we could all make that sort of mistake and, interpreting this psalm like him, turn from the world's vanities and concentrate on the essential, that is, on single-minded faith.

Leaving such questions to one side, let us continue our discussion of the interpretation handed down by our other predecessors, at the same time praying that, if they have wandered from the truth, the spirit of Jesus will honour us with a revelation which he has postponed until now; that spirit, which cherishes the humble, can reveal to little children what it has chosen to conceal from the mighty.[477] The Holy Scriptures are an inexhaustible vein of riches, as it were, from which there is always something new to be extracted, always some new exploration to be made. Thus I shall go on to apply this verse, which Augustine relates to the flesh, to the realm of the spirit. 'They have been multiplied by the ripening of their corn, their wine, and their oil': it is a simple matter to apply these words to the gospel food which, when the Jews' sacrifices were abolished, was distributed throughout the world by the communion of the sacred bread and the Lord's cup, and by the anointing of the Spirit.[478]

But now we must discuss how these words may be interpreted for the general edification of all Christians. I alluded briefly to this earlier on, but now I shall try to explain it more fully and at greater length. The distribution

* * * * *

476 *Confessions* 9.4 includes a paraphrase of the psalm as well as the information contained in the next two sentences; a catechumen is a candidate for baptism.
477 An echo of Matt 11:25
478 This symbolism is a central point in the very brief commentary by Arnobius; *Commentarii in psalmos* PL 53 330. Erasmus had edited Arnobius in 1522.

of this world's goods, called in the psalm 'multiplication,' creates envy. Grasping businessmen want the profits to be shared by just a few, and so they establish a monopoly. Those seeking a bride resent a great throng of other suitors; those who pass themselves off as professional philosophers are dismayed that there are many others who claim the same distinction. But the possession of spiritual goods has a very different result. Anyone who has obtained a share in them will be grieved that everyone does not share his portion; he is grateful for his share, of course, but at the same time he is delighted if others have more than he. The godly man therefore gives thanks because the banner of good hope is raised for all above the hopeless tangle of human affairs, and he says: 'The light of your countenance, O Lord, has appeared like a banner on high.' Then, observing that this banner has meant salvation for many, he gives thanks and says: 'You have brought joy to my heart.' The true Christian, in his charity, takes more delight in the conversion of sinners than in his own salvation. Therefore if someone asks him: 'Why this joy in your heart?' he replies: 'Because they have been multiplied by the ripening of their corn, wine, and oil.'

We should not, I think, gloss over the fact that the Hebrew text reads 'in the season' or 'from the season' (Jerome translates the former and Augustine reads the latter)[479] where the Septuagint version has 'by the ripening.' I imagine that this refers to fruit ripening in due season, just as in the First Psalm the blessed man is compared to a tree planted by the streams of the waters, which gives its fruit in its season.[480] Spiritual regeneration in Christ passes through several stages, or ages, as it were, beginning with infancy, when it is fed on milk and cannot yet take solid food.[481] For a while we are little children in Christ, until the time comes when our minds are strengthened by the bread of sounder doctrine and our hearts are gladdened by the wine of love. Nothing is too difficult for a lover, and love sweetens everything. Strength of mind and constancy are produced by faith, for the bread which is eaten with faith is full of life and power. To faith is added love, which produces a sober drunkenness, leading even to contempt for life; according to another psalm, wine gladdens the heart and oil makes the face shine.[482] The strength of this wine ensures that in the midst of suffering the mind exults with spiritual joy; the oil ensures that, however burdened with

* * * * *

479 Respectively in *Divina bibliotheca* PL 28 1130 (though both readings are found in different manuscripts of Jerome) and *Enarratio in psalmum 4* PL 36 82
480 Ps 1:3
481 Cf 1 Cor 3:1–2 and Heb 5:12–13.
482 Ps 103/104:15. On the concept of 'sober drunkenness,' see Screech 72–5.

cares we may be, we are still companionable and affable towards our fellow man.

It is no wonder that the Jews' minds are narrow and desiccated, weak and foolish, since they still go on nibbling at their barley cakes; no wonder that they are doleful, since they still drink the water which Hagar was given to console her in her exile,[483] and no wonder that they are so little welcome among their fellow men, since they disfigure their faces with hypocrisy and have no oil with which to make their faces shine.[484] But we eat the bread reserved for God's children,[485] we drink his powerful new wine, and the oil of spiritual joy is poured upon our heads; we must therefore be strong enough to resist the ills of this world, like those described by John in a letter: 'I am writing to you, young men, because God's word dwells in you; you are strong and have mastered the evil one.'[486] Let us be joyful in ourselves, through hope, and kind to our fellows, with gladness, for God loves those who give in this way.[487] The Jews go hungry; they spit out the grain of the gospel teaching and drink the stagnant water of the letter. But our bread, better far than manna, comes down from heaven to give us immortality.[488]

We become drunk on the produce of God's house, our water is changed into the best wine by Jesus, and ours is the true vine.[489] Zechariah speaks of this corn and wine: 'For what does he possess that is good and beautiful except the corn of the chosen people and the wine which produces maidens?'[490] The chosen people are the young men, tall and strong in Christ, who uphold sound doctrine, 'which is used to teach the truth and refute error, to rebuke, and to instruct in righteousness, so that the man of God may be made ready and able for good work of all kinds.'[491] But the maidens whom this wine produces are the unsullied minds which, always singing a new song, follow the lamb wherever he leads.[492] They are mentioned in Psalm 44: 'Maidens shall be brought to the king after her; her companions shall be brought to you, and they shall come in joy and exultation.'[493] How should they not

* * * * *

483 See Genesis 21.
484 See Matt 6:16–17.
485 Mark 7:27
486 1 John 2:14
487 Cf 2 Cor 9:7.
488 Based on John 6:49–51
489 Cf John 2:3–10 and 15:1.
490 Zech 9:17
491 2 Tim 3:16–17
492 Cf Rev 14:3–4.
493 Ps 44/45:14–15

rejoice, these children of the bridegroom, who is always at his people's side? Now, the usual opinion is that wine is not suitable for maidens, and does not produce maidens; on the contrary, it corrupts them. But the more you drink of the wine stored in our bridegroom's cellars, the more chaste you become. The singer in Solomon's Song had tasted this wine: 'The king led me to his wine cellar; he ordained love in me.'[494]

However, there are still some so-called Christians who eat nothing but chaff, the empty husks of ritual, and drink the water of the letter, and thus they remain weak and morose. I am afraid that Paul's reproach to the Corinthians could also be applied to us: 'For this reason many among you are weak and sickly, and many sleep, for when they eat the bread of the Lord's body unworthily, and drink from the cup of the Lord's blood unworthily, they receive weakness instead of strength and death instead of life. Let each man take stock of himself, and eat of the bread and drink of the cup in such a way that he emerges fresh and eager to serve Christ.'[495]

For the same reason many people, though they read, hear, and sing the Scriptures every day, are not fortified in spirit or warmed by the wine of love; they remain forever unfilled and unhappy, because they have tasted them with their lips, but have not swallowed them eagerly and communicated them to their innermost parts. We should all eat this corn and drink this wine in such a way that we too may say with the prophet: 'They have been multiplied by the ripening of their corn, their wine, and their oil.'

This interpretation is not invalidated by the fact that there is such a scarcity of true Christians nowadays; the numbers have been declining for some time, and now seem to be diminishing faster than ever. But if you think of the tiny flock from which Christianity sprang, and then count up the huge number of martyrs, virgins, and witnesses for the faith throughout the world, you will agree that it is not unreasonable for any godly man to say: 'They have been multiplied by the ripening of their corn, wine, and oil.' They may be few when compared with the throng of those who say: 'Who will show us these good things?' but they have grown and spread more widely than anyone would have believed possible. I am sure that there are more people in the world in whom we may justly take pride than is generally realized, for in the midst of the chaff lies hidden the grain of Jesus Christ.[496] This great throng, beginning in such a small way but for centuries growing daily larger amid the turmoil of persecution, demonstrates that our confidence

* * * * *

494 Song of Sol 2:4
495 1 Cor 11:30, followed by an adaptation of 1 Cor 11:27–9
496 Cf Matt 3:12 and Luke 3:17.

in the gospel's promises is not misplaced; for the moment they are merely sampled by the godly, but they will become manifest at the Lord's coming. Encouraged by the thought of this holy throng, each of us can say: 'I shall sleep in peace and take my rest.'

Another point: St Augustine suggested that the inclusion here of the possessive 'their' was intended to draw a distinction between bread from heaven and human bread, between God's wine, as described in Psalm 35: 'They shall be drunk on the produce of your house,' and human wine, which leads to excess; also between God's oil, of which it is written: 'You have anointed him with the oil of gladness above his fellows,' and the oil described in another psalm: 'The oil of the sinner shall not anoint my head.'[497] All this Augustine expounds with learning and piety, I admit, but it does not tie in with the interpretation I am pursuing. We all ask the heavenly Father for our daily bread, which will reinvigorate us in Christ, and each day we ask for the new wine of the Holy Spirit.[498] The possessive 'their' distinguishes spiritual produce from the produce of this world; the world has its own food supply, but it is both unfulfilling and unable to gladden the heart. Those who have devoted themselves entirely to God have another kind of harvest, from which they draw greater strength every day, and will continue to do so until the end of the world. But all this multitude is one body in Christ Jesus; the many are merged into one by the communion of the body and blood of the Lord, as Paul teaches in his letter to the Corinthians: 'When we bless the cup of blessing, are we not sharing the Lord's blood? When we break the bread, are we not sharing the Lord's body? Although we are many, we are one body because there is one bread; we all share in the one bread and the one cup.'[499]

It is not fanciful to say that the same thing can both make us more numerous and make us one. In a physical body the limbs can grow, but they cannot increase in number. It is different with a mystical body; the more limbs it has, the more it becomes one. The very sacraments, by which we are joined, demonstrate this. You can separate one grain of corn from another, but when a number of grains have been ground and kneaded to make bread, you cannot tell one from another. Similarly, it is possible to separate one grape from another, but when a number of grapes are pressed to make wine, there is nothing left to separate. The same could be said of oil, which is made by squeezing

* * * * *

497 *Enarratio in psalmum 4* PL 36 82; cf Ps 35/36:8, Ps 44/45:7, and Ps 140/141:5. See the discussion of this point 208–9 above. Erasmus prefers to apply this verse to the faithful, rather than to the impious as Augustine had done.
498 Cf Matt 6:11 and 9:17.
499 1 Cor 10:16–17

a pile of olives. We are all anointed with the same oil, kings and commoners, slaves and freemen, scholars and simpletons, Greeks and barbarians, men and women: we all eat the same bread and drink from the same cup.

Let us hope, my dear friends, let us earnestly hope that our lives may reflect the sacraments we receive. May those who are anointed with the same oil, who eat the same bread, and drink the same wine, feel the same way, believe the same things, and work together, as befits limbs belonging to the same body. Can sacraments and solemn oaths bind us together unless our hearts are united? But it will serve no purpose here to complain, as I have done so often,[500] that for centuries wars, hatred, dissent, and bigotry have brought Christian into conflict with Christian, conflicts more cruel than any Turk's, more savage than the wild beasts': there is no limit or end to this discord. And yet we still consider ourselves proper Christians, and make dire threats against the Turks.

But enough of complaints, we must finish the psalm! If you truly eat the bread of sacred doctrine, truly drink of the wine which the divine wisdom has pressed for us, and are truly anointed with the oil of spiritual joy; if you promote harmony in the church, working evil against no man, rejoicing in the success of the good, and ignoring the insults of the wicked, then you will be able to say: 'I shall sleep in peace and take my rest in it.' The Latin translator's 'in it' [in id ipsum][501] is in Greek ἐπὶ τὸ αὐτό, which is often translated elsewhere as 'in one'; sometimes this refers to a place where many people gather together, as in 1 Corinthians 11: 'Coming together into one [place].'[502] Similarly, in Acts 2: 'They were all together in the same place,'[503] where ἐπὶ τὸ αὐτό is translated 'in the same place.' Sometimes it describes a meeting of minds, as in Romans 12: 'Agreeing one with another,'[504] τὸ αὐτό; again, in Psalm 132: 'How good it is and how pleasant for brothers to live together,'[505] ἐπὶ τὸ αὐτό. Although it is a commonplace with many applications, it is none the less a symbol of concord.

* * * * *

500 See for example *Adagia* IV i 1: *Dulce bellum inexpertis, Institutio principis christiani* chapter 11 CWE 27 282–8, and *Querela pacis* CWE 27 293–322. Erasmus was to return to the subject of war against the Turks in his commentary on Ps 28/29, *De bello Turcico*, where he counselled war only as a last resort, and suggested that it would have little chance of success; given the current corruption in Christendom, God was unlikely to favour the enterprise.
501 Literally 'in it itself'; the Hebrew in fact means 'at once.'
502 1 Cor 11:20
503 Acts 2:1
504 Rom 12:16
505 Ps 132/133:1

Now it remains to reiterate, in order to fix it in your minds, my earlier discussion of the repetition 'in peace and in harmony.'[506] In order to sleep soundly, a Christian needs to be at peace both with God and with the church or his fellow men. Sin sows enmity between God and mankind, but Christ conquered sin and restored peace. It is a peace such as the world cannot give,[507] but which, on the contrary, it destroys; it is the peace for which Paul so often prays for his people: 'Grace and peace from God the Father and Jesus Christ our Lord.'[508] This peace is not for the wicked, however loudly they cry: 'Peace, peace!' The wicked are at war with God, and at peace only with Belial; there can be no treaty of peace between God and Belial.[509] But since there is perfect and everlasting concord between Christ and his Father, because they are one, so everyone's relationship with the Son must be the same as that with the Father. Christ's prayer in John 17 makes this clear: 'Holy Father, by the power of your name preserve those you have given me, that they may be one, as we are one.'[510] Anyone who subordinates his own will entirely to the divine will is at peace with God.

God has made his wishes known in his commandments; if there is anything in them, or elsewhere, that our minds cannot comprehend (for example when we are dogged by misfortune for no apparent reason), we must always say: 'May the Lord's will be done'[511] – in peace, to which is added: 'in it' or 'together.' Peace may come to us as individuals, but for it to be established 'in it' or 'together,' we must all gather in one congregation, as if in a house shared by all Christ's followers, and there brother may make his peace with brother. There is a natural logic in all this: who can quarrel with the Son when he is at peace with the Father? Who can be at peace with the head, if he is engaged in civil war with one of the limbs? If you side with sin, you cannot have peace with God or with the Son and the Holy Spirit; the authors of schisms and heresies cannot have peace with the church, which is the body of Christ;[512] the vengeful and self-loving, intolerant of others'

* * * * *

506 See 210 above; Erasmus is following his own advice about the utility of repetition!
507 John 14:27
508 Paul uses this formula at the beginning of most of his letters, for example Rom 1:7 and 1 Cor 1:3.
509 Cf 2 Cor 6:15.
510 John 17:11
511 Matt 6:10; the Lord's Prayer
512 Although this may be an allusion to contemporary controversies, it is probably inspired by 1 Cor 11:18–19 and 12:25, which concludes a passage on the old fable concerning 'civil war' within the body.

weaknesses, cannot have peace with their fellows. Christ asks even more of us: he asks that we love even our enemies,[513] and that is more demanding than simply keeping the peace. To sum up, only those can lie down and sleep in peace 'together' who wage war against sin, who bear no ill will towards anyone, and, as far as they can, show good will to all; only those who lie down to sleep in this way can find peace of mind in this life. Abraham's body had in this sense 'gone to its rest,' and Sara's womanly parts had ceased to live,[514] when there was born to them Isaac, whose name means 'joy,'[515] the joy of a conscience at ease with itself. We are dealing here with the death of the passions, not of the body.

None the less, although this interpretation can be applied to every part of Christian life, it is true that death provides a particularly striking example of this kind of peace, for death represents the final battle between the flesh and the spirit. I need not point out the obvious fact that in Holy Writ death is often called sleep.[516] It has frequently been said that sleep is a kind of image of death, and for that reason it is called 'peace of mind and a rest from care' by a most talented poet;[517] in the Apocalypse too, the Spirit calls blessed those who die in the Lord, because they rest from their labours.[518] Paul wished for the gift of death, that he might take his rest with Christ.[519] Because of the comparison between death and sleep, this Fourth Psalm is sung, according to church custom, before the time for sleep,[520] and thus it may be sung still more appropriately at the hour of death; the pagans call death eternal sleep,[521] whereas we, who are to live again, may more correctly call it 'the long sleep,' but not eternal.

It is at the moment of death in particular that it becomes clear which among us are the 'holy ones whom the Lord has made an object of wonder.'

* * * * *

513 Cf Matt 5:44 and Luke 6:27.
514 See Gen 17 and 21, 18:11–12.
515 Cf Jerome De nominibus Hebraicis PL 23 779.
516 Cf the Old Testament expressions 'to sleep with one's fathers' (eg Deut 31:16) and 'perpetual sleep' (eg Jer 51:37), and the New Testament euphemism 'to fall asleep' (eg Acts 7:60).
517 Ovid Metamorphoses 11.623–4; for the 'image of death,' cf Ovid Amores 2.9.41 and Cicero Tusculan Disputations 1.38.92.
518 Rev 14:13
519 See for example Rom 7:24 and 2 Cor 1:9.
520 Ps 4 is one of the psalms traditionally sung at compline, the last of the canonical hours, the final service of the day.
521 This phrase was often used in funerary inscriptions: cf A. Forcellini Lexicon totius Latinitatis 4 vols (Padua 1940) sv somnus II.4.7. 'The long sleep' is used by Horace Odes 3.11.38.

The general run of people try to get everything in, with frequent confession, just as frequent absolution, holy water and holy oil, consecrated candles, bedside confessors,[522] mourners, testaments, funeral feasts, solemn declarations, vows, bulls – and yet they die with unquiet minds. It is not that I mean to condemn such things, but on their own they cannot compare with the wine, corn, and oil of the true Christian.[523] On the other hand, anyone who has placed all his trust in the Lord, who has confidence in all the gospel's promises, who has spurned all worldly things, who is at peace with God, acknowledging his weakness and relying on God's mercy, and who wishes ill to no man: such a one, at the end, 'sleeps in peace and takes his rest in it.' You will see that such people are full of eagerness and confidence as they breathe their last, since they have truly practised all these things during their lives; you would say that they are not dying, but travelling on to a happier place. Why should they not lay down their lives with perfect equanimity, since they rely on God's promises and have certain hope of immortality? Why should they not freely and willingly lay down the burden of a feeble body, since they are certain that in place of their inglorious mortal form they are to put on a form that will be glorious and immortal?[524] Why should they not be glad to fall asleep in the Lord since, being limbs of Jesus Christ, they are assured that they cannot be cut off from the head?

All this, of course, is summed up in the last line: 'For you, O Lord, have set me apart, in hope.' God alone can grant this certainty to man, since he alone revives the dead, and has promised eternal life to all who believe in him. It cannot be obtained by human means, by solemn declarations, by bulls, or by foolish promises made to the dying by the mourners: 'You're dying, but cheer up: I'll stand bail for your soul with my own.'

It is not hard to reconcile the earlier phrase 'in it' or 'together' with the word used here, καταμόνας, meaning 'separately' or 'apart.' In this case it means that you will be preserved from the storm which will break over the wicked, and will instead sleep in the community of the saints. Being 'set apart' will not mean that you will be cut off from the fellowship of the

* * * * *

522 The word used is *assessor*, a legal term perhaps used jocularly here, since it means literally 'one who sits beside [the judge].' Augustine uses it (*Sermo* 58 PL 38 393) to describe Christ, at present God's 'assessor,' who intercedes on our behalf but who will later become our judge.

523 The two sentences 'The general run ... true Christian' were recommended for deletion in the *Index expurgatorius* LB X 1820B. The passage recalls the satire in the colloquy *Funus* and the discussion of confession in *Exomologesis*.

524 Cf 1 Cor 15:53.

blessed, but it will remove you from the dangers of contact with the wicked. As long as we stay in this world, the peace we find in the Lord is often endangered; but once he has removed us from the world, we may sleep in safety, free from all ills, and take our rest in the hope shared by all God's children.

The Holy Spirit has expressed the certainty of our hopes in three phrases: first, it names the source of hope when it says: 'You, O Lord'; then it adds 'apart,' meaning far removed from any danger; finally, it says κατῴκησας, that is, 'made me dwell' or 'gave me a home.' In the mystic writings, this word frequently signifies a secure refuge which no danger can threaten, as in: 'O Lord, who shall dwell in your tabernacle, or who shall rest on your holy mountain?'[525] Similarly, Moses says in Deuteronomy 33: 'Israel shall dwell in security and alone.'[526] Again, a safe refuge is promised to the Israelites in Jeremiah: 'And I shall make them dwell in safety, and they shall be my people, and I shall be their God.'[527] People can find rest in a place of their own, and may dwell in safety in a place far removed from the enemy's attacks. There is no perfect safety for the soul as long as we stay in the tabernacle of this feeble body, but when godly souls finally come to leave it, they begin to dwell in safety in the perfect security of the house which God has prepared for them. There, rescued from life's ills, they enjoy a blessed peace, as we read: 'In the eyes of fools, they appear to have died, but they are at peace, and their hopes are full of immortality.'[528] In fact the bliss of these godly souls is not yet complete, for they desire to put on once more the body they have laid down; but this desire does not torment them, and they take their rest in the certain hope which God gives them. Such is the death of those who truly have faith in the Lord; it is truly blessed and truly precious in the Lord's sight.[529] Very different is the death of those who have fixed their hopes on this world.

But now it is time to end a long sermon with a brief epilogue. Although it is short, this one psalm would enable us to win salvation, if we could manage to understand what we were reading, and put our understanding into practice. We have as our pattern Christ hanging on the cross; he cried out, was answered, and found relief; he called out again – for us, and then exhorted us all to direct our love towards heaven, to repent of our sinful love

* * * * *

525 Ps 14/15:1
526 Deut 33:28
527 Jer 32:37–8
528 Wisd 3:3–4, adapted
529 Ps 116:15

for the world, to hope for forgiveness, to ask for the gifts of the Spirit, to find peace of mind by mortifying the flesh, and to obtain the prize of immortality. My dear friends, let each one of us heed his advice, and, though beset by troubles and burdened with sin, let us cry out in perfect confidence to the Lord, entrusting to him the entire care of our souls – and he will relieve our hearts. Having tasted of his kindness, let us confess his gratuitous goodness towards us, and never cease to cry: 'Have mercy on me,' until we feel God's gift strengthen and grow within us. Then, when he has enlarged our hearts and fitted them to withstand suffering, when he has lifted up our thoughts so that, scorning the world, they aspire to heaven, then let us proclaim to others God's goodness towards us, that we may kindle in others the hope of a better life. But we must proclaim God's gifts in such a way that we claim no credit for ourselves, proving instead that God's goodness is available to all if they will seek his aid with trust.

May our exhortations strengthen the resolve of those who have already begun to be changed by repentance; when once they have conceived a firm hatred for sin, may they be careful to avoid a return to their wallowing in the mire of the flesh, from which they have been rescued by God's mercy; now, walking in newness of life, let them perform the works of righteousness, hoping that their good deeds will be rewarded, not by men, but by the Lord, and unmoved by the cries of those still subject to the flesh: 'Who will show us these good things?' On the contrary, encouraged by the light of the gospel promise and by the Spirit's pledge, let them constantly rejoice with the joy of the Spirit, and constantly progress towards better things until, fortified by the bread of heavenly doctrine, gladdened by the wine of eternal love, they may stoutly resist Satan, and enjoy the constant delights of a clear conscience; at the same time, let them minister, with all kindness and conscientiousness, to the weaknesses of their fellows. Thus, when the last day of this life dawns, may we journey, in certain hope of resurrection, from here to the Lord, who promised us all this through the prophets, who fulfilled many promises in person, and who has imparted the Holy Spirit to his people as a pledge for the promises that remain. Our Lord will fulfil all his promises with a generosity beyond our understanding, and in him we shall find peace and joy in this world; and to him, with the Father and the Holy Spirit, be praise without end. Amen.

WORKS FREQUENTLY CITED

SHORT-TITLE FORMS FOR ERASMUS' WORKS

INDEX OF BIBLICAL AND
APOCRYPHAL REFERENCES

GENERAL INDEX

WORKS FREQUENTLY CITED

This list provides bibliographical information for works referred to in short-title form in this volume. For Erasmus' writings see the short-title list following.

Allen — *Opus epistolarum Des. Erasmi Roterodami* ed P.S. Allen, H.M. Allen, and H.W. Garrod (Oxford 1906–58) 11 vols and index

ASD — *Opera omnia Desiderii Erasmi Roterodami* (Amsterdam 1969–   )

Boyle — M. O'Rourke Boyle *Erasmus on Language and Method in Theology* (Toronto 1977)

CEBR — *Contemporaries of Erasmus: A Biographical Register of the Renaissance and Reformation* ed Peter G. Bietenholz and Thomas B. Deutscher (Toronto 1985–7) 3 vols

Chantraine — G. Chantraine 'Erasme, lecteur des psaumes' in *Colloquia Erasmiana Turonensia* (Paris 1972) II 691–712

CWE — *Collected Works of Erasmus* (Toronto 1974–   )

LB — *Desiderii Erasmi Roterodami opera omnia* ed J. Leclerc (Leiden 1703–6) 10 vols

PG — *Patrologiae cursus completus ... series Graeca* ed J.P. Migne (Paris 1857–66) 162 vols

PL — *Patrologiae cursus completus ... series Latina* ed J.P. Migne (Paris 1844–64) 221 vols

Screech — M.A. Screech *Ecstasy and the Praise of Folly* (London 1980)

SHORT-TITLE FORMS FOR ERASMUS' WORKS

Titles following colons are longer versions of the same, or are alternative titles. Items entirely enclosed in square brackets are of doubtful authorship. For abbreviations, see Works Frequently Cited.

Acta: Acta Academiae Lovaniensis contra Lutherum *Opuscula* / CWE 71

Adagia: Adagiorum chiliades 1508, etc (Adagiorum collectanea for the primitive form, when required) LB II / ASD II-1, 4, 5, 6 / CWE 30–6

Admonitio adversus mendacium: Admonitio adversus mendacium et obtrectationem LB X

Annotationes in Novum Testamentum LB VI / CWE 51–60

Antibarbari LB X / ASD I-1 / CWE 23

Apologia ad Caranzam: Apologia ad Sanctium Caranzam, or Apologia de tribus locis, or Responsio ad annotationem Stunicae . . . a Sanctio Caranza defensam LB IX

Apologia ad Fabrum: Apologia ad Iacobum Fabrum Stapulensem LB IX / ASD IX-3 / CWE 83

Apologia adversus monachos: Apologia adversus monachos quosdam Hispanos LB IX

Apologia adversus Petrum Sutorem: Apologia adversus debacchationes Petri Sutoris LB IX

Apologia adversus rhapsodias Alberti Pii: Apologia ad viginti et quattuor libros A. Pii LB IX

Apologia contra Latomi dialogum: Apologia contra Iacobi Latomi dialogum de tribus linguis LB IX / CWE 71

Apologia de 'In principio erat sermo' LB IX

Apologia de laude matrimonii: Apologia pro declamatione de laude matrimonii LB IX / CWE 71

Apologia de loco 'Omnes quidem': Apologia de loco 'Omnes quidem resurgemus' LB IX

Apologiae contra Stunicam: Apologiae contra Lopidem Stunicam LB IX / ASD IX-2

Apologia qua respondet invectivis Lei: Apologia qua respondet duabus invectivis Eduardi Lei *Opuscula*

Apophthegmata LB IV

Appendix de scriptis Clithovei LB IX / CWE 83

Appendix respondens ad Sutorem LB IX

Argumenta: Argumenta in omnes epistolas apostolicas nova (with Paraphrases)

Axiomata pro causa Lutheri: Axiomata pro causa Martini Lutheri *Opuscula* / CWE 71

Carmina LB I, IV, V, VIII / ASD I-7 / CWE 85–6

Catalogus lucubrationum LB I

Ciceronianus: Dialogus Ciceronianus LB I / ASD I-2 / CWE 28

Colloquia LB I / ASD I-3 / CWE 39–40

Compendium vitae Allen I / CWE 4

Concionalis interpretatio (in Psalmi)

Conflictus: Conflictus Thaliae et Barbariei LB I

[Consilium: Consilium cuiusdam ex animo cupientis esse consultum] *Opuscula* / CWE 71

De bello Turcico: Consultatio de bello Turcico (in Psalmi)

De civilitate: De civilitate morum puerilium LB I / CWE 25

Declamatio de morte LB IV

Declamatiuncula LB IV

Declarationes ad censuras Lutetiae vulgatas: Declarationes ad censuras Lutetiae vulgatas sub nomine facultatis theologiae Parisiensis LB IX

De concordia: De sarcienda ecclesiae concordia, or De amabili ecclesiae concordia (in Psalmi)

De conscribendis epistolis LB I / ASD I-2 / CWE 25

De constructione: De constructione octo partium orationis, or Syntaxis LB I / ASD I-4

De contemptu mundi: Epistola de contemptu mundi LB V / ASD V-1 / CWE 66

De copia: De duplici copia verborum ac rerum LB I / ASD I-6 / CWE 24

De esu carnium: Epistola apologetica ad Christophorum episcopum Basiliensem de interdicto esu carnium LB IX / ASD IX-1

De immensa Dei misericordia: Concio de immensa Dei misericordia LB V / CWE 70

De libero arbitrio: De libero arbitrio diatribe LB IX / CWE 76

De praeparatione: De praeparatione ad mortem LB V / ASD V-1 / CWE 70

De pueris instituendis: De pueris statim ac liberaliter instituendis LB I / ASD I-2 / CWE 26

De puero Iesu: Concio de puero Iesu LB V / CWE 29

De puritate tabernaculi: De puritate tabernaculi sive ecclesiae christianae (in Psalmi)

De ratione studii LB I / ASD I-2 / CWE 24

De recta pronuntiatione: De recta latini graecique sermonis pronuntiatione LB I / ASD I-4 / CWE 26

De taedio Iesu: Disputatiuncula de taedio, pavore, tristicia Iesu LB V / CWE 70

Detectio praestigiarum: Detectio praestigiarum cuiusdam libelli germanice scripti LB X / ASD IX-1

De vidua christiana LB V / CWE 66

De virtute amplectenda: Oratio de virtute amplectenda LB V / CWE 29

[Dialogus bilinguium ac trilinguium: Chonradi Nastadiensis dialogus bilinguium ac trilinguium] Opuscula / CWE 7

Dilutio: Dilutio eorum quae Iodocus Clithoveus scripsit adversus declamationem suasoriam matrimonii CWE 83

Divinationes ad notata Bedae LB IX

Ecclesiastes: Ecclesiastes sive de ratione concionandi LB V / ASD V-4, 5

Elenchus in N. Bedae censuras LB IX

Enchiridion: Enchiridion militis christiani LB V / CWE 66

Encomium matrimonii (in De conscribendis epistolis)

Encomium medicinae: Declamatio in laudem artis medicae LB I / ASD I-4 / CWE 29

Epistola ad Dorpium LB IX / CWE 3 / CWE 71

Epistola ad fratres Inferioris Germaniae: Responsio ad fratres Germaniae Inferioris ad epistolam apologeticam incerto autore proditam LB X / ASD IX-1

Epistola ad graculos: Epistola ad quosdam imprudentissimos graculos LB X

Epistola apologetica de Termino LB X

Epistola consolatoria: Epistola consolatoria virginibus sacris, or Epistola consolatoria in adversis LB V / CWE 69

Epistola contra pseudevangelicos: Epistola contra quosdam qui se falso iactant
  evangelicos LB X / ASD IX-1
Euripidis Hecuba LB I / ASD I-1
Euripidis Iphigenia in Aulide LB I / ASD I-1
Exomologesis: Exomologesis sive modus confitendi LB V
Explanatio symboli: Explanatio symboli apostolorum sive catechismus LB V /
  ASD V-1 / CWE 70
Ex Plutarcho versa LB IV / ASD IV-2

Formula: Conficiendarum epistolarum formula (see De conscribendis epistolis)

Hyperaspistes LB X / CWE 76–7

In Nucem Ovidii commentarius LB I / ASD I-1 / CWE 29
In Prudentium: Commentarius in duos hymnos Prudentii LB V / CWE 29
Institutio christiani matrimonii LB V / CWE 69
Institutio principis christiani LB IV / ASD IV-1 / CWE 27

[Julius exclusus: Dialogus Julius exclusus e coelis] *Opuscula* / CWE 27

Lingua LB IV / ASD IV-1A / CWE 29
Liturgia Virginis Matris: Virginis Matris apud Lauretum cultae liturgia LB V /
  ASD V-1 / CWE 69
Luciani dialogi LB I / ASD I-1

Manifesta mendacia CWE 71
Methodus (see Ratio)
Modus orandi Deum LB V / ASD V-1 / CWE 70
Moria: Moriae encomium LB IV / ASD IV-3 / CWE 27

Novum Testamentum: Novum Testamentum 1519 and later (Novúm instrumentum
  for the first edition, 1516, when required) LB VI

Obsecratio ad Virginem Mariam: Obsecratio sive oratio ad Virginem Mariam in rebus
  adversis LB V / CWE 69
Oratio de pace: Oratio de pace et discordia LB VIII
Oratio funebris: Oratio funebris in funere Bertae de Heyen LB VIII / CWE 29

Paean Virgini Matri: Paean Virgini Matri dicendus LB V / CWE 69
Panegyricus: Panegyricus ad Philippum Austriae ducem LB IV / ASD IV-1 / CWE 27
Parabolae: Parabolae sive similia LB I / ASD I-5 / CWE 23
Paraclesis LB V, VI
Paraphrasis in Elegantias Vallae: Paraphrasis in Elegantias Laurentii Vallae LB I /
  ASD I-4
Paraphrasis in Matthaeum, etc (in Paraphrasis in Novum Testamentum)
Paraphrasis in Novum Testamentum LB VII / CWE 42–50
Peregrinatio apostolorum: Peregrinatio apostolorum Petri et Pauli LB VI, VII
Precatio ad Virginis filium Iesum LB V / CWE 69

Precatio dominica LB V / CWE 69
Precationes: Precationes aliquot novae LB V / CWE 69
Precatio pro pace ecclesiae: Precatio ad Dominum Iesum pro pace ecclesiae LB IV, V / CWE 69
Psalmi: Psalmi, or Enarrationes sive commentarii in psalmos LB V / ASD V-2, 3 / CWE 63–5
Purgatio adversus epistolam Lutheri: Purgatio adversus epistolam non sobriam Lutheri LB X / ASD IX-1

Querela pacis LB IV / ASD IV-2 / CWE 27

Ratio: Ratio seu Methodus compendio perveniendi ad veram theologiam (Methodus for the shorter version originally published in the Novum instrumentum of 1516) LB V, VI
Responsio ad annotationes Lei: Liber quo respondet annotationibus Lei LB IX
Responsio ad collationes: Responsio ad collationes cuiusdam iuvenis gerontodidas-cali LB IX
Responsio ad disputationem de divortio: Responsio ad disputationem cuiusdam Phimostomi de divortio LB IX / CWE 83
Responsio ad epistolam Pii: Responsio ad epistolam paraeneticam Alberti Pii, or Responsio ad exhortationem Pii LB IX
Responsio ad notulas Bedaicas LB X
Responsio ad Petri Cursii defensionem: Epistola de apologia Cursii LB X / Allen Ep 3032
Responsio adversus febricitantis libellum: Apologia monasticae religionis LB X

Spongia: Spongia adversus aspergines Hutteni LB X / ASD IX-1
Supputatio: Supputatio calumniarum Natalis Bedae LB IX

Tyrannicida: Tyrannicida, declamatio Lucianicae respondens LB I / ASD I-1 / CWE 29

Virginis et martyris comparatio LB V / CWE 69
Vita Hieronymi: Vita divi Hieronymi Stridonensis Opuscula / CWE 61

Index of
Biblical and Apocryphal References

General Index

Abraham: his trust in God lvi, 260;
name lengthened 15; acknowledged
by God 60; feast for Isaac 232;
patriarch of the Hebrews 238–9;
commanded to sacrifice Isaac 258;
peace of mind in old age 272

Absalom: as prototype of the renegade
154–5; as a tyrant 155; death of 157

Adrian vi, Pope lix

Adrianus, Matthaeus, Jewish convert
lv

Aesop *Fables* 118 n228

Agamemnon, king of Mycenae and
Argos 104, 190

Ahithophel, as prototype of Judas 155,
157

Alexander the Great 13 n27

Alypius, fellow catechumen of St
Augustine 265

Ambrose of Milan, conversion of 39

Amphictyons, Greek councillors 56

Anthony, St, of Egypt, founder of
monasticism 246

Apollinarist heresy 17 n51

apostles: prototypes of bishops xxxiv;
persecuted 58–9, 251; false apostles
94

Aquila, translator of the Old Testament
xx, 38, 245

Areopagites, Athenian judges 56

Arian heresy 16–17

Aristarchus of Samothrace, Greek
literary critic 71

Aristotle: an unreliable guide in
theology lviii, 31, 32, 40, 242, 244; as

a guide in ethics 3; his beliefs on the
soul and creation 196
– *De anima* 196 n119
– *De generatione* 196 n119
– *De partibus animalium* 102 n152
– *Physics* and *Metaphysics* 31
– *Politics* 258 n444

Arnobius *Commentarii in psalmos* lix,
66, 67, 92, 144, 171, 177, 207, 265
n478

Augustine, St: influence on Erasmus
xvii, xxviii n29, xlii, lxix, 2, 67, 171;
suspicion of Jerome xxi; conversion
of 39; on the authorship of the Psalms
77; on *diapsalma* 257; opposes Stoical
apathy 257
– *Confessions* xix, 39 n184, 265
– *Contra Faustum* 255 n432
– *De civitate Dei* 77, 257 n443
– *De doctrina christiana* xx, xxiv, 258
n444
– *De utilitate credendi* xxix
– *Enarratio in psalmum 1* 9, 22, 24 n90,
28 n119, 33 n147
– *Enarratio in psalmum 2* 86, 92, 101,
113, 124, 128, 132, 136, 138, 144
– *Enarratio in psalmum 3* 149
– *Enarratio in psalmum 4* 175 n3, 177,
181 n31, 200, 207 n192, 208, 211 n222,
235, 245 and n395, 252–3, 256, 257,
261, 266, 269
– *In primum psalmum annotatio* 9 n2, 74
n10, 76 n21, 77 n24
– *Sermo 58* 273 n522

Aulus Gellius 257 n441

This book

was designed by

VAL COOKE

based on the series design by

ALLAN FLEMING

and was printed by

University

of Toronto

Press